The Distributional Effects of Government Spending and Taxation

The Distributional Effects of Government Spending and Taxation

Edited by

Dimitri B. Papadimitriou
Jerome Levy Professor of Economics
Bard College, Annandale-on-Hudson, New York

Selection and editorial matter © Dimitri B. Papadimitriou 2006
Individual chapters © contributors 2006

First published 2006 by
PALGRAVE MACMILLAN
Houndmills, Basingstoke, Hampshire RG21 6XS and
175 Fifth Avenue, New York, N.Y. 10010
Companies and representatives throughout the world

PALGRAVE MACMILLAN is the global academic imprint of the Palgrave
Macmillan division of St. Martin's Press, LLC and of Palgrave Macmillan Ltd.
Macmillan® is a registered trademark in the United States, United Kingdom
and other countries. Palgrave is a registered trademark in the European
Union and other countries.

ISBN-13: 978–1–4039–9625–1 hardback
ISBN-10: 1–4039–9625–3 hardback

This book is printed on paper suitable for recycling and made from fully
managed and sustained forest sources.

A catalogue record for this book is available from the British Library.

Library of Congress Cataloging-in-Publication Data
The distributional effects of government spending and taxation/edited by
    Dimitri B. Papadimitriou.
      p.   cm.
    Includes bibliographical references and index.
    ISBN 1–4039–9625–3 (cloth)
    1. Income distribution—United States.   2. Distributive justice—
    United States.   3. Finance, Public—United States.   4. Fiscal
    policy—United States.   I. Papadimitriou, Dimitri B.
    HC110.I5.D533 2006
    339.20973—dc22   2005057768

10   9   8   7   6   5   4   3   2   1
15   14   13   12   11   10   09   08   07   06

Printed and bound in Great Britain by
Antony Rowe Ltd, Chippenham and Eastbourne

Contents

Part III   International Comparisons

The Levy Economics Institute of Bard College

Founded in 1986, The Levy Economics Institute of Bard College is an autonomous nonprofit public policy research organization. It is nonpartisan, open to the examination of diverse points of view and dedicated to public service.

The Institute believes in the potential for economic study to improve the human condition. Its purpose is to generate viable, effective public policy responses to important economic problems. It is concerned with issues that profoundly affect the quality of life in the United States, in other highly industrialized nations and in countries with developing economies.

The Institute's present research programs include such issues as financial instability, economic growth and employment, international trade, problems associated with the distribution of income and wealth, the measurement of economic well-being and the relationship between public and private investment and their effects on productivity and competitiveness.

The opinions expressed in this volume are those of the authors and do not necessarily represent those of the Institute or its Board of Governors.

Acknowledgements

I would like to thank the Board of Trustees of Bard College for sponsoring the Levy Economics Institute's ongoing research project on the *Distribution of Income and Well-Being*. As part of this project, many distinguished scholars, policymakers and business leaders visit the Institute and participate in seminars and conferences aimed at finding policy options to pressing economic problems. The chapters of this volume have been selected from papers delivered at these events and I want to thank the authors of these chapters for their promptness and their readiness in carrying out revisions. As always, I am indebted to my assistant Deborah C. Treadway, for her skill, loyalty and devotion, without which this book would not have been possible.

To her, my warm and sincere thanks.

Dimitri B. Papadimitriou

Notes on Contributors

Leonard E. Burman is co-director of the Tax Policy Center, Senior Fellow at the Urban Institute, and Visiting Professor at the Georgetown University Public Policy Institute. Dr Burman served as Deputy Assistant Secretary of the Treasury for Tax Analysis from 1998 to 2000, and as Senior Analyst at the Congressional Budget Office from 1988 to 1997. He is the author of a book, *The Labyrinth of Capital Gains Tax Policy: A Guide for the Perplexed*, and numerous articles, studies and reports. He is also a commentator for *Marketplace*. Recent research has examined the individual alternative minimum tax, the estate tax, the changing role of taxation in social policy, and tax incentives for savings, retirement and health insurance. He holds a PhD from the University of Minnesota and a BA from Wesleyan University.

Barbara A. Butrica, a labor economist with research interests in aging and income dynamics, is a Senior Research Associate at the Urban Institute. Dr Butrica has detailed knowledge of Social Security regulations and is currently involved in a number of projects that assess the impact of Social Security retirement and survivors' programs on the economic well-being of the aged. She previously served as an analyst at Mercer Human Resource Consulting and as an economist at the Social Security Administration. She holds a PhD from Syracuse University and a BA from Wellesley College.

Kwang Soo Cheong is an Assistant Professor of Finance in the Graduate Division of Business and Management at Johns Hopkins University. His research areas include public finance, corporate finance, industrial organization and income distribution. He received his Bachelor's and Master's degrees in economics from Seoul National University in South Korea, and his doctorate in economics from Stanford University. He previously taught at Stanford University and the University of Hawaii.

William G. Gale is the Arjay and Frances Fearing Miller Chair in Federal Economic Policy and the Deputy Director of the Economic Studies Program at the Brookings Institution. He is also co-director of the Tax Policy Center, a joint venture of the Urban Institute and Brookings. His areas of expertise include tax policy, budget and fiscal policy, public and private saving behavior and pensions. Before joining Brookings in 1992, Gale was an Assistant Professor in the Department of Economics at the University of California at Los Angeles, and a senior staff economist for the Council of Economic Advisers. Gale has written extensively in academic journals and popular outlets, and is co-editor of Rethinking Estate and Gift Taxation, Economic Effects of Fundamental Tax Reform, and Private Pensions and Public Policies.

Matthew Hall is an analyst in the Antitrust practice for NERA Economic Consulting. He previously worked as a research assistant at the Brookings Institution, specializing in federal tax and budget policy. He received a BA in Economics from Princeton University in 2002.

Ann Harding is Professor of Applied Economics and Social Policy and the inaugural Director of the National Centre for Social and Economic Modelling (NATSEM) at the University of Canberra. She is an internationally recognized expert in the fields of microsimulation modelling, income distribution and tax/transfer policy.

Howard M. Iams is the Director of the Division of Policy Evaluation in the Social Security Administration's research office. Since 1986 he has been conducting policy evaluations with survey data from the Census Bureau's Survey of Income and Program Participation (SIPP) matched to SSA administrative records of lifetime earnings and benefits. In collaboration with Steve Sandell, he designed and developed the Modeling Income in the Near Term (MINT) data system with matched SIPP data. SSA uses MINT to estimate the distributional impact of Social Security reform proposals and to project the baby boom and other future retirees in the twenty-first century.

Herwig Immervoll is Economist and Social Policy Analyst at the Organisation for Economic Co-operation and Development (OECD), Research Fellow at the Institute for the Study of Labor (IZA), a Research Associate at the Institute for Social and Economic Research (ISER) at the University of Essex, and an Affiliate of the European Centre for Social Welfare Policy. His responsibilities and research interests include analyzing and monitoring current trends in social and fiscal policies and their effects on poverty, income distribution and labor markets. He has worked extensively on microsimulation methods and their application to policy analysis in EU, OECD and developing countries.

Mathieu Lefèbvre is currently a research assistant in the Department of Economics of the University of Liège. He is working on a PhD thesis on Social Security and retirement in Belgium. He holds a BA in Economics from the University of Liège and an MA in economics from the Catholic University of Louvain.

Horacio Levy is a senior research officer at the Institute for Social and Economic Research, University of Essex, having previously been at the Department of Applied Economics at Universitat Autonoma of Barcelona. His research interests are on building and using tax-benefit microsimulation models in developed and developing countries, distributional effects of taxes and social policies and child poverty.

Christine Lietz is a research associate at the Institute of Advanced Studies, Vienna and was previously a research associate at the Microsimulation Unit, University of Cambridge. Her current research interests are tax-benefit microsimulation, income distribution and poverty.

Rachel Lloyd is a Principal Research Fellow at the National Centre for Social and Economic Modelling (NATSEM) at the University of Canberra. Since joining NATSEM six years ago, she has worked on a range of microsimulation and other modelling projects and conducted research into poverty, regional income distribution and factors affecting the use of telecommunications.

Daniela Mantovani is researcher of public economics at the University of Modena e Reggio Emilia (Italy). She previously worked for Microsimulation Unit, University of Cambridge. Her research interests include microsimulation, income inequality and poverty in developed countries.

Cathal O'Donoghue is Director of the Irish Rural Economy Research Centre and lectures in Economics at the National University of Ireland, Galway. He has published extensively in the field of microsimulation modelling and Economics of Social Policy.

Peter R. Orszag is the Joseph A. Pechman Senior Fellow in Economic Studies at the Brookings Institution; Co-Director of the Tax Policy Center, a joint venture of the Urban Institute and Brookings Institution; Director of The Retirement Security Project; and Research Professor at Georgetown University. He previously served as Special Assistant to the President for Economic Policy and as a Senior Economist and Senior Adviser on the Council of Economic Advisers, during the Clinton Administration. His current areas of research include pensions, budget and tax policy, Social Security, higher education, and homeland security. He was the co-editor of *American Economic Policy* in the 1990s (MIT Press, 2002), co-author of *Protecting the American Homeland: A Preliminary Analysis* (Brookings Institution Press, 2002), co-author of *Saving Social Security: A Balanced Approach* (Brookings Institution Press, 2004), and co-author of *Taxing the Future: Fiscal Policy Under the Bush Administration* (Brookings Institution Press, forthcoming).

Lars Osberg is currently the McCulloch Professor of Economics at Dalhousie University, Halifax, Canada. He received his PhD from Yale University after undergraduate work at Queen's University, Kingston and the London School of Economics and Political Science. His major fields of research interest have been the extent and causes of poverty and economic inequality, with particular emphasis in recent years on social policy, social cohesion and the implications of unemployment and structural change in labor markets. Among other professional responsibilities, he was President of the Canadian

Economics Association in 1999–2000 and is currently Review Editor for the *Review of Income and Wealth*.

Dimitri B. Papadimitriou is President of The Levy Economics Institute, Executive Vice President and Jerome Levy Professor of Economics at Bard College. His areas of special interest are community development banking, banking and financial structure, the Federal Reserve, monetary and fiscal policy, and the distribution of income and wealth in the United States. He has served as vice chairman of the congressional U.S. Trade Deficit Review Commission. Papadimitriou is general editor of the Levy Institute's book series and a member of the editorial board of *Challenge*. He received a PhD in economics from New School University.

Pierre Pestieau has had over 30 years of experience teaching and conducting research in public economics and population economics, first at Cornell and then at the University of Liège, since receiving his PhD from Yale. His major interests are pension economics, social insurance, inheritance taxation, redistributive policies and tax competition. His articles have been published in such leading journals as *Econometrica*, the *Journal of Economic Theory*, *Economica*, the *Journal of Public Economics*, the *Journal of Population Economics* and the *Scandinavian Journal of Economics*. His most recent book with Robert Fenge 'Social Security and Retirement' is to be published by the MIT Press.

Leon Podkaminer is a senior research fellow with the Vienna Institute for International Economic Studies (WIIW). Until 1993 he was associated with the Polish Academy of Sciences. He has published extensively in *Journal of Post Keynesian Economics*, *Journal of Comparative Economics*, *Banca Nazionale del Lavoro Quarterly Review*, *Review of Economics and Statistics*, *Cambridge Journal of Economics*.

Jonathan A. Schwabish joined the Congressional Budget Office in 2005. He is currently working on forecasting earnings and labor market behavior in the CBO's Long-Term Model, which is used to analyze the Social Security system in the United States. His other research interests include inequality, poverty and regional economics.

Timothy M. Smeeding is the Maxwell Professor of Public Policy, Professor of Economics and Public Administration, and Director of Maxwell's Center for Policy Research. He is also the Project Director of the Luxembourg Income Study (www.lisproject.org), a nonprofit research organization which he co-founded in 1983. Smeeding's research is focused on national and cross-national aspects of economic inequality, poverty, and public policy toward the family and vulnerable groups, such as children, the aged and the disabled. Additional unpublished papers and a complete curriculum vitae may be found on his website at http://www.cpr. maxwell.syr.edu/faculty/smeeding/.

Karen E. Smith is a Senior Research Associate at The Urban Institute. She has designed and developed microsimulation models for Social Security, taxation, wealth and savings, labor-supply, charitable giving, health expenditure, student aid and welfare reform. She received her BA from the University of Michigan and has done graduate work in statistics and econometrics at George Washington University. Prior to joining the Urban Institute, she was a manager in the Health Policy Economics Group at Price Waterhouse. She has also worked as a microsimulation modelling consultant to the New Zealand Treasury and as a Principal Analyst at the Congressional Budget Office.

Holly Sutherland is a Research Professor in the Institute for Social and Economic Research at the University of Essex. Her research is based on building and using microsimulation models. She has a particular interest in developing microsimulation as a tool for international comparative research and she coordinates the EU-wide EUROMOD project. Recent work is on the gendered effects of redistribution policies and on child poverty measurement and analysis.

Gerlinde Verbist works as a post-doctoral researcher at the Centre for Social Policy, University of Antwerp (UA). She is also visiting research associate at the Microsimulation Unit, University of Cambridge. Her main research interests are microsimulation modelling and applications, measurement of income inequality and redistribution, family policy and higher education policy, and the impact of personal income taxes on the welfare state in Belgium and Europe.

Neil Warren is Associate Professor of Economics in the Australian Taxation Studies Program (Atax), Faculty of Law, at the University of New South Wales and Research Director of the Australian Tax Research Foundation. His research interests lie in the area of public sector economics and, in particular, taxation and welfare policy and tax incidence. He received his PhD in Economics from the University of New South Wales in 1984.

Edward N. Wolff received his PhD from Yale University in 1974 and is professor of economics at New York University, where he has taught since 1974, and a Senior Scholar at the Levy Economics Institute of Bard College. He is also a Research Associate at the National Bureau of Economic Research. He served as Managing Editor of the *Review of Income and Wealth* from 1987 to 2004 and was a Visiting Scholar at the Russell Sage Foundation in New York (2003–04), President of the Eastern Economics Association (2002–03), a council member of the International Input-Output Association (1995–2003), and a council member of the International Association for Research in Income and Wealth (1987–2004). His principal research areas are income and wealth distribution and productivity growth.

Ajit Zacharias is a research scholar at the Levy Economics Institute working on the Levy Institute Measure of Economic Well-Being (LIMEW). The LIMEW is an alternative measure that can provide the foundation for a comprehensive view of the level and distribution of economic well-being. His research interests include concepts and measurement of well-being, effects of taxes and government spending on well-being, valuation of noncash transfers and time use. Zacharias received an MA from the University of Bombay, and a PhD from New School University.

List of Abbreviations and Acronyms

ABS	Australian Bureau of Statistics
ADS	Annual demographic supplement
AEU	Australian Education Union
AGI	Adjusted gross income
AIME	Average indexed monthly earnings
AMT	Alternative minimum tax
APSA	American Political Science Association
ASGF	Annual Survey of Government Finances
Atax	Australian Taxation Studies Program
AVGEN	Average generosity
CBO	Congressional Budget Office
CGE	Computable general equilibrium
CIT	Corporate income tax
CI	Comprehensive income
CIW	Wealth-adjusted comprehensive income
COG	Center of Gravity of income distribution
CPI	Consumer Price Index
CPS	Current Population Survey
DB	Defined benefit
DC Plan	Define contribution plan
DER	Detailed Earnings Record
DERGEN	Change in the effective age of retirement
DI	Disability Insurance
DIW	German Institute for Economic Research
DPOVGEN	Poverty alleviation generosity due to Social Security
EBF	Enquête sur les Budgets Familiaux
ECHP	European Community Household Panel
EGTRRA	Economic Growth and Tax Relief Reconciliation Act of 2001
ERGEN	Early retirement generosity
EU	European Union
EUROMOD	Tax-benefit microsimulation model for the European Union
FES	Family Expenditure Survey
GDP	Gross domestic product
GFS	Government Finance Statistics
GSOEP	German Socio Economic Panel Study
GST	Goods and Services Tax
HES	Household Expenditure Survey

INEGEN	Income share generosity
IRA	Individual Retirement Account
IRS	Internal Revenue Service
ISSP	International Social Survey Programme
JCT	Joint Committee on Taxation
JGTRRA	Jobs and Growth Tax Relief Reconciliation Act of 2003
KHPS	Korean Household Panel Study
KLIPS	Korean Labor and Income Panel Study
LIMEW	Levy Institute Measure of Economic Well-Being
LIS	Luxembourg Income Study
MICRESA	Micro Level Analysis of the European Social Agenda
MINT	Model of Income in Near Term
NATSEM	National Centre for Social and Economic Modelling
NHS	National Health Survey
NIPA	National Income and Product Accounts
OASID	Old-Age and Survivors Insurance and Disability Insurance
OECD	Organization for Economic Co-operation and Development
OLS	Ordinary least squares
ONS	Office of National Statistics
OTA	Office of Tax Analysis
PAYG	Pay-As-You-Go
PEU	Primary economic unit
PHI	Private Health Insurance
PIA	Primary insurance amount
PIT	Personal income tax
POVGEN	Poverty alleviation generosity
PSBH	Panel Survey of Belgian Households
PSELL-2	Socio-Economic Panel for Luxembourg
PUF	Public-use file
SCF	Survey of Consumer Finances
SEP	Socio-Economic Panel
SER	Summary Earnings Record
SHIW95	Survey of Household Income and Wealth
SILC	Statistics on Income and Living Standards (EU)
SIPP	Survey of Income Program Participation
Soc Ex	Social expenditures
SOI	Statistics of Income
SSA	Social Security Administration
SSI	Supplemental Security Income
TANF	Temporary Assistance for Needy Families
TB	Tax benefits
TOI	Trade openness indicator
TPC	Tax Policy Center
UHIES	Urban Household Income and Expenditure Survey

UK	United Kingdom
VAT	Value added tax
WIC	Women, Infants and Children
WIIW	Vienna Institute for International Economic Studies
WVS	World Value Survey

1
Government Effects on the Distribution of Income: An Overview

Dimitri B. Papadimitriou

A government's role, as it relates to taxation and public spending, has never gone unquestioned. Controversy arises from conservatives advocating fiscal responsibility and limited government intervention in a market economy. This supports the notion that taxes should be levied at the lowest possible level, specifically designated for the financing of the few public goods that only government can provide. However, there are advocates supporting an expanded role for government and arguing in favor of higher taxes to finance more public goods. They also argue for a social protection system of redistributive schemes that, to some extent, will correct the stark inequities in our society. Public provisioning of goods and services and redistribution policy can be defined according to different criteria, some of which have real economic significance while others are matters of convention and convenience. In general, 'public spending can be wise or foolish, appropriate or inappropriate, effective or ineffective but—the paradox first pointed out by Keynes—it cannot be more costly to the economy as a whole than doing nothing' (Nell, 1988, p. 228).

The provisioning of public goods and services can be wide ranging and can be classified into two broad categories:

1) *collective consumption goods*—goods and services affecting the entire population such as defense, the judicial system, police and fire protection, physical infrastructure and so on; and
2) *private consumption goods*—those affecting individuals that can also be provided by the private sector such as education and health care services, since they can meet the microeconomic criteria of excludability, positive supply curves and have no 'external effects' found in the collective consumption goods (Samuelson, 1966a, pp. 1223–5, emphasis in the original).

Moreover, the latter category of goods admittedly possesses 'an element of variability in the benefit that can go to one citizen *at the expense* of some other citizen,' but it is not necessarily synonymous to being optimally produced solely by the ordinary market process (Samuelson, 1966b, p. 1232, emphasis in the original). However, there can be a number of other arguments supporting their place within the functions of government. These arguments can include:

- market failure;
- basic needs considerations;
- externalities; and
- distributional considerations (Hare, 1988, p. 68).

Public finance projects, especially those involving education and health, cannot usually be determined or ranked on the basis of their rate of return, but rather on their discounted net benefits (Summers, 2003, p. 285). Education is subject to long-term decisions and the rates of return are assumed to be reflected in future earnings. Health care is fraught with incidence of adverse selection and moral hazard. Both result in inefficient markets or in absolute market failure, as they are in the realm of public provisioning.

The concept of basic needs enters into the argument for the public provisioning of goods that are required to maintain 'socially accepted norms or standards.' In the same way, minimum amounts of schooling and health to ensure social cohesion can be justified. Providing the elderly with a state pension may or may not be sufficient to cover their basic needs, the latter then requiring further public intervention (Hare, 1988, p. 69).

Externalities are hard to quantify, but they are nevertheless prominent if one assumes that returns to education result in the societal improvement, thus redounding in benefits to a larger segment of the population beyond the individuals whose human capital has increased the most. The same can be said for publicly provided health care, which not only positively affects those who fall ill, but also is beneficial to those who are well by reducing the risk of infection (ibid., pp. 69–70).

Income distribution has always been a dominant concern of the public sector. Governments are empowered to impose taxes on commodities, income and wealth and spend the resulting revenues in many ways to achieve a more equitable distribution. Targeted re-distributive transfers, such as assistance to the poor and the disabled, social insurance and pensions, and agricultural supports, can benefit either a large segment of the population or a narrow one. 'Similarly in the absence of a complete system of private markets for [particular goods and services] some public sector provision is likely to be justified on distributional grounds' (ibid., p. 70). The public supply of such goods and services is not tantamount to being provided only by state-run enterprises, but perhaps through partnerships between the private and public sectors. The financing of such programs can come from various sources of general tax revenues or special tax-surcharges.

In general, neither benefits from public goods and services nor costs are equally distributed. The wealthier constituency pays the larger share of the tax burden while poorer persons pay the smaller. Thus, their respective interests in the size of these programs are necessarily contradictory because the former prefer smaller programs while the latter prefer the more generous. These include various programs of the welfare state, unemployment and disability insurance, retirement benefits, and special purpose subsidies and transfers. Public spending represented as a fraction of gross domestic product (GDP) differs greatly across countries (Schwabish, Smeeding and Osberg, Chapter 9, this volume). Andrè Sapir (2005) for example, distinguishes four models of Western European welfare state systems:

1) The Nordic model of the Scandinavian countries and the Netherlands devotes the highest fraction of public expenditures on social protection and universal welfare provision.
2) The model of the Anglo-Saxon countries (Ireland and the United Kingdom) offers relatively large social assistance of last resort, with cash transfers directed mainly toward working age individuals.
3) The Continental model of Austria, Belgium, France, Germany and Luxembourg relies primarily on strong employment protection and provides generous unemployment insurance and retirement benefits.
4) Finally, the Mediterranean countries (Greece, Italy, Portugal and Spain) focus their social expenditures on old-age retirement programs with differences in the degree of eligibility and benefit amounts. Employment protection is heavily regulated and support for early-retirement provisions result in reducing the number of job seekers.

The latest figures for 2002, taken from the EU Commission *Public Finance Report* (2004), show public spending for the Nordic countries to average more than 53 percent, the Anglo-Saxon countries and Japan a little less than 40 percent, the Continental and Mediterranean countries close to 50 percent. All the above correspond to the 35 percent of Australia, Switzerland and the United States. Further, each country's composition of spending varies considerably. The 15 member states of the European Union (EU), before the last increase in membership, devoted 3 to 16 percent of total public spending on the unemployed, representing an income replacement rate of 20 to 90 percent. During the last three decades, a rapidly growing component of public spending in the United States, Europe and elsewhere has been assigned to public pensions, while public investment has been in the order of 3 percent of GDP. Of all components of government primary spending in the postwar period, especially in the years of 1960–82, transfers and subsidies had grown the most. By 1990, they averaged one-half of the total public expenditures. Tanzi and Schuknecht (1995, 1996), when tracking the historical development of subsidies and transfers, found that for the 17 industrialized democracies that they studied,[1] subsidies and transfers were immaterial in those countries a century ago. In the postwar period, in the Organisation for Economic Co-operation and Development (OECD, 2005) countries, the average transfer/subsidy share of GDP stood at about 9 percent around 1960, but grew to about 23 percent by around 1994. As noted earlier, the overall growth of welfare state programs was unprecedented but varied widely among many countries. In 1990, the GDP share in Japan was below 10 percent, whereas in the Netherlands it was close to 40 percent. In other areas, such as Latin America, some countries' public spending on social protection has been very small and devoted mainly to social insurance and directed, albeit disproportionately, to the upper middle class (Afonso, *et al.*, 2005; Persson and Tabellini, 2001; Rodrik, 2000; Tanzi and Schuknecht, 1997, 2000, 2003).

Beginning with the latter part of the nineteenth century, redistribution became one of the most important functions of government, requiring some form of imposed transfer of income and wealth from the better off to the less so. The first old-age pension system, for example, was instituted in Germany in the late 1880s. Ever since, public spending for redistributive purposes continued to a varying degree. Financing World War I meant the imposition of higher taxes that continued after the conflict and were used for funding higher public expenditures. It is during this time that many countries instituted social security systems. In the United States, following the Great Depression, the New Deal gave a boost to expansionary government expenditures, which included a number of work-related and income-assisted programs. Fast forward to the early 1970s, where the role and size of the public sector were questioned when the Keynesian advocated activist government faltered. Questions relating to public sector expenditure efficiency became a major topic in the policy discussion and economic research arenas. In the rapidly growing literature of academic research on this topic, performance and efficiency indicators were devised, institutions and rules were assessed and the optimal levels of government were suggested (Persson and Tabellini, 2001; Rodrik, 2000; Tanzi and Davoodi, 1997; Tanzi and Schuknecht, 2000, 2003). Besides public sector performance and efficiency, present-day societies play a crucial role in the economy in seeking to improve well-being and alleviate poverty.

Rising incomes have been associated with faster economic growth.[2] Until recently, it was assumed that poor and working families, even those with little or no education, could ascend into the middle class, and those less fortunate who were unemployed, disabled and the retired elderly would also be cared for by the modern welfare state. But even though most of the OECD countries saw their economies grow in the 1980s and 1990s, public expenditures were cut in concert with legislative mandates for deficit reduction and 'fiscal responsibility.' During the same period, a disturbing and marked increase in inequality was recorded. Especially in the United States, notwithstanding the robust economic growth, inequality has been distinctly higher. Yet if economic growth does not improve the human condition, then there is an expectation that modern society's redistributive policies have a positive impact on the level and distribution of household economic well-being together with an improvement in inequality. However, estimating the impact of the distributional effects of government policies is in itself a difficult task.

Part I of this book deals with public sector redistributive effects in the United States and opens with Wolff and Zacharias (Chapter 2). They note that the last study to measure the net effect of government expenditures and taxes on economic well-being was for the year 1970, more than three decades ago, in contrast to a significant number of theoretical papers published on the topic.[3] Traditionally, the Census Bureau has provided estimates of extended measures of disposable income reflecting the effects of taxes and transfer payments. Wolff and Zacharias argue that these measures do not represent an accurate estimate of economic well-being, which to them is defined as 'the magnitude of the command or access of the household over the products produced.' The proper measures of well-being—aside from various transfers between the state and households that include direct and indirect taxation—need to account for expenditures such as schooling and physical infrastructure among other things. That is, public consumption is in general attributable for the benefit of households and provided by the state. In addition, income must somehow include the employer contribution for various benefits and the imputed value from home and non-home wealth. In their analysis, Wolff and Zacharias proceed to construct two estimates of income, which they label 'pre-fiscal' and 'post-fiscal' income, respectively. Pre-fiscal income is defined as the income that enables households to command products entailing market and quasi-market transactions, while the post-fiscal income is pre-fiscal income and net government expenditures. It is important to underscore the particular years of their estimates, 1989 and 2000, since these represent the terminal years of the last two exceptionally high growth periods for the United States. Further, the 1990s is distinguished by a number of institutional and market changes being implemented, affecting both the tax and expenditure policy, including the 'end of welfare as we know it.'

The Wolff and Zacharias analysis shows that in 1989 and 2000, the effect of net government expenditures on the level and distribution of economic well-being was particularly significant. Overall, their results indicate that net government expenditure was negative and that Americans were taxed more than they received in benefits from either transfers or public consumption. They also found that the difference between the mean and median values of pre-fiscal and post-fiscal income was small, in the range of 4 percent, while the mean and median values of post-fiscal income were about 20 to 30 percent higher than the money income—the most widely accepted measure. When their overall estimates, however, are examined by various categories of income and household structure, their results are much more revealing. Other painstakingly documented estimates are based on (i) household characteristics, that is, race, age, family type and (ii) income deciles. Their conclusion, in contrast with the American notion of a small government—since size is positively correlated with inefficiency and waste, which has been shown to ring true for the better off—can be summed-up as yet another endorsement in favor of activist government redistributive policies as an effective instrument in reducing income inequality.

Old-age income security looms large on a government's agenda, whether it involves a state sponsored pension system or a framework within which incentives, such as tax preferred for retirement saving, can be promoted. Investigating the structure of privately funded retirement, in Chapter 3, Burman, Gale, Hall and Orszag note that there has always been government involvement in subsidizing retirement savings since the institution of income tax. Over the years, the US government, irrespective of party affiliation, has offered incentives to promote retirement savings. These fall under the rubric of tax-preferred schemes based on a fraction of labor income. The incentives encouraging saving for retirement differ widely and their effectiveness is dependent on the level of earnings and accumulated wealth. Thus, the distributional effects of such programs are important, since they may involve either reduction of consumption for the low-income, low-wealth households or shifting of assets for the high-income, high net-worth households. The analysis undertaken by Burman, Gale, Hall and Orszag focuses on the distributional effects of defined contribution pension plans that are either employer-sponsored or individually arranged. These authors, using the Tax Policy Center's microsimulation model of the US federal income tax system, produce estimates of contributions and benefits. Defined contribution retirement plans were introduced relatively late in the twentieth century, substituting for the long-implemented defined benefits plans that emulated those sponsored by the state. However, it turned out to be difficult to finance their actuarially determined liabilities, given the volatility of corporate profits and the relative freedom of investment adventuring. Defined contribution plans are based on investment income from contributions—employer/employee or individually arranged IRAs—as opposed to defined benefit plans based on length of service and earnings, especially late career earnings. The authors' detailed simulations show that the tax benefits of new contributions to the defined contribution retirement plans are skewed, being primarily favorable toward the highest income households, namely more than 50 percent of the benefits accrue to the top 10 percent. In contrast, the Individual Retirement Account (IRA) plans are much less so, with 60 percent of IRA tax benefits going to the top 20 percent of households and 85 percent of benefits accruing to the top 40 percent. The most disturbing finding is that the bottom 20 percent receives no benefit from the income tax incentives because few workers contribute. This is because the tax benefit per dollar contribution is low or zero due to the marginal income tax rate being low or zero. Similarly, the simulations of employer contributions show even skewer distributional patterns with the highest benefits going to the 0.1 percent of employees. The picture drawn from the Burman, Gale, Hall and Orszag study calls for a serious reconsideration in creating incentives for retirement savings. This should offer tax refunds to those in the lowest marginal income tax rate who contribute, which are more in concert with the reality facing the low-income segment of the population.

State sponsored retirement programs, such as the United States' Social Security system, are by far the most important mechanisms for achieving redistributive outcomes. Over the long run, projections of retiree benefits, given the variety of household characteristics, have spurned much debate in the policy-making arena. This is the main concern of Chapter 4, authored by Butrica, Iams and Smith. The authors analyze and contrast retiree incomes of various cohorts:

- current retirees (born in the 1926–35 period);
- near term retirees (born in 1936–45);
- early baby-boomer retirees (born in 1946–55); and
- late baby-boomers (born in 1956–65).

Using the Social Security Administration's Model of Income in the Near Term (MINT), and taking into account a number of demographic and socio-economic changes that have and are projected to take place in the foreseeable future, the authors project retiree incomes, income replacement rates and poverty rates for various population groups. Whereas Social Security was originally conceived as an insurance program with the objective to provide replacement income from work at retirement, it has over time expanded to include benefits for spouses, children and the disabled. Retirement benefits are not solely determined on the basis of earnings from employment, but reflect marriage history and status at retirement, and a spouse's earning history also. The projections documented in Chapter 4 include the changing trends of the typical family, which now includes two wage earners or is headed by a single female working parent. The family structure also involves divorces and multiple marriages, and rising life expectancy rates. When these trends are taken into account, the projections yield benefit changes for recent retirees and for those at future retirement. The MINT projections estimate:

- future per capita income that includes, in addition to Social Security benefits, private pension income, income from various assets, imputed rental income, earnings of both individuals and their spouses and income from non-spouse family members living at home;
- poverty rates;
- income replacement rates; and
- Supplemental Security Income.

The message of this analysis is that baby boomers will most likely have higher incomes and lower poverty rates than those of the current retirees, and their replacement income rates will be lower than those suggested by financial planning advocates. However, the projections for several subgroups of baby boomers show economic vulnerability for the old-aged divorced women, men who have never married, Hispanics, high school dropouts, those with marginal attachment to the labor force, and those with the lowest lifetime wages. Moreover, it is probable that a good number of them could be in poverty at retirement.

In evaluating the effectiveness of several key social programs, international comparisons become vital when assessing redistributive policies. Yet such comparisons are particularly difficult given the limitations and incompatibility of data. Parts II and III of this book, comprising Chapters 5–10, attempt to address this important task. In Chapter 5, a team of seven authors, Immervoll, Levy, Lietz, Mantovani, O'Donoghue, Sutherland, and Verbist, offer a comparison among the redistributive aspects of taxation and social benefits in the 15 'old' member countries of the EU, by using a microsimulation method of the European model, EUROMOD. Their cross-national analysis illustrates the effects of tax and social benefits programs on the level of household disposable income, as well as the corresponding income inequalities before and after taxation and benefits are applied. The authors are able to overcome the various problems with cross-national data limitations and incompatibilities, by partly harmonizing microdata with the use of well-established simulation techniques. Their methodology does not use data to directly extract the tax and benefits. Instead they use it as a basis to calculate tax liabilities and benefits entitlements in accordance with accepted rules, which would result in observations being close to those that would be officially determined. Their results are framed in such a way that particular comparisons can be drawn:

- the profile for the average household and that of either the top and the bottom quintiles is contrasted;
- the redistributive effects of four specific tax-benefit programs—means-tested benefits, non means-tested benefits, social contributions and income taxes—are determined; and
- the Gini coefficients are estimated to document changes in income inequalities, resulting from the redistributive effects of tax-benefit systems.

Their findings are striking in that there is extensive variation among the EU-15 countries. Pensions, for example, play a major role in reducing inequality in Austria, Germany, Luxembourg, France and Spain and a minor one in Ireland and the United Kingdom, with an even lesser one in Denmark.

Other findings show that non-means-tested benefits are very important in the redistributive process in all 15 countries, while the inequality reduction resulting from means-tested benefits varies significantly. Finally, the effect of income taxes on reducing inequality is high in the countries with the most equal distributions of disposable income, such as Austria, Belgium, Denmark, Finland, Germany, Luxembourg and the Netherlands, and also in Ireland and Spain. In summary, the Immervoll, *et al.*, analysis reaffirms the welfare state categorization of Andrè Sapir referred to earlier.

The next three chapters are country-specific sequential analyses of the tax-benefit distributional effects for Poland, Australia and Korea. Leon Podkaminer explores Poland's redistribution experiences for the pre- and post-socialist periods. The economic system of pre-socialist Poland, which he describes, was egalitarian in ensuring fairness in the distribution of income and consumption. Consequently, inequality in personal income and wealth was low and was complemented by a public pension system. The 'shock therapy' of 1990 brought with it declining fortunes exemplified by a precipitous drop in real wages, farmers' incomes and retirement bene-fits. These trends were halted for some years post-1991, that significantly improved matters, only to return in the latter part of the 1990s, instituting a new structure of public finance marked with low taxes—a *de facto* flat tax for all—and spending cuts including decreases in social transfers. The conclusion of that chapter suggests that, based on the Polish experience, the controversial proposition that high levels of redistribution can be good for growth and lessen inequality, should not be dismissed but be seriously reconsidered.

Australia's experience regarding its redistribution efforts is similar to other OECD countries, as evidenced in the analysis presented in Chapter 7. The country's tax-benefit program is not exemplary, but better than those found in most countries of the industrialized world. The winner/loser pairs vary depending on the taxes collected—some are progressive while others are regressive—and the benefits distributed. The winners, overall, are elderly Australians and sole parents, while couples with no children and single person households are net losers. Using data obtained from the Australian Bureau of Statistics and Household Expenditure Surveys in 1998–99 and running simulations for 2001–02, Ann Harding, Rachel Lloyd and Neil Warren cover a lot of ground in this chapter. They successfully estimate the social security cash transfers and family payments, income taxes, tax rebates and allowances such as the health insurance rebate, the Common-wealth Goods and Services Tax, all excise taxes and imputed values (non-cash) of health, welfare and education benefits. Their approach of estimating an expanded measure of household income is reminiscent of similar type measures of economic well-being—albeit with clearly distinct differences—employed by Wolff, Zacharias and Immervoll, *et al.*, previously seen in Chapters 2 and 5, respectively. Clearly, government intervention through collection of taxes and distribution of benefits lessens the gap between the poor and the better off. Moreover, the Harding, Lloyd and Warren study demonstrates that Australia's system of taxes and benefits is designed to assist households over their lifecycle, by redistributing income and benefits from times of relative plenty to times of relative indigence, such as when there are children and during retirement.

The empirical exploration of equity consequences of Korea's income tax system is the focus of Chapter 8. Kwang Soo Cheong's analysis uses new and novel methods of analyzing panel data in estimating the redistributive effects of the country's income tax system and the consequent changes in vertical equity and horizontal equity and tax-induced income re-ranking. Estimates of vertical equity demonstrate the degree of the tax progression while horizontal inequity is the result of tax-induced household income re-ranking. The author's findings reveal some undesirable redistributive effects of Korea's tax system affecting horizontal inequity, exemplified by the tax-induced household income re-ranking, in addition to re-affirming other studies findings of the moderate degree of tax progressivity.

The relationship between inequality and social spending form the theme of Chapter 9, which begins Part III of this book. In it, Jonathan Schwabish, Timothy Smeeding and Lars Osberg consider a number of important, interesting and intertwined issues relating to the questions they attempt to address. The focus surveys non-elderly social expenditures and subsequently tests their relationship to inequality. The authors construct a model, incorporating variables such as values (which they equate with trust), growth, institutions and immigrants. This model uses a dataset with 57 different sets of observations for 17 countries, drawn from data collected by the Luxembourg Income Study, the OECD and the World Value Survey. The reported results confirm Robert Reich's hypothesis who, referring to America's rich, noted that they 'feel increasingly justified in paying only what is necessary to insure that everyone in their community is sufficiently well educated and has access to the public services they need to succeed' (1991). Alas, the Schwabish, Smeeding and Osberg study shows that America's 'fortunate top fifth' is similar to those in other countries too.

The final chapter, Chapter 10 returns to the topic of pensions and attempts to estimate various aspects of generosity. Mathieu Lefèbvre and Pierre Pestieau perform a series of econometric tests to determine the correlation, evolution, and economic openness relations among three kinds of pension generosity based on average benefits, early retirement and poverty alleviation. The authors' results considered, perhaps, controversial indications that the three types of generosity are not correlated, that the evolution into contributory plans has made them more generous and beneficial to the poor, and that economic integration (openness) is not significantly linked with redistribution.

The chapters in this book present theories, findings and applied policies dealing with one or more issues of income distribution and well-being. While many readers may not agree with all of them, I hope the many lessons drawn from the success and failure of the tested social policies will help continue the search and development of better policies to improve economic inequality.

Notes

1. The countries include: Australia, Austria, Belgium, Canada, France, Germany, Ireland, Italy, Japan, the Netherlands, New Zealand, Norway, Spain, Sweden, Switzerland, The United Kingdom, and the United States.
2. In the words of United States President John F. Kennedy who, as he put it: 'A rising tide lifts all boats.'
3. See, Bowles and Gintis (1982), Shaikh and Tonak (1987, 1994).

References

Afonso, A., W. Ebert, L. Schuknecht and M. Thone (2005) 'Quality of Public Finances and Growth,' Working Paper 438 (Germany: European Central Bank).

Bowles, S. and H. Gintis (1982) 'The Crisis of Liberal Democratic Capitalism: The Case of the United States,' *Politics and Society* **11**: 51–93.

European Commission (2004) Public Finance Report, Brussels.

Hare, P.G. (1988) 'Economics of Publicly Provided Private Goods and Services,' in *Surveys in Public Sector Economics* (United Kingdom: Basil Blackwell Ltd.), pp. 68–101.

Nell, E. (1988) *Prosperity and Public Spending* (Boston: Unwin Hyman), p. 228.

OECD (2005) Annex Table 25. General government total outlays. *OECD Economic Outlook 77* (Paris: OECD).

Persson, T. and G. Tabellini (2001) 'Political Institutions and Policy Outcomes: What are the Stylized Facts?', mimeo.

Reich, R.B. (1991) 'Secession of the Successful', *New York Times Magazine* (January 20): 16–23. Reprinted at www.-personal.umich.edu/~gmarkus/secession.html.

Rodrik, D. (2000) 'Institutions for High-Quality Growth: What they are and How to Acquire them,' Working Paper 7540 (Cambridge, MA: National Bureau of Economic Research).

Samuelson, P.A. (1966a) 'The Pure Theory of Public Expenditure,' reprinted in J. Steiglitz (ed.) *The Collected Scientific Papers of Paul Samuelson, Vol. 2* (Cambridge, MA: The MIT Press), pp. 1223–5.

Samuelson, P.A. (1966b) 'Diagrammatic Exposition of a Theory of Public Expenditure,' reprinted in J. Stiglitz (ed.) *The Collected Scientific Papers of Paul Samuelson, Vol. 2* (Cambridge, MA: The MIT Press), pp. 1226–32.

Sapir, A. (2005) 'Globalisation and the Reform of European Social Models,' Policy Brief, 1 (Brussels: Bruegel).

Shaikh, A. and E.A. Tonak (1994) *Measuring the Wealth of Nations* (New York: Cambridge University Press).

Shaikh, A. and E.A. Tonak (1987) 'The Welfare State and the Myth of the Social Wage,' in R. Cherry *et al.* (eds), *The Imperiled Economy*, Book I (New York: Union for Radical Political Economics).

Summers, L.H. (2003) 'Comment,' in James J. Heckman and Alan B. Krueger, *Inequality in America* (Cambridge, MA: The MIT Press), pp. 69–70, 285.

Tanzi, V. and H. Davoodi (1997) 'Corruption, Public Investment, and Growth,' Working Paper 139 (Washington, DC: International Monetary Fund).

Tanzi, V. and L. Schuknecht (2003) 'Public Finances and Economic Growth in European Countries,' in *Fostering Economic Growth in Europe*, conference volume of the 31st Economics Conference of the Oestereichische Nationalbank, Vienna, 2003, pp. 178–196.

Tanzi, V. and L. Schuknecht (2000) *Public Spending in the 20th Century* (London: Cambridge University Press).

Tanzi, V. and L. Schuknecht (1997) 'Reconsidering the Fiscal Role of Government: The International Perspective,' *American Economic Review*, 87(2), 164–68.

Tanzi, V. and L. Schuknecht (1996) 'Reforming Government in Industrial Countries,' *Finance and Development* (September) 2–5.

Tanzi, V. and L. Schuknecht (1995) 'The Growth of Government and the Reform of the State in Industrial Countries,' Working Paper 130 (Washington, DC: International Monetary Fund).

Part I

Distributional Effects of Taxes and Government Spending in the United States

2

An Overall Assessment of the Distributional Consequences of Government Spending and Taxation in the United States, 1989 and 2000

Edward N. Wolff and Ajit Zacharias

2.1 Introduction and overview

This chapter assesses the effects of government expenditures and taxation on household economic well-being in the United States in 1989 and 2000 on the basis of household-level data.[1] While there is an enormous literature on particular aspects of government expenditures and taxation, there has been no recent study of the net effect of the government budget (expenditures less taxes) on household economic well-being. The last comprehensive estimates, for the year 1970, were published in 1981 (Ruggles and O'Higgins, 1981). Since the early 1980s, the Census Bureau has been publishing regular estimates of broader definitions of disposable household income that reflect the net effects of some taxes and transfers. However, the measures do not take into account public provisioning (government expenditures on schools, highways and so on), which has a crucial effect on economic well-being. The present study seeks to fill this gap in the existing literature by developing comprehensive estimates that take into account all relevant government expenditures and taxes for an admittedly remarkable period in recent US economic history (see Blinder and Yellen, 2001; Stiglitz, 2003).

Economic growth was notably strong during most of the 1990s and the unemployment rate fell to levels not seen since the 1960s. At the same time, economic inequality, as measured by inequality in earnings, gross money income or wealth, was also on the rise during much of this period (Wolff, 2004). Both these developments affected the revenue and expenditure sides of the budget. Net government saving, as measured in the national accounts, turned positive in the later part of the decade, after being in the red for almost all of the previous 30 years. A number of important institutional changes also affected the tax and expenditure policy since 1990 (for example, the Omnibus Budget Reconciliation Act of 1993 that raised marginal income tax rates, expenditure reductions stemming from the Budget Enforcement Act of 1990 and its extensions in 1993 and 1997, and the dramatic reduction in tax burden under the current administration). Welfare reform and the spectacular growth in medical spending have also changed the composition of expenditure significantly (Auerbach, 2000).

Given the changes in the economy and the policy environment, it is important to examine the net effect of government expenditures and taxation on the distribution of household economic well-being. We narrowly define the scope of the effects studied here by excluding two considerations. First, the public provisioning of goods and services exerts direct and indirect effects on household income via employment and output changes. For example, establishing a new public school yields jobs to individuals such as teachers and school staff, creates new demand for goods and services produced locally and elsewhere, and has ripple effects on employment and income. Second, tax and transfer payments incorporated in the budget may have indirect effects on household income by changing consumer preferences, individual decisions regarding labor market participation, and business decisions on the location and scale of activity (Ruggles, 1991). Exclusion of these considerations is in line with the previous research into this question (Gillespie, 1965).[2]

Most existing empirical studies aimed at answering the question 'how does government affect distribution' can be classified into two categories. Studies in the first category involve two steps in the allocation and distribution of taxes and government expenditures. First, assumptions are made regarding the incidence of various taxes on different categories of factor incomes and types of consumer expenditures, and also regarding on whose behalf government expenditures may be considered as being made. For example, a study may assume that taxes on corporate profits are borne entirely by those who earn property-type income and expenditures on public educations are incurred exclusively on behalf of households with students enrolled in public educational institutions. Such incidence assumptions are generally derived from a specific theoretical framework, a combination of theoretical predictions and empirical findings from testing theoretical predictions, or, when theoretical arguments and empirical evidence are inconclusive, just plain arbitrarily. In the second step, taxes and expenditures are distributed across households, grouped into different income groups, in accordance with the incidence assumptions and, when appropriate, other household-level characteristics relevant to the determination of tax liability and expenditure incidence (Musgrave, Case and Leonard, 1974).

The second category of studies is based on computable general equilibrium (CGE) models that allow for estimating the effects of all types of taxes and government expenditures simultaneously on factor and product prices (Piggot and Whalley, 1987). A CGE model does not need to make assumptions regarding the incidence of particular types of taxes because their incidence is determined endogenously (Ballard, *et al.*, 1985). Further, being based on explicit utility-maximizing behavior of households, such a model can also assess welfare losses from taxes suffered by different types of households and the deadweight loss from taxation. However, regarding public goods, the problem still remains because preferences for public goods have to be necessarily imputed. For example, in the study by Piggot and Whalley cited above (on the Australian tax-benefit system), preferences for public goods were derived by imputing 'private expenditures' on public goods according to two alternative imputation rules: proportional to income and equal dollar amount per household (Piggot and Whalley, 1987, p. 687).

Several criticisms have been advanced against both types of studies. A key issue plaguing the first category is the sensitivity of estimates to the incidence assumptions. Since models of tax incidence produce different results depending on whether they are static or dynamic, assume perfectly or imperfectly competitive markets, and a host of other specification details, this issue affects the validity of the whole exercise (Whalley, 1984). Some have also argued that by equating tax burden with actual tax payments, the approach does not allow for the assessment of welfare losses to households or the deadweight loss associated with the tax system (Fullerton and Metcalf, 2002, p. 26). Similar considerations also apply to the expenditure side. For example, expenditures on public education are widely believed to generate positive externalities, which are disregarded when such expenditures are considered as being incurred solely on behalf of students alone.

On the other hand, the specification of the underlying utility and production functions in a CGE model involves a degree of arbitrariness that may not be significantly different than what was involved in the traditional incidence assumptions (Whalley, 1984, p. 678). Further, as noted above, while purely theoretical studies can model the preferences for public goods in a general way (Pirttila and Tuomala, 2002, pp. 175–176, and references cited therein), a CGE model requires for its calibration very specific assumptions to be made regarding the distribution of public expenditures. Questionable assumptions of continuous full employment and perfectly competitive markets are generally made in both approaches to determine tax and expenditure incidence.

2.1.1 Overview

The next section presents the basic framework used in conceptualizing the relationship between the household sector and the government, as well as the measures of economic well-being (Section 2.2). We then outline the empirical methodology used in constructing the estimates of government spending and taxes at the level of the individual household and estimates of economic well-being (Section 2.3). The subsequent section (Section 2.4) reports and discusses our findings. We begin with the size and composition of net government expenditures (Section 2.4.1). Next, we examine how the major components of net government expenditures— transfers, public consumption and taxes—vary across population subgroups

(Section 2.4.2) and by deciles of income (Section 2.4.3). This is followed by a discussion of the distribution of 'post-fisc income' by household characteristics (Section 2.4.4). The level and distribution of economic well-being by alternative measures of well-being is analyzed next (Section 2.4.5). We then address the relationship between net government expenditure and overall inequality (Section 2.4.6). The final section contains our conclusions and caveats.

2.2   Net government expenditure and measures of economic well-being

The approach adopted in the present study might be described as a social accounting method (Hicks, 1946). Our aim is to account for the flows of purchasing power and products between the government sector and household sector during a given accounting period in an *ex post* fashion. We take the individual household as the unit of analysis and build estimates of how much the government spends for each household and how much the government takes from each household in taxes. In assessing the effect of net government expenditure on well-being, it is insufficient to examine only the distribution of net government expenditure. As has been observed, ultimately the result of the government's taxation and spending policies is to affect the distribution of economic well-being that prevails after the effects of these policies have been taken into account (Lambert and Pfahler, 1988, p. 198).

For the purposes of this study, economic well-being is defined as the magnitude of the command or access exercised by members of a household over the products produced (excluding self-provisioning by households) in a modern market economy during a given period of time.[3] In all modern economies, the state intervenes in determining the household's command over commodities. Apart from cash transfers, noncash transfers from the government to the households constitute government payments for commodities on behalf of the recipients. Through the system of direct (including negative income tax such as the Earned Income Tax Credit) and indirect taxes, the state affects the command that the household can exercise over commodities. Admittedly, commodities only form a portion, though a critical one, of the entire set of products produced and distributed in an economy. Apart from influencing the command over commodities, the state also plays a crucial role in the direct provisioning of products (as in the case of schooling and highways).

Government expenditures considered here consists of cash transfers, noncash transfers and public consumption. The social accounting approach to government expenditures yields the generally accepted conclusion in the case of government cash transfers—they are to be considered entirely as part of money incomes of the recipients. Our approach to noncash transfers is that they must be distributed among recipients on the basis of the appropriate average cost incurred by the government. However, it has been argued on theoretical grounds that the income-value for the recipient from a given noncash transfer is, on average, less than the average cost incurred by the government in providing that benefit (see Canberra Group, 2001, pp. 24, 65). In practice, a method of imputation consistent with this argument (often referred to as the cash-equivalent method) involves estimating how much the household could have paid for the transfer, after meeting its expenditures on some basic items (such as food, clothing and so on), with the maximum payment for the transfer set equal to the average cost incurred by the government.

The alternative is not pursued by us primarily because of its important implication that households with incomes below the minimum threshold and participating in the program are presumed to receive no benefit from a good or service that they actually consume. This is inconsistent with our goal of measuring the household's access or command over products. Further, unlike the social accounting approach, the alternative method would not, by definition, yield the actual total government expenditure when aggregated across recipients. Such a feature is incompatible with our goal of estimating net government expenditures using a consistent methodology.

The third type of government expenditure that we consider as part of our measure of well-being are public expenditures ('public consumption'). In deciding to allocate these expenditures to the household sector we attempt to follow, as far as possible, the general criterion that a particular expenditure must be considered as incurred directly on behalf of the households and as expanding their consumption possibilities. The implementation of the approach is carried out in two stages.

We begin with a detailed functional classification of government expenditures (excluding transfer payments) and exclude certain functions entirely because they fail to satisfy the general criterion. Most such functions form part of general social overhead and their major effect is to keep the ship of state afloat (for example, national defense, general public service, law courts and prisons, and so on). Expenditures under other functional categories also may not meet the general criterion fully because part of such expenditures can be considered as being incurred on behalf of the business sector (for example, transportation, energy, natural resources and so on). We estimate the household sector's share in such expenditures using data on the utilization or consumption of services or goods provided via the expenditures.[4] Finally, expenditures under certain functional categories are considered as incurred completely on behalf of the household sector, such as health.

In the second stage, the relevant totals for each functional category are distributed among the households. The distribution procedures followed by us build on the earlier studies employing the government cost approach (see Ruggles and O'Higgins, 1981) in that some expenditures are distributed, in the same way as the split was made between the household and other sectors, on the basis of estimated patterns of utilization or consumption[5] and some expenditures are distributed equally among the relevant population.[6]

The final step in constructing net government expenditure is concerned with taxes. Our approach is to determine, mainly in an accounting sense, the distribution of the actual tax payments by households among those in different income and demographic groups, rather than incidence in a strict theoretical sense. However, for the bulk of the taxes paid by households— individual income taxes—most theoretical models of incidence concur that the tax is borne by the taxpayer (Fullerton and Metcalf, 2002). In addition we also consider property taxes on owner-occupied housing, payroll taxes (both employee and employer portion), and consumption taxes as a part of the household tax burden. Inclusion of the property taxes is required for consistency with the inclusion of imputed rental cost on the income side.

It should be noted that we include both the employee and employer portions of the payroll tax. According to the National Income and Product Accounts (NIPA) conventions, payroll taxes are not considered as taxes. Instead they are considered as contributions for government social insurance and are excluded from personal income. Excluding payroll taxes from personal income allows for the consistent derivation of measures of personal saving and disposable personal income in the NIPA. We treat the employee portion of the payroll tax as directly reducing the purchasing power of households. The employer portion is considered as paid ultimately out of labor income, and so the employer portion of the payroll tax is included in both the income side and the tax side.

Consumption taxes also reduce the potential command that households could exercise over commodities. Finally, taxes on corporate profits, taxes on business-owned property, and other business taxes and nontaxes were not allocated to the household sector because they are considered as paid out of the incomes of the business sector.

In sum, in the social accounting approach, taxes paid by the household sector are considered as reducing the command over products. Symmetrically, transfers and public provisioning received by the household sector are considered as expanding the command over products. The difference between the government expenditures incurred on behalf of the household sector and the taxes paid by that sector is defined as net government expenditure. This approach is similar in several practical respects to the methods used by the national statistical agencies in the United Kingdom and Australia to assess annually the effects of taxes, transfers and some public expenditures on household income as well as by the OECD for estimating net social expenditure (Adema, 2001; Australian Bureau of Statistics, 2001; Lakin, 2002). A similar approach has also been employed in estimating the impact of net government expenditures on the functional distribution of income between labor and capital (Shaikh, 2003).

We construct two measures of economic well-being. One, which may be called 'pre-fisc' income, reflects primarily the actual or potential command over products that the members of the household derive from market or quasi-market transactions. The other, called 'post-fisc' income is the sum of pre-fisc income and net government expenditure.[7]

Gross money income—the yardstick used in the current official measures of poverty and income inequality—is not a measure of pre-fisc income because it includes government cash transfers. Therefore, the first step in constructing the pre-fisc income measure is to subtract cash transfers from gross money income. In the second step, we need to add the value of employer-provided fringe benefits that enhance the current command of the household over commodities but are not included in gross money income. Finally, the property income component of gross money income has to be replaced by an alternative component that better reflects the economic advantage derived from asset ownership. To this end, we add an 'annuity' component derived from nonhome wealth (see below) as well as the imputed rental cost of owner-occupied housing. The latter reflects the replacement cost of the services derived from owner-occupied housing, that is, a rental equivalent.

2.3 Empirical methodology

Our empirical strategy is to begin with the public-use datafiles developed by the U.S. Bureau of the Census from the Current Population Survey's Annual demographic supplement (ADS).[8] The calculation of the income measures to be used in the study involves a set of imputations based on additional information available from other sources, such as household surveys on wealth and NIPA. Sources and methods used in constructing these estimates are described below.

2.3.1 Imputed rent and annuities

The ADS contains no information on household wealth.[9] Therefore, we estimate it by statistically matching the 1989 and 2001 rounds of the Survey of Consumer Finances (SCF) conducted by the Federal Reserve Board with the ADS for 1989 and 2000 respectively.[10] Each household record in the SCF is matched with a household record in the ADS, where a match represents a similar unit. The strata variables used in the matching procedure are the race of the household head (white versus non-white), the homeownership status of the household (owns or buying versus rents), the family type (married couples, single males, single females) and age of the household head (age difference within a range of two, five, ten or more). Within these strata, records are matched by minimizing a distance function based on the education and occupation of the household head, and total income and size of the household. The weights of the distance function are the coefficient estimates from an ordinary least squares (OLS) regression of wealth that includes all of the variables mentioned above as regressors.

After matching the datafiles we estimated imputed rent and annuities. Imputed rent is the replacement cost of the services derived from owner-occupied housing. We estimate this amount by distributing the total amount of imputed rent on nonfarm owner-occupied housing in the GDP (available from the Bureau of Economic Analysis)[11] to homeowners in the ADS, based on the gross values of their houses.

Each household was assigned a lifetime annuity flow—reflecting the benefit or loss from nonhome wealth. The latter was computed in two steps. In the first step, we estimated the annuity flow generated by each component of nonhome wealth using average total real rates of return for each component from 1960 to 2000. Then, we calculated the weighted sum of the annuity flows for each household with the portfolio shares of the components serving as weights to take into account differences between households in portfolio composition. The annuity amount calculated is such that:

- it is the same for all remaining years of the younger spouse's life;[12] and
- brings wealth down to zero at the end of the expected lifetime.

Formally, the annuity value of non-home wealth can be written as the product of (1×6) and (6×1) vectors: $A_i = [f_i(r_j, race_i, sex_i, age_i)] * [W_j]$. Each element f_i of the first vector gives the annuity flow that household i would receive each year if it held \$1 in wealth component j. This amount is a function of the real total rate of return on the non-home wealth component, r_j, and of the race, sex and age of the younger spouse. Multiplying this factor, f_i, by the total amount of money held in the jth component, W_j, gives us the total annuity generated by this component.

The rationale for using long-run average rates of return (instead of using the rate of return in an arbitrarily chosen year) is that the annuity value estimated in this way is a better indicator of the resources available to the household on a sustainable basis over its lifetime. The total rates of return data we use are inclusive of the incomes generated by the assets. Therefore, in order to avoid double counting, we net out from the total income measure any property income already included in money income (see Wolff, Zacharias, and Caner, forthcoming, for more details).

2.3.2 Government transfers

Government transfers to be estimated for the study are 'NIPA-consistent,' meaning that in the aggregate they are equal to the appropriate NIPA benchmarks. The latter are derived from the NIPA Table 3.12 'Government social benefits' by making adjustments for differences in definition and coverage. These adjustments are made for old-age, survivors and disability insurance, unemployment insurance, Supplemental Security Income, veterans' payments, workers' compensation and the cash-component of public assistance on the basis of the estimates in Roemer (2000). Adjustments are made for NIPA expenditures on Medicare and Medicaid to exclude expenditures on institutionalized recipients based on administrative data.

Transfers for which actual or imputed amounts are reported in the ADS are aggregated across recipients and compared against the benchmarks.[13] Any discrepancy between the ADS total and the NIPA benchmark for a given transfer payment is distributed across recipients according to the distribution of that transfer payment in the ADS. Rather than reflecting any assumptions about misreporting in the survey, this procedure was chosen merely to avoid changing the distribution of transfers among recipients identified in the ADS as a result of the NIPA adjustment.[14]

Transfers for which there are no actual or imputed amounts reported in the ADS can be divided into two categories: those for which recipients are identified in the ADS itself and those for which we had to impute recipiency. For the first category our approach is to distribute the relevant NIPA amount across households equally, adjusted by the number of participants in a household. For the second category, we distribute the NIPA amount equally among households selected using appropriate eligibility criteria. Transfers that fall into the two categories are:

- the noncash component of public assistance (applicable only since the 1996 welfare reform);
- Women, Infants and Children (WIC) program;
- employment and training;
- military-related transfers (veterans' life insurance and, medical payments for retired and active armed forces personnel and their dependents at nonmilitary facilities); and
- payments to nonprofit institutions.

Expenditures on WIC, payments to nonprofit institutions and payments for medical services for retired military personnel and their dependents at nonmilitary facilities are not reported separately in the NIPA table on transfers. We estimate these amounts using unpublished information from the Bureau of Economic Analysis (made available to us for strictly research purposes).[15]

2.3.3 Public consumption

Estimates of public consumption by households are constructed in three steps.

1) expenditure totals by function and level of government are obtained;
2) expenditure totals are allocated between the household sector and other sectors of the economy; and
3) expenditures allocated to the household sector are distributed among households.

Table 2.1 summarizes the functional classifications used in the study and the allocation and distribution assumptions associated with each function.

Table 2.1 Allocation and distribution of government consumption expenditures and gross investment by function

No.	Function	Allocation	Distribution
	General public service		
1	Executive and legislative	Non-household	
2	Tax collection and financial management	Non-household	
3	Other public service	Non-household	
4	National defense	Non-household	
	Public order and safety		
5	Police	Household and non-household (50:50)*	Population
6	Fire	Household and non-household (50:50)*	Population
7	Law courts	Non-household	
8	Prisons	Non-household	
	Economic affairs		
9	General economic and labor affairs	Household	Population
10	Agriculture	Share of family farms in total sales of farm products	Farm income
11	Energy	Share of household sector in total energy consumption	Energy expenditures
12	Water resources (federal only)	Households	Population
13	Land conservation and management (federal only)	Households	Population
14	Forestry (State and local only)	Households	Population
15	Fish and game (State and local only)	Households	Population
16	Pollution control and abatement	Share of household sector in total pollution[1]	Polluting consumption expenditures[2]
17	Highways	Share of passenger vehicles in total highway costs	Vehicle miles traveled
18	Air	Share of commercial air carrier miles in total air carrier miles	Person-miles traveled
19	Railroad	Share of passenger car-miles in total car-miles	Person-miles traveled
20	Public transit	Household	Person-miles traveled

21	Postal service (federal only)	Household	Expenditures on postage and stationery
22	Parking facilities (state and local only)	Household	Vehicle owning households
23	Liquor stores (state and local only)	Household	Expenditures on alcohol
24	Miscellaneous commerce (state and local only)	Household	Population
	Housing and Community Services		
25	Water supply (state and local only)	Domestic-use share of total deliveries from the public water supply	Expenditures on water and other public services by households receiving public water supply
26	Sewerage (state and local only)	Domestic share of total water discharges from all sectors	Expenditures on water and other public services by households using public sewerage
27	Solid waste management (state and local only)	Residential share of total municipal solid waste	Expenditures on nondurables and entertainment (less fees and admissions)
28	Other housing and community development	Household	Recipients of government housing assistance
	Health		
29	Public Health	Household	Population
30	Public hospitals	Household	Population
31	Occupational safety and health	Household	Employed
32	Administrative costs of Medicare	Household	Medicare recipients
33	Medical and related services for veterans	Household	Veterans
34	Recreation and culture	Household	Population
	Education		
35	Elementary and secondary education	Household	Elementary and secondary public-school students
36	Higher education	Household and non-household	Higher education students residing in households
37	Other education	Household	Population
38	Libraries (State and local only)	Household	Population

Table 2.1   (Continued)

No.	Function	Allocation	Distribution
	Income Security		
39	Disability assistance	Household	Recipients of public disability assistance
40	Retirement	Household	Recipients of Social Security
41	Welfare and social services	Household	Recipients of means-tested public assistance
42	Unemployment	Household	Recipients of unemployment insurance
43	Other public welfare	Household	Recipients of means-tested public assistance
44	Welfare institutions (state and local only)	Household	Population

Notes: * Expenditures split equally between the two sectors.
[1] Average household contribution to four pollution types: air, CO_2, water and municipal solid wastes.
[2] Expenditures on non-durable goods, energy, water and other public services, public transportation and entertainment (less fees and admissions).

2.3.3.1   *Expenditure by function and level of government*

The expenditure category used here is the same that appearing on the product side of the NIPA: government consumption expenditures and gross investment. In order to allocate government expenditures to the households and distribute it among these households, it is essential to have expenditures grouped according to purpose. We adopt the functional classification given in the NIPA Table 3.15 'Government consumption expenditures and gross investment by function,' with minor modifications.

Since the disparities in state and local expenditures that exist across US states could possibly have effects on the distribution of economic well-being, we distribute the NIPA aggregate of state and local expenditures among the states. This distribution is accomplished using the Annual Survey of Government Finances (ASGF) conducted by the U.S. Bureau of the Census. We use the ASGF to determine the proportion in which the total state and local expenditure given in the NIPA for each function (such as education) is divided among the states. Care is taken to ensure that the expenditure concept formed from the ASGF and the grouping of the ASGF functions conform as closely as possible to the NIPA expenditure and function concepts.

2.3.3.2   *Allocation of expenditures to the household sector*

Our data allow us to construct a schema consisting of 44 functions by level of government (federal versus state and local). Allocation of expenditures between the household and other sectors is done on the basis of two sets of assumptions regarding these functions. The first involves the designation of a particular function as involving activities that do not expand the potential amenities available to the household sector at all or that expand only that sector's potential amenities. General public service, National defense, and, Law courts and Prisons are the prominent examples of functions that are assumed to provide no directly useable services to the household sector. In contrast, functions such as elementary and secondary education or public retirement income (Social Security) are assumed to directly expand amenities available only to the household sector.

The second type of assumption concerns functions that can potentially serve the household and non-household sectors. Costs incurred in the performance of these functions are allocated to the household sector in accordance with the extent of its 'responsibility' in generating such costs. We made judgments regarding the extent of responsibility, as far as possible, on the basis of available empirical information.[16] The allocation between the sectors in terms of the NIPA major functions is summarized in Table 2.2.

Of the 1.1 trillion dollars of government expenditure in 1989, we estimate that 485.2 billion dollars or 44 percent directly benefits households or individuals and thus constitutes public consumption. Total government expenditures grew to 1.75 trillion dollars in 2000, of which 892 billion dollars or 51 percent are estimated to directly benefit households or individuals. The increase in the share of public consumption reflects mainly the decline in the share of defense expenditures. In fact, public consumption is about two-thirds of non-defense expenditures in both years. The decline in the share of defense expenditures is also reflected in the increase in the share of federal expenditures devoted to public consumption from 13 percent in 1989 to 21 percent in 2000. As shown in the bottom two lines of Table 2.2, state and local government services are by far the largest component of public consumption—87 percent in 1989 and 86 percent in 2000. Moreover, in contrast to federal expenditures, the majority of state and local government spending directly benefits households.

2.3.3.3 *Distribution of allocated expenditure among households*

Once government expenditure allocated to the household sector ('public consumption') under different functions was determined, we proceed to distribute it among households. In distributing public consumption among households, we attempt to follow as much as possible, the same principles of direct usage and cost responsibility that were employed in splitting total government expenditures between the household and non-household sectors. Since household-level information required for a number of variables is simply not available in the ADS, various assumptions have to be made.

There are two major categories of public consumption to be distributed among households: those distributed equally among persons and those distributed according to household-level or person-level characteristics.

Table 2.2 Government consumption and gross investment expenditures by function (in billions of current dollars): total expenditure and the amount and share (in percent) allocated to the household sector

Function[1]	1989			2000		
	Total	Allocated	Household share	Total	Allocated	Household share
General public service	88.9	0.0	0	172.5	0.0	0
National defense	363.2	0.0	0	374.9	0.0	0
Public order and safety	92.0	24.3	26	203.2	52.9	26
Economic affairs	161.8	96.5	60	278.7	165.6	59
Housing and Community Services	23.6	16.5	70	28.1	19.3	69
Health[2]	57.5	56.8	99	92.7	91.6	99
Recreation and culture[2]	13.2	13.2	100	25.2	24.9	99
Education[3]	270.8	248.8	92	511.8	474.9	93
Income security[2]	29.1	29.1	100	63.9	62.5	98
Total government expenditures	1,100.1	485.2	44	1,751.0	891.8	51
Memo:						
Federal expenditures	482.5	63.4	13	589.2	124.2	21
State & Local expenditures	617.8	421.9	68	1,161.7	767.7	66

Note: Subtotals may not add up to totals due to rounding.
[1] The components of each function, where applicable, are shown in Table 2.1.
[2] Household share may be slightly different than 100 percent due to population weighting.
[3] The higher education component is adjusted for the fact that some students do not live in households.

The first class of expenditures pertains to functions that we consider, at least in principle, as equally available to all individuals in the form of a universal in-kind benefit. The person-level or household-level characteristics used in the distribution procedures for the second class of expenditures are the amount and type of income, employment status, shares in consumption expenditures on relevant items, public school enrollment, vehicle ownership and transportation usage.

Information on the type and amount of income as well as employment status of individuals was obtained directly from the ADS. All other characteristics were imputed to individuals or households in the ADS sample from information gathered from external sources. The relative importance of each allocation method in distributing public consumption is shown in Table 2.3. In both 1989 and 2000, a little over one fourth of public consumption was allocated to households on a straight per capita basis while a little less than three-fourths was allocated on the basis of specific household characteristics such as car ownership and miles driven.

2.3.4 Taxes

The household tax burden consists of federal and state individual income taxes, property taxes on owner-occupied housing, payroll taxes, and state and local consumption taxes (excise and sales). Federal and state individual income taxes, property taxes on owner-occupied housing, and employee portion of payroll taxes have imputed values in the ADS (estimated by the Census Bureau).[17] The ADS aggregates of these taxes are aligned with their

Table 2.3 Classification of public consumption expenditures by distribution method: total expenditure (in billions of current dollars) and share (in percent) of total expenditure allocated to the household sector

	1989		2000	
	Amount	Share	Amount	Share
Public consumption	485.3	100.0%	891.8	100.0%
A. General	134.2	27.7%	235.3	27.0%
Police and Fire	24.3	5.0%	52.9	5.7%
Public health and hospitals	53.3	11.0%	88.7	9.9%
Other	56.6	11.7%	93.7	10.5%
Memo: Federal	42.7	8.8%	88.7	9.9%
Memo: State and local	91.5	18.9%	149.7	16.8%
B. Specific	351.1	72.3%	656.6	73.6%
Highways	43.8	9.0%	77.4	8.7%
Elementary and secondary education	207.8	42.8%	403.2	45.2%
Other	99.4	20.5%	176.0	19.7%
Memo: Federal	20.7	4.3%	35.5	4.0%
Memo: State and local	330.4	68.1%	619.6	69.5%

NIPA counterparts by distributing the discrepancy between the NIPA and ADS aggregate for each tax among households according to the share of each household in the ADS aggregate.[18]

State and local consumption taxes are calculated on the basis of estimates published by the Institute on Taxation and Economic Policy (McIntyre *et al.*, 2003). For each of the 50 states, estimates are available for the average tax rates for 'General Sales-Individuals' and 'Other sales and excise-Individuals' differentiated for households in each quintile of the household income distribution and selected portions of the top quintile. We assigned the average tax rates to households in the corresponding positions in the ADS household income distribution.

Table 2.4 Derivation of post-fiscal income

1	Census money income[1]
2	*Less:*
3	Government cash transfers[1]
4	Property income[1]
5	*Plus:*
6	Employer contributions for health insurance[1]
7	Employer portion of payroll taxes[2]
8	Consumption taxes (state)[2]
9	*Equals:*
10	Base income
11	*Plus: Income from wealth*
12	Imputed annuity from non-home wealth[2]
13	Imputed rent on owner-occupied housing[2]
14	*Equals:*
15	Wealth-adjusted, pre-fisc income
16	*Plus: Government cash and noncash transfers*[3]
17	*Equals:*
18	Wealth-adjusted, comprehensive income (CIW)
19	*Plus:*
20	Public consumption[2]
21	*Less: Taxes*
22	Income taxes[3]
23	Payroll taxes (employer and employee)[3]
24	Property taxes[3]
25	Consumption taxes (state)[2]
26	*Equals:*
27	Wealth-adjusted, post-fisc income

Notes:
[1] Estimates reported in the ADS.
[2] Authors' estimates.
[3] Estimates reported in the ADS and modified by the authors. The modifications were (a) alignment with the NIPA benchmarks, and (b) for noncash transfers, valuation by government cost rather than fungible value.

The NIPA aggregate of employer portion of payroll taxes is distributed among the wage and salary workers in the ADS in accordance with the distribution of the employee portion of such taxes among them. The latter is available in the ADS.

2.3.5 Pre-fisc and post-fisc income measures

Table 2.4 shows the derivation of the income measures used in this study. We first subtract government cash transfers and property income—both as measured in the ADS—from Census gross money income and then add in the employer contribution for health insurance, the employer portion of payroll taxes and state-level consumption taxes to obtain 'base income.' We then add income from wealth as imputed rent on owner-occupied housing and the imputed annuity on non-home wealth to obtain 'wealth-adjusted pre-fisc income.' Government cash and noncash transfers are then added to obtain 'comprehensive income' (line 18).[19] This income measure differs substantially from the Census money income in that it includes employer contributions for health insurance, the employer portion of the payroll tax, noncash government transfers, and a broader definition of income from wealth. Finally, we add in public consumption and subtract income, payroll, property, and consumption taxes to obtain 'post-fisc income.'

2.4 Findings

2.4.1 Size and composition of net government expenditures

Table 2.5 shows the composition of net government expenditures. In both 1989 and 2000, the value of total government transfers and that of public consumption were close—the latter was 4 percent higher in 1989 and 2 percent lower in 2000 than the former. Social security comprised 47 percent of total transfers in 1989 but only 42 percent in 2000. This was offset by a rise in the share of Medicare from 20 to 23 percent over this period and an even larger increase in the share of Medicaid from 10 to 17 percent.

Education is by far the largest component of public consumption, comprising 53 percent in 2000—up from 51 percent in 1989. The next largest items in 2000 were public health and hospitals (10 percent), highways (9 percent) and police and fire departments (6 percent). While total public consumption rose by 15 percent between 1989 and 2000, expenditures for police and fire departments grew by a notable 36 percent and education increased by a more modest 19 percent. The remaining components of public consumption rose at below average rates—a paltry growth of 2 percent for public health and hospitals, and 10 percent for highways.

Table 2.5 Composition of net government expenditures, 1989 and 2000

Components	Mean (in 2000 dollars)			Shares (in percent)		
	1989	2000	Change	1989	2000	Change
Government transfers	6,912	8,421	22%	100	100	0
Social Security	3,248	3,562	10%	47	42	−5
Medicare	1,391	1,895	36%	20	23	2
Medicaid	718	1,392	94%	10	17	6
All others	1,555	1,573	1%	23	19	−4
Public consumption	7,211	8,242	14%	100	100	0
Police and Fire	361	489	36%	5	6	1
Public Health and Hospitals	794	811	2%	11	10	−1
Education	3,698	4,389	19%	51	53	2
Highways	651	714	10%	9	9	0
All others	1,708	1,839	8%	24	22	−1
Taxes	15,440	19,655	27%	100	100	0
Federal income taxes	6,705	9,231	38%	43	47	4
State income taxes	1,382	1,853	34%	9	9	0
Payroll taxes—Employee	2,847	3,311	16%	18	17	−2
State consumption taxes	1,269	1,578	24%	8	8	0
Property taxes	885	906	2%	6	5	−1
Payroll taxes—Employer	2,352	2,775	18%	15	14	−1
Net Government Expenditures	−1,318	−2,992	127%			

If we consider both transfers and public consumption jointly, then education still ranks first in 2000, at 26 percent of government spending, followed by health spending (including Medicare, Medicaid, and public health and hospitals) at 25 percent (up from 21 percent in 1989), and then Social Security at 21 percent (down from 23 percent in 1989). It seems clear that health spending will soon surpass education as the largest government expenditure.

The largest component of the taxes paid by households and individuals are federal income taxes. They comprised 47 percent of total taxes in 2000, up from 43 percent in 1989. The second largest component is payroll taxes (employee plus employer), which fell from 34 to 31 percent in 2000. State income taxes accounted for another 9 percent in the two years, state consumption taxes another 8 percent, and property taxes between 5 and 6 percent.

The most notable finding from Table 2.5 is that the total benefits to persons from government activity fell short of total personal tax payments. In 1989, mean net government expenditures amounted to −1318 dollars or −9 percent of personal tax payments. In 2000, mean net government expenditures more than doubled to about −3000 dollars or −15 percent or personal tax payments. This change reflected a much more rapid growth in taxes than in either transfers or public consumption.

2.4.2 Transfers, public consumption, and taxes by household characteristics

We next investigate the distribution of the components of net government expenditure by household characteristics. For comparisons, we also show both mean and median gross money income by the same set of characteristics in Table 2.6. Both mean and median values of government transfers

Table 2.6 Money income (in 2000 dollars) by household characteristics, 1989 and 2000

Characteristic	1989		2000		Percent change	
	Mean	Median	Mean	Median	Mean	Median
Race						
White	52,435	42,974	60,975	45,176	16.29	5.12
Non-white	38,687	29,180	46,455	34,350	20.08	17.72
Family type						
Married couples	62,419	53,604	74,677	59,280	19.64	10.59
Single females	31,625	23,955	36,346	28,160	14.93	17.55
Single males	50,452	42,011	55,163	42,000	9.34	−0.03
Housing tenure						
Own	58,066	49,019	66,606	51,038	14.71	4.12
Rent	34,394	27,774	37,248	28,000	8.30	0.81
Age of householder						
Less than 35	43,319	37,495	49,926	39,225	15.25	4.61
35–50 years	61,540	53,896	69,592	55,000	13.08	2.05
50–56 years	58,325	47,302	67,090	50,168	15.03	6.06
65 or older	32,290	21,749	34,645	23,128	7.30	6.34
Income						
Less than $20,000	11,261	11,340	11,168	11,623	−0.83	2.49
$20,000–50,000	34,214	33,966	33,701	33,017	−1.50	−2.80
$50,000–75,000	61,401	60,825	61,151	60,605	−0.41	−0.36
$75,000–100,000	86,037	85,235	85,606	85,000	−0.50	−0.28
$100,000 or more	140,482	127,524	166,515	130,770	18.53	2.55
Education of householder						
Less than high school	27,995	20,621	28,786	20,360	2.83	−1.27
High school degree	44,144	37,634	44,307	35,382	0.37	−5.98
Some college	53,324	46,584	56,092	45,000	5.19	−3.40
College degree	77,345	66,807	90,637	71,000	17.19	6.28
Household size						
One person	27,662	20,478	30,555	21,309	10.46	4.06
Two persons	51,261	41,461	59,476	44,356	16.03	6.98
Three or more persons	60,829	52,933	72,247	57,646	18.77	8.90
All households	49,570	40,167	57,140	42,000	15.27	4.56

by household characteristics are shown in Table 2.7. Transfer payments, as might be expected, are generally equalizing. They are larger for low-income groups and lower for high-income ones.

In 1989, mean government transfer payments were 14 percent greater for non-white households than for white households.[20] Between 1989 and 2000,

Table 2.7 Government transfers (in 2000 dollars) by household characteristics, 1989 and 2000

Characteristic	1989		2000		Percent change	
	Mean	Median	Mean	Median	Mean	Median
Race						
White	6,711	153	8,360	137	24.57	−10.44
Non-white	7,675	1,074	8,591	1,491	11.95	38.83
Family type						
Married couples	6,404	141	8,147	120	27.21	−14.59
Single females	10,298	5,779	11,655	5,603	13.17	−3.04
Single males	7,204	971	8,881	2,157	23.28	122.22
Housing tenure						
Own	7,084	153	8,560	137	20.84	−10.44
Rent	6,604	591	8,130	1,086	23.10	83.69
Age of householder						
Less than 35	3,049	47	3,838	66	25.86	39.00
35–50 years	2,906	105	4,106	82	41.31	−21.96
50–56 years	5,421	129	6,409	104	18.23	−19.50
65 or older	18,891	16,984	22,654	19,798	19.92	16.57
Income						
Less than $20,000	11,516	11,707	13,818	13,219	20.00	12.92
$20,000–50,000	7,127	400	9,239	1,220	29.64	204.72
$50,000–75,000	4,133	105	5,471	82	32.37	−21.96
$75,000–100,000	3,672	117	4,326	66	17.79	−43.87
$100,000 or more	3,466	117	4,517	66	30.31	−43.87
Education of householder						
Less than high school	12,563	12,065	14,784	12,855	17.68	6.55
High school degree	6,436	412	9,236	1,880	43.52	356.07
Some college	4,897	129	6,939	120	41.69	−6.76
College degree	3,482	47	5,051	66	45.07	39.00
Household size						
One person	6,985	2,078	8,189	486	17.24	−76.59
Two persons	8,984	854	10,693	891	19.02	4.31
Three or more persons	5,319	153	6,719	153	26.32	0.33
All households	6,912	307	8,421	332	21.84	8.09

transfer payments grew faster for white households, so that by 2000 the differential had fallen to 3 percent. In comparison, mean non-white gross money income averaged about three-fourths of white income in the two years.[21] Mean transfers were greatest for single females, followed by single males and then married couples. In contrast, mean gross money income is by far the highest for married couple households, followed by female-headed families and families headed by a single male adult.

Mean government transfers averaged only 5 to 7 percent less for renters than for home owners, whereas the mean gross money income of renters was only 56 to 59 percent that of home owners. Mean transfers were by far the largest for elderly households than younger ones (roughly 270 percent of overall mean transfers), whereas the mean gross money income of the elderly varied from 61 to 65 percent of the overall mean. Not surprisingly, mean transfer payments declined almost monotonically with household money income (with one slight exception). Mean transfer payments also declined monotonically with the education of the householder—a direct reflection of their relative income levels.

Public consumption by population subgroups is shown in Table 2.8. Both mean and median public consumption was considerably greater for non-white than white households. In 2000, mean public consumption was 46 percent greater for non-whites and the median 61 percent greater. The higher public consumption of non-whites is mainly a reflection of the differences in household size and composition. On average, non-white households have more members and more children of school age. In addition, the incidence of means-tested welfare—the administrative costs of which are included in public consumption—is also higher for non-white households. Both mean and median public consumption were almost identical for home owners as for renters. Public consumption was highest among the 35–50 age group—largely due to the large number of school-age children in this age group. For similar reasons, public consumption was greatest among households of three or more individuals than among smaller households. Both mean and median public consumption increased with household income, though differentials in public consumption across income classes were considerably smaller than in money income.

As shown in Table 2.9, differences in taxes paid by household group largely reflect differences in household income. In 2000, mean taxes paid by white households was 37 percent greater than taxes paid by non-whites, while their mean income was 31 percent greater. Average taxes paid by homeowners was almost exactly twice as great as renters in 2000, while their money income was 79 percent greater. Tax burdens by age class vary systematically with incomes by age class. However, the elderly had a particularly low tax burden relative to income. In 2000, their ratio of mean taxes to mean income was only 23 percent, compared to an overall ratio of 34 percent. Both mean and median taxes paid varied systematically by

Table 2.8 Public consumption (in 2000 dollars) by household characteristics, 1989 and 2000

Characteristic	1989		2000		Percent change	
	Mean	**Median**	**Mean**	**Median**	**Mean**	**Median**
Race						
White	6,533	3,092	7,347	3,196	12.45	3.36
Non-white	9,785	5,058	10,735	5,152	9.71	1.86
Family type						
Married couples	8,630	4,166	10,120	4,603	17.27	10.48
Single females	11,608	9,432	13,559	11,029	16.81	16.93
Single males	8,412	4,889	10,659	7,927	26.72	62.16
Housing tenure						
Own	7,177	3,330	8,185	3,443	14.06	3.42
Rent	7,272	3,220	8,360	3,481	14.97	8.13
Age of householder						
Less than 35	7,438	3,642	8,955	4,279	20.40	17.50
35–50 years	10,872	9,432	12,393	10,668	13.99	13.11
50–56 years	5,753	2,941	6,015	3,045	4.56	3.54
65 or older	3,130	2,450	3,319	2,635	6.05	7.54
Income						
Less than $20,000	6,123	2,436	6,402	2,483	4.56	1.93
$20,000–50,000	6,710	3,037	7,709	3,244	14.90	6.83
$50,000–75,000	7,924	3,747	9,137	4,062	15.31	8.42
$75,000–100,000	8,955	4,512	9,761	4,568	9.00	1.23
$100,000 or more	8,598	4,414	10,280	5,064	19.57	14.72
Education of householder						
Less than high school	6,958	3,038	8,711	3,455	25.19	13.76
High school degree	7,300	3,385	8,097	3,402	10.91	0.50
Some college	7,583	3,457	8,602	3,662	13.44	5.93
College degree	7,027	3,291	7,755	3,342	10.36	1.56
Household size						
One person	2,166	1,738	2,217	1,880	2.34	8.13
Two persons	3,744	2,692	4,136	2,982	10.47	10.78
Three or more persons	12,689	10,841	15,442	13,025	21.70	20.14
All households	7,211	3,297	8,242	3,452	14.30	4.71

income class, though taxes rose more than proportionately with income. A similar pattern is evident with tax burdens and income by educational groups.

Table 2.10 shows the net effects of government spending and taxation by demographic group. Here, the results are striking. As noted before and shown in the last line of the table, overall both mean and median net

Table 2.9 Taxes (in 2000 dollars) by household characteristics, 1989 and 2000

Characteristic	1989		2000		Percent change	
	Mean	Median	Mean	Median	Mean	Median
Race						
White	16,547	11,476	21,166	12,811	27.91	11.63
Non-white	11,234	6,766	15,446	8,972	37.50	32.60
Family type						
Married couples	19,898	14,986	26,426	17,727	32.81	18.29
Single females	8,061	4,583	10,230	6,242	26.91	36.18
Single males	15,366	10,979	18,257	11,579	18.81	5.46
Housing tenure						
Own	18,599	13,583	23,437	14,926	26.01	9.89
Rent	9,797	6,450	11,707	7,022	19.50	8.86
Age of householder						
Less than 35	13,509	10,618	17,221	11,422	27.48	7.57
35 – 50 years	20,906	16,248	25,577	17,059	22.34	4.99
50 – 56 years	19,143	13,153	24,246	15,378	26.66	16.92
65 or older	6,656	2,111	7,985	2,429	19.97	15.03
Income						
Less than $20,000	1,767	1,127	1,897	1,284	7.33	13.92
$20,000–50,000	8,435	8,236	8,667	8,367	2.75	1.58
$50,000–75,000	18,516	18,529	19,528	19,353	5.47	4.45
$75,000–100,000	28,217	28,328	31,254	31,250	10.76	10.31
$100,000 or more	55,934	45,695	68,689	53,390	22.80	16.84
Education of householder						
Less than high school	6,526	2,806	7,458	3,439	14.27	22.54
High school degree	12,864	9,720	13,797	9,189	7.25	−5.46
Some college	16,695	13,107	18,901	12,681	13.21	−3.25
College degree	27,686	20,992	34,766	24,040	25.58	14.52
Household size						
One person	8,438	4,188	10,090	4,852	19.59	15.84
Two persons	15,685	10,194	20,233	12,147	29.00	19.16
Three or more persons	19,260	14,758	25,304	16,690	31.39	13.09
All households	15,440	10,430	19,655	11,589	27.30	11.11

government expenditure was negative in both 1989 and 2000. The first notable finding is that non-white households were net beneficiaries of the fiscal system, whereas white households were net losers. However, between 1989 and 2000, mean net government expenditures declined by 38 percent and its median value by 36 percent among non-whites (net government spending also become more negative among white households).

Table 2.10 Net government expenditures (in $ dollars) by household characteristics, 1989 and 2000

Characteristic	1989		2000		Percent change	
	Mean	Median	Mean	Median	Mean	Median
Race						
White	−3,303	−2,717	−5,459	−3,185	65	17
Non-white	6,226	4,206	3,881	2,693	−38	−36
Family type						
Married couples	−4,863	−4,367	−8,159	−5,474	68	25
Single females	13,845	10,786	14,984	11,782	8	9
Single males	250	175	1,283	2,190	414	1,154
Housing tenure						
Own	−4,339	−3,080	−6,692	−3,698	54	20
Rent	4,079	1,030	4,783	1,664	17	62
Age of householder						
Less than 35	−3,022	−4,586	−4,428	−4,242	47	−7
35–50 years	−7,129	−6,000	−9,077	−6,580	27	10
50–56 years	−7,969	−6,169	−11,822	−8,390	48	36
65 or older	15,366	15,987	17,989	17,878	17	12
Income						
Less than $20,000	15,871	14,236	18,323	16,078	15	13
$20,000–50,000	5,402	1,379	8,282	3,798	53	176
$50,000–75,000	−6,459	−9,960	−4,920	−9,649	−24	−3
$75,000–100,000	−15,590	−19,072	−17,168	−20,993	10	10
$100,000 or more	−43,870	−37,686	−53,892	−43,363	23	15
Education of householder						
Less than high school	12,994	13,426	16,037	15,433	23	15
High school degree	872	−560	3,536	2,333	305	−516
Some college	−4,215	−4,614	−3,360	−3,240	−20	−30
College degree	−17,177	−12,699	−21,960	−14,806	28	17
Household size						
One person	714	690	316	−91	−56	−113
Two persons	−2,957	−2,813	−5,403	−3,980	83	41
Three or more persons	−1,252	−1,557	−3,144	−649	151	−58
All households	−1,318	−1,302	−2,992	−1,454	127	12

Married couple families were net losers in terms of net government spending whereas single male- and single female-headed families were net beneficiaries. Single male families also enjoyed the greatest percentage growth in net government expenditures over the 1989–2000 period of any of the household groups shown in Table 2.10. Renters were also net beneficiaries of the fiscal system, whereas homeowners were considerable losers in the two years.

Looking at age of householder, we see that the only age group in the black was the elderly, who enjoyed substantial net benefits from government expenditures and taxation.[22] Only the bottom two income groups recorded positive net government expenditures. In contrast, the top income group had an extremely high negative level of net government spending (a mean value of almost –$54,000). Likewise, net government expenditures were positive for only the bottom two educational groups (a high school degree or less) and were very negative for college graduates.

2.4.3 Transfers, public consumption, and taxes by income decile

We next group households by income decile. For convenience, we use wealth-adjusted comprehensive income (CIW) as the income definition.[23] Table 2.11 shows the distribution of transfers by income decile (also see Figure 2.1). Total government transfers are extremely progressive, falling monotonically from 56 percent of CIW for the lowest decile to 2.5 percent for the top decile in 1989 and from 50 to 2.6 percent in 2000. The same pattern holds for the largest government transfer, social security benefits, which fall continuously from 25 to 1.4 percent of CIW in 1989 and from 21 to 1.3 percent in 2000. The other transfer payments show almost identical patterns (with one or two exceptions).

Public consumption is also highly progressive, though not quite as strongly as transfers (see Table 2.12 and Figure 2.2). Unlike transfers, the absolute amount of public consumption does not fall as we move to the higher income deciles. Only the ratio of public consumption to income falls, reflecting the fact that the disparity in income is far larger than the disparity in public consumption. Total public consumption falls monotonically from 39 percent of CIW for the lowest decile to 3.5 percent for the top decile in 1989 and from 34 to 3.0 percent in 2000. The same pattern holds for the largest source of public consumption, educational expenses, which fall continuously from 17 to 1.8 percent of CIW in 1989 and from 16 to 1.5 percent in 2000. The other types of public consumption all also show a similar pattern by income decile.

The federal income tax was uniformly progressive in 1989, as shown in Table 2.13 and Figures 2.3A and 2.3B. The average federal income tax rate rises from 2.5 percent in the bottom decile to 12.7 percent in the top decile, while in 2000 the average tax rate increases steadily from 2.2 percent in the first decile to 13.8 percent in the ninth and then drops slightly to 13.5 percent in the top decile. State income taxes are also progressive (with two exceptions), with average tax rates rising from 0.6 to 2.5 percent in both years. Payroll taxes, as a percent of CIW, increases modestly between the first and eighth deciles and then declines over the top two deciles. State consumption taxes are (not unexpectedly) regressive in the two years, with average tax rates falling across deciles from 3.4 to 0.9 percent

Table 2.11 Distribution of government transfers by wealth-adjusted, comprehensive income (CIW) decile, 1989 and 2000 (all dollar amounts are in 2000 dollars; the italicized amounts are percentages of mean CIW)

1989

	Lowest	Second	Third	Fourth	Fifth	Sixth	Seventh	Eighth	Ninth	Top	All
Government transfers	6,476	9,652	9,501	8,880	8,168	6,690	4,945	4,692	4,520	5,743	6,912
	55.8	*44.7*	*32.3*	*23.8*	*17.7*	*11.9*	*7.2*	*5.6*	*4.2*	*2.5*	*9.9*
Social Security	2,851	4,021	4,116	4,136	4,024	3,277	2,385	2,326	2,145	3,242	3,248
	24.6	*18.6*	*14.0*	*11.1*	*8.7*	*5.8*	*3.5*	*2.8*	*2.0*	*1.4*	*4.6*
Medicare	1,468	1,812	1,862	1,790	1,685	1,324	942	866	874	1,309	1,391
	12.7	*8.4*	*6.3*	*4.8*	*3.7*	*2.4*	*1.4*	*1.0*	*0.8*	*0.6*	*2.0*
Medicaid	721	1,404	1,297	1,042	856	656	436	320	311	173	718
	6.2	*6.5*	*4.4*	*2.8*	*1.9*	*1.2*	*0.6*	*0.4*	*0.3*	*0.1*	*1.0*
All others	1,435	2,415	2,226	1,912	1,602	1,433	1,181	1,180	1,190	1,018	1,555
	12.4	*11.2*	*7.6*	*5.1*	*3.5*	*2.5*	*1.7*	*1.4*	*1.1*	*0.4*	*2.2*

2000

	Lowest	Second	Third	Fourth	Fifth	Sixth	Seventh	Eighth	Ninth	Top	All
Government transfers	6,653	10,019	9,413	10,369	9,091	8,591	8,061	6,897	6,829	8,242	8,421
	49.7	*38.9*	*27.0*	*23.6*	*16.8*	*13.1*	*10.1*	*7.0*	*5.4*	*2.6*	*9.8*
Social Security	2,817	3,966	3,750	4,026	3,718	3,449	3,300	2,998	3,269	4,298	3,562
	21.0	*15.4*	*10.7*	*9.2*	*6.9*	*5.3*	*4.1*	*3.1*	*2.6*	*1.3*	*4.1*
Medicare	1,826	2,285	2,077	2,284	1,958	1,778	1,693	1,487	1,530	1,978	1,895
	13.6	*8.9*	*5.9*	*5.2*	*3.6*	*2.7*	*2.1*	*1.5*	*1.2*	*0.6*	*2.2*
Medicaid	738	1,734	1,706	2,179	1,724	1,660	1,545	1,113	879	686	1,392
	5.5	*6.7*	*4.9*	*5.0*	*3.2*	*2.5*	*1.9*	*1.1*	*0.7*	*0.2*	*1.6*
All others	1,271	2,034	1,879	1,880	1,692	1,705	1,523	1,298	1,151	1,280	1,573
	9.5	*7.9*	*5.4*	*4.3*	*3.1*	*2.6*	*1.9*	*1.3*	*0.9*	*0.4*	*1.8*

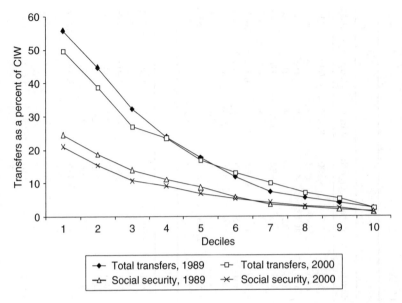

Figure 2.1 Social Security payments and total government transfers as a percent of wealth-adjusted comprehensive income (CIW) by CIW decile, 1989 and 2000

in 1989 and from 3.7 to 0.8 percent in 2000. Property taxes are generally regressive in the two years. This reflects the fact that though house values rise with income, they decline as a *percent* of income across income classes.

Overall, total personal taxes by decile are generally progressive. In 1989, total personal taxes as a percent of CIW declined slightly between the first and second decile, from 13.7 to 12.8 percent and then rose steadily to 26.0 percent in the ninth decile before shrinking to 22.1 percent in the top decile. In 2000, the average personal tax rate rose continuously from 13.6 percent in the lowest decile to 28.3 percent in the ninth decile and then plummeted once again to 22.0 percent in the top decile. The sharp drop off in the average tax rate between the ninth and tenth deciles is largely a reflection of the correspondingly sharp decline in the average payroll tax between these two deciles.

The distribution of net government expenditures by decile is shown in Table 2.14 and Figures 2.4A and 2.4B. In both 1989 and 2000, net government spending is extremely progressive. Net government spending as a percent of CIW plummets from 81 percent for the lowest decile to –16 percent for the top in 1989 and from 70 to –16 percent in 2000. It is also of note that net government expenditure is positive for the lowest six deciles and negative for the top four deciles.

Table 2.12 Distribution of public consumption by wealth-adjusted, comprehensive income (CIW) decile, 1989 and 2000 (all dollar amounts are in 2000 dollars; the italicized amounts are percentages of mean CIW)

1989

	Lowest	Second	Third	Fourth	Fifth	Sixth	Seventh	Eighth	Ninth	Top	All
Public consumption	4,478	5,846	6,713	6,994	7,167	7,632	7,977	8,500	8,577	8,099	7,211
	38.6	*27.1*	*22.8*	*18.7*	*15.5*	*13.5*	*11.7*	*10.1*	*7.9*	*3.5*	*10.3*
Police and Fire	218	264	308	332	357	379	404	429	451	455	361
	1.6	*1.0*	*0.9*	*0.8*	*0.7*	*0.6*	*0.5*	*0.4*	*0.4*	*0.1*	*0.4*
Health	532	640	738	790	842	883	935	988	1,033	1,046	845
	4.0	*2.5*	*2.1*	*1.8*	*1.6*	*1.3*	*1.2*	*1.0*	*0.8*	*0.3*	*1.0*
Education	2,001	2,622	3,245	3,464	3,605	4,000	4,409	4,761	4,702	4,091	3,698
	15.0	*10.2*	*9.3*	*7.9*	*6.7*	*6.1*	*5.5*	*4.9*	*3.7*	*1.3*	*4.3*
Highways	342	429	537	619	728	789	766	815	770	699	651
	2.6	*1.7*	*1.5*	*1.4*	*1.3*	*1.2*	*1.0*	*0.8*	*0.6*	*0.2*	*0.8*
All others	1,384	1,890	1,885	1,788	1,635	1,581	1,464	1,507	1,622	1,807	1,657
	11.9	*8.8*	*6.4*	*4.8*	*3.5*	*2.8*	*2.1*	*1.8*	*1.5*	*0.8*	*2.4*

2000

	Lowest	Second	Third	Fourth	Fifth	Sixth	Seventh	Eighth	Ninth	Top	All
Public consumption	4,584	6,309	7,514	8,096	8,683	9,191	9,506	9,584	9,746	9,748	8,242
	34.2	*24.5*	*21.5*	*18.4*	*16.1*	*14.0*	*11.9*	*9.8*	*7.7*	*3.0*	*9.6*
Police and Fire	296	359	425	461	500	535	561	583	600	599	489
	2.2	*1.4*	*1.2*	*1.0*	*0.9*	*0.8*	*0.7*	*0.6*	*0.5*	*0.2*	*0.6*
Health	534	640	750	809	871	924	961	995	1,020	1,015	847
	4.0	*2.5*	*2.1*	*1.8*	*1.6*	*1.4*	*1.2*	*1.0*	*0.8*	*0.3*	*1.0*
Education	2,154	3,097	3,846	4,125	4,638	5,042	5,377	5,445	5,635	4,906	4,389
	16.1	*12.0*	*11.0*	*9.4*	*8.6*	*7.7*	*6.7*	*5.5*	*4.4*	*1.5*	*5.1*
Highways	369	525	680	795	822	855	844	840	756	715	714
	2.8	*2.0*	*1.9*	*1.8*	*1.5*	*1.3*	*1.1*	*0.9*	*0.6*	*0.2*	*0.8*
All others	1,231	1,687	1,813	1,906	1,852	1,834	1,763	1,720	1,737	2,513	1,803
	9.2	*6.5*	*5.2*	*4.3*	*3.4*	*2.8*	*2.2*	*1.8*	*1.4*	*0.8*	*2.1*

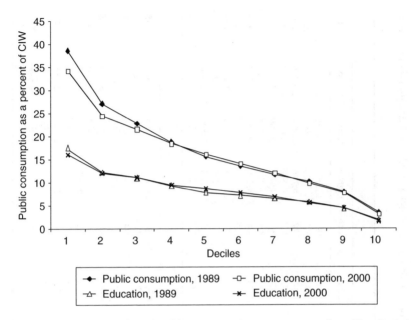

Figure 2.2 Education and total public consumption as a percent of wealth-adjusted comprehensive income (CIW) by CIW decile, 1989 and 2000

2.4.4 The distribution of post-fisc income by household characteristics

In the next stage of the analysis, we add net government spending to pre-fisc income to produce post-fisc income (see Table 2.4). Table 2.15 shows mean and median wealth-adjusted post-fisc income in the two years by household characteristics and Table 2.16 shows comparable statistics for equivalent wealth-adjusted post-fisc income.[24] The differences in measured disparities among households by selected characteristics are also shown in Figure 2.5. It is evident that measured racial disparities are considerably reduced when we consider post-fisc income instead of Census gross money income. In 2000, the ratio of non-white to white mean post-fisc income was 81 percent compared to a ratio of 76 percent for money income and the ratio of median post-fisc income was 87 percent compared to 76 percent for money income. It is also of note that both mean and median post-fisc income grew faster for non-whites than whites between 1989 and 2000. The non-white to white ratio of equivalent post-fisc income was lower than that of standard post-fisc income—73 percent for the ratio of means and 78 percent for the ratio of medians in 2000. This is mainly a reflection of the larger family sizes for non-whites than whites. Mean equivalent post-fisc income grew faster for non-whites than whites, while median equivalent post-fisc income grew at the same pace over the period.

Table 2.13 Distribution of taxes by wealth-adjusted, comprehensive income (CIW) decile, 1989 and 2000 (all dollar amounts are in 2000 dollars; the italicized amounts are percentages of mean CIW)

1989

	Lowest	Second	Third	Fourth	Fifth	Sixth	Seventh	Eighth	Ninth	Top	All
Taxes	1,595	2,754	4,416	6,554	8,975	12,013	16,184	21,008	28,240	50,786	15,440
	13.7	*12.8*	*15.0*	*17.6*	*19.4*	*21.3*	*23.7*	*25.0*	*26.0*	*22.1*	*22.0*
Federal income taxes	294	542	1,047	1,790	2,790	3,990	5,777	8,146	12,294	29,325	6,705
	2.5	*2.5*	*3.6*	*4.8*	*6.0*	*7.1*	*8.5*	*9.7*	*11.3*	*12.7*	*9.6*
State income taxes	66	118	225	396	615	872	1,280	1,781	2,559	5,701	1,382
	0.6	*0.5*	*0.8*	*1.1*	*1.3*	*1.5*	*1.9*	*2.1*	*2.4*	*2.5*	*2.0*
Payroll taxes	532	1,073	1,841	2,725	3,693	4,996	6,664	8,208	10,055	11,723	5,199
	4.6	*5.0*	*6.3*	*7.3*	*8.0*	*8.9*	*9.8*	*9.8*	*9.2*	*5.1*	*7.4*
State consumption taxes	399	666	883	1,072	1,240	1,369	1,546	1,667	1,824	1,961	1,269
	3.4	*3.1*	*3.0*	*2.9*	*2.7*	*2.4*	*2.3*	*2.0*	*1.7*	*0.9*	*1.8*
Property taxes	303	355	419	572	638	786	918	1,205	1,508	2,076	885
	2.6	*1.6*	*1.4*	*1.5*	*1.4*	*1.4*	*1.3*	*1.4*	*1.4*	*0.9*	*1.3*

2000

	Lowest	Second	Third	Fourth	Fifth	Sixth	Seventh	Eighth	Ninth	Top	All
Taxes	1,822	3,831	6,062	8,298	11,324	14,829	19,305	26,003	36,093	70,548	19,655
	13.6	*14.9*	*17.4*	*18.9*	*21.0*	*22.6*	*24.2*	*26.5*	*28.3*	*22.0*	*22.9*
Federal income taxes	290	806	1,464	2,372	3,565	5,100	7,294	11,047	17,604	43,196	9,231
	2.2	*3.1*	*4.2*	*5.4*	*6.6*	*7.8*	*9.2*	*11.3*	*13.8*	*13.5*	*10.7*
State income taxes	76	211	391	604	878	1,199	1,642	2,239	3,212	8,180	1,853
	0.6	*0.8*	*1.1*	*1.4*	*1.6*	*1.8*	*2.1*	*2.3*	*2.5*	*2.5*	*2.2*
Payroll taxes	637	1,537	2,591	3,416	4,647	5,933	7,412	9,291	11,439	14,748	6,087
	4.8	*6.0*	*7.4*	*7.8*	*8.6*	*9.0*	*9.3*	*9.5*	*9.0*	*4.6*	*7.1*
State consumption taxes	492	863	1,154	1,330	1,518	1,704	1,877	2,045	2,237	2,716	1,578
	3.7	*3.3*	*3.3*	*3.0*	*2.8*	*2.6*	*2.4*	*2.1*	*1.8*	*0.8*	*1.8*
Property taxes	328	414	462	575	717	893	1,080	1,380	1,602	1,709	906
	2.4	*1.6*	*1.3*	*1.3*	*1.3*	*1.4*	*1.4*	*1.4*	*1.3*	*0.5*	*1.1*

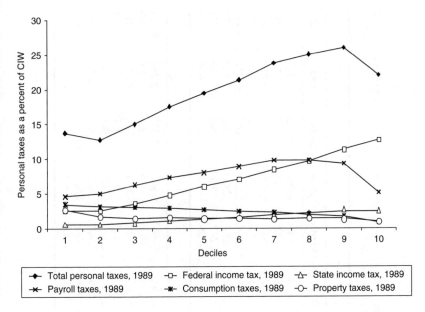

Figure 2.3A Personal taxes as a percent of wealth-adjusted comprehensive income (CIW) by CIW decile, 1989

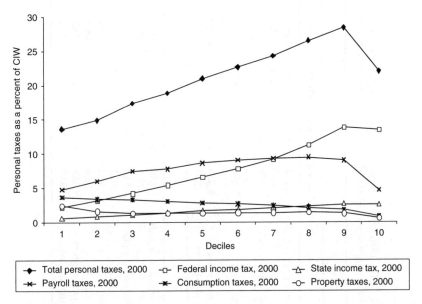

Figure 2.3B Personal taxes as a percent of wealth-adjusted comprehensive income (CIW) by CIW decile, 2000

Table 2.14 Distribution of net government expenditures by wealth-adjusted, comprehensive income (CIW) decile, 1989 and 2000 (All dollar amounts are in 2000 dollars; the italicized amounts are percentages of mean CIW)

1989

	Lowest	Second	Third	Fourth	Fifth	Sixth	Seventh	Eighth	Ninth	Top	All
Government transfers	6,476	9,652	9,501	8,880	8,168	6,690	4,945	4,692	4,520	5,743	6,912
	55.8	*44.7*	*32.3*	*23.8*	*17.7*	*11.9*	*7.2*	*5.6*	*4.2*	*2.5*	*9.9*
Public consumption	4,478	5,846	6,713	6,994	7,167	7,632	7,977	8,500	8,577	8,099	7,211
	38.6	*27.1*	*22.8*	*18.7*	*15.5*	*13.5*	*11.7*	*10.1*	*7.9*	*3.5*	*10.3*
Taxes	1,595	2,754	4,416	6,554	8,975	12,013	16,184	21,008	28,240	50,786	15,440
	13.7	*12.8*	*15.0*	*17.6*	*19.4*	*21.3*	*23.7*	*25.0*	*26.0*	*22.1*	*22.0*
Net government expenditures	9,359	12,744	11,799	9,320	6,360	2,309	−3,262	−7,816	−15,142	−36,945	−1,318
	80.7	*59.1*	*40.1*	*25.0*	*13.8*	*4.1*	*−4.8*	*−9.3*	*−13.9*	*−16.0*	*−1.9*

2000

	Lowest	Second	Third	Fourth	Fifth	Sixth	Seventh	Eighth	Ninth	Top	All
Government transfers	6,653	10,019	9,413	10,369	9,091	8,591	8,061	6,897	6,829	8,242	8,421
	49.7	*38.9*	*27.0*	*23.6*	*16.8*	*13.1*	*10.1*	*7.0*	*5.4*	*2.6*	*9.8*
Public consumption	4,584	6,309	7,514	8,096	8,683	9,191	9,506	9,584	9,746	9,748	8,242
	34.2	*24.5*	*21.5*	*18.4*	*16.1*	*14.0*	*11.9*	*9.8*	*7.7*	*3.0*	*9.6*
Taxes	1,822	3,831	6,062	8,298	11,324	14,829	19,305	26,003	36,093	70,548	19,655
	13.6	*14.9*	*17.4*	*18.9*	*21.0*	*22.6*	*24.2*	*26.5*	*28.3*	*22.0*	*22.9*
Net government expenditures	9,415	12,497	10,865	10,167	6,450	2,954	−1,739	−9,522	−19,518	−52,559	−2,992
	70.3	*48.5*	*31.1*	*23.1*	*11.9*	*4.5*	*−2.2*	*−9.7*	*−15.3*	*−16.4*	*−3.5*

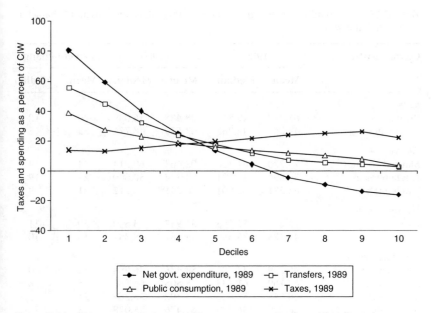

Figure 2.4A Net government expenditure as a percent of wealth-adjusted comprehensive income (CIW) by CIW decile, 1989

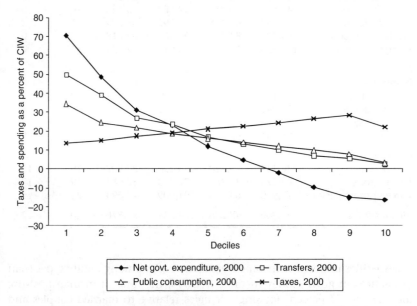

Figure 2.4B Net government expenditure as a percent of wealth-adjusted comprehensive income (CIW) by CIW decile, 2000

Table 2.15 Wealth-adjusted, post-fisc income (2000 dollars) by household characteristics, 1989 and 2000

Characteristic	1989		2000		Percent change	
	Mean	Median	Mean	Median	Mean	Median
Race						
White	65,237	49,815	78,488	56,039	20	12
Non-white	49,251	42,283	63,529	48,774	29	15
Family type						
Married couples	75,720	61,126	93,663	69,914	24	14
Single females	50,896	42,591	63,234	50,800	24	19
Single males	63,281	52,001	76,295	56,912	21	9
Housing tenure						
Own	73,512	57,195	87,932	63,550	20	11
Rent	41,173	35,359	46,387	38,837	13	10
Age of householder						
Less than 35	46,739	42,781	54,436	46,984	16	10
35–50 years	68,169	61,133	78,508	64,566	15	6
50–56 years	68,545	52,666	83,192	56,269	21	7
65 or older	66,019	36,279	81,476	45,078	23	24
Income						
Less than $20,000	28,638	22,211	33,983	24,585	19	11
$20,000–50,000	47,803	40,940	52,682	43,146	10	5
$50,000–75,000	73,457	63,405	73,898	65,294	1	3
$75,000–100,000	94,235	83,858	94,300	84,018	0	0
$100,000 or more	140,533	115,177	183,917	122,134	31	6
Education of householder						
Less than high school	46,134	35,703	54,920	39,951	19	12
High school degree	56,042	46,520	60,721	48,574	8	4
Some college	63,896	51,757	68,939	54,775	8	6
College degree	85,831	66,918	108,405	73,129	26	9
Household size						
One person	36,442	25,020	43,290	27,907	19	12
Two persons	65,273	47,288	77,753	52,984	19	12
Three or more persons	73,942	63,790	91,909	72,694	24	14
All households	61,906	48,226	74,537	53,876	20	12

Disparities in post-fisc income were also smaller among family types than differences in gross money income. In 2000, the ratio of median post-fisc income was 73 percent for single females relative to married couples and 81 percent for single males relative to married couples. The comparable ratios for median equivalent post-fisc income were 76 percent and

Table 2.16 Wealth-adjusted, post-fisc income (equivalence scale adjusted) by household characteristics (2000 dollars), 1989 and 2000

Characteristic	1989		2000		Percent change	
	Mean	Median	Mean	Median	Mean	Median
Race						
White	88,882	67,031	108,041	76,113	22	14
Non-white	58,659	52,310	78,579	59,589	34	14
Family type						
Married couples	89,208	69,874	111,307	79,671	25	14
Single females	61,490	51,412	74,703	60,563	21	18
Single males	76,893	62,974	90,323	66,357	17	5
Housing tenure						
Own	96,425	71,959	116,860	80,316	21	12
Rent	57,860	50,668	65,374	55,941	13	10
Age of householder						
Less than 35	61,029	54,958	69,352	59,150	14	8
35–50 years	79,601	70,241	92,188	75,526	16	8
50–56 years	90,185	70,114	113,684	78,651	26	12
65 or older	106,967	60,460	133,234	73,224	25	21
Income						
Less than $20,000	46,684	37,499	56,675	42,274	21	13
$20,000–50,000	68,229	56,693	75,917	60,745	11	7
$50,000–75,000	95,144	77,362	95,215	81,070	0	5
$75,000–100,000	114,104	95,988	117,498	98,649	3	3
$100,000 or more	167,411	128,675	229,074	142,275	37	11
Education of householder						
Less than high school	63,050	49,491	74,124	53,986	18	9
High school degree	73,241	60,330	81,279	65,007	11	8
Some college	84,521	68,028	91,478	72,063	8	6
College degree	115,943	87,279	147,394	95,698	27	10
Household size						
One person	78,699	54,038	93,495	60,273	19	12
Two persons	99,662	72,203	118,693	80,805	19	12
Three or more persons	72,025	62,884	89,569	71,234	24	13
All households	82,585	63,511	100,259	71,189	21	12

83 percent, respectively. In contrast, the ratio for median gross money income in 2000 was 48 percent between single females and married couples and 71 percent between single males and married couples.

Renters also seem to be better off relative to home owners on the basis of median post-fisc income than median money income, though not in terms of mean levels. In 2000, the ratio of renter to owner mean post-fisc income

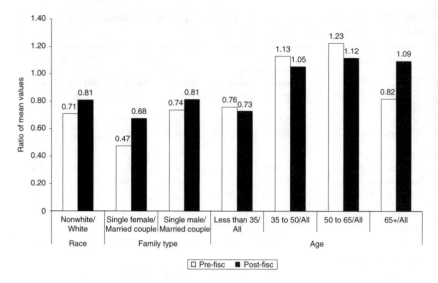

Figure 2.5 Disparities by selected characteristics and income measure, 2000 (pre-fisc income versus post-fisc income)

was 53 percent and the ratio of median post-fisc income was 61 percent, compared to 56 percent and 55 percent, respectively, for money income. In terms of equivalent post-fisc income, renters look somewhat better off, with a ratio of 56 percent for mean values and 70 percent for median values. This is a reflection of the smaller family sizes of renters.

The elderly turn out better off with regard to post-fisc income relative to money income while the other age groups appear worse off. In 2000, the ratio of the median post-fisc income of the elderly to the overall median was 84 percent and that of median equivalent post-fisc income to the overall median was 103 percent, in comparison to a ratio of 55 percent for gross money income. The ratios of median post-fisc and equivalent post-fisc income for the other age groups to the overall median were smaller than the corresponding ratios of gross money income. Moreover, median post-fisc income and equivalent post-fisc income grew faster over the 1989–2000 period for the elderly than for any of the other age groups. These patterns may be traced to the relatively higher values of annuities and noncash transfers (due to Medicare) for the elderly.

Differentials in post-fisc income by money income class were noticeably smaller than differentials in gross money income.[25] For example, in 2000 the median post-fisc income of the top income class was 2.3 times the overall median while the ratio of median money income was 3.1. The ratio of median post-fisc income of the bottom income class was 46 percent, compared to 28 percent for money income. A similar pattern is evident for post-fisc equivalent income. Similar results also hold by educational attainment. In 2000, the ratio of median post-fisc income of college graduates to the overall median was 1.36 while the corresponding ratio of median money income was 1.69. Likewise, the ratio of median post-fisc income of those with less than a high school degree to the overall median was 74 percent, in comparison to 49 percent for money income.

2.4.5 Level and distribution of economic well-being by income measure

The picture of economic well-being as conveyed by the Census money income and three of our wealth-adjusted measures are shown in Table 2.17. The average level of well-being (as measured by either the mean or median) is the lowest for the money income measure. The adjustments made to money income (replacing property income with our imputed income from wealth, adding the employer share of payroll taxes, employer contributions and consumption taxes, and subtracting government cash transfers) to arrive at pre-fisc income have the effect of increasing the average level relative to money income. As expected, CIW, calculated by adding government transfers to pre-fisc income, shows average levels that are still higher. As suggested by the evidence on taxes and public consumption presented above (see Table 2.5), post-fisc income has an average level that is lower relative to CIW. The fact that net government expenditures were negative in both years is reflected in the mean values of post-fisc income being less than that of pre-fisc income. Conversely, the redistributive impact of net government expenditure is reflected in the median values of post-fisc income being higher than of pre-fisc income. It is also noteworthy that the mean and median values of money income are substantially lower than that of post-fisc income.

The percentage change for alternative measures of well-being over the 1989–2000 period is also shown in Table 2.17. While median money income increased by 5 percent over the period, median CIW grew notably faster, by 13 percent. The reason is the surge of annuity income from wealth over this period. Similar differences prevail between gross money income and CIW based on mean values and also on mean and median equivalence scale adjusted values. However, in all four cases post-fisc income grew slower than CIW over the 1989–2000 period. This difference is largely due to the rapid increase in personal taxes over the period and the consequent decline in net government expenditure (actually becoming more negative over the period).

We next consider changes in the three wealth-adjusted income measures by decile. As shown in Table 2.18, the percentage change in CIW between 1989 and 2000 is fairly uniform among the bottom nine deciles and is almost double for the top decile. This reflects both the large surge in annuity income from wealth and its extreme concentration in the top decile. In contrast, the percentage change in pre-fisc income shows a pronounced decline over the bottom six deciles (from 88 to 15 percent), flattens outs over

Table 2.17 Income measures, mean and median values in 1989 and 2000 (2000 dollars)

Income measure	Median			Mean		
	1989	2000	Change	1989	2000	Change
Money Income (MI)	40,167	42,000	5%	49,570	57,140	15%
Pre-Fisc Income (Wealth-adjusted)	45,972	50,631	10%	63,224	77,528	23%
Comprehensive income (Wealth-adjusted)	51,508	58,041	13%	70,136	85,950	23%
Post-Fisc Income (Wealth-adjusted)	48,226	53,876	12%	61,906	74,537	20%
Equivalence Scale Adjusted:						
Money Income	53,655	57,095	6%	65,659	76,235	16%
Pre-Fisc Income (Wealth-adjusted)	61,102	68,309	12%	84,345	104,344	24%
Comprehensive income (Wealth-adjusted)	69,238	78,601	14%	94,704	116,999	24%
Post-Fisc Income (Wealth-adjusted)	63,511	71,189	12%	82,585	100,259	21%

the next three deciles and then shows a dramatic increase for the top decile. Since transfer income is excluded in the construction of pre-fisc income, these differences largely reflect the concentration of the largest component of money transfer income, Social Security, among the middle deciles of the income distribution and its growth over the 1989–2000 period.

Like CIW, the percentage change in post-fisc income is almost flat among the bottom nine deciles and then surges once again for the top decile. However, the percentage change in post-fisc income is uniformly lower than CIW by decile. The only exception is at the 95th percentile, where post-fisc income actually grew slightly faster than CIW (see Figure 2.6). This primarily reflects the large decline in overall net government expenditures over the period (which became more negative). In fact, mean post-fisc income grew by 20.4 percent while CIW gained 22.5 percent, and median post-fisc income increased by 11.7 percent in comparison to a 12.7 percent growth in median comprehensive income.

Further details on the distributional changes in income measures are provided in Figures 2.7 through 2.9. Each line in these graphs represents the percent change in the percentile cut-offs at five-percentile increments. Figure 2.5 shows the percentage change of CIW and after-tax CIW between 1989 and 2000. Here it is apparent that average tax rates rose over the period for the bottom 85 percentiles. At the 90th percentile, average tax rates remained unchanged, while at the 95th percentile, the average tax rate

Table 2.18 Mean values across deciles by income measure, 1989 and 2000 (Mean values in 2000 dollars)

Decile	Pre-FIW			CIW			Post-FIW		
	1989	2000	% Change	1989	2000	% Change	1989	2000	% Change
Lowest	1,074	2,023	88.4	11,600	13,385	15.4	12,167	13,944	14.6
Second	8,857	12,308	39.0	21,570	25,767	19.5	22,658	26,157	15.4
Third	18,957	24,079	27.0	29,449	34,922	18.6	30,066	34,951	16.2
Fourth	29,118	35,171	20.8	37,335	43,998	17.8	37,043	43,287	16.9
Fifth	39,794	46,642	17.2	46,153	53,991	17.0	44,427	51,752	16.5
Sixth	51,469	59,314	15.2	56,333	65,606	16.5	52,221	60,856	16.5
Seventh	64,354	74,143	15.2	68,232	79,687	16.8	61,292	71,126	16.0
Eighth	80,420	93,381	16.1	84,038	98,151	16.8	73,073	84,010	15.0
Ninth	105,271	122,539	16.4	108,704	127,344	17.1	90,635	104,042	14.8
Top	224,698	315,080	40.2	230,243	321,012	39.4	193,979	263,480	35.8
All: Mean	63,224	77,528	22.6	70,136	85,950	22.5	61,906	74,537	20.4
All: Median	45,972	50,631	10.1	51,508	58,041	12.7	48,226	53,876	11.7

Key: Pre-FIW = Pre-fisc income adjusted for wealth.
CIW = Comprehensive income adjusted for wealth.
Post-FIW = Post-fisc income adjusted for wealth.

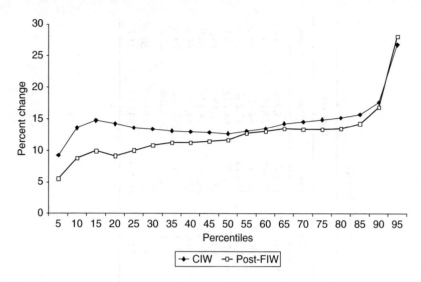

Figure 2.6 percent change from 1989 to 2000 in wealth-adjusted, comprehensive income (CIW) and wealth-adjusted, post-fiscal income (Post-FIW)

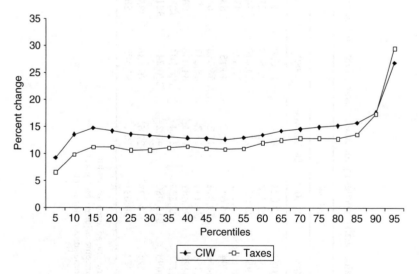

Figure 2.7 percent change from 1989 to 2000 in wealth-adjusted, comprehensive income (CIW) and wealth-adjusted, comprehensive income less taxes (Taxes)

declined. As a result, only above the 90th percentile was the percentage increase in after-tax CIW greater than that of CIW.

Figure 2.6 shows the percentage change in both CIW and CIW-less-transfers over the same period. Here the pattern is different. Transfers

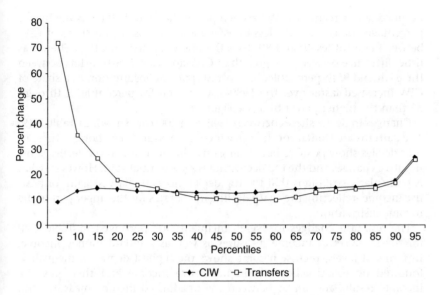

Figure 2.8 percent change from 1989 to 2000 in wealth-adjusted, comprehensive income (CIW) and wealth-adjusted, comprehensive income less transfers (Transfers)

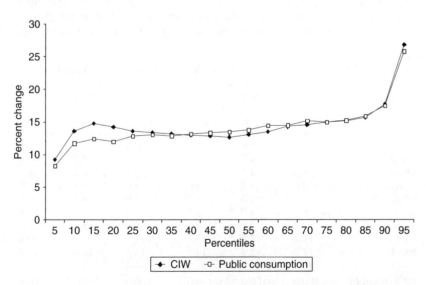

Figure 2.9 percent change from 1989 to 2000 in wealth-adjusted, comprehensive income (CIW) and wealth-adjusted, comprehensive income plus public consumption (Public consumption)

declined as a percent of CIW between percentiles 1 and 30 (thus the higher percentage change in CIW-less-transfers) and increased as a share of CIW between percentiles 40 and 80 (thus the higher growth in CIW). There was little difference between the growth of CIW and CIW-less-transfers between the 85th and 95th percentile. In contrast, public consumption as a share of CIW increased faster over the 1989–2000 period for percentiles 1 through 35 than the higher percentiles (see Figure 2.7).

Changes in decile shares between 1989 and 2000 are shown in Table 2.19. The patterns are similar for the three income measures. The bottom three or four deciles show positive but small gains, the next five to six deciles show negative changes and the top decile shows a substantial gain. However, what is particularly striking is that the top decile shows the largest gain for post-fisc income, reflecting the sharp decline in tax rates for the upper part of the income distribution.

The resultant changes in overall inequality are portrayed in Table 2.20 for the same set of income measures as well as standard money income. In terms of levels, pre-fisc income shows the highest degree of inequality, followed by wealth-adjusted comprehensive income and then post-fisc income (results are similar between the unadjusted income measures and those adjusted by the equivalent scale). The reason for the former is that, overall, transfers are highly progressive, so that their exclusion results in a higher level of measured inequality (pre-fisc versus CIW). The rationale for the latter is that the combined effect of adding in-kind benefits and public consumption to income and netting out taxes is also highly progressive, so that their addition lowers measured inequality (CIW versus post-fisc

Table 2.19 Shares of deciles by income measure, 1989 and 2000 (in percent)

Decile	1989			2000		
	Pre-FIW	CIW	Post-FIW	Pre-FIW	CIW	Post-FIW
Lowest	0.2	1.6	1.9	0.3	1.7	2.1
Second	1.4	3.0	3.7	1.7	3.2	3.9
Third	3.0	4.2	4.9	3.2	4.2	4.9
Fourth	4.6	5.2	6.0	4.6	5.1	5.9
Fifth	6.3	6.6	7.2	5.8	6.2	6.7
Sixth	8.1	8.0	8.4	7.4	7.2	7.6
Seventh	10.2	9.7	9.8	8.9	8.9	8.8
Eighth	12.7	12.0	11.7	11.4	11.0	10.4
Ninth	17.0	15.9	14.8	15.4	14.6	13.3
Top	36.7	33.7	31.6	41.2	38.1	36.4
All households	100.0	100.0	100.0	100.0	100.0	100.0

Key: Pre-FIW = Pre-fisc income adjusted for wealth.
CIW = Comprehensive income adjusted for wealth.
Post-FIW = Post-fisc income adjusted for wealth.

Table 2.20 Inequality by income measure, 1989 and 2000 (Gini coefficient × 100)

Income measure	Gini coefficient × 100		Change
	1989	2000	
Money Income (MI)	41.8	46.0	4.2
Pre-Fisc Income (Wealth-adjusted)	51.3	54.7	3.3
Post-Fisc Income (Wealth-adjusted)	40.4	44.4	4.0
Comprehensive income (Wealth-adjusted)	44.0	47.7	3.8
Equivalence Scale Adjusted:			
Money Income	40.0	44.1	4.1
Pre-Fisc Income (Wealth-adjusted)	51.2	54.4	3.2
Post-Fisc Income (Wealth-adjusted)	38.2	42.3	4.1
Comprehensive income (Wealth-adjusted)	43.0	46.7	3.7

income). The difference in Gini coefficients among these three measures is large. Moreover, both pre-fisc and CIW show a higher degree of inequality than standard money income—a result that is largely due to the addition of annuities to income.

It is next apparent that the Gini coefficient shows a marked rise over the 1989–2000 period according to all income measures. However, of the three new measures, post-fisc income shows the greatest rise over the period, followed by CIW and then pre-fisc income. The widening gap between the Gini coefficients for post-fisc income and CIW may be indicative of a fall in the equalizing effect of adding public consumption to income. Similarly, the larger gap between the Gini coefficients for pre-fisc income and CIW is suggestive of a fall in the equalizing effect of transfers between the two years. These issues are examined in greater detail in the next section.

2.4.6   Inequality and net government expenditures

Two central issues regarding the relationship between overall inequality and net government expenditures are addressed here. The first is the differences in the degree of inequality among alternative measures of economic well-being. The second issue relates to incremental effects or the expected change in inequality resulting from a slight proportionate change in one of the components of the measure, with other components remaining the same.

2.4.6.1   *Reranking and redistribution*

The change in the Gini coefficient between measures (or income definitions) can be decomposed into effects from the reranking of households and changes in the income gaps between households.[26] The method developed by Lerman and Yitzhaki (1995) is one way of decomposing the change in the Gini coefficient into reranking and gap-narrowing effects, with the latter considered as an index of redistribution. While earlier literature characterized the reranking component as an index of horizontal inequity (Plotnick, 1981), several later contributions have argued that the reranking component is not pertinent for horizontal equity. Instead, they split the redistribution effect itself into components of vertical and horizontal equity (Aronson and Lambert, 1994), based on a notion of 'equal tax rates for equals.' For our purposes here, we follow the method advanced by Lerman and Yitzhaki.

In particular, assume that A and B are two measures of well-being that are related to each other by addition or subtraction of individual components (for example, pre-tax and post-tax income). Let G_a the Gini coefficient for A, G_b be the Gini coefficient for B, and C_{ba} the concentration coefficient for B with respect to A. Then, the difference between the Gini coefficients can be written as:

$$G_b - G_a = (G_b - C_{ba}) + (C_{ba} - G_a),$$

with the first term indicating the reranking effect and the second indicating the gap-narrowing effect of moving from definition A to definition B.

Results from deploying this method are shown in Table 2.21. The top panel provides the 'big picture' regarding net government expenditures. We begin with wealth-adjusted pre-fisc income (Y_1) and then subtract taxes to obtain after-tax pre-fisc income (Y_2). We then subtract the Gini coefficient of Y_2 from that of Y_1 and report it under 'total effect.' As can be seen from the first line of the table, the total effect of the movement from pre-fisc income to post-tax pre-fisc income is a slight *increase* in the Gini coefficient (-0.6 in 1989 and -0.8 in 2000).[27] This is mainly a reflection of the sharp drop in the overall average tax rate between the ninth and tenth decile. Reading along the same line reveals that the increase in inequality would have been even higher if not for the reranking effect (0.7 in both years) offsetting some of the regressive redistributive effect or 'gap reduction' (-1.3 in 1989 and -1.5 in 2000) of taxation. Therefore, the tax system as a whole seems to be neutral at best and slightly regressive at worst.

The next line of the top panel shows the effect of moving from pre-fisc income less taxes to an income definition that now adds in transfers (Y_3). Reranking and redistributive components now work in the same direction (with the latter dominating) and bring about a substantial decline in the Gini coefficient in both years. However, the progressive redistributive effect declines from 1989 to 2000, while the reranking effect remains about the same. As a result, the total reduction in inequality due to transfers was lower in 2000 than in 1989.

The effect of moving from pre-fisc to post-fisc income (Y_4) is shown in the last line of the top panel. Inequality falls further when public consumption

Table 2.21 Decomposition of the changes in the Gini coefficient (×100) from adding net government expenditures, 1989 and 2000

	A. Net government expenditures					
	1989			2000		
	Total Effect	Reranking	Gap-reduction	Total Effect	Reranking	Gap-reduction
Y1 to Y2	−0.6	0.7	−1.3	−0.8	0.7	−1.5
Y2 to Y3	8.7	2.3	6.3	8.0	2.5	5.5
Y3 to Y4	2.9	0.9	2.0	3.0	0.8	2.2
Y1 to Y4	11.0	4.5	6.5	10.2	4.6	5.6

	B. Gini coefficients (×100)			
	Y1	Y2	Y3	Y4
1989	50.9	51.5	42.8	39.9
2000	54.2	55.0	47.0	44.0

Key: Y1 = Pre-fisc income, Y2 = Pre-fisc income less taxes, Y3 = Income after taxes and transfers, Y4 = Income after net government expenditure (Y3 plus public consumption).
Note: 'Total effect' for each pair of income definitions is obtained by subtracting the Gini ratio of the second income definition from the Gini ratio of the first income definition. For example, total effect on inequality for moving from definition Y1 to Y2 is calculated by subtracting the Gini ratio of Y2 from that of Y1. The reranking effect for each pair of income definitions is calculated by subtracting the concentration ratio of the first definition from the Gini ratio of the first definition and the gap-reduction effect is calculated by subtracting the Gini ratio of the second definition from the concentration ratio of the first definition. The concentration ratio of the first definition is calculated using the ranks of households according to the second definition.

is added to the income measure, but the inequality-reduction from this source is smaller relative to that induced by transfers. Comparison between 1989 and 2000 suggests that the impact of net government expenditures in reducing inequality has weakened somewhat as a result of the fall in the progressive redistributive effect.

It is also interesting to examine the impact of the major individual components of taxes, transfers and public consumption on pre-fisc inequality (Table 2.22). As shown in panel A of the table, the progressive effect of income taxes is substantially reduced when payroll taxes are added to the household tax burden. The inclusion of property taxes and consumption taxes makes the distribution of after-tax income more unequal than pre-fisc income. For transfers, estimates reported in panel B suggest that the two major social insurance programs of the federal government—Social Security and Medicare—mainly benefiting the elderly have a large inequality-reducing impact. Together, they accounted for 4.3 points out of the 6.8 percentage point difference between pre-fisc income and pre-fisc

Table 2.22 Decomposition of the changes in the Gini coefficient ($\times 100$) from taxes, transfers and public consumption, 1989 and 2000

	A. Taxes					
	1989			2000		
	Total effect	Reranking	Gap-reduction	Total effect	Reranking	Gap-reduction
Y_1 to Y_{t1}	1.3	0.5	0.8	1.5	0.3	1.2
Y_1 to Y_{t2}	0.1	0.2	−0.1	0.2	0.3	−0.1
Y_1 to Y_{t3}	−0.3	0.3	−0.5	−0.3	0.3	−0.6
Y_1 to Y_{tx}	−0.6	0.7	−1.3	−0.8	0.7	−1.5

Key: Y1 = Pre-fisc income, Yt1 = Pre-fisc income less income taxes, Yt2 = Pre-fisc income less income and payroll taxes, Yt3 = Pre-fisc income less income, payroll and property taxes, Ytx = Pre-fisc income less all taxes (Yt3 minus consumption taxes).

	B. Transfers					
	1989			2000		
	Total effect	Reranking	Gap-reduction	Total effect	Reranking	Gap-reduction
Y_1 to Y_{tr1}	3.5	0.5	3.0	3.0	0.4	2.6
Y_1 to Y_{tr2}	4.8	0.9	3.9	4.3	0.8	3.5
Y_1 to Y_{tr3}	5.8	1.0	4.8	5.7	1.1	4.5
Y_1 to Y_{tr}	7.3	1.3	5.9	6.8	1.4	5.4

Key: Y1 = Pre-fisc income, Ytr1 = Pre-fisc income plus Social Security, Ytr2 = Pre-fisc income plus Social Security and Medicare, Ytr3 = Pre-fisc income plus Social Security, Medicare and Medicaid, Ytr = Pre-fisc income plus all transfers (Ytr3 plus all other transfers).

	C. Public consumption					
	1989			2000		
	Total effect	Reranking	Gap-reduction	Total effect	Reranking	Gap-reduction
Y_1 to Y_{pc1}	0.2	0.0	0.2	0.3	0.0	0.3
Y_1 to Y_{pc2}	0.8	0.0	0.8	0.7	0.0	0.7
Y_1 to Y_{pc3}	2.4	0.4	1.9	2.4	0.4	2.0
Y_1 to Y_{pc4}	2.7	0.4	2.3	2.8	0.4	2.4
Y_1 to Y_{pc}	3.8	0.6	3.2	3.7	0.6	3.1

Key: Y1 = Pre-fisc income, Ypc1 = Pre-fisc income plus police and fire, Ypc2 = Pre-fisc income plus police, fire and health, Ypc3 = Pre-fisc income plus police, fire, health and education, Ypc4 = Pre-fisc income plus police, fire, health, education and highways, Ypc = Pre-fisc income plus all public consumption (Ypc4 plus all other public consumption).

	Memo: net government expenditures					
	1989			2000		
	Total effect	Reranking	Gap-reduction	Total effect	Reranking	Gap-reduction
Pre-fisc to post-fisc	11	4.5	6.5	10.2	4.6	5.6

Note: See the 'Note' to Table 2.21 for definitions of the total effect, the reranking effect, and the gap-reduction effect.

income plus transfers in 2000. Education appears to be the main inequality-reducing component of public consumption (see panel C). While the contribution of public consumption to a reduction in pre-fisc inequality is smaller compared to transfers, it is striking that pre-fisc income after income taxes is more unequally distributed than pre-fisc income adjusted for expenditures on public safety, health and education.

2.4.6.2   Incremental effects

We now turn to the issue of incremental effects—perhaps the most interesting one from a policy standpoint as far as overall inequality is concerned, since policy changes typically operate at the margin. We estimated the incremental effects using the so-called 'natural decomposition' method (Lerman, 1999; Yao, 1999). The incremental impact of a particular component of post-fisc income is the proportionate change in post-fisc income inequality due to an incremental, proportionate change in each household's income from that component. It is equal to the difference between a component's share in inequality and its share in post-fisc income.[28] Since the results are similar for both years, only the results for 2000 are shown here (Table 2.23).

The results suggest that base income (dominated by labor income) reduces pre-fisc inequality at the margin. This is because income from wealth (especially annuities), the other component of pre-fisc income, is distributed more unequally than base income. Thus, the inequality-enhancing marginal effect of pre-fisc income is entirely due to income from wealth. Taxes, transfers and public consumption have incremental effects that are similar in direction to their global effects. Since taxes tend to increase inequality slightly at the margin, the inequality-reducing effect of net government expenditure is entirely attributable to government expenditures. Among transfers, Social Security and Medicare play prominent equalizing roles, accounting for roughly 70 percent of the marginal effect of transfers. Education expenditure is the largest item in public consumption and accounts for nearly 30 percent of the marginal effect of public consumption.

Table 2.23 Decomposition of the Gini coefficient for wealth-adjusted post-fisc income, 2000

	Share of income	Amount of inequality	Share of inequality	Incremental effect
Pre-fisc income	1.040	0.520	1.170	0.130
Base income	0.754	0.300	0.676	−0.078
Income from wealth	0.286	0.219	0.494	0.208
Net government expenditure	−0.040	−0.076	−0.170	−0.130
Transfers	0.113	0.009	0.019	−0.093
Social Security	0.048	0.003	0.006	−0.041
Medicare	0.025	0.000	0.001	−0.025
Medicaid	0.019	0.003	0.006	−0.012
All others	0.021	0.003	0.006	−0.015
Public consumption	0.111	0.029	0.066	−0.045
Police and Fire	0.007	0.001	0.003	−0.004
Health and Hospitals	0.011	0.002	0.004	−0.007
Education	0.059	0.021	0.047	−0.012
Highways	0.010	0.001	0.002	−0.008
All others	0.024	0.005	0.011	−0.013
Taxes	−0.264	−0.113	−0.255	0.008
Federal income taxes	−0.124	−0.066	−0.148	−0.024
State income taxes	−0.025	−0.013	−0.028	−0.003
Payroll taxes	−0.082	−0.028	−0.064	0.018
State consumption taxes	−0.021	−0.004	−0.010	0.011
Property taxes	−0.012	−0.002	−0.005	0.007
Total	1.000	0.444	1.000	0.000

2.5 Conclusion

Net government expenditure was negative in both 1989 and 2000 and became more negative over the two years. Parenthetically, we might note that these results seem to suggest that Americans are not getting a good deal from the government—they pay more in taxes than they receive in benefits, either in the form of transfers or public consumption. This result may help to explain why Americans are generally upset with the government. Indeed, comparisons with Europe would be enlightening—in particular, Americans most likely pay an excessive amount for national defense compared to Europeans and receive much less in the way of income transfers and public consumption.

Our results also indicate that the level and distribution of economic well-being is altered considerably by net government expenditure. While *mean* post-fisc income is about 2 to 4 percent less than *mean* pre-fisc income, post-fisc income is *greater* than pre-fisc income at the *median*—by about 4 to

6 percent. Indeed, while net government expenditure was positive for the bottom six income deciles it was negative for the top four. However, the mean and median values of post-fisc income are about 20 to 30 percent higher than money income. Pre-fisc and post-fisc income both grew faster than money income between the two years, with the former growing twice as fast at the median level. The relatively smaller difference between the levels of pre-fisc and post fisc incomes on the one hand, and the much larger disparity between either measure and money income on the other, suggests that the crucial factor here is not the inclusion of net government expenditures, but the treatment of income from wealth. When the advantage from non-home wealth is reckoned in terms of annuities (rather than actual property income), the level and growth of median economic well-being becomes much higher than the official measure.[29]

Disparities between households, grouped according to certain salient social and economic characteristics are also considerably affected by net government expenditure. Racial disparity (measured here between non-whites and whites) is considerably less according to the post-fisc as compared to pre-fisc income. Similarly, the disparity between married couple family households and family households with a single female householder is less by post-fisc income as against by pre-fisc income. Disparities among households according to the age of the householder also show some marked differences between pre-fisc and post-fisc income. In particular, the elderly appear to be better off relative to the average household in the case of post-fisc income. Net government expenditure is also found to be positive for non-whites but negative for whites, positive for singles but negative for married couples, positive for renters but negative for home owners, and positive for the elderly but negative for all other age groups.

The distribution of both pre- and post-fiscal income became more unequal in the 1989–2000 period, with post-fisc inequality rising by a somewhat larger amount (0.7 percentage point). Net government expenditures played an important progressive role by reducing inequality in both years. As compared to pre-fisc income, the Gini coefficient for post-fisc income is lower by 10 to 11 points. Decomposing this change by the components of net government expenditures reveals that transfers (especially Social Security and Medicare) are extremely progressive, public consumption (especially expenditures on education and health) is very progressive but less so than transfers, and that taxation does not contribute to this reduction at all because of the regressive effects of payroll, property and consumption taxes. In fact, while average tax rates increase between the first and ninth decile of income, they drop off sharply at the tenth decile. The decomposition analysis also shows that reranking of households plays a substantial role in the reduction of inequality from pre-fisc to post-fisc income by accounting for about 40 to 45 percent of such reduction, with the remainder occurring from redistribution.

Our analysis of the marginal effects of the components of post-fisc income suggests that government expenditures for the household sector are far more potent in their inequality-reducing effect as compared to taxes. The asymmetry between taxes and expenditure in reducing inequality is reminiscent of the elementary macroeconomic proposition that, in a situation of deficient aggregate demand, government spending has a larger multiplier than tax cuts. We also found that base income (primarily composed of labor income) has an inequality-reducing effect at the margin. Thus, post-fisc income inequality is most affected by the inequalities in income from wealth. These findings suggest that to consider economic inequality as shaped predominantly by inequalities in labor income may be misleading from a policy standpoint. Reductions in the inequality of non-home wealth can have a significant impact on overall economic inequality, globally and marginally.

Several limitations of the estimates reported here must be noted. Estimates of pre-fisc income are obtained from a statistically matched dataset because of the need for imputing income from wealth. While our matching procedure was able to reproduce the main features of wealth distribution, admittedly it cannot be as good as the information from a single unified household survey. Estimates of the distribution of income, payroll and property taxes in the ADS are based on the amounts imputed by the Census Bureau rather than those reported by taxpayers. Among other things, these imputations have the effect of narrowing the variation in taxes among households of similar demographic characteristics. As in previous studies, the allocation and distribution of government consumption and gross investment expenditures were done on the basis of assumptions that, in our judgment, are reasonable and based on the best available empirical information. It is indeed possible that other equally reasonable assumptions could be made and they can result in substantially different estimates of public consumption and consequently net government expenditures. The sensitivity of the results reported here to alternative treatments of the government sector and income from wealth is a line of work that we are currently pursuing.

Notes

1. We have chosen to study 1989 and 2000 because they can be considered as the terminal years of the last two economic expansions in the United States. The two phases of economic expansion, defined here as consecutive quarters of positive real GDP growth, may be dated respectively as 1983:1 to 1990:2 and 1991:2 to 2000:4. This makes the years 1989 and 2000 the last full years before the 1990–1991 and 2001 recessions. It may also be noted that the unemployment rate hit its troughs during 1989 and 2000.
2. Regulation of factor and product markets, conduct of monetary and fiscal policies, operation of public enterprises, and the exercise of judicial and executive authority have profound impact on the level and growth of household economic

well-being. Our study follows the traditional demarcation of government intervention (Musgrave and Musgrave, 1980: 4) and focuses on the effects of the government budget on the level and distribution of economic well-being.

3. For a discussion of a measure that also includes self-provisioning, see Wolff, Zacharias and Caner, 2004a.
4. For example, for highways we split the expenditures between the business and household sectors using estimates from highway cost allocation studies that split expenditures between vehicle types.
5. In the example of highways, as in the previous note, we distribute the total expenditure allocated to the household sector among the households on the basis of estimated person-miles traveled. The latter are estimated from household surveys of personal travel.
6. The relevant population may be the entire US population (as in the case of public health expenditures) or a specific demographic group (for example, administrative costs of Medicare are distributed among Medicare recipients).
7. We borrow the terms 'pre-fisc income' and 'post-fisc income' from Reynolds and Smolensky (1977).
8. From 2003, this has been renamed Annual Social and Economic Supplement.
9. Wealth is defined here as net worth. Assets included are homes, real estate and businesses, liquid assets, financial assets, and retirement assets (excluding defined-benefit pensions and Social Security). Liabilities included are mortgage debt and other debt.
10. We are grateful to Asena Caner for performing the necessary computer programming.
11. NIPA Table 8.21, line 172.
12. Information on remaining lifetimes comes from the tables on vital statistics. (U.S. Bureau of the Census, 2002, Table 93.)
13. The only exception to this procedure is educational assistance, for which we lack information to split the NIPA amount between recipients residing in households and student-housing (such as dormitories). Hence no modification is made to the amount reported in the ADS.
14. In the case of Medicaid and Medicare, this procedure involves altering the 'person market value' (the average government cost) in a manner such that the relative values remain the same across risk classes.
15. We wish to thank Michelle Robinson and Alyssa Holdren of the Bureau for their generous help.
16. A prominent example of this type of function is highways where we estimated that about 60 percent of expenditures were incurred on behalf of households. Our estimates were based on the 1997 Federal Highway Administration study that calculated costs per mile and miles traveled by vehicle type.
17. Payroll taxes paid by the self-employed are also included here.
18. Our calculations indicate that the resulting aggregates for consumption taxes are lower than the NIPA counterparts published in NIPA Table 3.5. However, since we have no independent estimate of the household shares in the NIPA totals, it is impossible to align the household consumption tax burden with any portion of the NIPA total.
19. See Congressional Budget Office 2003 also for the use of the term 'comprehensive income.' The CBO definition of pre-tax comprehensive income includes all cash income (both taxable and tax-exempt), taxes paid by businesses, employee contributions to 401(k) retirement plans, and the value of income received in kind from various sources (including employer-paid health insurance premiums, Medicare and Medicaid benefits, and food stamps, among others).

20. The category 'white' includes only non-Hispanic whites, whereas the non-white category includes all other racial and ethnic groups.
21. Because of the large number of households with zero values, the median values of government transfers are not meaningful enough to use here.
22. It should be noted that this result partially reflects the fact that we are using current accounting and hence current taxes rather than accrual accounting and hence accumulated payroll taxes to assess the tax burden. If accrual accounting were used, the social security benefits received by the elderly would be compared to the accumulated value of social security taxes paid by them over their working years.
23. The results reported below are similar when gross money income or comprehensive income (CI) is used. CI is similar to CIW, except that income from non-home wealth in CI is equal to the sum of net realized capital gains and property income.
24. The equivalence scale used here is the three-parameter scale currently used in the Census Bureau's experimental poverty measures. For single parents, the scale is $(A + 0.8 + 0.5*(C-1))^{0.7}$, while for all other households, it is $(A + 0.5*C)^{0.7}$, where A is the number of adults and C is the number of children.
25. Since households are grouped into money income classes, disparities will always be lower if an alternative income definition is used. The notable finding is the extent to which the disparities are reduced when using the post-fisc income definition.
26. In contrast, the Musgrave-Thin index of progressivity is simply the difference between the Gini coefficients for pre-tax and post-tax income.
27. In general, the results of this type of decomposition are sensitive to the order in which the different components are introduced. However, we have also done this decomposition with different orderings and the results remain similar.
28. The share of an income component in inequality is calculated as the contribution of that component divided by the overall Gini coefficient. In turn, the contribution of a component to inequality is calculated as the product of its concentration coefficient and its share in total income. In interpreting the results it is useful to note that the marginal effects are calculated on the assumption that no reranking occurs as a result of a slight proportionate change in a particular component and the method of calculation ensures that the sum of marginal effects is equal to zero.
29. For a discussion of alternative approaches to the treatment of income from wealth and its implications for the distribution of economic well-being, see Wolff, Zacharias and Caner, 2004b.

References

Adema, W. (2001) 'Net Social Expenditure,' 2nd Edn, Labor Market and Social Policy Occasional Papers 52, OECD.

Aronson, J. Richard and Peter Lambert (1994) 'Decomposing the Gini Coefficient to Reveal the Vertical, Horizontal, and Reranking Effects of Income Taxation,' *National Tax Journal* **47**(2): 273–94.

Auerbach, A. J. (2000) 'Formation of Fiscal Policy: The Experience of the Past Twenty-Five Years,' *Federal Reserve Bank of New York Economic Policy Review* (April) 9–23.

Australian Bureau of Statistics (2001) Government Benefits, Taxes and Household Income (Australia: Canberra).

Ballard, C. L., D. Fullerton, J. B. Shoven and J. Whalley (1985) *A General Equilibrium Model for Tax Policy Evaluation* (Chicago: University of Chicago Press).

Blinder, A. S. and J. L. Yellen (2001) *The Fabulous Decade: Macroeconomic Lessons from the 1990s* (New York: The Century Foundation Press).

Canberra Group (2001) 'Expert Group on Household Income Statistics: Final Report and Recommendations' (Ottawa).

Congressional Budget Office (2003) 'Effective Tax Rates, 1997–2000' (August) The Congress of the United States: Washington, D.C. Available on the internet at http://www.cbo.gov/showdoc.cfm?index=4514&sequence=0.

Fullerton, D. and G. E. Metcalf (2002) 'Tax Incidence,' Working Paper 8829 (Cambridge, MA: National Bureau of Economic Research).

Gillespie, W. (1965) 'The Effect of Public Expenditure on the Distribution of income: An Empirical Investigation', in *Essays in Fiscal Federalism*, Richard Musgrave (ed.) (Washington, D.C.: Brookings Institution).

Hicks, U. K. (1946) 'The Terminology of Tax Analysis,' *The Economic Journal* 56(221): 38–50.

Lakin, C. (2002) 'The Effects of Taxes and Benefits on Household Income, 2000–1,' Social Analysis and Reporting Division, Office for National Statistics, United Kingdom. http://www.statistics.gov.uk/.

Lambert, P. J. and W. Pfahler (1988) 'On Aggregate Measures of the Net Redistributive Impact of Taxation and Government Expenditure,' *Public Finance Quarterly* 16(2): 178–202.

Lerman, Robert I. (1999) 'How do Income Sources Affect Income Inequality?,' in Silber, Jacques (ed.), *Handbook on Income Inequality Measurement* (Boston, MA: Kluwer Academic Publishers).

Lerman, Robert I. and Shlomo Yitzhaki (1995) 'Income Inequality Effects by Income Source: A New Approach and Applications to the United States,' *The Review of Economics and Statistics* 67(1): 151–6.

McIntyre, R. S., R. Denk, N. Francis, M. Gardner, W. Gomaa, F. Hsu and R. Sims (2003) *Who Pays? A Distributional Analysis of the Tax Systems in All 50 States*, 2nd Edn (Washington, D.C.: Institute on Taxation and Economic Policy).

Musgrave, R. and P. Musgrave (1980) *Public Finance in Theory and Practice*, 3rd Edn (New York: McGraw-Hill).

Musgrave, R., K. E. Case and H. Leonard (1974) 'The Distribution of Fiscal Burdens and Benefits,' *Public Finance Quarterly* 2(3): 259–311.

Piggott, J. and J. Whalley (1987) 'Interpreting Net Fiscal Incidence Calculations,' *The Review of Economics and Statistics* 69(4): 685–94.

Pirttila, J. and M. Tuomala (2002) 'Publicly Provided Private Goods and Redistribution: A General Equilibrium Analysis,' *Scandinavian Journal of Economics* 104(1): 173–88.

Plotnik, Robert (1981) 'A Measure of Horizontal Inequity,' *Review of Economics and Statistics* 63: 283–8.

Reynolds, M. and E. Smolensky (1977) *Public Expenditures, Taxes, and the Distribution of Income* (New York: Academic Press).

Roemer, M. I. (2000) *Assessing the quality of the March Current Population Survey and the Survey of Income and Program Participation income estimates, 1990–1996*, Staff paper (Washington, D.C.: U.S. Bureau of the Census). Available at http://www.census.gov/hhes/www/income/assess1.pdf.

Ruggles, P. (1991) 'The Impact of Government Tax and Expenditure Programs on the Distribution of Income in the United States,' in Lars Osberg (ed.) *Economic Inequality and Poverty: International Perspectives* (Armonk, NY: M. E. Sharpe) pp. 220–45.

Ruggles, P. and M. O'Higgins (1981) 'The Distribution of Public Expenditure Among Households in the United States,' *Review of Income and Wealth* 27(2): 137–64.

Shaikh, A. (2003) 'Who Pays for the "Welfare" in the Welfare State? A Multicountry Study,' *Social Research* **70**(2): 531–50.

Stiglitz, J. (2003) *The Roaring Nineties: A New History of the World's Most Prosperous Decade* (New York: W. W. Norton & Co).

U.S. Bureau of the Census (2002) *Statistical Abstract of the United States, 2002.* (Washington, D.C.: USGPO).

Whalley, J. (1984) 'Regression or Progression: The Taxing Question of Incidence Analysis,' *The Canadian Journal of Economics* **17**(4): 654–82.

Wolff, E. N. (2004) 'Recent Trends in the Standard of Living in the United States,' in Edward N. Wolff (ed.), *What has Happened to the Quality of Life in the Advanced Industrialized Nations?* (Northampton, MA: Edward Elgar Publishing).

Wolff, E. N., A. Zacharias and A. Caner (2004a) *The Levy Institute Measure of Economic Well-Being, Concept, Measurement and Findings: United States, 1989 and 2000* (Levy Institute) (February).

Wolff, E. N., A. Zacharias and A. Caner (2004b) *The Levy Institute Measure of Economic Well-Being, How Much Does Wealth Matter for Well-Being: Alternative Measures of Income from Wealth* (Levy Institute) (September).

Wolff, E. N., A. Zacharias and A. Caner (2005) 'Household Wealth, Public Consumption, and Economic Well-Being in the United States,' *Cambridge Journal of Economics*, 29(6), 1073–90.

Yao, Shujie (1999) 'On the Decomposition of Gini Coefficients by Population Class and Income Source: A Spreadsheet Approach and Application,' *Applied Economics* **31**: 1249–64.

3
Distributional Effects of Defined Contribution Plans and Individual Retirement Arrangements

Leonard E. Burman, William G. Gale, Matthew Hall and Peter R. Orszag*

3.1 The distributional effects of defined contribution plans and individual retirement accounts

Since the origins of income tax in 1913, the federal government has subsidized retirement saving relative to other saving. In 2003, the present value of the federal revenue loss from new contributions to employer pensions exceeded $184 billion (Office of Management and Budget, 2004, Table 18.4). Despite the magnitude of these revenue losses and the sizable role of tax-deferred saving in providing retirement income, the distributional effects of these programs have received little attention.[1] This chapter helps fill that gap. We describe the development of a retirement saving module in the Tax Policy Center (TPC) microsimulation model and present estimates of the current distribution of benefits from defined contribution plans and individual retirement arrangements.[2]

The distribution of pension benefits is not only an issue of fairness. First, evidence suggests that high-income, high-wealth households are more likely to finance contributions to tax-preferred accounts by shifting assets from other sources, rather than reducing their current consumption. Moderate-income households are more likely to finance contributions by reducing consumption.[3] Thus, retirement saving incentives targeted at high-income households may be relatively ineffective ways to raise private and national saving. Second, evidence suggests that high-income and high-wealth households are more likely to accumulate adequate private wealth to maintain their preretirement living standards in retirement. Low- and middle-income households are more likely to face problems accumulating adequate amounts for retirement. Thus, retirement saving programs targeted at households with high income and high wealth will not encourage saving where it is most needed.[4]

Measuring the benefits that workers receive from tax preferences for saving is not a simple task, however. For an Individual Retirement Account (IRA), for example, the benefit depends on marginal tax rates at the time of contribution, the time of withdrawal, and during the accumulation period. Also, the benefit depends on the length of time the contribution is held in the account, the nominal and real rate of return and the timing and form of withdrawals. For employer-sponsored plans, the effects are substantially more complex. The benefit depends on the nature of any wage offsets to employer pension contributions. It also depends on the economic incidence of nondiscrimination rules, since that incidence indicates how one party's contribution affects the applicable or allowable contributions for other parties.[5]

We found that about 70 percent of tax benefits from new contributions to defined contribution (DC) plans accrued to the highest-income 20 percent of tax filing units in 2004, and more than half went to the top 10 percent. Because eligibility for IRAs was subject to income limits, the tax benefits associated with IRAs were somewhat less skewed by income than contributions to DC plans. Even so, almost 60 percent of IRA tax benefits accrued to the top 20 percent of households and more than 85 percent of benefits went to households in the top 40 percent.

By income level, the largest benefits as a share of after-tax income accrued to households with income between $100,000 and $200,000. Sizable benefits also accrued to households with income between $75,000 and $500,000. Thus, pensions provide the largest benefits, relative to income, for households roughly in the 80th to 99th percentiles of the income distribution. The benefits provided to the wealthiest households are a significantly smaller share of their income, but are larger in dollar terms, than the benefits provided to the 80th to 99th percentiles.

The next section summarizes the major tax incentives for saving addressed in this chapter. The second section describes the TPC microsimulation model. The third section and the appendix summarize the steps taken to model retirement saving programs. The fourth section provides the central results. The final section concludes.

3.2 Tax incentives for saving

We model most, but not all, defined contribution plans and individual retirement arrangements. Because of recent legislation—most notably, the Economic Growth and Tax Relief Reconciliation Act of 2001 (EGTRRA) and the Taxpayer Relief Act of 1997—a variety of retirement saving rules are evolving over time. We focus on the structure of saving incentives as of 2004.[6]

In a 401(k) plan, the most commonly defined contribution arrangement, both employees of for-profit private entities and their employers can make tax-deductible contributions. In 2004, employees could contribute up to $13,000 and workers aged 50 and over in 2004 were permitted additional 'catch-up contributions' of $3000 a year. Employer plus employee contributions to all defined contribution plans for a given worker were limited in

2004 to $41,000 or 100 percent of earnings, whichever was lower. Employer contributions, if any, could be dependent on employee contributions (that is, the employer could match employee contributions up to a certain point). Employers could choose to limit the amount contributed by employees to less than the statutory maximum. Assets in 401(k) plans were not taxed until they were withdrawn, when they faced ordinary income taxes. If the account holder was younger than $59\frac{1}{2}$ at the time of withdrawal, an additional 10 percent penalty was imposed, unless special hardship rules applied.

Separate code sections govern defined contribution plans similar to 401(k) plans that are offered by tax-exempt entities (Section 403(b) plans) and state and local governments (Section 457 plans). A Keogh account can be created by self-employed individuals and is subject to the same tax rules as a 401(k).

We model traditional and Roth individual retirement arrangements, also known as IRAs. Traditional IRAs are taxed in roughly the same way as 401(k) plans, although contribution limits are lower. An individual under the age of $70\frac{1}{2}$ can make a tax-deductible contribution of up to $3000 (but not more than earnings), subject to income limits. For taxpayers with access to an employer plan, eligibility for deductible IRA contributions phases out with income between $65,000 to $75,000 for married taxpayers that file joint returns, $45,000 to $55,000 for singles and heads of household, and $0 to $10,000 for married couples that file separate returns. The phaseout range for a married filing joint taxpayer without access to an employer plan, whose spouse is covered by an employer plan, is $150,000–$160,000. Asset accumulations are not subject to tax until withdrawal, but distributions from IRAs are generally subject to income tax. Withdrawals before the age of $59\frac{1}{2}$ are also subject to a 10 percent penalty unless they are used for specified purposes.[7] Minimum distribution rules stipulate that withdrawals must begin by age $70\frac{1}{2}$ and impose other conditions on the frequency and size of withdrawals.

Contributions to a Roth IRA are not deductible, but qualified distributions are tax-free. In general, a withdrawal is a qualified distribution if it is taken at least five years after the initial contribution and the account owner reaches age $59\frac{1}{2}$, is disabled, or spends the proceeds to purchase a primary residence (subject to the same rules as apply to a traditional IRA; see footnote 8). In addition, withdrawals made by a beneficiary upon death are not subject to the penalty. Other withdrawals are subject to a 10 percent penalty. There is no age limit for contributions to a Roth IRA, and minimum distribution rules do not apply. The maximum contribution to a Roth IRA phases out over the following income ranges:

- $95,000 to $110,000 for single and head of household returns;
- $150,000 to $160,000 for married filing joint returns; and
- $0 to $10,000 for married filing separate.

The limit for total annual contributions to all types of IRAs is $3000.

The 'saver's credit' is a nonrefundable tax credit for low-income people who contribute to an IRA or an employer defined contribution pension plan (see Gale *et al.*, 2004).[8] The maximum contribution eligible for the credit is $2000 (not indexed for inflation). The maximum credit rate is 50 percent, with the rate declining with income. The credit is available to individuals aged 18 or over who are not full-time students or claimed as a dependent on another taxpayer's return. The credit is in addition to any deduction or exclusion that would otherwise apply. The maximum income eligible for a credit is $50,000 on joint returns, $37,500 on head of household returns, and $25,000 on single returns.

3.3   The Tax Policy Center microsimulation model

The TPC has developed a large-scale microsimulation model of the US federal income tax system to produce revenue and distribution estimates. The model is similar to those used by the Congressional Budget Office (CBO), the Joint Committee on Taxation (JCT), and the Treasury's Office of Tax Analysis (OTA). The model consists of three components:

1) a database of tax returns from 1999 supplemented with demographic information;
2) a statistical routine that 'ages' or extrapolates the data to create a representative sample of filers and nonfilers for future years; and
3) a detailed tax calculator and set of incidence assumptions that computes tax liability and tax burdens for filers under current law and alternative proposals.

3.3.1   Data

The tax model uses two data sources:

1) the 1999 public-use file (PUF) produced by the Statistics of Income (SOI) Division of the Internal Revenue Service (IRS); and
2) the 2000 Current Population Survey (CPS).

The PUF contains 132,108 income tax records with detailed information from federal individual income tax returns filed in the 1999 calendar year. It provides key data on the level and sources of income and deductions, income tax liability, marginal tax rates, and use of particular credits. However, it excludes most information about pensions and IRAs, as well as demographic information such as age.

Additional information is mapped on to the PUF through a constrained statistical match with the March 2000 CPS of the U.S. Census Bureau. The statistical match provides important information not reported on tax returns, including measures of earnings for head and spouse separately, their ages, the ages of their children, and transfer payments. The statistical match also generates a sample of individuals who do not file income tax returns ('nonfilers'). By combining the dataset of filers with the dataset of estimated nonfilers from the CPS, we are able to carry out distributional analysis on the entire population rather than just the subset that files individual income tax returns.

3.3.2 Aging and extrapolation process

For the years from 2000 to 2013, we 'age' the data based on forecasts and projections for the growth in various types of income from the CBO, the growth in the number of tax returns from the IRS, and the demographic composition of the population from the Bureau of the Census. We use actual 2000 and 2001 data when available. A two-step process produces a representative sample of the filing and nonfiling population in years beyond 1999. First, the dollar amounts for income, adjustments, deductions, and credits on each record are inflated by their appropriate per capita forecasted growth rates. For the major income sources such as wages, capital gains, and various types of nonwage income such as interest, dividends, Social Security benefits and others, we have specific forecasts for per capita growth. Most other items are assumed to grow at CBO's projected per capita personal income growth rate. In the second stage of the extrapolation process, the weights on each record are adjusted using a linear programming algorithm to ensure that the major income items, adjustments, and deductions match aggregate targets. For the years beyond 1999 we do not target distributions for any item. Wages and salaries, for example, grow at the same per capita rate regardless of income.

3.3.3 Tax calculator

Based on the extrapolated data set, we simulate policy options using a detailed tax calculator that captures most features of the federal individual income tax system, including the alternative minimum tax (AMT). The model reflects the major income tax legislation enacted through to 2003, including the Jobs and Growth Tax Relief Reconciliation Act of 2003 (JGTRRA), the Job Creation and Worker Assistance Act of 2002, and EGTRRA.

The model incorporates most major provisions of EGTRRA and JGTRRA. This includes the 10 percent tax bracket, the changes in marginal tax rates, credits for children and for dependent care, itemized deduction limitations, personal exemption phaseouts, the AMT, and the marriage penalty provisions, which increased the standard deduction, 15 percent bracket, and earned income tax credit for married couples. It also includes JGTRRA's changes to the taxation of dividends and capital gains. The model assumes that the payer bears the burden of the individual income tax, the payroll tax, and the estate tax, and that owners of capital bear the burden of corporate income taxes.

3.4 Modeling retirement saving

We model the benefits of retirement saving in three steps:

1) For each adult head and spouse in a tax unit, we use new data sources to generate estimates of defined contribution coverage and, conditional on coverage, the employer and employee contributions, if any. We also generate estimates of IRA participation by type of IRA, and contributions conditional on participation.
2) We use the results of the estimation procedures to impute coverage and contributions to records in the PUF/CPS database.
3) We develop methods of calculating the value of the tax benefits associated with contributions.

3.4.1 Data sources

To model retirement saving, we supplement the PUF and CPS data described above with information from the 2001 Federal Reserve Board of Governors' Survey of Consumer Finances (SCF) and the Survey of Income and Program Participation (SIPP).

Our principal data source for type of pension, pension participation, and contributions by employers and employees is the SCF, a stratified sample of about 4400 households with detailed data on wealth and savings. The SCF has the best available data on pensions for a broad cross-section of the population, but does not report enough information to determine eligibility for deductible IRA contributions.

To measure eligibility and contributions to individual retirement accounts, we use pooled data from the 1984, 1990, 1992, and 1996 SIPP. We selected individuals who were full-time workers, not self-employed, and between 25 and 55 years old. We dropped records where tax, IRA, or pension data were missing. This yielded a sample of 40,188 households. SIPP participants are re-interviewed every four months for two years, creating new 'waves' of data with additional information. Data on IRAs were derived from wave seven, and they refer to the tax year following the sample year—so the 1996 SIPP yields IRA data for tax year 1997. We calibrate our estimates for IRA participation and contributions to match data from Sailer and Nutter (2004).

3.4.2 Estimation and imputation of retirement saving activity

The appendix describes the procedures used to estimate retirement saving activity in the SCF and SIPP and impute the results to records in the PUF/CPS database. Although the procedures are somewhat complex in practice, the basic approach is straightforward in principle. For defined contribution plans, we estimate the probability of coverage as a function of variables shared by the SCF and PUF/CPS database. Conditional on coverage, we use a similar set of variables to estimate actual and desired employer contributions and employee contributions. For IRAs, we estimate participation in each type of IRA, controlling for the fact that we observe some people already participating in traditional IRAs in the PUF. Then we estimate actual and desired contributions, given participation. With these estimates, we impute values for coverage and contributions on to the records in the PUF/CPS database.

3.4.3 Attributing the value of a retirement saving incentive

Once coverage and contributions are imputed on to the PUF/CPS database, it is still not obvious how to measure the distribution of tax benefits from saving incentives. The primary reason is that the tax savings tend to be spread over many years, whereas distributional tables tend to be annual.

Looking only at changes in annual tax liability (the approach currently employed by the JCT) is not a helpful solution because it can make economically equivalent tax breaks for saving appear different. For example, traditional IRAs provide an up-front deduction and tax-free earnings during the accumulation phase, but withdrawals are taxable. Roth IRAs provide no up-front deduction, but earnings and withdrawals are tax-free. However, even though the pattern of tax payments is different, the expected present value of lifetime taxes paid on the two accounts is equivalent for an equal after-tax contribution for taxpayers whose tax rates do not change, and both accounts provide identical after-tax retirement income under those assumptions.[9] Thus, it would be inappropriate and highly misleading to present the traditional IRA as a larger tax subsidy in the contribution phase and an additional tax during withdrawal, and the Roth IRA as the opposite.

Instead of looking at the current annual tax break, our methodology is similar to that developed by the U.S. Department of the Treasury (Cronin, 1999). We define the benefit received by a tax filing unit in a given year as the present value of the tax benefits associated with their own contributions in that year to IRAs, plus their own and their employer's contributions in that year to defined contribution pensions. Thus, a taxpayer with a positive balance in a 401(k) in 2004 but no employer or employee contributions in 2004 would be attributed no benefit from the 401(k) in 2004. The benefit from the 401(k) balances would be attributed to the years when contributions were made.

To undertake these calculations, we assume that the taxpayer's marginal tax rate does not change over time, and that amounts contributed will be left in the tax-free account until age 65, when they will be withdrawn in equal installments over the remaining life expectancy (17 years for men and 20 years for women).

We measure the value of tax subsidies in terms of the discounted present value of tax savings compared with an equivalent contribution made to a taxable account. For example, for a $2000 contribution made to a traditional IRA by a taxpayer in the 25-percent tax bracket, the actual net-of-tax cost of the contribution is $1500 ($2000 minus the $500 in tax savings). Assuming a 6 percent rate of return on both accounts, that the tax bracket does not change, and that the taxpayer holds the account for 20 years and then withdraws it in equal installments over the next 10, he or she would pay taxes over a lifetime equal to $435.74 in present-day value. Put differently, the IRA would finance an after-tax benefit that is worth $435.74 more in present value than the taxable account financed with the same initial after-tax investment. Thus, in this case, the tax subsidy would be worth about 22 percent of the initial contribution (see the Appendix).

Several aspects of these estimates are worth noting. First, the estimated distributional effect ignores the extent to which contributions represent net additions to private saving, though the net effect on saving will affect the household's utility.[10] Second, we do not allow IRA eligibility or pension coverage—even in the absence of participation—to provide any 'option value' to the worker. Third, for employer-based arrangements, we assume not only that workers as a whole bear the burden of employer contributions via wage adjustments, but also that each worker bears the burden of employer contributions made to his or her account. Lastly, we do not make any adjustments for the presence or operation of nondiscrimination rules.

3.5   Results

3.5.1   Distribution by cash income

We present the model results in terms of 'cash income,' a measure of income that is broader than adjusted gross income, better reflects economic status, and is similar to the measures used by government agencies.[11] Tables 3.1–3.9 and 3.11–3.14 report results by cash income percentile. For similar results by cash income level, see the Appendix (Tables 3.A.1–3.A.13).

The present value of tax benefits attributable to contributions into DC plans and IRAs is substantial. Contributions made to the accounts in 2004 reduce the present value of income taxes by an average of $528 per tax filing unit, an average 1.2 percent of after-tax income (Table 3.1). The tax benefits are concentrated at high incomes, where 70 percent goes to the top quintile and 90 percent to the top 40 percent of the income distribution. By comparison, the bottom quintile gets almost no benefit from the income tax exclusion because few people in this category contribute to pensions or IRAs. Those who do tend to contribute smaller shares of their income than do

Table 3.1 Tax Benefits of Defined Contribution Plans and IRAs[1] by Cash Income Percentile, 2004

Cash income percentile[2]	% of Tax units with benefit[3]	Benefit as % of after-tax income[4]	Share of total benefits	Average benefit ($)
Lowest Quintile	2.0	0.1	0.2	−6
Second Quintile	12.7	0.4	2.9	−77
Middle Quintile	24.9	0.7	7.9	−208
Fourth Quintile	43.0	1.1	19.3	−509
Top Quintile	61.0	1.4	69.7	−1,838
All	28.7	1.2	100.0	−528
Addendum				
Top 10%	63.8	1.4	48.6	−2,566
Top 5%	61.9	1.2	30.4	−3,211
Top 1%	53.3	0.6	7.8	−4,111
Top 0.5%	51.6	0.4	4.0	−4,252
Top 0.1%	51.4	0.2	0.9	−4,645

Source: Urban-Brookings Tax Policy Center Microsimulation Model.
[1] Distribution of the present value of lifetime tax benefits for new contributions made in 2004.
[2] Tax units with negative cash income are excluded from the lowest income class but are included in the totals. Visit http://www.taxpolicycenter.org/TaxModel/income.cfm for a description of cash income.
[3] Both filing and non-filing units are included. Filers who can be claimed as dependents by other filers are excluded from the analysis.
[4] After-tax income is cash income less individual income tax net of refundable credits, payroll and estate tax liability, and imputed, burden from corporate taxes.

higher-income contributors, and the tax benefit per dollar of contribution is smaller, and in some cases worthless, because they face low or zero marginal income tax rates.[12] The distribution of the tax benefits from pensions is similar to the distribution of all federal taxes by quintile.[13]

Although taxpayers with very high incomes receive the largest benefit in dollar terms (for example, $4111 on average in the top 1 percent), benefits decline as a share of income at the very top. Benefits amount to 0.2 percent of income for the highest-income 0.1 percent of tax filing units, compared with about 1.4 percent for the top 10 percent. This decline as a share of income occurs because contributions are limited and thus decline as a share of income for those with very high incomes. IRAs are subject to even lower contribution limits than DC plans and are only available on a tax-deductible basis to those with very high incomes if they and their spouse do not have access to an employer pension.[14]

Appendix Table 3.A.1 shows the distribution by cash income levels. The largest benefits, as a share of income, accrue to taxpayers with cash income between $75,000 and $500,000, who collectively receive about two-thirds of the benefits. The 0.6 percent of taxpayers with income above $500,000 receive 4.4 percent of the benefits. The 14 percent of tax units with income between $50,000 and $75,000 receive 15 percent of the benefits, as do the 65 percent of households with income below $50,000.

3.5.1.1   Defined contribution plans

The vast majority of tax benefits from contributory pension plans (92 percent) arise from DC plans sponsored by employers. As a result, the distribution of tax benefits from these plans is similar to the distribution of DC and IRA plans together (Compare Table 3.2 to Table 3.1).

Table 3.3 shows estimates for pension participation and contributions for married households with a head of working age (18 to 64) in 2001.[15] The likelihood of participating in an employer DC plan and the average contribution amount grow steadily with income. About 41 percent of household heads in the top quintile participate in DC plans, compared with only 4 percent in the bottom quintile. The participation rate is not markedly higher at the top, but average contributions among participants grow steadily with income.

Employer contributions for heads of households follow a similar pattern, although the likelihood of an employer contribution grows even within the top quintile. About 48 percent of heads in the top 0.1 percent get an employer contribution, averaging almost $26,000, compared with only 28 percent overall, who get an average contribution of about $4200.

For spouses, the probability of participating generally grows with income, but it actually declines within the top quintile. Spouses in the top 0.1 percent

Table 3.2 Tax Benefits of Defined Contribution Plans by Cash Income Percentile, 2004

Cash income percentile	% of Tax units with benefit	Benefit as % of after-tax income	Share of total benefits	Average benefit ($)
Lowest Quintile	1.8	0.1	0.2	−6
Second Quintile	11.6	0.4	2.8	−69
Middle Quintile	21.7	0.6	7.5	−182
Fourth Quintile	36.8	0.9	18.6	−452
Top Quintile	53.0	1.3	70.8	−1,722
All	25.0	1.1	100.0	−486
Addendum				
Top 10%	55.8	1.3	50.0	−2,433
Top 5%	54.8	1.2	32.0	−3,108
Top 1%	48.2	0.6	8.3	−4,031
Top 0.5%	46.7	0.4	4.3	−4,176
Top 0.1%	47.0	0.2	0.9	−4,587

Source: Urban-Brookings Tax Policy Center Microsimulation Model. See notes to Table 3.1.

Table 3.3 Participation and Contributions to Defined Contribution Plans[1] Married Filing Joint Returns, by Cash Income Percentile, 2004

Cash income percentile	Tax units Working age population (thousands)	% of total	Elective deferral head % Participating	Average contribution[2]	Elective deferral spouse % Participating	Average contribution[2]	Employer contribution head % Participating	Average contribution[2]	Employer contribution spouse % Participating	Average contribution[2]
Lowest Quintile	3,467	7.5	3.5	816	3.0	499	4.2	683	2.7	384
Second Quintile	4,044	8.8	10.7	1,343	8.2	876	10.9	1,048	8.6	644
Middle Quintile	5,756	12.5	17.1	2,154	15.1	1,348	18.5	1,653	14.9	1,024
Fourth Quintile	12,329	26.8	27.3	3,401	24.7	2,193	27.8	2,507	25.4	1,819
Top Quintile	20,155	43.9	41.7	7,405	35.2	4,399	40.9	5,949	33.8	3,555
All	45,955	100.0	28.5	5,627	24.7	3,390	28.5	4,166	24.3	2,700
Addendum										
Top 10%	10,522	22.9	45.4	9,160	36.1	5,312	44.7	7,788	33.7	4,382
Top 5%	5,243	11.4	46.6	11,036	34.5	6,305	46.5	10,553	31.2	5,374
Top 1%	997	2.2	42.6	12,937	27.7	8,621	46.5	19,733	23.8	8,484
Top 0.5%	499	1.1	41.7	13,149	21.1	9,244	47.5	23,035	18.0	10,394
Top 0.1%	100	0.2	43.5	13,558	17.4	10,966	48.5	25,802	15.6	15,337

Source: Urban-Brookings Tax Policy Center Microsimulation Model. See notes to Table 3.1.
[1] Sample is limited to households where the head is between 18 and 64 years of age. Percentile groups are in terms of the entire population.
[2] Among those who contribute to a defined contribution plan.

are half as likely to contribute to a DC pension plan as those in the top 10 percent overall. This may reflect the fact that spouses married to people with very high incomes are less likely to work in a high-paying job than those with moderately high incomes.

The average contribution of spouses who participate in a DC plan grows steadily with income, but the amount is always smaller than for similar heads, because spouses tend to have lower earnings. Similarly, the employer contribution follows the same pattern as for household heads, but is smaller for spouses.

The results for working-age singles (Table 3.4) are similar to those for household heads. The notable difference is in the overall averages, which are much lower for singles. This is because singles as a group have lower incomes than married people—that is, the average is more heavily weighted toward those with lower incomes.

3.5.1.2 IRAs

As noted, new contributions to IRAs were a very small factor compared with DC pension plans in 2004. On average, contributions to IRAs in 2004 (not counting rollovers) garnered tax benefits worth only about $42 per tax filing unit (Table 3.5). The main reason the figure is so low is that the vast majority of low- and middle-income households did not contribute, even though they were eligible for tax-deductible contributions. In addition, most high-income households were ineligible for the deductions, and the contribution limit for IRAs was much lower than the combined employer and employee limit for DC plans. About 83 percent of the tax benefits of IRAs were concentrated between the 60th and 99th percentiles of the income distribution.

Overall, we estimate that only about 3 percent of tax units contributed to a traditional IRA in 2004 and about the same percentage contributed to a Roth IRA (Table 3.6). The likelihood of contributing to an IRA increases with income up to a point and then declines because most people with very high incomes are ineligible (especially for Roth IRAs). Among contributors, the average contribution to both kinds of accounts increases with income. The likelihood of making the maximum contribution also generally increases with income, although the trend is not so even.[16]

3.5.1.3 Saver's credit

Table 3.7 shows the distributional effects of the saver's credit. The credit is used by about 5 percent of tax filing units overall, including roughly 7 to 9 percent of filing units in the middle three quintiles. The benefits are very modest as a share of after-tax income. About one-third of the benefits goes to each of the three middle quintiles (see Gale *et al.*, 2004, for further discussion).

Table 3.4 Participation and Contributions to Defined Contribution Plans[1] Single and Head of Household Returns, by Cash Income Percentile, 2004

Cash income percentile	Tax units		Elective deferral		Employer contribution	
	Working age population (thousands)	% of total	% Participating	Average contribution[2]	% Participating	Average contribution[2]
Lowest Quintile	18,489	27.1	5.4	701	5.3	611
Second Quintile	17,371	25.4	14.9	1,292	14.5	1,103
Middle Quintile	16,651	24.4	23.1	2,141	22.4	1,745
Fourth Quintile	11,251	16.5	35.7	3,611	33.2	2,768
Top Quintile	4,224	6.2	40.4	7,335	38.9	6,129
All	68,311	100.0	19.2	2,968	18.4	2,357
Addendum						
Top 10%	1,715	2.5	41.1	9,558	40.2	8,661
Top 5%	810	1.2	40.2	11,321	38.8	11,934
Top 1%	160	0.2	35.4	12,311	36.5	20,214
Top 0.5%	81	0.1	34.4	12,814	34.7	22,558
Top 0.1%	18	0.0	37.0	13,462	38.6	25,514

Source: Urban-Brookings Tax Policy Center Microsimulation Model. See notes to Table 3.1.
[1] Sample is limited to households where the head is between 18 and 64 years of age. Percentile groups are in terms of the entire population.
[2] Among those who contribute to a defined contribution plan.

Table 3.5 Tax Benefits of Roth and Traditional IRAs by Cash Income Percentile, 2004

Cash income percentile	% of tax units with benefit	Benefit as % of after-tax income	Share of total benefits	Average benefit ($)
Lowest Quintile	0.2	0.0	0.2	0
Second Quintile	1.3	0.0	3.5	−7
Middle Quintile	4.0	0.1	11.5	−24
Fourth Quintile	8.4	0.1	26.8	−56
Top Quintile	12.7	0.1	58.0	−121
All	5.3	0.1	100.0	−42
Addendum				
Top 10%	13.3	0.1	34.9	−145
Top 5%	10.8	0.0	15.2	−126
Top 1%	5.9	0.0	2.0	−83
Top 0.5%	6.0	0.0	1.0	−84
Top 0.1%	4.4	0.0	0.1	−59

Source: Urban-Brookings Tax Policy Center Microsimulation Model. See notes to Table 3.1.

3.5.1.4 Policy changes

The model may be used to simulate the effects of policy options. We considered two here:

1) making the saver's credit refundable in 2004; and
2) accelerating the phased in pension and IRA limit increases to 2004.

Making the saver's credit refundable (available to tax filers even if they do not owe income tax) would provide 87 percent of its benefits to the bottom 60 percent of taxpayers (Table 3.8). The middle quintile would get 34 percent of the benefits, and the second quintile 38 percent, but even the bottom 20 percent would get 15 percent of the tax savings. This is because many low-income taxpayers, especially those with children, owe little or no income tax and thus obtain limited or no benefit from a nonrefundable tax credit. The largest benefits from making the saver's credit refundable accrue to the second quintile because, among taxpayers who can benefit from refundability, they are most likely to have qualifying contributions.

Accelerating the EGTRRA limit increases would provide little benefit to the bottom half of the income distribution (Table 3.9). More than half of the benefits would go to the top 10 percent of the income distribution.

Table 3.6 Participation and Contributions to Roth and Traditional IRAs by Cash Income Percentile, 2004

Cash income percentile	Tax units		% who contribute	Traditional IRA		% who contribute	Roth IRA	
	Number (thousands)	% of total		Average contribution[1]	% of contributors at limit		Average contribution[1]	% of contributors at limit
Lowest Quintile	28,143	19.6	0.2	1,918	40.0	0.3	2,189	29.6
Second Quintile	28,701	20.0	0.9	2,236	50.4	0.8	2,911	45.5
Middle Quintile	28,703	20.0	2.9	2,596	50.2	1.4	2,883	38.5
Fourth Quintile	28,704	20.0	4.5	2,868	36.8	4.0	3,117	36.9
Top Quintile	28,701	20.0	5.2	3,610	44.3	7.6	3,552	38.6
All	143,509	100.0	2.7	3,032	43.4	2.8	3,296	38.3
Addendum								
Top 10%	14,351	10.0	5.5	4,015	51.9	7.9	3,723	41.2
Top 5%	7,176	5.0	5.7	4,244	59.7	5.1	3,889	53.9
Top 1%	1,435	1.0	4.6	5,022	77.3	1.4	5,371	84.6
Top 0.5%	718	0.5	4.5	5,058	78.1	1.6	5,928	98.3
Top 0.1%	144	0.1	4.3	5,000	77.4	0.2	6,141	100.0

Source: Urban-Brookings Tax Policy Center Microsimulation Model. See notes to Table 3.1.
[1] Among those who contribute to an IRA.

Table 3.7 Tax Benefits of the Savers' Credit by Cash Income Percentile, 2004

Cash income percentile	% of tax units with benefit	Benefit as % of after-tax income	Share of total benefits	Average benefit ($)
Lowest Quintile	1.2	0.0	2.6	−2
Second Quintile	7.1	0.1	28.4	−20
Middle Quintile	9.1	0.1	36.7	−26
Fourth Quintile	8.0	0.0	31.2	−22
Top Quintile	0.2	0.0	1.1	−1
All	5.1	0.0	100.0	−14
Addendum				
Top 10%	0.2	0.0	0.6	−1
Top 5%	0.1	0.0	0.1	0
Top 1%	0.0	0.0	0.0	0
Top 0.5%	0.0	0.0	0.0	0
Top 0.1%	0.0	0.0	0.0	0

Source: Urban-Brookings Tax Policy Center Microsimulation Model. See notes to Table 3.1.

Table 3.8 Tax Benefits of Making the Savers' Credit Refundable[1] by Cash Income Percentile, 2004

Cash income percentile	% of tax units with benefit	Benefit as % of after-tax income	Share of total benefits	Average benefit ($)
Lowest Quintile	4.8	0.2	14.6	−17
Second Quintile	8.6	0.3	38.2	−44
Middle Quintile	7.0	0.1	34.3	−39
Fourth Quintile	2.5	0.0	8.9	−10
Top Quintile	0.3	0.0	2.6	−3
All	4.6	0.1	100.0	−23
Addendum				
Top 10%	0.2	0.0	1.3	−3
Top 5%	0.1	0.0	0.4	−2
Top 1%	0.1	0.0	0.1	−1
Top 0.5%	0.1	0.0	0.0	−1
Top 0.1%	0.1	0.0	0.0	−2

Source: Urban-Brookings Tax Policy Center Microsimulation Model. See notes to Table 3.1.
[1] Baseline is current law.

3.5.2 Distribution by age

The tax benefits of IRAs and DC pension plans vary by age for several reasons. Younger people stand to gain the most from deferral of tax liability because they can hold on to their accounts for many years before they are required

Table 3.9 Tax Benefits of Accelerating DC and IRA Contribution Limit Increases[1] by Cash Income Percentile, 2004

Cash income percentile	% of tax units with benefit	Benefit as % of after-tax income	Share of total benefits	Average benefit ($)
Lowest Quintile	0.0	0.0	0.1	0
Second Quintile	0.6	0.0	2.1	−2
Middle Quintile	1.7	0.0	7.5	−7
Fourth Quintile	3.1	0.0	18.8	−18
Top Quintile	9.6	0.1	71.5	−69
All	3.0	0.0	100.0	−19
Addendum				
Top 10%	14.6	0.1	54.4	−104
Top 5%	22.2	0.1	38.1	−146
Top 1%	34.8	0.0	10.7	−205
Top 0.5%	36.2	0.0	4.7	−182
Top 0.1%	39.1	0.0	0.7	−142

Source: Urban-Brookings Tax Policy Center Microsimulation Model. Sec notes to Table 3.1.
[1] Baseline is current law.

to begin making withdrawals. Earnings peak in the 40s and 50s, so older workers have more income available to defer and are also more likely to be working for an employer that offers a 401(k)-type plan. Older workers also face higher tax rates on average and thus benefit most from salary deferral, especially if they expect their tax rate to decline in retirement, although this is not accounted for in our estimates.

On balance, it appears that the tax benefits for DC plans and IRAs (including saver's credit) are worth the most to workers between 35 and 54 years of age. In 2004, the present value of such tax benefits averaged about $900 for households with a head between 35 and 44 years old, and almost $800 for those between 45 and 54 (see Table 3.10). The benefits are largest as a share of income—1.7 percent—for those between 25 and 44. The fraction declines for older workers, in part because they are more likely to have defined benefit (DB) plans and thus contribute less to a DC plan. Not surprisingly, benefits are virtually nil for those over age 64 (recall that these estimates only apply to new contributions) and small for those under age 25.

3.5.2.1 Sensitivity analysis

Besides reporting the main results by cash income percentile (Table 3.1) and level (Appendix Table 3.A.1), we report several different sensitivity analyses here. One concern is that cross-sectional results may be artificially skewed because they combine differences in income among households that are the same age with differences in income among households that are on the same

Table 3.10   Tax Benefits of Defined Contribution Plans and IRAs by Age of Household Head, 2004

Age bracket	Tax units			Benefit as % of after-tax income[3]	Share of total benefits	Average benefit ($)
	Number (thousands)	% of total	% with benefit			
Less than 25	19,029	13.3	16.4	1.2	7.9	−316
25–34	26,480	18.5	34.3	1.7	22.9	−654
35–44	29,677	20.7	43.9	1.7	35.3	−900
45–54	23,920	16.7	43.5	1.3	24.9	−789
55–64	15,160	10.6	30.0	0.7	7.7	−384
65+	29,243	20.4	3.5	0.1	1.3	−33
All	143,509	100.0	28.7	1.2	100.0	−528

Source: Urban-Brookings Tax Policy Center Microsimulation Model. See notes to Table 3.1.

Table 3.11   Tax Benefits of DC Plans and IRAs Among Household Heads Aged 45 to 54 by Cash Income Percentile, 2004

Cash income percentile	% of tax units with benefit	Benefit as % of after-tax income	Share of total benefits	Average benefit ($)
Lowest Quintile	2.5	0.1	0.1	−7
Second Quintile	17.0	0.5	1.5	−85
Middle Quintile	32.6	0.8	4.7	−218
Fourth Quintile	51.9	1.1	15.3	−509
Top Quintile	73.1	1.5	78.4	−1,970
All	43.5	1.3	100.0	−789
Addendum				
Top 10%	75.6	1.5	57.8	−2,722
Top 5%	74.4	1.3	36.6	−3,476
Top 1%	65.8	0.6	8.3	−4,448
Top 0.5%	63.5	0.5	4.6	−4,765
Top 0.1%	61.8	0.2	0.9	−4,871

Source: Urban-Brookings Tax Policy Center Microsimulation Model. See notes to Table 3.1.

life-cycle income path but are currently of different ages. To address this concern, Table 3.11 examines the distribution of benefits among households aged 45 to 54. Comparing Tables 3.1 and 3.11 shows that participation in pensions and the net average benefit ($789) are substantially higher in the 45 to 54 age group than in the population as a whole. Because households in this age group tend to have higher incomes and more access to pensions than the population at large, the benefits are somewhat more skewed by income. About 78 percent of pension and IRA tax subsidies accrue to 45 to 54-year-olds in the top quintile, compared with 69 percent for the whole population.[17]

Table 3.12 reports the distributional effects of DC plans and IRAs, but classifies households by their economic income rather than their cash income. Economic income is a more comprehensive measure still, similar to the measure used by the Treasury Department from the early 1980s until 2001 (Cronin, 1999). The primary difference relative to cash income is that economic income includes the imputed return to assets rather than the actual realized return reported on income tax returns.[18] In addition, income is adjusted for family size.[19] A comparison of Tables 3.12 and 3.1 shows that the distribution of benefits is broadly similar across economic income percentiles and cash income percentiles. There is a somewhat higher concentration of benefits in the 80th to 99th percentile when classifying households by cash income.

The last two tables examine sensitivity to different parametric assumptions. Table 3.13 examines the distribution of benefits assuming that the tax rate that would have applied to the investment income from the contributions had they remained in taxable accounts was 10 percent, rather than the base case assumption that the household's statutory marginal tax rate would

Table 3.12 Tax Benefits of Defined Contribution Plans and IRAs by Economic Income Percentile, 2004

Economic income percentile[1]	% of tax units with benefit	Benefit as % of after-tax income	Share of total benefits	Average benefit ($)
Lowest Quintile	3.6	0.2	0.5	−13
Second Quintile	15.9	0.8	4.3	−115
Middle Quintile	26.0	1.1	9.3	−246
Fourth Quintile	42.0	1.7	21.8	−574
Top Quintile	56.1	1.8	64.0	−1,689
All	28.7	1.5	100.0	−528
Addendum				
Top 10%	57.9	1.6	41.9	−2,213
Top 5%	55.7	1.3	25.3	−2,672
Top 1%	46.0	0.6	6.2	−3,286
Top 0.5%	43.2	0.4	3.2	−3,400
Top 0.1%	43.2	0.1	0.7	−3,700

Source: Urban-Brookings Tax Policy Center Microsimulation Model. See notes to Table 3.1.
[1] Visit http://www.taxpolicycenter.org/TaxModel/income.cfm for a description of economic income.

Table 3.13 Tax Benefits of Defined Contribution Plans and IRAs Using a 10% Tax Rate by Cash Income Percentile, 2004

Cash income percentile	% of tax units with benefit	Benefit as % of after-tax income	Share of total benefits	Average benefit ($)
Lowest Quintile	5.5	0.2	0.7	−13
Second Quintile	14.5	0.5	4.4	−81
Middle Quintile	25.3	0.6	9.9	−183
Fourth Quintile	43.2	0.8	20.2	−374
Top Quintile	61.0	0.9	64.7	−1,197
All	29.9	0.8	100.0	−370
Addendum				
Top 10%	63.8	0.9	43.6	−1,614
Top 5%	61.9	0.7	27.1	−2,004
Top 1%	53.0	0.3	6.5	−2,403
Top 0.5%	51.3	0.2	3.2	−2,377
Top 0.1%	50.6	0.1	0.7	−2,534

Source: Urban-Brookings Tax Policy Center Microsimulation Model. See notes to Table 3.1.

Table 3.14 Tax Benefits of Defined Contribution Plans and IRAs Using a 9% Rate of Return by Cash Income Percentile, 2004

Cash income percentile	% of tax units with benefit	Benefit as % of after-tax income	Share of total benefits	Average benefit ($)
Lowest Quintile	2.0	0.1	0.2	−7
Second Quintile	12.7	0.5	2.7	−93
Middle Quintile	25.0	0.9	7.7	−262
Fourth Quintile	43.0	1.4	19.7	−668
Top Quintile	61.0	1.8	69.7	−2,367
All	28.7	1.5	100.0	−679
Addendum				
Top 10%	63.8	1.8	48.4	−3,289
Top 5%	62.0	1.5	30.1	−4,092
Top 1%	53.4	0.8	7.7	−5,244
Top 0.5%	51.7	0.5	4.0	−5,454
Top 0.1%	51.7	0.2	0.9	−5,986

Source: Urban-Brookings Tax Policy Center Microsimulation Model. See notes to Table 3.1.

apply. Table 3.14 calculates the distribution of benefits with a nominal rate of return of 9 percent rather than the base case assumption of 6 percent. Comparing these two tables to Table 3.1 shows that the changes naturally affect the estimated level of the benefit, but have little impact on the distribution of benefits.

3.6 Conclusion

A key, but underexamined, aspect of tax policy toward pensions is how such benefits are distributed across the population. This chapter develops an enhanced version of the TPC microsimulation tax model to examine this question. We find that about 70 percent of such tax benefits accrued to the highest-income 20 percent of tax filing units in 2004 and more than half went to the top 10 percent. Because eligibility for IRAs was subject to income limits, the tax benefits are less skewed by income than contributions to DC plans. Even so, almost 60 percent of IRA tax benefits accrue to the top 20 percent of households. As a share of income, the benefits from DC plans and IRAs are highest in households with income between $75,000 and $500,000, roughly the 80th to 99th percentile of the income distribution.

Several areas for further research could be fruitful. First, the distributional effects of DC plans could be enhanced by refining assumptions about the incidence of employer contributions, the option value of pension coverage and IRA eligibility, the role of nondiscrimination rules, and the relation between the benefit received and the net impact on saving. Second, the analysis could be extended to defined benefit plans. Third, for both types of pensions, the target effectiveness of tax subsidies for retirement saving could be examined by linking the income-related distribution of tax benefits from pension plans with income-related differences in both the effects of pensions on saving and the adequacy of current saving for retirement. All these issues represent promising directions for future research.

Appendix

This Appendix provides details on estimation, imputation, and valuation procedures used to determine the distribution of retirement saving incentives.

Defined contribution plans

Estimation

We use the probit maximum likelihood estimator to estimate the likelihood of being covered by a DC plan. Under the probit model, the coverage is observed if and only if $X_1\beta_1 + \varepsilon_1 > 0$, where ε_1 is assumed to be a standard normal random variable with mean 0 and variance 1, X is a vector of explanatory variables, and β is a vector of parameters to be estimated. Conditional on coverage, we estimate contributions as a function of a similar set of variables.

The procedure is similar to the Heckman two-step estimator, with two differences. First, we estimate the second stage equation using censored regression techniques to account for the fact that contributions are limited by law. Second, we omit a Mills ratio correction in the second stage. This may yield biased coefficient estimates in the second stage, but that is not a relevant concern because we are interested in producing the best fit, conditional on the explanatory variables, rather than the best coefficient estimates.

For employee and employer contributions, we estimate an equation of the form $ln(y^*) = X_2\beta_2 + \varepsilon_2$, where y^* is the desired contribution (before application of statutory limits), and ε_2 is assumed to be normal with mean 0 and variance σ^2. The latent variable, y^*, is not observed. Instead, we observe y, defined as y^* when $y^* < L$, and L if $y^* > L$, where L is the statutory contribution limit. The upper limits for the censored regression are based on the law in effect in 2000. The maximum elective contribution to a 401(k) was the lesser of $10,500 or 25 percent of earnings, and the maximum total qualifying contribution (including both employer and employee contributions) was $30,000.[20]

The list of exogenous variables for each probit and censored regression is designed to be an exhaustive set of relevant variables that exist on both the SCF and the PUF. These variables include number of dependents, age (included as 10-year bracket dummies), income (as defined for purposes of the SCF), and the following components of income: income from a farm or business, tax-exempt interest income, taxable interest income, rental income from schedule E, pension income, taxable dividends, and realized capital gains (all defined as the natural logarithm of the income item plus one). We include dummies for zero values of each income item: dummies for negative overall income; negative income from a business or farm; and negative capital income. We also include interactions between the negative income dummies and the appropriate negative income amount (defined as the natural logarithm of the absolute value of the income item plus one). In addition, we include dummies for whether the individual itemizes deductions on his or her federal tax return, and dummies for whether certain federal tax schedules are filed (C for business income, E for rental income, and F for farm income). The list of explanatory variables is identical for each equation, except for the employer contribution probit and level equations. Those equations include the natural logarithm of employee contributions as an explanatory variable, under the logic that employer contributions are often matching.

Equations are estimated separately for head of household and spouse, but are based on household-level values for the explanatory variables with the exception of age and earnings.[21] It is not appropriate in the SCF to simply run regressions or probits on the entire dataset because of its approach to missing variables. The SCF imputes missing values for a number of fields. To reflect the variance introduced by that process, the SCF database includes five replicates of each observation. Missing values are drawn randomly for each replicate from the estimated probability distribution of the imputed value, whereas non-missing values are simply repeated. We estimate coefficients by computing each estimate separately for each sample replicate and then averaging the coefficient estimates.[22]

Imputation

Given the estimates of coverage and contributions from the SCF, we impute values to tax filing units in the PUF/CPS database. Imputation is done in three steps:

1) We simulate whether the taxpayer has the item. For consistency, pension contributions are attributed only to tax returns that are not shown ineligible by virtue of

their IRA contributions.[23] Using the estimated coefficients from the probit estimation and values of explanatory variables in the tax model database, we calculate Xb_1 (where b_1 refers to the probit estimate for β_1). We then calculate the threshold probability, $z = \Phi^{-1}(X_1 b_1)$, where Φ is the cumulative standard normal probability distribution, and draw a uniform random number, p, between 0 and 1. If $z < p$, we assign a nonzero value for the item.[24]

2) We estimate employer and employee contribution levels for taxpayers with $z < p$. Using the estimated coefficients from the level equation (b_2) and values for explanatory variables in the PUF, we calculate Xb_2, the desired value for the item, y. In the limit, $E(y^*) = \exp(Xb_2 + s^2/2)$, where s is the estimated standard error for the level regression. However, in finite samples, $\exp(Xb_2 + s^2/2)$ can be a biased estimator, and the biases can be large if the errors are in fact non-normal. We follow Duan (1983) and instead use a robust empirical 'smearing adjustment' to match the sample means of predicted values with the sample mean of the actual SCF data. The adjustment basically amounts to multiplying $\exp(Xb_2)$ by a constant chosen to align the sample means.

3) We adjust the imputed aggregates to match SCF totals. After the adjustment, the number of participants and the size of employer and employee contributions match approximately the totals reported in the SCF.

Calculating gross wages

After the imputation process is complete, we calculate gross wages by adding employer and employee contributions to DC pension plans to reported taxable wages and salaries. Unlike taxable wages, gross wages are invariant with respect to tax changes, assuming that employer contributions to pension plans and other fringe benefits are paid out of wages. By the same logic, we subtract the employer's portion of additional payroll taxes due on the additional cash compensation from gross wages. We use gross wages as a component of cash income.

IRAs

IRAs raise special issues for three reasons:

1) IRA contributions are not reported on the SCF, which we resolve by using the 1996 SIPP.
2) No questions were asked about Roth IRAs in the 1996 SIPP (since the Roth IRA was first enacted in 1997) and there is currently no cross-section information available on Roth IRA contributions.
3) 1997 legislation phased in substantial increases to the income limits for contributions to traditional IRAs—not fully effective until 2007. This last point means that baseline contributions can be significantly greater in later years than the observed values for taxpayers who are at the limit in 1997.

To calculate the IRA participation and contributions, we use a similar method to the one described above, modified to use information on the PUF about contributions to traditional IRAs. We distinguish between individuals who already contribute to a tax-deductible IRA in the PUF and all others.

Individuals who contribute to a tax-deductible IRA as indicated on the PUF in 1999 are assumed to also contribute to such an account in later years. For those who contribute the limit to an IRA in 1999, the desired contribution is at least the limit amount. We calculate the desired contribution based on the estimates from the censored regression equation. Suppose the limit in 1999 was L, the actual contribution was I, the vector of explanatory variables is X, the coefficient vector from the censored regression is denoted as β_3, and the error as ε_3, a random variable with mean 0 and variance σ_3^2. Let $\ln(I^*) = X\beta_3 + \varepsilon_3$ represent the desired contribution. The dependent variable is upward censored at $\ln(L)$, so the observed variable is $\ln(I) = \ln(I^*)$ when $I^* < L$ and $\ln(I) = \ln(L)$ otherwise. For limit contributors, the expectation of I^* is

$$E(I^*|I \geq L) = E(e^{X\beta_3 + \varepsilon_3}|\varepsilon_3 \geq \ln(L) - X\beta_3).$$

It may be shown that

$$E(I^*|I \geq L) = e^{X\beta_3 + \sigma_3^2/2} \frac{1 - \Phi\left(\dfrac{\ln L - X\beta_3 - \sigma_3^2}{\sigma_3}\right)}{1 - \Phi\left(\dfrac{\ln L - X\beta_3}{\sigma_3}\right)}.$$

We calculate a consistent estimator for this expected value using the estimates for the coefficient vector and standard error generated by the censored regression equation. This procedure guarantees that predicted contributions are at least as great as the 1999 limit, which means that these people will contribute more when the limit increases.[25]

For all other tax filing units, IRA participation depends on the results of probit equations estimated on the 1997 SIPP data (as described above for 401(k) plans), and the desired level of contribution depends on the predictions of a censored regression equation also estimated on the SIPP. To simplify, we assume that, when eligible for both types of IRA, these households all contribute to Roth IRAs, even if they become eligible for traditional IRAs as the limits increase. Because the present value of Roth and traditional IRAs is equivalent for an equal after-tax contribution (as discussed below), this assumption does not affect the distribution of tax benefits from IRAs overall. It may, however, lead to an overestimate of the share of IRA contributions in Roth IRAs, especially for those with higher incomes.[26]

We use the estimated probit equation and censored regression estimates to predict whether tax filing units contribute to a Roth IRA and the amount of desired pre-tax contribution (since the traditional IRAs were all made on a pre-tax basis). The procedure is identical to that outlined for 401(k) participation and contributions, except for two modifications:

1) The contribution is converted from a pre-tax to an after-tax contribution based on the taxpayer's marginal tax rate (subject to the applicable Roth IRA limit).
2) The estimates for participation and contribution levels are calibrated to match estimates based on IRS data from 2000 (Sailer and Nutter, 2004).

Other policies

The saver's credit

The saver's credit is a nonrefundable tax credit equal to a share of employee contributions to DC pensions and contributions to IRAs. We model this credit simply as a reduction in tax based on the credit formula. Following standard distributional analysis conventions, no behavioral response is assumed—that is, we do not assume that saving increases when people have access to the credit. Thus, the credit calculation follows directly from our estimates of IRA and retirement plan contributions. For some scenarios, we assume that the credit is refundable. That means that tax filers get the full benefit of the credit, even if it exceeds their income tax liability—even if they do not owe income tax at all.

Changes in contribution and income limits

We simulate the effects of higher contribution limits and changes in income eligibility rules using an analogous procedure. We assume that people who are eligible to contribute in the baseline but do not contribute will not decide to contribute if their contribution limit increases (this assumption could be wrong if there are transaction costs). However, those who do contribute in the baseline and are at the limit will increase their contribution, according to their desired contribution equation and adjustments described above. Changes in income limits for IRA contributions could also increase the number of contributors as some newly eligible people would contribute depending on the prediction of the probit participation equation, as discussed above.[27]

The present value of tax benefits from IRAs and pensions

Theoretical determination

We calculate the value of pension and IRA tax benefits by comparing the taxation to a taxable account holding a similar level of after-tax contributions. Consider a contribution of $1000 to a traditional (deductible) IRA. The cost of that contribution is $1000(1-\tau)$. Call that amount V_0. Assuming that, alternatively, that money would be contributed to a taxable account paying a rate of return r and taxed at constant rate, τ, the account would be worth

$$V_t = V_0(1 + r(1-\tau))^t \tag{A.1}$$

after t years, where $t = 1, \ldots, N$, and N is the year at which withdrawals start (at the end of the year). Assuming discounting at rate r, the present value of taxes during the N-year accumulation phase is

$$PV_N = \left[1 - \left(\frac{1 + r(1-\tau)}{1+r} \right)^N \right] V_0 \tag{A.2}$$

If the money were withdrawn in a lump sum at the end of year N, this would be the present value of the tax benefits. We follow Cronin (1999) in assuming that the contribution period is until age 65 and then the money is withdrawn in equal portions starting at age 66 until the end of the life expectancy. Withdrawals are assumed to occur at the end of the year, after interest has accrued.

If life expectancy at age 65 is $65 + T$, then the annual withdrawal, A, will solve the following equation:

$$V_N = A\left[1 - (1 + r(1 - \tau))^{-T}\right]\frac{1 + r(1 - \tau)}{r(1 - \tau)} \qquad (A.3)$$

where V_N is the value of the taxable account at age 65 (at the end of the year). It may be shown that the value of the taxable account during the retirement period is

$$V_{N+j} = \gamma^j\left[V_N - A\frac{1 - \gamma^{-j}}{1 - \gamma^{-1}}\right] \qquad (A.4)$$

where $\gamma \equiv 1 + r(1 - \tau)$. Tax in period $N + j$ is

$$\theta_{N+j} = \gamma^{j-1}\left[V_N - A\frac{1 - \gamma^{-j}}{1 - \gamma^{-1}}\right]r\tau \qquad (A.5)$$

Thus, the present value of the taxes saved is

$$PV = PV_N + \sum_{j=1}^{T}\frac{\theta_{N+j}}{(1 + r)^{N+j}}. \qquad (A.6)$$

Parameter assumptions

For a deductible IRA or 401(k) contribution, V_0 is the after-tax cost of the contribution (i.e., multiplied by $1 - \tau$). For a Roth IRA or 401(k), V_0 is the amount of the contribution. Thus, for someone in the 25 percent tax bracket, a $2000 contribution to a traditional IRA would be analogous to a $1500 contribution to a taxable account ($V_0 = 1500$). A $2000 contribution to a Roth IRA would be analogous to a $2000 contribution to the taxable account ($V_0 = 2000$).

For this calculation, τ should be the marginal tax rate on earnings. For simplicity, assume that the tax rate on savings outside of retirement accounts is also τ (as assumed in the calculation above). In fact, the effective rate might be lower if, for example, the account pays returns in the form of capital gains or dividends. This assumption will thus tend to overstate the value of the retirement tax incentives.

We make a conservative assumption about the rate of return on the taxable account. We assume that r is 6 percent—3 percent inflation plus 3 percent real growth—as assumed in the 2003 Social Security Association (SSA) trustees report. To the extent that the taxable account would be invested in stocks or commercial bonds, there would be a risk premium that would raise the expected return. Thus, this assumption will tend to understate the value of retirement tax incentives, and so offset the bias from assuming full taxation of returns. Tables 3.13 and 3.14 show that the net effects of these two assumptions on the distribution of benefits are small.

Table 3.A.1 Tax Benefits of Defined Contribution Plans and IRAs[1] by Cash Income Level, 2004

Cash income level (thousands of 2003 dollars)[2]	Tax units[3]			% Change in after-tax income[4]	Share of total benefit	Average benefit ($)
	Number (thousands)	% of total	% with benefit			
Less than 10	20,428	14.2	1.1	0.0	0.0	−2
10–20	26,467	18.4	8.7	0.3	1.6	−45
20–30	20,379	14.2	18.5	0.6	3.7	−137
30–40	15,377	10.7	27.0	0.7	4.6	−225
40–50	11,446	8.0	34.7	0.9	5.3	−353
50–75	20,054	14.0	46.0	1.1	14.9	−564
75–100	11,395	7.9	57.4	1.4	15.2	−1,009
100–200	13,281	9.3	65.0	1.9	34.8	−1,985
200–500	3,339	2.3	59.5	1.6	15.4	−3,495
500–1,000	527	0.4	52.2	0.8	2.9	−4,165
More than 1,000	257	0.2	50.7	0.2	1.5	−4,428
All	143,509	100.0	28.7	1.2	100.0	−528

Source: Urban-Brookings Tax Policy Center Microsimulation Model.
[1] Distribution of the present value of lifetime tax benefits for new contributions made in 2004.
[2] Tax units with negative cash income are excluded from the lowest income class but are included in the totals. For a description of cash income, visit http://www.taxpolicycenter.org/TaxModel/income.cfm.
[3] Includes both filing and non-filing units. Tax units that are dependents of other taxpayers are excluded from the analysis.
[4] After-tax income is cash income less individual income tax net of refundable credits, payroll and estate tax liability, and imputed burden from corporate taxes.

Table 3.A.2 Tax Benefits of Defined Contribution Plans[1] by Cash Income Level, 2004

Cash income level (thousands of 2003 dollars)	Tax units			% Change in after-tax income	Share of total benefit	Average benefit ($)
	Number (thousands)	% of total	% with benefit			
Less than 10	20,428	14.2	1.0	0.0	0.0	−2
10–20	26,467	18.4	8.0	0.3	1.6	−41
20–30	20,379	14.2	16.6	0.5	3.5	−121
30–40	15,377	10.7	23.4	0.7	4.4	−197
40–50	11,446	8.0	29.7	0.8	5.2	−315
50–75	20,054	14.0	39.2	1.0	14.4	−500
75–100	11,395	7.9	49.6	1.3	15.0	−918
100–200	13,281	9.3	56.2	1.7	35.0	−1,839
200–500	3,339	2.3	53.4	1.5	16.3	−3,404
500–1,000	527	0.4	47.2	0.8	3.1	−4,083
More than 1,000	257	0.2	46.1	0.2	1.6	−4,365
All	143,509	100.0	25.0	1.1	100.0	−486

Source: Urban-Brookings Tax Policy Center Microsimulation Model. See notes to Table 3.A.1.

Table 3.A.3 Participation and Contributions to Defined Contribution Plans[1] Married Filing Joint Returns by Cash Income Level, 2004

Cash income level (thousands of 2003 dollars)	tax units		Elective deferral head		Elective deferral spouse		Employer contribution head		Employer contribution spouse	
	Working age population (thousands)	% of total	% Participating	Average contribution[2]	% Participating	Average contribution[2]	% Participating	Average contribution[2]	% Participating	Average contribution[2]
Less than 10	2,590	5.6	2.8	791	2.5	386	3.3	612	2.3	285
10–20	3,419	7.4	8.3	1,156	6.3	682	8.4	906	6.5	547
20–30	3,257	7.1	12.8	1,628	10.7	1,075	13.4	1,257	11.1	769
30–40	3,206	7.0	18.4	2,208	16.4	1,333	20.1	1,707	16.1	1,075
40–50	3,469	7.5	22.8	2,663	19.4	1,689	23.7	1,992	19.6	1,319
50–75	9,598	20.9	28.4	3,543	26.0	2,300	28.7	2,604	26.8	1,910
75–100	7,463	16.2	36.4	4,827	34.2	3,174	35.8	3,319	34.0	2,522
100–200	9,788	21.3	44.6	7,471	37.4	4,572	42.9	5,085	35.7	3,673
200–500	2,417	5.3	46.4	12,157	32.8	6,746	47.2	11,422	29.2	5,666
500–1,000	366	0.8	42.3	12,929	24.8	8,909	47.1	21,208	20.8	9,185
More than 1,000	177	0.4	40.7	13,448	17.7	10,062	47.7	25,810	15.2	13,206
All	45,955	100.0	29.0	5,744	24.9	3,444	29.0	4,501	24.5	2,762

Source: Urban-Brookings Tax Policy Center Microsimulation Model. See notes to Table 3.A.1.
[1] Sample is limited to households where the head is between 18 and 64 years of age.
[2] Among those who contribute to a defined contribution plan.

Table 3.A.4 Participation and Contributions to Defined Contribution Plans[1] Single and Head of Household Returns by Cash Income Level, 2004

Cash income level (thousands of 2003 dollars)	Tax units		Elective deferral		Employer contribution	
	Working age population (thousands)	% of total	% Participating	Average contribution[2]	% Participating	Average contribution[2]
Less than 10	13,923	20.4	4.0	590	3.9	519
10–20	15,901	23.3	12.4	1,083	12.2	926
20–30	12,301	18.0	19.0	1,659	18.5	1,399
30–40	8,841	12.9	24.6	2,256	23.8	1,816
40–50	5,889	8.6	30.1	2,905	28.2	2,293
50–75	6,879	10.1	38.0	3,939	35.4	2,986
75–100	2,135	3.1	40.4	5,595	37.8	4,136
100–200	1,670	2.4	41.1	8,256	40.6	6,241
200–500	360	0.5	39.1	12,119	38.6	13,315
500–1,000	58	0.1	34.1	12,685	33.7	21,440
More than 1,000	30	0.0	36.0	13,129	37.4	24,560
All	68,311	100.0	19.3	2,989	18.5	2,403

Source: Urban-Brookings Tax Policy Center Microsimulation Model. See notes to Table 3.A.1.
[1] Sample is limited to households where the head is between 18 and 64 years of age.
[2] Among those who contribute to a defined contribution plan.

Table 3.A.5 Tax Benefits of Roth and Traditional IRAs by Cash Income Level, 2004

Cash income level (thousands of 2003 dollars)	Tax units			% Change in after-tax income	Share of total benefit	Average benefit ($)
	Number (thousands)	% of total	% with benefit			
Less than 10	20,428	14.2	0.1	0.0	0.0	−0
10–20	26,467	18.4	0.8	0.0	1.8	−4
20–30	20,379	14.2	2.5	0.1	5.1	−15
30–40	15,377	10.7	4.4	0.1	6.6	−26
40–50	11,446	8.0	6.5	0.1	7.2	−37
50–75	20,054	14.0	9.1	0.1	21.2	−63
75–100	11,395	7.9	11.6	0.1	16.6	−87
100–200	13,281	9.3	15.5	0.2	35.2	−158
200–500	3,339	2.3	6.8	0.0	5.2	−93
500–1,000	527	0.4	6.1	0.0	0.7	−83
More than 1,000	257	0.2	5.5	0.0	0.4	−82
All	143,509	100.0	5.3	0.1	100.0	−42

Source: Urban-Brookings Tax Policy Center Microsimulation Model. See notes to Table 3.A.1.

Table 3.A.6 Participation and Contributions to Roth and Traditional IRAs by Cash Income Level, 2004

Cash income level (thousands of 2003 dollars)	Tax units		Traditional IRA			Roth IRA		
	Number (thousands)	% of total	% who contribute	Average contribution	% of contributors at limit	% who contribute	Average contribution	% of contributors at limit
Less than 10	20,428	14.2	0.2	1,631	27.4	0.3	2,210	27.0
10–20	26,467	18.4	0.6	2,213	50.4	0.6	2,852	47.2
20–30	20,379	14.2	1.7	2,578	56.8	1.1	2,956	39.8
30–40	15,377	10.7	3.2	2,584	49.4	1.5	2,904	37.7
40–50	11,446	8.0	4.0	2,284	32.0	2.8	2,731	32.3
50–75	20,054	14.0	4.8	3,092	39.3	4.4	3,206	38.6
75–100	11,395	7.9	4.7	3,078	34.2	7.0	3,320	36.0
100–200	13,281	9.3	5.5	3,638	43.1	10.0	3,632	39.0
200–500	3,339	2.3	5.6	4,680	70.1	1.4	4,613	61.4
500–1,000	527	0.4	4.5	5,040	79.3	1.7	5,704	95.1
More than 1,000	257	0.2	4.3	5,065	77.8	1.3	6,348	98.2
All	143,509	100.0	2.7	3,032	43.4	2.8	3,296	38.3

Source: Urban-Brookings Tax Policy Center Microsimulation Model. See notes to Table 3.A.1.
[1] Among those who contribute to an IRA.

Table 3.A.7 Tax Benefits of the Savers' Credit by Cash Income Level, 2004

Cash income level (thousands of 2003 dollars)	Tax units			% Change in after-tax income	Share of total benefit	Average benefit ($)
	Number (thousands)	% of total	% with benefit			
Less than 10	20,428	14.2	0.4	0.0	0.1	0
10–20	26,467	18.4	5.0	0.1	19.9	–16
20–30	20,379	14.2	10.1	0.1	24.5	–25
30–40	15,377	10.7	7.8	0.1	19.2	–26
40–50	11,446	8.0	11.6	0.1	16.0	–29
50–75	20,054	14.0	6.5	0.0	19.1	–20
75–100	11,395	7.9	0.2	0.0	0.5	–1
100–200	13,281	9.3	0.2	0.0	0.6	–1
200–500	3,339	2.3	0.0	0.0	0.0	0
500–1,000	527	0.4	0.0	0.0	0.0	0
More than 1,000	257	0.2	0.0	0.0	0.0	0
All	143,509	100.0	5.1	0.0	100.0	–14

Source: Urban-Brookings Tax Policy Center Microsimulation Model. See notes to Table 3.A.1.

Table 3.A.8 Tax Benefits of Makings the Savers' Credit Refundable[1] by Cash Income Level, 2004

Cash income level (thousands of 2003 dollars)	Tax units			% Change in after-tax income	Share of total benefit	Average benefit ($)
	Number (thousands)	% of total	% with benefit			
Less than 10	20,428	14.2	3.8	0.2	8.4	−14
10–20	26,467	18.4	8.3	0.3	29.2	−36
20–30	20,379	14.2	8.0	0.2	30.1	−49
30–40	15,377	10.7	6.8	0.1	17.2	−37
40–50	11,446	8.0	4.7	0.1	6.7	−19
50–75	20,054	14.0	1.6	0.0	4.3	−7
70–100	11,395	7.9	0.3	0.0	1.0	−3
100–200	13,281	9.3	0.3	0.0	1.4	−3
200–500	3,339	2.3	0.2	0.0	0.2	−2
500–1,000	527	0.4	0.1	0.0	0.0	−1
More than 1,000	257	0.2	0.1	0.0	0.0	−2
All	143,509	100.0	4.6	0.1	100.0	−23

Source: Urban-Brookings Tax Policy Center Microsimulation Model. See notes to Table 3.A.1.
[1] Baseline is current law.

Table 3.A.9 Tax Benefits of Accelerating DC and IRA Contribution Limit Increases[1] by Cash Income Level, 2004

Cash income level (thousands of 2003 dollars)	Tax units			% Change in after-tax income	Share of total benefit	Average Benefit ($)
	Number (thousands)	% of total	% with benefit			
Less than 10	20,428	14.2	0.0	0.0	0.0	0
10–20	26,467	18.4	0.3	0.0	0.8	–1
20–30	20,379	14.2	1.1	0.0	3.4	–5
30–40	15,377	10.7	1.9	0.0	4.6	–8
40–50	11,446	8.0	2.0	0.0	4.0	–10
50–75	20,054	14.0	3.6	0.0	15.6	–21
75–100	11,395	7.9	4.2	0.0	12.2	–29
100–200	13,281	9.3	8.0	0.1	31.4	–65
200–500	3,339	2.3	27.8	0.1	22.8	–188
500–1,000	527	0.4	35.5	0.0	3.8	–200
More than 1,000	257	0.2	37.2	0.0	1.5	–156
All	143,509	100.0	3.0	0.0	100.0	–19

Source: Urban-Brookings Tax Policy Center Microsimulation Model. See notes to Table 3.A.1.
[1] Baseline is current law.

Table 3.A.10 Defined Contribution Plan and IRA Tax Benefits Among Household Heads Aged 45 to 54 by Cash Income Level, 2004

Cash income level (thousands of 2003 dollars)	Tax units			% Change in after-tax income	Share of total benefit	Average benefit ($)
	Number (thousands)	% of total	% with benefit			
Less than 10	2,373	9.9	1.3	0.0	0.0	−2
10–20	3,114	13.0	11.7	0.4	0.8	−51
20–30	2,350	9.8	25.1	0.7	1.9	−154
30–40	2,346	9.8	33.6	0.8	2.8	−224
40–50	1,953	8.2	42.2	0.9	3.6	−343
50–75	4,159	17.4	55.3	1.1	12.4	−562
75–100	2,688	11.2	70.1	1.4	14.0	−980
100–200	3,690	15.4	76.3	2.0	40.3	−2,059
200–500	956	4.0	71.0	1.7	19.3	−3,807
500–1,000	132	0.6	65.7	0.9	3.3	−4,663
More than 1,000	66	0.3	62.5	0.3	1.7	−4,910
All	23,920	100.0	43.5	1.3	100.0	−789

Source: Urban-Brookings Tax Policy Center Microsimulation Model. See notes to Table 3.A.1.

Table 3.A.11 Tax Benefits of Defined Contribution Plans and IRAs by Economic Income Level, 2004

Economic income level (thousands of 2003 dollars)[1]	Tax units			% Change in after-tax income	Share of total benefit	Average benefit ($)
	Number (thousands)	% of total	% with benefit			
Less than 10	23,851	16.6	2.4	0.1	0.3	−8
10–20	29,715	20.7	15.1	0.7	4.0	−102
20–30	23,401	16.3	22.9	1.0	6.5	−209
30–40	18,325	12.8	34.0	1.3	8.8	−362
40–50	13,246	9.2	43.5	1.7	10.6	−606
50–75	17,593	12.3	52.7	2.3	24.1	−1,038
75–100	7,009	4.9	58.9	2.5	14.5	−1,567
100–200	6,822	4.8	59.8	2.3	20.2	−2,239
200–500	2,086	1.5	52.0	1.5	8.7	−3,176
500–1,000	347	0.2	42.4	0.7	1.5	−3,212
More than 1,000	177	0.1	42.7	0.2	0.9	−3,667
All	143,509	100.0	28.7	1.5	100.0	−528

Source: Urban-Brookings Tax Policy Center Microsimulation Model. See notes to Table 3.A.1.
[1] For a description of economic income, visit http://www.taxpolicycenter.org/TaxModel/income.cfm.

Table 3.A.12 Tax Benefits of Defined Contribution Plans and IRAs Using a 10% Tax Rate[1] by Cash Income Level, 2004

Cash income level (thousands of 2003 dollars)	Tax units			% Change in after-tax income	Share of total benefit	Average benefit ($)
	Number (thousands)	% of total	% with benefit			
Less than 10	20,428	14.2	4.3	0.1	0.3	−8
10–20	26,467	18.4	11.5	0.4	2.7	−54
20–30	20,379	14.2	19.1	0.6	5.0	−130
30–40	15,377	10.7	27.3	0.6	5.7	−196
40–50	11,446	8.0	35.0	0.7	5.9	−271
50–75	20,054	14.0	46.2	0.8	15.6	−412
75–100	11,395	7.9	57.6	1.0	15.6	−727
100–200	13,281	9.3	65.1	1.2	31.6	−1,264
200–500	3,339	2.3	59.4	1.0	14.1	−2,239
500–1,000	527	0.4	52.1	0.5	2.3	−2,360
More than 1,000	257	0.2	50.1	0.1	1.2	−2,435
All	143,509	100.0	29.9	0.8	100.0	−370

Source: Urban-Brookings Tax Policy Center Microsimulation Model. See notes to Table 3.A.1.

Table 3.A.13 Tax Benefits of Defined Contribution Plans and IRAs Using a 9% Rate of Return by Cash Income Level, 2004

Cash income level (thousands of 2003 dollars)	Tax units			% Change in after-tax income	Share of total benefit	Average benefit ($)
	Number (thousands)	% of total	% with benefit			
Less than 10	20,428	14.2	1.1	0.0	0.0	−2
10–20	26,467	18.4	8.7	0.4	1.5	−54
20–30	20,379	14.2	18.5	0.7	3.5	−168
30–40	15,377	10.7	27.0	0.9	4.5	−286
40–50	11,446	8.0	34.7	1.2	5.3	−456
50–75	20,054	14.0	46.0	1.5	15.3	−742
75–100	11,395	7.9	57.4	1.9	15.4	−1,316
100–200	13,281	9.3	65.0	2.4	35.0	−2,566
200–500	3,339	2.3	59.6	2.0	15.1	−4,410
500–1,000	527	0.4	52.3	1.1	2.9	−5,329
More than 1,000	257	0.2	50.9	0.3	1.5	−5,697
All	143,509	100.0	28.7	1.5	100.0	−679

Source: Urban-Brookings Tax Policy Center Microsimulation Model. See notes to Table 3.A.1.

Notes

* The authors thank Jeffrey Rohaly for numerous helpful discussions, Paul Smith for helpful comments, and the American Association of Retired Persons for financial support. This paper was previously published in the *National Tax Journal*, September 2004, and is reprinted here with permission.

1. For exceptions to this general rule, see Congressional Budget Office (2003b), Even and MacPherson (2003), Gustman and Steinmeier (1998), and Joulfaian and Richardson (2001).
2. We note that the tax treatment of pensions is a subsidy relative to an income tax, not a consumption tax.
3. Early research on 401(k)s found that the saving plans raised saving at all levels of income (Poterba, Venti, and Wise, 1995). Subsequent research, which has addressed a number of econometric issues in earlier work, tends to find that 401(k) plans have not raised the wealth of relatively high-income households, but may have raised wealth of low-income households (Benjamin, 2001; Engen and Gale, 2000; Chernozhukov and Hansen, 2004).
4. Congressional Budget Office (2003a) and Engen, Gale, and Uccello (1999) review the literature on the adequacy of saving. For an important recent contribution, reaching a much more optimistic view than much of the previous literature on the adequacy of saving, see Scholz, Seshadri, and Khitatrakun (2003).
5. In a utility-based model, the benefits of tax-deferred saving contributions would also depend on the extent to which the contribution represents a net addition to private saving and whether there is an option value associated with pension coverage, even for those who do not actually participate. These issues, as well as the issues related to nondiscrimination rules, do not arise in standard distributional analysis, but are interesting avenues for future research.
6. For an overview of tax incentives for saving, see Gale and Orszag (2003).
7. The penalty is waived if:

   - the funds are used by an unemployed account holder to pay medical insurance premiums;
   - the withdrawal is used to pay for higher education expenses of a dependent, spouse, or grandchild;
   - the withdrawal (up to $10,000) is used to buy a first-time primary residence; or
   - the withdrawal is taken in the form of an annuity.

8. In 2004, the saver's credit is allowed only after all other nonrefundable tax credits, including the child tax credit, have been claimed, and only to the extent of remaining income tax liability. Legislation passed in 2002 allowed the saver's credit to be taken before the child tax credit, which increased its value for some households eligible for the refundable child credit.
9. For example, a contribution of X to a traditional IRA costs $X(1-\tau)$ after accounting for the value of the tax deduction (τX), where τ is the tax rate. If the balance in the account grows tax-free at interest rate r for N years, it will be worth $X(1+r)^N$, but withdrawals are fully taxed, so the after-tax proceeds are $X(1+r)^N(1-\tau)$ assuming that the money is withdrawn in a lump sum. If, instead, the same after-tax

amount—$X(1-\tau)$—were deposited into a Roth IRA, it would also grow tax-free at rate r, to a value of $X(1-\tau)(1+r)^N$. Withdrawals from the Roth IRA are not taxable, so the after-tax proceeds are the same in each case. The equivalence also holds if proceeds are withdrawn as an annuity. The Roth IRA would be worth more in retirement if tax rates rise, and less if they fall. Also, the same dollar contribution is worth more if made to a Roth IRA as explained below. See Burman, Gale, and Weiner (2001) for more discussion.

10. That is, the tables implicitly assume that the subsidy is entirely a windfall—that is, that taxable savings now become nontaxable. To the extent that taxpayers are being induced to alter their behavior and reduce current consumption, there is an opportunity cost to the new saving so the net gain will be less than the tax savings. This would imply that the actual distribution of benefits from retirement tax incentives would be more skewed toward the wealthy than illustrated in the table, since they are least likely to have to alter their behavior to take advantage of the subsidy.

11. Cash income includes wages and salaries, employee contribution to tax-deferred retirement savings plans, business income or loss, farm income or loss, Schedule E income, interest income, taxable dividends, realized net capital gains, social security benefits received, unemployment compensation, energy assistance, Temporary Assistance for Needy Families (TANF), worker's compensation, veteran's benefits, supplemental security income, child support, disability benefits, taxable IRA distributions, total pension income, alimony received, and other income including foreign earned income. Cash income also includes imputed corporate income tax liability and the employer's share of payroll taxes. This puts the income measure on a pretax basis. visit http://www.taxpolicycenter.org/TaxModel/income.cfm for more discussion of income measures. Note that since cash income is a broader measure than adjusted gross income (AGI), some people with low reported AGI actually appear in higher income quintiles because they have other income such as pension contributions or tax-exempt bond interest that does not appear in AGI. As a result, some people in higher income quintiles are eligible for income-tested tax benefits, and more people in the bottom quintile of cash income are subject to income tax than in the bottom quintile of AGI.

12. The assumption that tax rates remain constant over a lifetime may distort the measured present value of tax benefits. For example, some low-income people may contribute to Roth IRAs in expectation that their contribution would otherwise be taxable when they reach retirement age. For them, the tax benefit can be significant as they can effectively contribute out of pre-tax income, while all earnings and withdrawals are tax-free. On the other hand, individuals in the bottom quintile, who contribute to a traditional IRA or DC plan account, may pay tax upon withdrawal if their income increases, even though they got no tax benefit from the contribution. In that case, their effective tax rate can be higher than it would have been on a contribution to a taxable account. Similarly, high-income people may contribute to a traditional IRA with the expectation that their tax rate in retirement will be lower. In that case, the actual tax benefit will be larger than reflected in our calculations.

13. Estimates from the TPC model indicate that in 2004, the top 20 percent of households paid 70 percent of all federal taxes, the fourth quintile paid 18 percent, and the middle quintile paid 8 percent.

14. Highly compensated employees may also benefit from nonqualified deferred compensation plans. These plans are not limited in size, but employers may not

claim a corporate tax deduction for amounts in the plan until they are actually paid out as compensation (at which point they are taxable to the recipient). There are also no payroll tax advantages. If employer and employee are taxed at the same rate, these plans provide no net tax benefit, but they can be beneficial when the employee expects to be taxed at lower rates in the future or if the employer can shelter its income from tax. Measuring the tax benefits of nonqualified plans is beyond the scope of this chapter.

15. The Congressional Budget Office (2003b) looked at participation in and contribution to pension and IRA plans based on data from 1997. Their tables show statistics at the worker level rather than for households or tax units, but are broadly consistent with the estimates we present. CBO's participation rates are somewhat higher, especially for 401(k) type plans, but that is presumably because their sample is restricted to workers, whereas our sample includes all tax filing units, including those that are out of the work force (for example, because they are in school, retired, or unemployed). Contribution levels are lower, which may have occurred because contribution limits for IRAs and DC plans were significantly lower in 1997.

16. Possibly the explanation for this anomaly is that some taxpayers in the phaseout range for contributions to IRAs choose not to contribute the exact amount that they are eligible for. For example, it may be easy to decide to contribute $2000, but a tax filer who discovers he or she is eligible to contribute $1300 may choose to round down to $1000.

17. We note that age is imputed on our database.

18. Economic income includes wages and salaries, other returns to labor, returns to capital, and other income. Returns to labor are measured as a percentage of business income, farm income, rental income, farm rental income, partnership income and income from small business corporation. Returns to capital are assumed to be the nominal risk-free rate on capital, measured as 6 percent of net worth. Other income includes royalty income, Social Security benefits received, unemployment compensation, supplemental security income, alimony received, TANF, worker's compensation, veteran's benefits, disability benefits, child support, energy assistance, food stamps, and school lunches. Finally, including employer's share of payroll taxes and corporate tax liability puts the income measure on a pretax basis. This measure is adjusted for family size using the CBO methodology. See, for example, footnotes to Congressional Budget Office 2004. This comprehensive measure is divided by the square root of the family size. So a married filing joint return, with two children, earning $100,000 would have the same family-size adjusted economic income as single person earning $50,000. For more discussion, see 'Description of Income Measures' at http://www.taxpolicycenter.org/TaxModel/income.cfm.

19. To adjust for family size, we use the methodology of CBO. Economic income is divided by the square root of family size—a rough adjustment for differences in ability to pay. See, for example, footnotes to tables in Congressional Budget Office (2004). No family size adjustment is done to compute cash income.

20. In some cases, earnings reported separately for each spouse were inconsistent with total household earnings. In that case, total earnings were apportioned among the spouses in proportion to their reported separate earnings. If positive household earnings were reported, but the individuals did not report earnings separately, we attributed the total amount to the head of household. Some employees reported

contributing more than the limit. We assumed that any excess contributions were made to a nonqualifying pension plan.

21. The SCF is a household-based survey that records only total income and wealth items for all individuals in the 'primary economic unit' (PEU); it does not attribute shares of those amounts to individuals within the PEU. This provides a slight complication for those PEUs that consist of two unmarried individuals living together (with or without other financially interdependent members of the PEU). These individuals will show up in the income tax file as two single tax returns but will show up in the SCF as one unit. We assume that an unmarried couple living together with shared finances behaves like a married couple and thus include them in the married category when running the regressions. The results do not change significantly if these individuals are dropped from the analysis.

22. We also correct the standard errors using the procedure supplied by the Federal Reserve Board, but it is not a particularly important adjustment given that we are not interested in the parameter estimates. The corrected estimates and standard errors from that procedure, as well as a measure of goodness-of-fit from the first replicate, are available upon request.

23. Tax returns include data on contributions to traditional IRAs. Since taxpayers above certain AGI thresholds may not make contributions to IRAs if their employers offer a pension, any in those categories who report IRA contributions must not participate in an employer plan.

24. Without adjustment, this process can produce too many or too few individuals with pension contributions on the PUF dataset. We force the numbers to match published totals by shifting the threshold probabilities by a constant (up or down) so the simulated number of contributors matches the estimates on the SCF.

25. For alternative methods of imputing desired contributions, see Gale and Scholz (1994) and Venti and Wise (1990).

26. On the other hand, it may be that an increasing number of higher-income people will shift from traditional IRAs to Roth IRAs over time as awareness of the new (in 1997) program grows. In addition, those who would like to make an after-tax contribution of more than $L(1-\tau)$, where L is the contribution limit and τ is the marginal income tax rate, can only do so through a Roth IRA. So, on balance, this simplifying assumption seems plausible until further data are available.

27. This feature would be used to model recent proposals to eliminate income limits entirely for eligibility for contributions to Roth IRAs.

References

Benjamin, D. (2001) *Does 401(k) Eligibility Increase Saving? Evidence from Propensity Score Subclassification* (London: London School of Economics).

Burman, L. E., W. G. Gale and D. Weiner (2001) 'The Taxation of Retirement Saving: Choosing between Front-Loaded and Back-Loaded Options,' *National Tax Journal* 54(3): 689–702.

Chernozhukov, V. and C. Hansen (2004) 'The Impact of 401(k) Participation on the Wealth Distribution,' *The Review of Economics and Statistics* 86(3): 735–51.

Congressional Budget Office (2003a) 'Baby Boomers' Retirement Prospects: An Overview' (Washington, D.C.: Congressional Budget Office).

Congressional Budget Office (2003b) 'Utilization of Tax Incentives for Retirement Saving' (Washington, D.C.: Congressional Budget Office).

Congressional Budget Office (2004) *Effective Federal Tax Rates: 1979–2001* (Washington, D.C.: Congressional Budget Office).

Cronin, J.-A. (1999) 'U.S. Treasury Distributional Analysis Methodology,' OTA Paper 85 (Washington, D.C.: U.S. Department of the Treasury), http://www.ustreas.gov/offices/tax-policy/library/ota85.pdf.

Duan, N. (1983) 'Smearing Estimate: A Nonparametric Retransformation Method,' *Journal of the American Statistical Association* 78(383): 605–10.

Engen, E. and W. G. Gale (2000) 'The Effects of 401(k) Plans on Household Wealth: Differences across Earnings Groups,' NBER Working Paper 8032 (Cambridge, MA: National Bureau of Economic Research).

Engen, E., W. G. Gale and C. E. Uccello (1999) 'The Adequacy of Household Saving,' *Brookings Papers on Economic Activity* 2: 65–165.

Even, W. and D. MacPherson (2003) 'The Distributional Consequences of the Shift to Defined Contribution Plans,' Working Paper (Tallahassee, FL: Florida State University).

Gale, W. G. and P. R. Orszag (2003) 'Private Pensions: Issues and Options,' in Henry J. Aaron, James N. Lindsay and Pietro S. Nivola (eds.), *Agenda for the Nation* (Washington, D.C.: The Brookings Institution).

Gale, W. G. and J. K. Scholz (1994) 'IRAs and Household Saving,' *American Economic Review* 84(5): 1233–60.

Gale, W. G., J. M. Iwry and P. R. Orszag (2004) 'The Saver's Credit: Issues and Options,' *Tax Notes* 103(5): 597–612.

Gustman, A. L. and T. L. Steinmeier (1998) 'Changing Pensions in Cross-Section and Panel Data: Analysis with Employer-Provided Plan Descriptions,' NBER Working Paper W6854 (Cambridge, MA: National Bureau of Economic Research).

Joulfaian, D. and D. Richardson (2001) 'Who Takes Advantage of Tax-Deferred Saving Programs? Evidence from Federal Income Tax Data,' *National Tax Journal* (54:3) 669–88.

Office of Management and Budget (2004) *Analytical Perspectives, Fiscal Year 2005* (Washington, D.C.: Office of Management and Budget).

Poterba, J. M., S. F. Venti and D. A. Wise (1995) 'Do 401(k) Contributions Crowd Out Other Personal Saving?,' *Journal of Public Economics* (58:1) 1–32.

Sailer, P. J. and S. E. Nutter (2004) 'Accumulation and Distribution of Individual Retirement Arrangements, 2000,' Statistics of Income Bulletin.

Scholz, J. K., A. Seshadri and S. Khitatrakun (2003) 'Are Americans Saving "Optimally" for Retirement?,' NBER Working Paper W10260 (Cambridge, MA: National Bureau of Economic Research).

Venti, S. F. and D. A. Wise (1990) 'Have IRAs Increased U.S. Saving? Evidence from Consumer Expenditure Surveys,' *Quarterly Journal of Economics* (105:3) 661–98.

4

The Changing Impact of Social Security on Retirement Income in the United States*

Barbara A. Butrica, Howard M. Iams and Karen E. Smith

4.1 Introduction

As members of the baby-boom cohort—individuals born in 1946 to 1964—approach retirement age, their economic well-being at that time is of particular concern to policymakers. Baby boomers grew up in a different era than did current retirees—one accompanied by considerable changes in marriage patterns, earnings and work patterns, retirement policy, and the economy. Although these changes will undoubtedly affect baby-boomer retirees, it is difficult to know exactly how they will influence their economic well-being.

Historically, social insurance in the form of Social Security benefits has played a major role of income support for the elderly in the United States. However, because Social Security benefits are programmatically linked to marital and earnings histories, they may be especially affected by the social, demographic, and labor market changes that have transformed retirement expectations for the baby-boom cohort. Although it plays a smaller role of income support, a supplementary welfare program in the form of Supplemental Security Income (SSI) benefits also provides a safety net for elderly individuals who have low incomes and limited assets.

This analysis evaluates the role of these government income programs in protecting the economic security of baby boomers at retirement. Accordingly, it assesses the contribution of these programs to the expected income of:

- current retirees (those born in 1926 to 1935);
- near-term retirees (those born in 1936 to 1945);
- early baby-boomer retirees (those born in 1946 to 1955); and
- late baby-boomer retirees (those born in 1956 to 1965).[1]

Supported by employers and tax laws, pensions and retirement accounts are the main alternatives to public programs when it comes to income support for the elderly. In the latter part of the twentieth century, the majority of employer-sponsored pension plans switched from defined benefit to defined contribution pensions (Employee Benefit Research Institute, 2003; Munnell and Sundén, 2004). Defined benefit pensions are based on years of service and earnings, usually emphasizing late career earnings. In contrast, defined contribution pensions are based on investment income from the worker's private accounts. The essence of defined contribution pension plans is to increase an individual's responsibility for his or her own retirement saving and to shift investment risk from employers to employees. This means that the trend away from defined benefit plans and toward defined contribution plans may affect the relative importance of government programs, such as Social Security and SSI. For that reason, this analysis also compares the proportion of overall income from Social Security and SSI benefits with defined benefit pensions and retirement accounts (including defined contribution pensions, individual retirement accounts, and Keoghs), as well as other income sources.

This analysis uses projections of the major sources of income at age 67 from the Social Security Administration's Model of Income in the Near Term (MINT) model. MINT starts with data from the U.S. Census Bureau's Survey of Income and Program Participation (SIPP) for 1990 to 1993 matched to the Social Security Administration's (SSA) earnings and benefit records through to 1999. MINT directly measures the experiences of survey respondents from the early 1990s—representing the first third to the first half of the lives of the baby-boom cohort—and statistically projects their income and characteristics into the future, adjusting for expected demographic and socioeconomic changes.

Results from this analysis suggest that while baby-boomer retirees can expect higher incomes and lower poverty rates than current retirees, their replacement rates—postretirement income as a share of preretirement income—will be lower. Although the contribution of Social Security and SSI benefits to overall income remains relatively constant across cohorts, the decline in replacement rates is driven, in part, by a decline in Social Security replacement rates.

4.2 Social security program

When first adopted in 1935, Social Security was designed as a social insurance program aiming to provide income security to the aged through retirement benefits. At the time, an individual's retirement benefits were based entirely on his or her own career earnings. Although the primary function of the Social Security program continued to be replacement of income from work due to retirement, over time the program expanded to include benefits for spouses, survivors and the disabled. These programmatic changes meant that the Social Security benefits were no longer entirely linked to an individual's own earnings history, but also to his or her marriage history and spouse's earnings history.[2]

While the original Social Security program was designed for the typical family, which included a working husband, a stay-at-home mother and their children, the average baby-boomer family entering retirement in the twenty-first century is headed by two working parents or by a single working mother (Steuerle and Bakija, 1994). Further, the Social Security provisions for spouses and survivors were originally intended to provide family benefits to retirees with one lifetime marriage. However, marriage trends in the second half of the twentieth century reflect sharply increased divorce rates and multiple marriages (Cherlin, 1992; Ruggles, 1997). These trends are accompanied by rising life expectancy (U.S. Board of Trustees, 2004). Accordingly, future retirees are more likely to be never married or divorced and less likely to be married or widowed. Because Social Security benefits are linked, in part, to marriage histories, changes in marriage trends will result in changes in benefit patterns among more recent cohorts.

The pattern of lifetime earnings also changed greatly in the latter half of the twentieth century. The increased labor force participation of women over the past 30 years (Farley, 1996; Levy, 1998; Henretta and O'Rand, 1999) resulted in more women in the baby-boomer cohort with lifetime earnings and with entitlement to their own retired-worker benefits. In addition, average earnings (adjusted for inflation) grew at an average annual rate of about 2 percent–3 percent per year between 1947 and 1973. Between the mid-1970s and early 1990s, there was little real growth in earnings. However, earnings grew faster for women than men (Levy and Murnane, 1992; Levy, 1998). Earnings have been growing steadily since the early 1990s, with the largest increases in the late 1990s, but the Board of Trustees of the Federal Old-Age and Survivors Insurance and Disability Insurance (OASDI or Social Security) Trust Funds is not expecting the high growth rate of the 1990s to be sustained in the future. In fact, the Board reported negative real wage growth between 2001 and 2003 (Board of Trustees, 2004, Table V.B1). Because the Social Security benefit base is indexed to wages, continued wage growth will result in increased benefits for future retirees—*ceteris paribus*. However, since benefit reductions for early retirement are scheduled to gradually increase for cohorts born between 1938 and 1960, any increases in benefits over time due to wage growth will be offset for individuals who retire before their full retirement age (Social Security Administration, 2001; Butrica, Iams, and Smith, 2003).

The lifetime benefits paid by Social Security have been declining relative to the lifetime contributions among more recent birth cohorts entering retirement (Leimer, 1995). Smith, Toder, and Iams (2003/2004) use historical and projected data from the MINT model to estimate the 'return' of lifetime benefits relative to lifetime contributions (or Social Security payroll taxes) for individuals born in 1931 to 1960. They find that the overall return declines among more recent cohorts of individuals, from 4.2 percent of contributions for retirees in the 1931–1935 birth cohort to 1.4 percent among those in the 1956–1960 birth cohort. The decline in returns primarily affects retirees in the second or higher quintile of lifetime earnings, with those in the lowest quintile being virtually unaffected (Smith, Toder, and Iams, 2003/2004, Table 4, Chart 4). These findings suggest that although Social Security is becoming less generous over time, it is becoming more progressive. It is projected to become a less important source of income to retirees on a life-time basis. Net lifetime benefits as a share of permanent income are projected to decline from 7.2 percent for retirees in the 1931–1935 birth cohort to –3.5 percent among those in the 1956–1960 birth cohort (Smith, Toder, and Iams, 2003/2004, Table 10, Chart 10).[3]

4.3   Supplemental Security Insurance program

Established in 1974, the SSI program provides benefits to aged and disabled individuals with very low income and assets (Social Security Administration, 2001). Although SSI indexes the maximum benefit to yearly changes in living costs, the asset level limits have remained constant since 1989. The impact is that as wages and prices increase over time, fewer individuals qualify for the program because their assets are well above the asset level limits.

4.4   Methodology

MINT projects the income of individuals, born in 1926 to 1965, from the early 1990s until 2032. It was developed by SSA's Office of Research, Evaluation, and Statistics, with substantial assistance from the Brookings Institution, the RAND Corporation, and the Urban Institute. (For more information, see Panis and Lillard, 1999; Toder *et al.*, 1999; Butrica *et al.*, 2001.) This analysis uses projections based on MINT3, the most recent version of MINT (Toder *et al.*, 2002; Butrica, Iams, and Smith, 2003).

MINT begins with data from the 1990 to 1993 panels of the SIPP, matched to SSA administrative records on earnings, benefits, and mortality. MINT then projects demographic processes such as marital changes, mortality, entry to and exit from the Social Security Disability Insurance (DI) program rolls, age of first receipt of Social Security retirement benefits, living arrangements, and immigration. It also projects expected income, such as Social Security benefits, defined benefit pension income, asset income,[4] earnings, SSI, imputed rent,[5] and income from nonspouse co-resident family members, for individuals and married couples. The results of this article reflect MINT projections of the future retiree population and its income based on the Census Bureau's SIPP survey matched to SSA administrative data.

Using projections of these income sources at age 67, this analysis compares baby-boomer cohorts with previous generations on the overall level, distribution, and composition of their income at age 67 and on the adequacy of this income in maintaining their economic well-being. The focus of this analysis is on the changing impact of Social Security and SSI on retirement income. All reported income projections are in 2003 dollars.

4.5   Results

The results of this article reflect MINT projections of the future retiree population. We begin with a description of the projected characteristics of retirees in each of the 10-year birth cohorts. Then we consider their economic well-being based on per capita family income, poverty rates, and replacement rates. Finally, we examine the extent to which Social Security and SSI, as well as other income sources, affect these measures of economic well-being. Since nonmarried women are particularly at risk of poverty in retirement, we analyze their projected economic status separately from the larger retiree population.

4.5.1   Characteristics of current and future retirees

MINT projects that characteristics of retired individuals will change over the next 20 years (Table 4.1). Compared with current retirees and near-term

Table 4.1   Projected characteristics for individuals at age 67, by birth cohort

Characteristic	Current retirees (1926–1935)	Near-term retirees (1936–1945)	Early baby boomers (1946–1955)	Late baby boomers (1956–1965)
Total percent	100	100	100	100
Sex				
Female	54	54	53	54
Male	46	46	47	46
Marital status				
Never married	4	5	6	8
Married	71	69	67	64
Widowed	16	12	11	11
Divorced	9	15	17	17
Gender and marital status				
Female				
Never married	2	3	3	4
Married	33	32	31	30
Widowed	13	10	8	9
Divorced	6	9	10	10

Male				
Never married	2	2	2	3
Married	38	36	36	34
Widowed	2	2	2	2
Divorced	4	6	7	7
Race and ethnicity				
Non-Hispanic white	82	79	76	72
Non-Hispanic black	8	8	9	10
Hispanic	7	8	9	12
Asian and Native American	4	5	6	7
Education				
High school dropout	28	19	11	12
High school graduate	54	58	58	60
College graduate	18	24	31	28
Benefit type				
Nonbeneficiary	12	8	7	7
Auxiliary only	10	6	3	2
Dually entitled	18	19	18	15
Retired worker	60	67	73	76
Mean values				
Years in the labor force	26	29	32	32
Own lifetime earnings (thousands of 2003 dollars)[a]	22	32	41	46
Shared lifetime earnings (thousands of 2003 dollars)[b]	23	32	41	45

Source: Authors' tabulations of MINT (see text for details).

[a] Own lifetime earnings is the average of an individual's wage-indexed earnings between ages 22 and 62.

[b] Shared lifetime earnings is the average of wage-indexed shared earnings between ages 22 and 62, where shared earnings are computed by assigning each individual half the total earnings of the couple in the years when the individual is married and his or her own earnings in years when not married.

retirees, baby-boomer retirees are less likely to be married or widowed at age 67 and more likely to be divorced or never married. They are also less likely to be non-Hispanic white and more likely to be minority, especially Hispanic. Baby-boomer retirees are also less likely to be high school dropouts and more likely to be college graduates. MINT projects that baby boomers will spend more years in the labor force and have higher lifetime earnings (both as individuals and together with their spouse(s)). As a result, a higher percentage of baby boomers will be entitled to their own Social Security retired-worker benefits.

4.5.2   Projected economic well-being

In this section, we consider the economic well-being of current and future retirees based on per capita family income, poverty rates, and replacement rates. Our measure of per capita family income includes Social Security benefits, pension income, asset income, earnings, SSI, imputed rental income, and income from nonspouse co-resident family members. As with the U.S. Bureau of the Census, we do not include imputed rent in the family income measure used to determine poverty rates. Also excluded are imputed rent and co-resident income from the family income measure used to determine replacement rates, since these income flows (unlike Social Security and pensions, for example) are not derived from preretirement earnings.

MINT projects that on average baby-boomer retirees will be economically better off than current or near-term retirees. This is suggested by their per capita income in 2003 dollars and poverty rates (Table 4.2). First, family income at age 67 is projected to be higher for baby-boomer retirees than for current retirees. Mean per capita family income at age 67 will increase from about $29,000 for current retirees to $44,000 for early boomers and $48,000 for late boomers. More typical is the experience of the median 10 percent of income recipients (those with per capita family income in the 45th–55th percentiles) for whom average per capita income is projected to increase by about 50 percent (from $23,000 to about $34,000) between current and baby-boomer retirees.[6] However, the degree of change varies across subgroups with minorities, the less educated, and the nonmarried experiencing smaller increases and even decreases in income across cohorts (Butrica, Iams, and Smith, 2003, Tables 4.2 and 4.3). Second, MINT projects that baby-boomer retirees are less likely than current retirees to be in severe economic need. The poverty rate, a measure of severe economic need, is expected to decrease by half between the current retiree and baby-boom cohorts. This reduction partly reflects the indexing of the poverty rate by prices, which are expected to increase over time at a slower rate than wages (Butrica, Iams, and Smith, 2003).

A completely different measure of economic well-being captures the extent to which retirees are able to maintain their preretirement living standards. Replacement rates compare postretirement income with preretirement income. Although the requisite replacement rate depends upon expected needs (TIAA-CREF 2002, Chapter 2), the financial planning literature often recommends having enough postretirement income to be able to replace 70 to 80 percent of preretirement income (TIAA-CREF, 1994, 12; Hinden, 2001, H1).

This analysis computes replacement rates for individuals as the ratio of per capita family income at age 67 to average wage-indexed earnings (both Social Security covered and noncovered earnings) from ages 22 to 62 where couples share their earnings in years of marriage.[7] Because of intermittent employment over a lifetime and partial or total labor force withdrawal before

Table 4.2 Projected measures of economic well-being at age 67 for all retirees and nonmarried women, by birth cohort

Measure	Current retirees (1926–1935)	Near-term retirees (1936–1945)	Early baby boomers (1946–1955)	Late baby boomers (1956–1965)
	All retirees			
Per capita income (thousands of 2003 dollars)				
Average of the overall group	29	35	44	48
Average of the median 10 percent[a]	23	28	33	34
Poverty rate (percent)	8	6	4	4
Average replacement rate of the median 10 percent[b]	93	82	80	81
Percentage below 3/4 replacement	35	44	45	44
Percentage below 1/2 replacement	12	17	17	17
	Nonmarried women			
Per capita income (thousands of 2003 dollars)				
Average of the overall group	30	36	44	48
Average of the median 10 percent[a]	22	26	31	33
Poverty rate (percent)	15	12	9	8
Average replacement rate of the median 10 percent[b]	100	84	80	83
Percentage below 3/4 replacement	32	43	46	44
Percentage below 1/2 replacement	13	17	19	19

Source: Authors' tabulations of MINT (see text for details).
[a] This measure is computed as the average per capita family income of individuals with per capita family income in the 45th–55th percentiles (the median 10 percent of income recipients).
[b] This measure is computed as the average replacement rate of individuals whose replacement rates are in the 45th–55th percentiles (the median 10 percent).

the take-up of Social Security benefits, lifetime earnings provides a more stable base for estimating preretirement income than does the measure of recent earnings (Smith, 2002). Further, it is reasonable to assume that such earnings are the basis of postretirement income since, in one way or another, most individuals pay for their retirement with wages earned over their lifetimes.[8]

MINT projects that average replacement rates for those with replacement rates in the 45th–55th percentiles will be at least 80 percent. However, while incomes are projected to increase across cohorts, replacement rates are projected to decrease. Replacement rates are projected to be 93 percent for current retirees, but only about 80 percent for baby-boomer retirees.[9] Because the average does not represent the distribution, this analysis estimated the percentage of individuals at age 67 whose incomes will replace less than three-quarters and less than half of their lifetime earnings. Based on the financial planning literature, a 50 percent replacement rate represents a shortfall that could create economic challenges and necessitate lifestyle adjustments. MINT projects an increasing proportion of more recent cohorts whose income will replace less than three-quarters of lifetime earnings. A little over a third of current retirees but over two-fifths of near-term and baby-boomer retirees will replace less than three-quarters of their preretirement income. About a tenth of current retirees and almost a fifth of near-term and baby-boomer retirees will replace less than half of their preretirement income.

The retirement experience of nonmarried women is a common focus of policy discussions, because older women are more often economically vulnerable. MINT projects that the per capita income of nonmarried women will be similar to that of other retirees.[10] However, their projected poverty rates are almost twice as high as those for the total sample, indicating that a larger proportion of nonmarried women will experience economic stress.[11]

Nonmarried women are also expected to have similar replacement rates of lifetime earnings as other retirees. A similar proportion is expected to replace less than three-quarters of their income—about a third of current retirees and about two-fifths of near-term and baby-boomer retirees. The share replacing less than half of their income is also similar to the total sample, although slightly higher in the baby-boomer cohorts. However, as indicated by their poverty rates, similar replacement rates do not necessarily mean that nonmarried women are as equally well off as other retirees. A retiree with $80,000 in postretirement income and $100,000 in preretirement earnings has the same replacement rate (80 percent) as a retiree with $8000 in postretirement income and $10,000 in preretirement earnings. Yet the former retiree would be considered well off, while the latter would be considered poor.

4.5.3   Composition of projected income

The previous results showed that although baby boomers will have higher incomes and lower poverty rates at retirement than current retirees have, they will not have higher replacement rates. Next, this analysis considers the extent to which Social Security and SSI, as well as other income sources, affect these measures of economic well-being. Income sources are grouped into retirement and nonretirement sources. Retirement income sources include Social Security benefits, defined pension benefits, and personal retirement accounts.

Nonretirement income sources include income from nonhousing, nonpension assets, imputed rental income, earnings, SSI, and co-resident income. MINT projects that at age 67 most retirees will live in families receiving income from both retirement and nonretirement sources (Table 4.3).

Table 4.3 also shows each income source's contribution to per capita family income for the median 10 percent of income recipients and how these vary by cohort. The middle panel of Table 4.3 presents the mean per capita income by source and the bottom panel presents the share of per capita family income held by each source.

Among current retirees, $14,000 of mean per capita family income comes from retirement income sources and $8000 comes from nonretirement income sources (Table 4.3). Although retirement income is projected to increase by more than 40 percent to $20,000 for late baby-boomer retirees, nonretirement income is expected to increase by 75 percent to $14,000. Thus, the share of per capita family income from retirement sources is projected to decrease from 63 percent among current retirees to about 58 percent among late baby-boomer retirees.

Social Security is the most important retirement income source for all retirees. About 91 percent of current retirees, 92 percent of near-term retirees, and 94 percent of baby-boomer retirees receive Social Security benefits (either their own or their spouse's). MINT projects that average per capita Social Security benefits for median individuals will increase from $9000 for current retirees to about $14,000 for baby-boomer retirees. However, the share of total family income from Social Security benefits will remain stable at about 40 percent.

MINT projects trends in pension benefits that reflect the well-known shift from defined benefit to defined contribution pension plans (Munnell and Sundén, 2004; Employee Benefit Research Institute, 2003). The percentage of retirees with defined benefit pensions (either their own or their spouse's) is expected to decrease from 53 percent among current retirees to around 40 percent among baby-boomer retirees. At the same time, the percentage with retirement accounts will increase from 46 to 59 percent. Although MINT projects that together defined benefit pensions and retirement accounts will provide about $6000 of total income for all cohorts, their relative contribution to total family income will change over time. Average defined benefit pensions among the median 10 percent of income recipients represent 20 percent of per capita family income for current retirees, but only 9 percent of per capita family income for baby-boomer retirees. Although the contribution of retirement accounts to family income more than doubles between cohorts (from 3 percent among current retirees to 8 percent among late baby boomers), the increase is not large enough to completely offset the decreased importance of defined benefit pensions.[12]

Earnings will be the most important nonretirement income source at age 67. MINT projects that 44 percent of current retirees, 47 percent of near-term retirees, and 49 percent of baby-boomer retirees will have earnings

Table 4.3 Per capita family income for the median 10 percent of income recipients at age 67, by source

Source	Current retirees (1926–1935)	Near-term retirees (1936–1945)	Early baby boomers (1946–1955)	Late baby boomers (1956–1965)
	Percentage with family income			
Total (percent)	100	100	100	100
Retirement income	95	95	96	97
Social Security benefits	91	92	94	94
Defined benefit pensions	53	45	43	40
Retirement accounts	46	53	57	59
Non-retirement income	98	99	99	99
Income from assets	90	91	93	94
Earnings	44	47	49	49
Supplemental Security Income	5	3	2	2
Imputed rental income	80	82	85	84
Co-resident income	17	16	14	14
	Mean per capita family income (thousands of 2003 dollars)			
Total	23	28	33	34
Retirement income	14	16	19	20
Social Security benefits	9	11	13	14
Defined benefit pensions	5	4	4	3
Retirement accounts	1	1	2	3

Non-retirement income	8	11	14	14
Income from assets	3	3	4	4
Earnings	3	4	6	6
Supplemental Security Income	0	0	0	0
Imputed rental income	2	2	2	2
Co-resident income	1	2	2	2
Share of mean per capita family income (percent)				
Total (percent)	100	100	100	100
Retirement income	63	59	57	58
Social Security benefits	40	41	40	41
Defined benefit pensions	20	13	11	9
Retirement accounts	3	5	7	8
Non-retirement income	37	41	43	42
Income from assets	12	12	12	12
Earnings	12	15	18	17
Supplemental Security Income	0	0	0	0
Imputed rental income	7	7	7	6
Co-resident income	6	6	5	6

Note: These are individuals whose per capita family income is in the 45th–55th percentiles.
Source: Authors' tabulations of MINT (see text details).

(either their own or their spouse's). Average per capita family earnings for median individuals will double from $3000 to $6000 between current retiree and baby-boomer cohorts. Social Security program rules encourage beneficiaries to work by allowing unlimited earnings for those at or above the full retirement age (rising from age 65 to age 67 for the late baby-boom cohort).[13] MINT projects that earnings will be a more important source of income at age 67 for baby-boomer retirees than for current retirees. Family earnings represent 12 percent of median per capita family income for current retirees, 15 percent for near-term retirees, and about 17 percent for baby-boomer retirees. The relative importance of income from assets, imputed rental income, and co-resident income remains fairly constant across cohorts.

Another nonretirement income source is SSI benefits. SSI, the main public program for the low-income aged and disabled, is expected to provide benefits to about 5 percent of current retirees but only 2 percent of baby-boomer retirees. This decline probably reflects the increasing restrictiveness of SSI limits on resources and income exclusions due to rising wages and prices over time. In contrast to Social Security, SSI on average does not make a noticeable contribution to per capita family income.

Given the high poverty rates of nonmarried women that were reported in Table 4.2, it is not surprising that these women are less likely than the overall group of retirees to have most income sources (Table 4.4). The main exception is the higher prevalence of SSI benefit receipt and co-resident income, particularly among current retirees. MINT projects that 10 percent of nonmarried women in this cohort will receive SSI benefits and 24 percent will have co-resident income. In contrast, only 3 percent of nonmarried women in the late baby-boom cohort will receive SSI benefits and only 19 percent will have co-resident income.

Among the median 10 percent of income recipients, however, SSI benefits and co-resident income are no more important to nonmarried women than they are to the larger retiree population. In contrast, Social Security benefits play a larger role in total income for nonmarried women.

Next, this analysis considers the relative contribution of income sources to overall replacement rates (Table 4.5). For individuals with replacement rates between the 45th and 55th percentiles, we compute the ratio of their mean income to their mean shared lifetime earnings for each income component.[14] As already shown, replacement rates are projected to decline across cohorts. Table 4.5 shows that the decline is driven by retirement income. Social Security benefits, defined benefit pensions and retirement accounts replace 63 percent of shared lifetime earnings for current retirees. However, these sources of income replace only 53 percent of shared lifetime earnings for near-term retirees, 50 percent for early baby boomers and 51 percent for late baby boomers. Social Security benefits replace 38 percent of shared lifetime earnings among current retirees, but only 31 percent of shared lifetime earnings among baby-boomer retirees. This may be partly

Table 4.4 Per capita family income for nonmarried women with the median 10 percent of income at age 67, by source

Source	Current retirees (1926–1935)	Near-term retirees (1936–1945)	Early baby boomers (1946–1955)	Late baby boomers (1956–1965)
	Percentage with family income			
Total (percent)	99	99	99	99
Retirement income	92	92	94	95
Social Security benefits	86	88	91	92
Defined benefit pensions	41	32	32	30
Retirement accounts	32	39	44	45
Non-retirement income	96	96	98	99
Income from assets	81	82	86	89
Earnings	28	29	32	33
Supplemental Security Income	10	7	4	3
Imputed rental income	67	68	73	73
Co-resident income	24	21	19	19
	Mean per capita family income (thousands of 2003 dollars)			
Total	22	26	31	33
Retirement income	15	17	19	21
Social Security benefits	10	13	15	16
Defined benefit pensions	4	3	3	3
Retirement accounts	1	1	2	2

Table 4.4 (Continued)

Source	Current retirees (1926–1935)	Near-term retirees (1936–1945)	Early baby boomers (1946–1955)	Late baby boomers (1956–1965)
Non-retirement income	8	9	11	12
Income from assets	2	3	4	5
Earnings	2	2	4	3
Supplemental Security Income	0	0	0	0
Imputed rental income	2	2	3	3
Co-resident income	2	1	1	1
Share of mean per capita family income (percent)				
Total (percent)	100	100	100	100
Retirement income	65	66	63	63
Social Security benefits	46	49	48	48
Defined benefit pensions	16	12	9	9
Retirement accounts	2	5	6	7
Non-retirement income	35	34	37	37
Income from assets	9	11	13	15
Earnings	9	9	12	9
Supplemental Security Income	1	0	0	0
Imputed rental income	9	9	9	8
Co-resident income	7	5	4	5

Note: These are individuals whose per capita family income is in the 45th–55th percentiles.
Source: Authors' tabulations of MINT (see text for details).

Table 4.5 Average replacement rates for individuals with the median 10 percent of replacement rates at age 67, by source

Source	Current retirees (1926–1935)	Near-term retirees (1936–1945)	Early baby boomers (1946–1955)	Late baby boomers (1956–1965)
	All retirees			
Total (percent)	93	82	80	81
Retirement income	63	53	50	51
Social Security benefits	38	34	32	31
Defined benefit pensions	21	14	12	10
Retirement accounts	4	6	7	9
Nonretirement income	30	29	30	30
Income from assets	15	14	15	15
Earnings	15	14	15	15
Supplemental Security Income	0	0	0	0
	Nonmarried women			
Total (percent)	100	84	80	83
Retirement income	72	62	58	58
Social Security benefits	50	45	41	39
Defined benefit pensions	17	11	11	11
Retirement accounts	4	6	6	7
Nonretirement income	27	23	22	25
Income from assets	15	14	13	15
Earnings	12	8	9	10
Supplemental Security Income	1	0	0	0

Note: Replacement rates are calculated as the ratio of income at age 67 to shared lifetime earnings. Shared lifetime earnings is the average of wage-indexed shared earnings between ages 22 and 62, where shared earnings are computed by assigning each individual half the total earnings of the couple in the years when the individual is married and his or her own earnings in years when not married. Replacement rate income omits imputed rent and co-resident income.

These are individuals whose replacement rates are in the 45th–55th percentiles.

Source: Authors' tabulations of MINT (see text for details).

explained by the increasing full retirement age for beneficiaries born after 1937. Defined benefit pensions are expected to replace about one-fifth of lifetime earnings for current retirees, but only about one-tenth for baby-boomer retirees. This decrease will be partially offset by a rise in the proportion of lifetime earnings replaced by retirement accounts—4 percent for current retirees and 9 percent for baby-boomer retirees.

In all birth cohorts, nonretirement income at age 67 (including income from assets, earnings, and SSI benefits) is expected to replace about 30 percent of preretirement earnings. Not surprising, given that SSI is focused on those with very low income, is that SSI on average does not contribute measurably to the replacement of preretirement income.

MINT projects similar patterns for nonmarried women. However, the percentages differ from those for the larger retiree population. In particular, MINT projects that Social Security benefits replace a much larger percentage of preretirement income for nonmarried women—50 percent for current retirees, decreasing to about 40 percent for baby-boomer retirees.

4.6   Conclusion

The Social Security Administration's MINT model projects measures of well-being through to 2032 for birth cohorts born between 1926 and 1965. Using projections of income at age 67 from MINT, this analysis assesses the role of major government income programs in the economic well-being of baby-boomer retirees and their predecessors. The analysis focuses on Social Security and SSI benefits and their contribution to overall income since Social Security, in particular, is likely to be impacted by social, demographic, and labor market changes that have transformed retirement expectations for the baby-boom cohort.

The analysis suggests that baby boomers can expect higher incomes and lower poverty rates at retirement than current retirees have. Similar to current retirees, Social Security will account for about two-fifths of projected total income and will be received by almost all baby-boomer retirees. SSI, which on average contributes almost nothing to total income, will be received by 5 percent of current retirees and only 2 percent of baby-boomer retirees. The projections also suggest that baby boomers are less likely than current retirees to have enough postretirement income to maintain their preretirement living standards. The financial planning literature often recommends having enough postretirement income to replace 70 percent to 80 percent of preretirement income. However, over two-fifths of baby-boomer retirees will replace less than three-quarters of their preretirement earnings and almost a fifth will replace less than half of their preretirement earnings. The decline in replacement rates for baby-boomer retirees relative to current retirees is partly driven by a decline in Social Security replacement rates. On a per capita basis, the experiences of nonmarried women will be similar to the larger retiree population, with the exception that nonmarried women are more likely to be economically challenged and in poverty at retirement.

A previous analysis suggested that despite their gains, certain baby-boomer subgroups are expected to remain economically vulnerable at retirement (Butrica, Iams, and Smith, 2003). These subgroups include divorced women, men that never married, Hispanics, high school dropouts, Social Security non-beneficiaries and auxiliary beneficiaries, those with weak labor force attachments, and those with the lowest lifetime earnings. Although they sometimes have higher than average replacement rates, high replacement rates do not ensure economic well-being.

Notes

*This paper was presented at The Levy Economics Institute of Bard College conference entitled 'The Distributional Effects of Government Spending and Taxation' and subsequently published in the Social Security Bulletin, Volume 65, No. 3, 2003/2004, pp. 1–13.

1. The baby-boom cohort is typically represented as those born in 1946 to 1964. However, for analytical purposes we define the baby-boom cohort as those born in 1946 to 1965.
2. Briefly, the aged receive Social Security benefits either as retired workers, spouses, divorced spouses or widow(er)s (Social Security Administration, 2001). Retired-worker benefits are computed by wage indexing annual earnings over an individual's working life and then calculating the average indexed monthly earnings (AIME) and primary insurance amount (PIA)—the benefit payable at the full retirement age, currently 65 and 10 months for someone born in 1942. The benefit is weighted to provide a higher proportion of benefits relative to a person's wages for those with low lifetime earnings and a lower proportion of benefits for those with high lifetime earnings. Individuals with 40 or more quarters of coverage over their working lives are considered fully insured and receive retired-worker benefits. Auxiliary benefits are paid to spouses, divorced spouses and widow(er)s of retired workers. Spouse benefits are effectively one-half of the spouse's PIA, unless reduced for early retirement or a family maximum. Divorced spouse benefits, paid to those with at least 10 years of marriage, are effectively one-half of the ex-spouse's PIA, with a reduction for early retirement. Widow(er) benefits are effectively equal to the deceased spouse's PIA, unless reduced for early retirement. Retired workers are dually entitled if their auxiliary benefits as spouses, divorced spouses or widow(er)s are larger than their retired-worker benefits. The dually entitled receive only the highest benefit to which they are entitled.
3. Net lifetime benefits are total lifetime benefits after age 61 minus lifetime Social Security taxes. Permanent income reflects income from age 62 until death, including covered earnings of beneficiaries, Social Security retirement benefits, defined benefit pensions and actuarially fair joint and survivor annuities from wealth at age 62.
4. Asset income reflects what economic resources from nonpension, nonhousing assets (including retirement accounts such as defined contribution pensions,

individual retirement accounts (IRAs), and Keoghs) could be available as a source of income, rather than predicting who actually draws on these resources in the future. In each year from retirement until death, MINT takes the stock of wealth in nonpension, nonhousing assets and:

1) depreciates it based on age-wealth patterns in the SIPP to represent the spend-down of assets in retirement; and
2) converts it into income by calculating the annuity a couple or individual could buy if they annuitized 80 percent of their total wealth.

Thus, asset income is derived from a series of annuity estimates based on a declining stock of wealth in retirement.

5. MINT estimates imputed rent as 3 percent of projected housing wealth.
6. This measure is computed as the average per capita family income of those with per capita family income in the 45th–55th percentiles. Not only does this measure overcome the problem of skewing from high income outliers that is typical of the mean, but also it is a more stable statistic than the median because it maintains a distribution of values.
7. Income is measured as a proportion of the national average wage at age 67, while earnings are measured as a proportion of the national average wage in each year between ages 22 and 62. This indexes the numerator and denominator to a common metric defined by the national average wage and expected wage growth. Wage-indexed earnings account for both past inflation and real wage growth and measure a family's actual standard of living. In contrast, price-indexed earnings take account of past inflation and measure a family's ability to attain a fixed standard of living. Because replacement rates gauge a family's ability to maintain preretirement living standards, wage-indexed earnings seem more appropriate than price-indexed earnings. Replacement rates would be greater than 100 percent if lifetime wages were indexed instead to annual prices that reflect purchasing power (Butrica, Iams, and Smith, 2003, Table 16). Historical earnings in MINT come from two sources of SSA administrative data. Earnings between 1951 and 1981 come from the Summary Earnings Record (SER) and include only Social Security covered earnings. Earnings between 1982 and 1999 come from the Detailed Earnings Record (DER) and include earnings from both Social Security covered and noncovered jobs. The DER also includes earnings over the Social Security taxable maximum. Projected earnings in MINT are based on the DER. We tested the sensitivity of our results to different sources of earnings data. Because it captures total earnings, not just Social Security covered earnings, the DER has fewer years of zero earnings and higher earnings on average than the SER. However, these data sources exhibit similar earnings patterns over time.
8. In reality, most individuals invest their wages in financial instruments, pensions or housing. Therefore, it is income from these sources, and not precisely earnings, which tends to finance retirement. Also, a number of individuals finance retirement with income generated through inheritances and gifts. However, MINT does not measure these income sources. Finally, some individuals without earnings may actually collect government transfers, such as welfare, unemployment insurance or Social Security DI benefits. Because this analysis does not account for these transfer payments, it may understate preretirement income and overstate replacement rates. In the case of Social Security DI benefits, the impact on overall replacement rates was negligible.

9. As discussed in a previous analysis, median replacement rates vary by subgroup (Butrica, Iams, and Smith, 2003, Table 10). These data show that widow(er)s will replace the highest proportion of lifetime earnings of any marital group, while those who are divorced will replace the lowest. Asian and Native Americans will have the highest replacement rates of any racial/ethnic group, fully replacing or replacing more than their lifetime earnings. Except for current retirees, MINT projects that high school graduates will replace a lower percentage of preretirement earnings than either high school dropouts or college graduates. Finally, median replacement rates will be highest for those with lower levels of lifetime labor force attachment and earnings and those with higher levels of total income.

10. It is important to consider that this analysis focuses on retirement income at age 67. Not only does the proportion of nonmarried women increase at older ages, but also their economic well-being tends to worsen.

11. This is because per capita income is based on the assumption that there are no economies of scale for larger families. In other words, those who are married need twice as much income to live equally as well as those who are nonmarried. In contrast, the US poverty thresholds for individuals aged 65 or older assume that those who are married need only 1.26 times more income to live equally as well as those who are nonmarried. Butrica, Iams, and Smith (2003) find that married retirees have less than twice the income as nonmarried retirees. However, they have more than 1.26 times the income of nonmarried retirees.

12. There are statutory limits on the amount individuals can contribute to retirement accounts. MINT assumes these limits remain fixed at current levels.

13. Those who are below the full retirement age face benefit reductions only if their earnings exceed the exempt amount ($11,604 in 2004).

14. Again, the replacement rate calculations omit imputed rent and co-resident income from income estimates in the numerator. Neither of these income sources is derived from lifetime preretirement earnings, which is the denominator for replacement rates.

References

Board of Trustees of the Federal Old-Age and Survivors Insurance and Disability Insurance Trust Funds (2004) *Annual Report* (Washington, DC: U.S. Government Printing Office).

Butrica, B. A., H. M. Iams and K. Smith (2003) 'It's All Relative: Understanding the Retirement Prospects of Baby Boomers,' Center for Retirement Research at Boston College. Available at http://www.bc.edu/crr.

Butrica, B. A., H. M. Iams, J. Moore and M. Waid (2001) *Methods in Modeling Income in the Near Term (MINT)*, ORES Working Paper 93 (Washington, DC: Social Security Administration, Office of Policy).

Cherlin, A. J. (1992) *Marriage, Divorce, and Remarriage* (Cambridge, MA: Harvard University Press).

Employee Benefit Research Institute (2003) *EBRI Research Highlights: Retirement Benefits* (Washington, DC: Employee Benefit Research Institute).

Farley, R. (1996) *The New American Reality: Who We Are, How We Got Here, Where We Are Going* (New York, NY: Russell Sage Foundation).

Henretta, J. C. and A. M. O'Rand (1999) *Age and Inequality: Diverse Pathways Through Later Life* (Boulder, CO: Westview Press).

Hinden, S. (2001) '12 Important Decisions You Must Make Before Retiring: Will You Be Ready?,' *The Washington Post* (January 14), Section H, pp. H1, H4.

Leimer, D. (1995) 'A Guide to Social Security Money's Worth Issues,' *Social Security Bulletin* 58(2): 3–20.

Levy, F. (1998) *The New Dollars and Dreams: American Incomes and Economic Change* (New York: The Russell Sage Foundation).

Levy, F. and R. J. Murnane (1992) 'U.S. Earnings Levels and Earnings Inequality: A Review of Recent Trends and Proposed Explanations,' *Journal of Economic Literature* 30(3): 1333–81.

Munnell, A. H. and A. Sundén (2004) *Coming Up Short: The Challenge of 401(k) Plans* (Washington, DC: Brookings Institution Press).

Panis, C. and L. Lillard (1999) 'Near Term Model Development,' Final Report, SSA Contract No: 600-96-27335 (Santa Monica, CA: RAND).

Ruggles, S. (1997) 'The Rise of Divorce and Separation in the United States, 1880–1990,' *Demography* 34(4): 455–66.

Smith, K. E., E. J. Toder and H. M. Iams (2003/2004) 'Lifetime Distributional Effects of Social Security Retirement Benefits,' *Social Security Bulletin* 65(1): 33–61.

Smith, K. E. (2002) 'How Will Recent Patterns of Earnings Inequality Affect Future Retirement Incomes?,' Final Report for AARP (Washington, DC: The Urban Institute).

Social Security Administration (2001) *Social Security Handbook,* 14th Edn (Washington, DC: U.S. Government Printing Office).

Steuerle, C. E. and J. M. Bakija (1994) *Retooling Social Security for the 21st Century: Right and Wrong Approaches to Reform* (Washington, DC: The Urban Institute Press).

TIAA-CREF (2002) 'Retirement Strategies,' Financial Series 4 (New York, NY).

TIAA-CREF (1994) 'Looking Ahead to Retirement,' The Library Series 3 (New York, NY).

Toder, E., L. Thompson, M. Favreault, R. Johnson, K. Perese, C. Ratcliffe, K. Smith, C. Uccello, T. Waidmann, J. Berk and R. Woldemariam (2002) 'Modeling Income in the Near Term: Revised Projections of Retirement Income Through 2020 for the 1931–1960 Birth Cohorts,' Final Report, SSA Contract No: 600-96-27332 (Washington, DC: The Urban Institute).

Toder, E., C. Uccello, J. O'Hare, M. Favreault, C. Ratcliffe, K. Smith, G. Burtless and B. Bosworth (1999) 'Modeling Income in the Near Term-Projections of Retirement Income Through 2020 for the 1931–1960 Birth Cohorts,' Final Report, SSA Contract No: 600-96-27332 (Washington, DC: The Urban Institute).

Part II
Distributional Effects in Other Countries

5

Household Incomes and Redistribution in the European Union: Quantifying the Equalizing Properties of Taxes and Benefits[1]

Herwig Immervoll, Horacio Levy, Christine Lietz, Daniela Mantovani, Cathal O'Donoghue, Holly Sutherland and Gerlinde Verbist

5.1 Introduction

Taxes and social benefits affect household income through several different channels and these effects can be assessed in a number of ways. This chapter focuses on the influence of social and fiscal policies on income inequality. In particular, we analyze how tax and benefit payments alter the distribution of household incomes in the European Union (EU). Our aim is to provide evidence on the effectiveness of a wide range of different policy configurations at reducing disparities of household resources.

The novelty of the analysis is that it encompasses both taxes and benefits and is undertaken for all 15 pre-2004 member countries of the EU. We employ a microsimulation approach, which allows us to better address some of the measurement problems normally encountered in comparative research on income inequality. Results are conceptually consistent and comparable across countries so that, in addition to country-specific results, inequality measures can be reported for the EU-15 as a whole. We analyze separately the distributive properties of different types of tax-benefit instruments, including income taxes, social contributions and public pensions, as well as other non-means-tested and means-tested benefits.

While the scope of this chapter is wider than that of most previous studies, it shares a number of relevant conceptual choices, two of which are worth noting in particular. First, taxes and benefit payments are assessed in terms of their *direct* impact on household resources. Focusing on observable tax and benefit payments in this way does, of course, provide a partial measure of how transfers between households and governments affect incomes (Boadway and Keen, 2000) and this should be kept in mind when interpreting results and comparing them across countries. On the one hand, the existence of taxes and benefits generally causes changes in both market prices and household behavior. Therefore this has an influence on pre tax-benefit market incomes (and economic welfare), which is not captured by looking at the amounts of taxes and benefits alone. On the other hand, in-kind transfers (to individual households or provided as collective goods and services) represent a significant portion of the resources transferred from governments to households.

Second, we measure incomes and inequality at a particular point in time. The analysis is therefore *static* and does not attempt to measure the distribution of lifetime incomes or separate the 'within-cohort' and 'between-cohort' components of cross-sectional inequality. This point is relevant because some of the tax-benefit instruments analyzed here (pensions and other contingency- or insurance-based benefits, as well as the taxes earmarked to finance them) are largely designed to redistribute across the lifecycle rather than across individuals. However, while the long-term or dynamic aspects of inequality are interesting, the same is true for disparities observed at any given point in time. Policy instruments that are designed to redistribute inter-temporally can, as shown here, also have important consequences for cross-sectional inequality. Indeed, the perceived impact on the distribution of *current* incomes can have important implications for the political feasibility of introducing these measures in the first place. In addition, the extent of income disparities at any given point in time is a measure of the effectiveness of social policies providing financial assistance subject to certain contingencies.

The remainder of this chapter is organized as follows. Section 5.2 provides some background by describing previous methods and existing sources of data for making international comparisons of the redistributive properties of tax and/or benefit systems. The advantages of using microsimulation methods are explained and Section 5.3 goes on to describe the method in more detail, including the European model, EUROMOD. Section 5.4 introduces some of the key issues to be addressed when comparing redistributive effects across different underlying populations and introduces the definitions and assumptions to be used in the analysis that follows. The results are presented in three stages. The first, in Section 5.5.1, illustrates the extent to which the components of tax and benefit systems vary in their importance across countries and according to the level of household disposable income. This is followed in Section 5.5.2 by an analysis which shows that inequality before the operation of taxes and benefits varies *less* across the countries considered than it does after they take effect. It also shows how the relative equalizing effects of the tax and benefit systems as a whole depend on whether public pensions are considered as part of the redistributive system. Finally, Section 5.5.3 considers the redistributive roles of sub-components of the tax-benefit systems, focusing particularly on the contrasting effects of means-tested and non-means-tested benefits. Section 5.6 concludes.

5.2 Sources and methods for the assessment and comparison of redistribution

International comparisons of social policies are often made using calculations based on model families (Eardley, *et al.*, 1996; OECD, 2004) or macroindicators (for example, share of social expenditures in gross domestic product, GDP). While useful for understanding the structure and certain relevant features of complex policy measures, such studies say little about their distributional impact. Research based on representative microdata is, however, often limited to one particular country. Comparisons of national datasets are difficult, as available data are typically not designed to be comparable across countries (Smeeding and Grodner, 2000). International studies relying on these data—which can for instance differ in terms of population coverage, unit of analysis or the definition of individual income components—are then subject to these limitations (Burniaux, *et al.*, 1998; Deleeck, *et al.*, 1992).

In a recent study covering 27 OECD (Organization for Economic Co-operative and Development) countries, Förster and Mira d'Ercole (2005) report household income inequality before and after taxes and social benefits. The analysis is based on indicators provided by individual country experts and on different types of microdata. Standardized terms of reference are used to ensure consistency of concepts and definitions but due to the different data sources, comparability *across* countries is necessarily limited. Hence, Förster and Mira d'Ercole focus specifically on changes of income inequality *over time* and how the observed longitudinal patterns differ internationally. Several international studies of the redistributive effects of taxes also use country-specific data.[2] However, they ignore the role of social benefits and generally do not consider tax-like payments such as compulsory social contributions. Where a large number of countries are covered, results tend to be based on a mix of administrative data and different types of survey sources. As a result, the populations that these data represent differ between countries. In addition, the unit of analysis is often dictated by data collection methods and so can vary between countries as well. For instance, household income, which is widely accepted as the appropriate measure of monetary well-being (Canberra Group, 2001), cannot be analyzed where tax data do not contain information on the incomes of all household members.

Comparative research on income inequality has been greatly helped by efforts to harmonize national data sets ex-post (Luxembourg Income Study, LIS) and by prioritizing comparability in the context of newly designed multi-country data collection activities, especially in the EU

(European Union Household Panel (ECHP) and Statistics on Income and Living Standards (SILC)).[3] Atkinson *et al.* (1995) use LIS data for a comparison of income inequality in OECD countries. Results are also available from later waves of LIS data (Smeeding and Grodner, 2000). The ex-post harmonization of the LIS data does, however, present some problems when analyzing the redistributive effects of tax and benefit policies. Notably, the quality and level of detail of information about taxes paid vary considerably across countries. Researchers using the ECHP have to confront similar issues. While data are more detailed than LIS in some respects (for instance, more information is provided separately for each household member), income variables tend to be more aggregated across sources of income. Most importantly, incomes are recorded *net* of taxes and information on tax liabilities is not provided. Therefore, redistribution studies cannot consider the redistributive impact of taxes and have to focus on social transfers alone (Heady, *et al.*, 2001).

The approach used in this chapter addresses several of the problems described here and arguably provides more comprehensive and comparable results than previous studies. The main difference lies in the combination of partly harmonized microdata with well-established simulation techniques. Rather than taking tax and benefit amounts directly from the data, the microdata are used instead as a basis for *calculating* tax liabilities and benefit entitlements. This is done in accordance with detailed legal rules to ensure that results for each observation correspond as closely as possible to the taxes and benefits that would be determined by tax authorities and benefit agencies. For instance, income taxes are computed by first determining, for each taxpayer identified in the data, taxable income as well as other tax-relevant circumstances (employment status, number of children and so on) and then applying legal income tax rules in order to find resulting tax liabilities.

Given limited information in available microdata on detailed tax and benefit amounts, tax-benefit microsimulation models generally provide a richer basis for assessing the distributive impact of taxes and benefits. The most obvious advantage of this approach is that it permits an analysis of taxes and benefits based on datasets that do not provide information on these variables at all, or not with the desired level of detail.[4] Moreover, the simulation approach is particularly attractive in a comparative setting as it makes the analysis of taxes and benefits less dependent on the precise definition of these target variables and less influenced by differences in these definitions across countries. By ensuring a consistent application of legal policy rules across countries, the resulting tax and benefit amounts are potentially more comparable than tax and benefit variables recorded in the microdata itself. Finally, the simulation approach provides greater analytical flexibility, as it allows categories of taxes and benefits to be defined consistently across countries and independently of definitions adopted by the data providers. While some countries have a long tradition of using microsimulation models for these types of analysis (see e.g. Duclos, 1993), a conceptually consistent comparison across countries has so far been inhibited by the lack of suitable multi-country tax-benefit models.

5.3 Tax-benefit models and EUROMOD

A microsimulation model is a representation of a socioeconomic reality aiming, among other things, at gaining insights into the functioning of existing policies as well as the consequences of proposed policy changes (Atkinson and Sutherland, 1988; Krupp, 1986). Tax-benefit models (or 'static' microsimulation models) are based on household microdata from representative sources. They calculate disposable income for each household in the dataset. This calculation is made up of elements of income taken from the underlying microdata (for example, employee earnings) combined with components that are simulated by the model (taxes and benefits). The main advantages of such a microsimulation model is that it allows one to focus accurately on the objectives of social and economic policy, on the instruments employed, and on the precise change experienced by those to whom the measures apply. Regulations are incorporated into the model as accurately as possible, so that the impact on each unit (person, family, household) is identified. A particular advantage of this method is that it allows for the study of a set of policy measures from two distinct perspectives. On the one hand, one can focus on the net, cumulative effect of the various policy instruments, and therefore also on the impact of the entire set of transfer-oriented measures. On the other hand, a microsimulation model offers the possibility of dissecting complex measures (for example, through a step-by-step tax calculation for a household), so that the impact of each step may be considered separately. The level of aggregation—both across units of analysis and across income components—may be chosen according to the question being posed.

All simulation models have inherent limitations. Most of them use empirical data that are obtained either from surveys or from administrative sources. As such, the accuracy of the results depends on the quality of the data. Generally, these data do not refer to the period of interest and must be updated in some way, a process that is inherently prone to some error. Factors affecting the administrative effectiveness of tax and benefit systems cannot be captured precisely, meaning that the non-take up of benefits and tax evasion may not be fully accounted for—and are typically not accounted for at all.

In this chapter, we use EUROMOD, the static tax-benefit model covering the 15 Member States of the pre-May 2004 EU.[5] It represents a concerted attempt to reduce the lack of comparability across datasets and to apply a consistent modeling strategy to these data. EUROMOD provides measures of direct taxes, social contributions and cash benefits, where benefits may be categorized according to function or other characteristics. The datasets used as the basis for the simulations in this chapter are listed in Appendix Table 5.A.1. They were chosen on the grounds that they provide the best quality input for a tax-benefit model and are at the same time available and accessible to an international scientific project. Although they include data collected at various points in the time 1993–1999, they have all been adjusted to 1998 prices and incomes and the policies simulated are those prevailing in mid-1998.

All benefits and taxes are computed, based on the assumption that the legal rules apply and that the costs of compliance are zero. They do not take into account any non-take up of benefits or tax evasion that may occur in practice. In some countries, EUROMOD is known to over-estimate taxes collected (for example, Greece) and in others it over-estimates the amount of means-tested benefits paid (for example, in the United Kingdom and Ireland and to some extent in Germany and Sweden). This is obviously more of an issue in countries that rely more heavily on these types of instrument. Mantovani and Sutherland (2003) provide a detailed assessment of the factors affecting the reliability of EUROMOD estimates of household disposable income.[6]

5.4 Measuring inequality and redistribution

We use a range of standard measures in order to explore the direct effects of tax and benefit payments on income inequality. For the purpose of this chapter, and following common usage of the term in the literature, the reduction of inequality achieved by the tax-benefit system as a whole (or of individual components) is termed 'redistribution' or 'redistributive effect,' which is therefore used synonymously with 'equalizing effect.' It is worth emphasizing that redistribution in this sense does not require anybody to be better off. A pareto-worsening policy measure (a progressive tax on everybody) thus constitutes 'redistribution' in the technical sense of the term, even before any of the tax revenues are redistributed in the form of transfers or collective goods or services.

In this chapter, income redistribution is measured in relation to the standard Gini coefficient.[7] In particular, the redistributive effect, RE of taxes and/or benefits (TB) is measured as the difference between the Gini coefficients of income before (G_X) and after taxes and/or benefits (G_{X+TB}):

$$RE = G_X - G_{X+TB}$$

Since measuring the redistributive effect of a policy instrument involves a comparison of incomes before and after this instrument, it is evident that redistribution measures are sensitive to the definition of the 'base' or 'pre-instrument' income (X in our notation). For example, the redistributive effect of an income tax can differ significantly from what one might expect if pre-tax and transfer market income is used as X. Since some benefits may be taxable, individuals with zero market income can have positive tax liabilities. As a result, income taxes will seem less redistributive if market income is taken as the base than if all of taxable income is the starting point.

One implication of this is that the assumed sequence of different instruments matters when decomposing the redistributive effect of the entire tax-benefit system into the contribution of each individual tax and benefit. Obviously, studies looking at only one type of instrument, such as taxes, do not encounter this problem. However, given the wider scope of this chapter, we do have to make a decision on the appropriate sequence. Unfortunately, choosing any particular sequence would be arbitrary to some extent since different sequences will generally be appropriate in each country (for instance, means-tested benefits can be taxable in some countries but may depend on after-tax income in others). Any particular choice would be hard to justify and so we do not attempt to decompose effects of all tax-benefit instruments simultaneously. Instead, we investigate the equalizing properties of different types of instrument by focusing on one instrument at a time. Rather than assessing the contribution of each type of tax or benefit to the overall effect of the tax-benefit system, we ask for each type of tax and benefit, starting from a situation where this instrument does not exist, what are the distributive effects of introducing it? Hence, we measure the redistributive effect of individual taxes and benefits by comparing disposable income after all taxes and benefits ($X + TB$ in the above notation) with disposable income minus the effect of the instrument of interest (X).

We exploit EUROMOD's capacity to identify individual taxes and benefits in order to explore the contribution of each main component of tax-benefit systems to redistribution. We use two different definitions of 'base' or 'pre tax-benefit' income as our starting points. One is 'market income' as conventionally defined. This includes gross earnings (pre-tax and not including employer social contributions), self-employment income and income from capital plus private pensions and transfers from other households. The second starting point also includes income from public pensions. This dual perspective is taken for two reasons. First, one can argue that public pension income is not properly part of the redistributive system and should be considered as deferred earnings or compulsory savings. This applies particularly to insurance-based systems.

The second reason is more pragmatic. In some countries, private pensions substitute for public pensions. This occurs under varying degrees of regulation, compulsion and state subsidy, and also to varying extents. Drawing the line between 'public' and 'private' is difficult. Our data do not allow us to identify private pension income with any precision and so this, together with other income from capital, is included in market income under both starting points. For reasons of comparability, the second starting point treats public pensions in the same way.

The transformation of market income to disposable income is defined in the following steps:

	(1)	market income
+	(2)	state pensions
+	(3)	non means-tested benefits
+	(4)	means-tested benefits
−	(5)	employee and self-employed social insurance contributions
−	(6)	income taxes
=	(7)	disposable income

The first of our two starting points is market income (1) and the second is after the addition of public pension income (2). Public pension income is defined to be restricted to those aged 65 or more and to benefits specifically intended to provide income during old age or to replace earnings during retirement. Any other pensions paid to younger people or other benefits paid to the elderly are included in one or other of the cash benefit categories (3) or (4), rather than as pension income. Cash benefits have been sub-divided into those that are means-tested—designed to redistribute to low-income individuals or households—and those that are not specifically targeted by income (or assets). In practice, in some cases the distinction can be somewhat arbitrary, especially where a means test applies to a relatively minor top-up component of a more general benefit. Appendix discusses these definitions in more detail and lists the income components that are considered to be 'pension' and 'means-tested' benefits in each country. Remaining cash benefits are classified as non-means-tested benefits (3). Employee and self-employed social contributions are deducted (5) as are direct taxes—mainly income taxes, but also including other direct, personal taxes that exist in some countries—(6).[8] This results in disposable income (7).

Throughout, income is aggregated across household members. When comparing average incomes across countries (as in Section 5.5.1), income is aggregated across all (weighted) households, without adjustment for household size and composition. All distributional analysis is conducted at the person level, allocating household income and its components to each person in the household. For this purpose, incomes and income components are equivalized using the modified OECD scale.[9] Statistics for EU-15 are constructed applying population weights and adjusting income for differences in purchasing power across countries.[10]

5.5 Results

This section considers in turn:

(a) The size of the various components of the redistributive systems. The picture for average households is contrasted with that for the bottom and top quintiles.
(b) Income inequality and the redistributive effects of tax-benefit systems as a whole, using the two alternative 'starting points' (excluding and including public pensions).
(c) The redistributive effect of the four main tax-benefit components (means-tested benefits, non-means-tested benefits, social contributions and income taxes).

5.5.1 The composition of household income across the income distribution

First, we demonstrate the extent to which each income source varies in size across countries. Figure 5.1 shows the composition of disposable income in terms of market income, income taxes, social contributions and the three categories of benefits and public pensions that we consider. Incomes are not equivalized and are measured per household rather than across persons. This

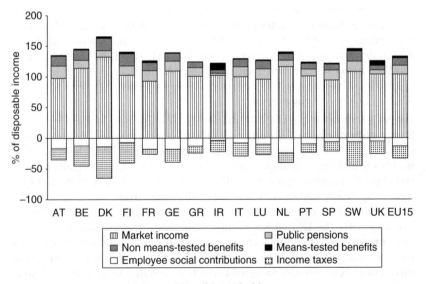

Figure 5.1 Income composition 1998: all households
Source: EUROMOD (visit http://www.iser.essex.ac.uk/msu/emodstats/).

gives a 'budgetary' perspective rather than a welfare perspective to the overall redistributive mechanisms. Nevertheless, it is important to note that these estimates should not be interpreted in terms of budget deficits or surpluses, as major parts of government revenue (for example, employer contributions, indirect taxes, corporate taxes) and spending (in-kind benefits, spending on public services) are not included. One way of interpreting the information in Figure 5.1 is as showing the composition of 100 euro of disposable income. How much market income is necessary on average to achieve this level of disposable income, and how much is deducted as taxes and added as benefits?

For eight countries, market income forms on average between 95 percent and 105 percent of disposable income. This means that in most countries, the state 'takes' about the same amount in income taxes and employee contributions[11] as it 'gives' in cash benefits shown here. Market income makes up more than 105 percent of disposable income in Belgium, Denmark, the Netherlands, Germany and Sweden. This means that deductions from gross market incomes are significantly higher than the sum of all shown benefits. This is especially the case in Denmark, where non-cash benefits— which are not included—play an important role. On the other hand, Spanish and French households receive on average notably more benefits than they pay in taxes, as their original income is less than 95 percent of disposable income.

Public pensions form more than 15 percent of average disposable income in Austria, France, Germany, Italy, Luxembourg, Spain and Sweden. On average, non-means-tested benefits make up a greater proportion of disposable income than means-tested benefits, except in the case of Ireland and the United Kingdom. On the burden side we find that income taxes are dominant in all countries, except France, the Netherlands and Greece, where social contributions are relatively more important.

5.5.1.1 Low income households

Figure 5.2 shows the same information for low income households: those in the bottom quintile group of the distribution (defined on the basis of equivalized household disposable income at the person level). The situation is entirely different. In about half of the EU countries, market income and state transfers each account for half of disposable income. Greece and Italy have a relatively higher share of market income (around 2/3). A considerably smaller share of market income is found in Belgium, Denmark, Finland and especially the United Kingdom and Ireland. In these latter two countries, means-tested benefits form a large proportion of household income for those in the bottom quintile (in Ireland even more than 50 percent). In all other countries, non-means-tested benefits represent a larger share of household incomes than means-tested cash transfers, even for these low income households. Compared to average households, public pensions make up a

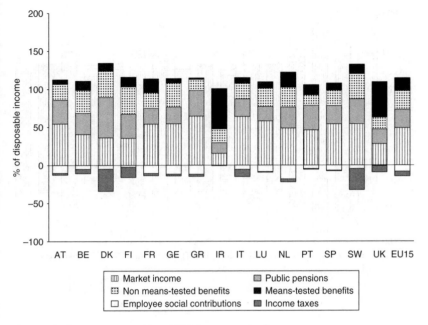

Figure 5.2   Income composition 1998: bottom quintile
Source: EUROMOD (visit http://www.iser.essex.ac.uk/msu/emodstats/).

larger share of household income in the bottom quintile, indicating that an important proportion of the low income population consists of pensioners.

Although most income tax systems are progressive, this does not mean that people with low incomes pay no taxes. Especially in Denmark and Sweden, the tax burden for the bottom quintile is relatively high. In the Netherlands they pay rather high social contributions, which follows from the fact that the Dutch also pay contributions on pensions and on an important part of their other state transfers (see Verbist, 2005). Ireland is the only country where the group with the lowest 20 percent of incomes pays virtually no taxes or contributions.[12]

5.5.1.2   High income households

As might be expected, and as shown in Figure 5.3, market income is greater than 100 percent of disposable income in the top quintile (by 80 percent in Denmark). This is mirrored by the high level of taxes paid by these relatively rich households, especially in Denmark and Belgium. Contributions are far less important than for the average household, due to the upper limit on earnings that is applied in most social contribution systems.

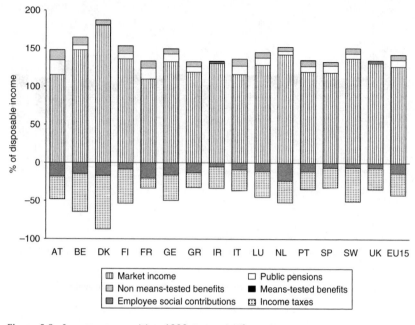

Figure 5.3   Income composition 1998: top quintile
Source: EUROMOD (visit http://www.iser.essex.ac.uk/msu/emodstats/).

Benefits only make up a small part of disposable income and are particularly low in Ireland and the United Kingdom. Naturally, means-tested benefits are low. But they are not entirely absent, as means tests are usually applied to income of the couple or inner family rather than the household as a whole. Thus low income pensioners may receive means-tested benefits while living in high income households. It is also striking that, except maybe for Austria, public pensions are far less important than for the other income groups (in Ireland and Denmark, they are almost zero). This is consistent with studies that show how pensioners are under-represented at the top of the income distribution (Whitehouse, 2000).

5.5.2   Income inequality and the redistributive effect of tax-benefit systems

Clearly tax-benefit systems operate differently for the rich and the poor across countries. In order to examine explicitly the redistributive effects of the systems as a whole, inequality levels before and after adding in taxes and benefits are shown in Figure 5.4 (see also Table 5.1). As explained in Section 5.4, we use the standard Gini coefficient to measure inequality and this is plotted for three different income concepts: market income, market

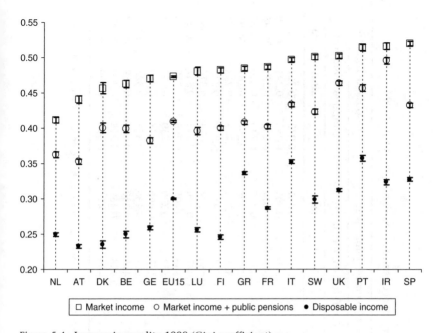

Figure 5.4 Income inequality 1998 (Gini coefficient)

Note: The statistical reliability of the estimates is shown using confidence intervals that have been constructed to be significant at the 5 percent level: that is, $+/-1.96 \times$ estimated standard error.

Source: EUROMOD countries are ranked by market income inequality.

plus public pension income and disposable income. Countries are ranked by market income inequality and confidence intervals, calculated using boot-strap techniques are also shown.[13] The differences between the square and circle shaped markers show the reduction in inequality that arises once public pensions are added to market income.

This is a graphical representation of calculating the redistributive effect as the difference between G_X and G_{X+TB}. The redistributive effect of all instruments, where X is market income and TB is the sum of all taxes and benefits, is given by the distance between the markers for market income and disposable income on Figure 5.4. The effect of all instruments, except public pensions (that is, $X =$ market and public pension income, and $TB =$ all taxes and benefits except public pensions), is given by the distance between the circle- and dot-shaped markers in Figure 5.4. An alternative picture is provided in Figure 5.5, which expresses the redistributive effect as a percentage of G_X in order to take account of country differences in the levels of market income inequality. In Figure 5.5, countries are ranked from high to low disposable income inequality. A third perspective is provided

Table 5.1 Gini coefficients for market income, market income including public pensions and disposable income, 1998

		Market income			Market income + public pensions			Disposable income		
			Confidence interval			Confidence interval			Confidence interval	
			min	max		min	max		min	max
Austria	AT	0.441	0.431	0.450	0.353	0.345	0.361	0.233	0.227	0.239
Belgium	BE	0.462	0.452	0.473	0.399	0.389	0.409	0.250	0.241	0.258
Denmark	DK	0.457	0.442	0.471	0.400	0.387	0.414	0.235	0.225	0.245
Finland	FI	0.482	0.474	0.489	0.400	0.393	0.407	0.246	0.240	0.252
France	FR	0.486	0.480	0.492	0.402	0.397	0.408	0.287	0.283	0.291
Germany	GE	0.470	0.461	0.479	0.383	0.375	0.391	0.259	0.253	0.264
Greece	GR	0.484	0.478	0.491	0.408	0.402	0.414	0.336	0.332	0.341
Ireland	IR	0.516	0.507	0.525	0.495	0.486	0.504	0.324	0.316	0.331
Italy	IT	0.497	0.490	0.504	0.434	0.427	0.440	0.352	0.347	0.358
Luxembourg	LU	0.481	0.470	0.491	0.396	0.386	0.405	0.256	0.250	0.263
Netherlands	NL	0.412	0.404	0.420	0.362	0.354	0.370	0.250	0.245	0.255
Portugal	PT	0.514	0.504	0.524	0.457	0.447	0.466	0.358	0.349	0.366
Spain	SP	0.520	0.514	0.526	0.433	0.427	0.438	0.328	0.323	0.332
Sweden	SW	0.501	0.493	0.508	0.423	0.416	0.430	0.299	0.289	0.309
United Kingdom	UK	0.502	0.496	0.508	0.464	0.458	0.469	0.313	0.309	0.317
EU-15		0.473	0.471	0.476	0.409	0.406	0.412	0.300	0.299	0.302

Note: The statistical reliability of the estimates is shown using confidence intervals that have been constructed to be significant at the 5 percent level: that is, $+/-1.96 \times$ estimated standard error.
Source: EUROMOD.

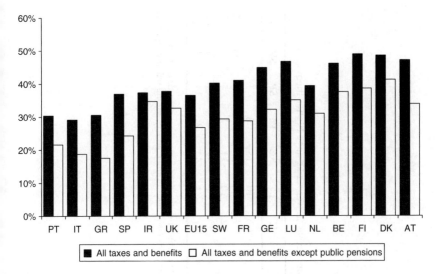

Figure 5.5 Redistributive effect of tax-benefit systems 1998 (% change in Gini)
Source: EUROMOD countries are ranked in descending order of inequality of disposable income.

by Table 5.2, which shows the positions in the country ranking by level of inequality for the three measures of income.

Looking first at the overall impact of the tax-benefit systems, including public pensions, on market income inequality, we can see that all systems reduce income inequality substantially, though to different extents. This is illustrated by the fact that the difference between the lowest and the highest levels of inequality is smaller for market income (a difference of 0.108 between the Gini coefficients for the Netherlands and Spain) than for disposable income (a difference of 0.125 between Austria and Portugal).

The tax-benefit system is highly redistributive in Finland, Denmark, Belgium, Austria, Luxembourg and Germany (*RE* of 45 percent or more, relative to market income inequality—shown by the darker bars in Figure 5.5). These are also the countries with the lowest levels of disposable income inequality. On the other hand, Greece, Italy and Portugal have a low degree of redistribution (*RE* of about 30 percent of market income inequality), being the countries with the highest inequality of disposable incomes. France, Sweden, the Netherlands, Ireland, United Kingdom and Spain form a middle group in terms of the extent of redistribution, although the Netherlands starts with the lowest market income inequality and Spain starts with the highest market income inequality. The observation that countries with relatively equal distributions of disposable incomes tend to exhibit the largest redistributive effects, illustrates the importance of redistributive mechanisms built into tax-benefit systems.[14]

Table 5.2 Inequality ranking of countries for market income and disposable income, 1998 (lower ranks have higher inequality)

	AT	BE	DK	FI	FR	GE	GR	IR	IT	LU	NL	PT	SP	SW	UK
market income (1a)	14	12	13	9	7	11	8	2	6	10	15	3	1	5	4
market income + pensions (1b)	15	11	9	10	8	13	7	1	4	12	14	3	5	6	2
disposable income (2)	15	12	14	13	8	9	3	5	2	10	11	1	4	7	6
re-ranking (1a)—(2)	1↓	↔	1↓	4↓	1↓	2↑	5↑	3↓	4↑	↔	4↑	2↑	3↓	2↑	2↓
re-ranking (1b)—(2)	↔	1↓	5↓	3↓	↔	4↑	4↑	4↓	2↑	2↑	3↑	2↑	1↑	1↓	4↓

Note: The first three rows show the position of each country in the ranking by inequality (Gini coefficient) using three measures of income and with the lowest rank indicating the highest inequality. The last two rows indicate with arrows the direction of movement in the country ranking when comparing the ranks under the two alternative market income measures with that for disposable income.
Source: EUROMOD.

The size of the redistributive effect is highly sensitive to whether public pensions are included as part of the redistributive system. Pensions play a particularly important role in reducing market income inequality in Austria, Germany, Luxembourg, France and Spain and a particularly minor role in Ireland, the United Kingdom and to a lesser extent, Denmark. The ranking of the amount of redistribution achieved is therefore somewhat altered if public pensions are considered as part of market income and not part of the redistributive system. Belgium, Denmark and Finland remain in the group of the three most redistributive countries (*RE* of 36 percent or more). Austria, Germany and Luxembourg now form an 'upper-middle' group (with *RE* between 30 percent and 36 percent) along with three of the countries that are classified as middle-ranking when pensions are included in the redistributive system: Ireland, the Netherlands and the United Kingdom. Without public pensions, the Spanish system is relatively less redistributive and joins the other southern countries in the low redistribution group (*RE* of under 25 percent). The remaining two countries—France and Sweden—achieve redistribution at an intermediate level between 25 percent and 30 percent.

Taking the EU-15 countries as a whole, 'European' market income inequality lies between that of the fifth and sixth most equal countries (Germany and Luxembourg) once national levels of income have been adjusted for purchasing power differences. The redistributive effect of the system as a whole is similar to that of the middle-ranking group of countries and if public pensions are not considered as part of the redistributive system, the equalizing effect is lower and commensurate with that of Spain.

Comparison of the measures of inequality for these two income concepts indicates that the equalizing effect of pensions varies greatly over countries. In Ireland and the United Kingdom, it turns out to be very small. As we have seen, these are also the countries with the lowest proportion of public pensions in household income (as shown in Figures 5.1 to 5.3). This distinction emphasizes the fact that pensions are primarily provided through the private sector in Ireland and the United Kingdom. Unsurprisingly, in countries where the state is a more important provider of retirement incomes, public pensions are more effective at reducing income disparities. Clearly, the accounting period is highly relevant here. Even if there were no interpersonal redistribution in state pensions over the lifetime at all (so that they would be equivalent to unsubsidized private pensions), pensions would appear highly redistributive in a cross-sectional perspective, as they are often the main income source for the elderly.[15]

5.5.3 Redistributive effects of individual policy measures

In a similar way, we now calculate the redistributive effect of each component of the tax-benefit systems separately. Thus X becomes market income, including all taxes and benefits except the instrument concerned, that is, in turn, non-means-tested benefits (not including public pensions), means-tested benefits, social contributions and income taxes. As explained in Section 5.4, the question that we are asking is, starting from the situation without the instrument in question, how much is inequality reduced by introducing it? We ask this question for each of the four types of instrument in turn, and the results are shown in Figure 5.6 (see also Table 5.3).[16]

Of these four instruments, non-means-tested benefits have a leading role in the redistributive process in almost all countries (and the EU-15 as a whole). Especially in the Scandinavian countries, Austria and Belgium, these benefits have a large equalizing effect. In Ireland and the United Kingdom, means-tested benefits are the most important redistributive instruments. The inequality reduction due to means-tested benefits is much smaller in all other countries, although the redistributive effect can still be sizable and is larger than that of income taxes in France and Sweden.

Social insurance contributions have relatively the weakest redistributive power, as in most countries they are levied on a more or less proportional base, at least within the most relevant parts of the earnings distribution.

The contribution of income taxes to inequality reduction is relatively high in the countries with the most equal distributions of disposable incomes (Austria, Belgium, Denmark, Finland, Germany, Luxembourg and the Netherlands) and also in Ireland and Spain. It is interesting to relate these results to the relative importance of income taxes shown in Figure 5.1. Income tax burdens are high in Belgium, Denmark and Finland. Given the size of the

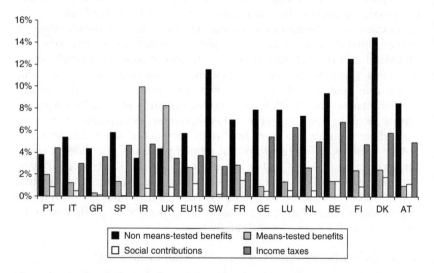

Figure 5.6   Redistributive effect of tax-benefit instruments 1998 (change in Gini)
Source: EUROMOD countries are ranked in descending order of inequality of disposable income.

Table 5.3 Gini coefficients with confidence intervals (ci)

	disposable income (di)	di excl. pensions	di excl. all benefits	di excl. non means-tested benefits	di excl. means-tested benefits	di excl. social insurance contributions	di excl. taxes
AT	0.233	0.359	0.331	0.318	0.243	0.245	0.283
ci	0.230 0.236	0.353 0.365	0.326 0.335	0.313 0.322	0.240 0.246	0.242 0.248	0.279 0.286
BE	0.250	0.344	0.360	0.343	0.263	0.263	0.317
ci	0.245 0.254	0.339 0.350	0.355 0.365	0.338 0.349	0.259 0.268	0.259 0.267	0.312 0.322
DK	0.235	0.324	0.414	0.380	0.259	0.253	0.293
ci	0.230 0.240	0.318 0.331	0.407 0.420	0.374 0.386	0.254 0.265	0.248 0.258	0.287 0.300
FI	0.246	0.366	0.402	0.371	0.270	0.255	0.294
ci	0.243 0.249	0.361 0.370	0.398 0.406	0.367 0.375	0.267 0.273	0.252 0.258	0.291 0.297
FR	0.287	0.389	0.390	0.356	0.316	0.302	0.309
ci	0.285 0.289	0.386 0.391	0.388 0.392	0.354 0.359	0.314 0.318	0.300 0.304	0.306 0.312
GE	0.259	0.362	0.349	0.338	0.268	0.264	0.313
ci	0.256 0.262	0.358 0.366	0.345 0.353	0.334 0.341	0.265 0.271	0.261 0.266	0.309 0.317
GR	0.336	0.423	0.384	0.380	0.339	0.337	0.372
ci	0.334 0.339	0.420 0.426	0.381 0.386	0.377 0.383	0.337 0.342	0.335 0.340	0.369 0.375
IR	0.324	0.346	0.463	0.358	0.423	0.331	0.371
ci	0.320 0.327	0.342 0.350	0.459 0.468	0.354 0.362	0.419 0.427	0.327 0.334	0.367 0.376

Table 5.3 (Continued)

	disposable income (di)		di excl. pensions		di excl. all benefits		di excl. non means-tested benefits		di excl. means-tested benefits		di excl. social insurance contributions		di excl. taxes	
IT	0.352		0.430		0.419		0.406		0.364		0.357		0.382	
ci	0.349	0.355	0.426	0.433	0.416	0.422	0.403	0.409	0.361	0.367	0.354	0.360	0.379	0.385
LU	0.256		0.365		0.351		0.335		0.269		0.262		0.319	
ci	0.253	0.260	0.360	0.370	0.347	0.355	0.331	0.339	0.266	0.273	0.259	0.265	0.314	0.324
NL	0.250		0.311		0.352		0.323		0.276		0.255		0.300	
ci	0.247	0.252	0.308	0.315	0.348	0.356	0.319	0.326	0.273	0.279	0.253	0.258	0.296	0.304
PT	0.358		0.420		0.416		0.396		0.377		0.366		0.401	
ci	0.353	0.362	0.415	0.424	0.412	0.421	0.391	0.400	0.373	0.381	0.362	0.370	0.397	0.406
SP	0.328		0.426		0.400		0.386		0.341		0.328		0.374	
ci	0.325	0.330	0.423	0.429	0.398	0.403	0.383	0.388	0.339	0.344	0.326	0.330	0.371	0.377
SW	0.299		0.427		0.458		0.415		0.336		0.301		0.326	
ci	0.294	0.304	0.422	0.432	0.454	0.463	0.409	0.420	0.331	0.340	0.296	0.305	0.322	0.330
UK	0.313		0.354		0.448		0.356		0.395		0.321		0.347	
ci	0.310	0.315	0.352	0.357	0.445	0.451	0.353	0.358	0.392	0.397	0.319	0.323	0.345	0.350
EU-15	0.300		0.376		0.388		0.358		0.327		0.312		0.338	
ci	0.299	0.301	0.374	0.377	0.387	0.390	0.357	0.359	0.326	0.328	0.311	0.313	0.337	0.339

Note: The statistical reliability of the estimates is shown using confidence intervals that have been constructed to be significant at the 5 percent level: that is, +/− 1.96 × estimated standard error.
Source: EUROMOD.

tax burdens in these countries there is, therefore, considerable potential to alter the distribution of incomes and so a progressive income tax will tend to be highly redistributive. Yet Figure 5.6 also shows that the other countries with a highly redistributive income tax achieve a similar reduction of the Gini coefficient despite much lower income tax burdens, indicating a higher degree of tax progressivity in these countries.[17] A moderate degree of redistribution through income taxes is achieved in Greece, Portugal and the United Kingdom (in Portugal income taxes are nevertheless the most redistributive of all instruments). The redistributive effect of taxes is low in Italy, France and—despite large tax burdens—Sweden.[18]

Summarizing, we find that countries with a relatively low level of disposable income inequality, are characterized by a high redistributive effect of both non-means-tested benefits and income taxes. Countries with a relatively high level of disposable income inequality either show a low redistributive effect for all instruments (such as Southern Europe) or a high redistributive effect for means-tested benefits only (Ireland and United Kingdom).

5.6 Conclusion

The variation in size and structure of direct taxes and cash benefits in the Member States of the EU is one of the prime determinants of differences in income inequality across countries. In this chapter we have investigated the role of different components of tax-benefit systems in the cross-sectional inequality of disposable household income. Unlike many other international studies, the analysis encompasses both direct taxes and cash benefits, and it covers all 15 pre-2004 member countries of the EU in a manner that provides results which are conceptually consistent and comparable across countries. A microsimulation approach is employed, which allows some of the measurement problems normally encountered in comparative research on income inequality to be addressed. The most obvious advantage is that this approach permits an analysis of taxes and benefits based on datasets that do not provide information on these variables at all, or not with the desired level of detail. More generally, it makes the analysis of taxes and benefits less dependent on the precise definition of these variables in the underlying data and differences in the definitions across countries. By ensuring a consistent application of the legal rules governing tax liabilities and benefit entitlements across countries, the resulting tax and benefit amounts are potentially more comparable than tax and benefit variables recorded in the original microdata sources. Further, the simulation approach provides greater analytical flexibility as it allows sub-categories of taxes and benefits to be defined consistently across countries and independently of definitions adopted by the data providers. Thus, analytical choices are not simply driven by data availability. In this study we explore separately the effects of income taxes, social contributions, public pensions and other non-means-tested and means-tested benefits. Finally, the generation of results at the micro-level for all 15 countries allows inequality measures to be reported for the EU-15 as a whole, as well as for each country.

For the EU-15 as a whole, the Gini coefficient for market income (0.47) is similar to that of Belgium, Finland, Germany or Luxembourg. Public pensions reduce this to 0.41 while the redistribution achieved by all tax and benefit components taken together reduces inequality to a level comparable to Sweden (0.30). The overall redistributive effect is in absolute terms of similar size to that in the Netherlands and the United Kingdom and in relative terms (taking account of the starting level of market inequality) closest to that of Spain.

Countries that achieve a high level of inequality reduction through their tax-benefit system do this mainly by using non-means-tested benefits and taxes. This is the case for the Scandinavian countries and most of the continental welfare states. A low degree of redistribution is achieved in Southern Europe, except in the case of Spain, if pensions are considered as part of the redistributive system. The redistributive effect of taxes and transfers is somewhat higher in Ireland and the United Kingdom, which mainly rely on means-tested benefits.

Pensions can be considered as a redistributive instrument between individuals at a point in time or as a means of saving by a single individual over time. Both aspects are present to some extent in all pension systems. While it is not possible to distinguish the savings function of pensions from the redistributive, we have shown that the equalizing effect of public pensions within a particular year is small in Ireland and the United Kingdom, where pensions are primarily provided through the private sector. However, in all other countries our results show that state pensions have a strong equalizing effect, which justifies some consideration of their redistributive role at a moment in time.

The analysis presented here raises questions to be explored in further work. First, we have relied on the standard Gini coefficient to measure inequality. Other measures, with different sets of welfare preferences embodied in them, could result in different rankings of countries. Second, we have focused on the redistributive, or equalizing, properties of taxes and benefits without investigating the extent to which the size and design of the instruments play a role. Unpacking the redistributive effect into components corresponding to the progressivity of the instrument, the size of the instrument and the extent of re-ranking when the instrument is applied, would inform our understanding of how and why some systems are more equalizing than others. Finally, the key equalizing role of non-means-tested benefits in many systems deserves further investigation. Non-means-tested benefits consist mainly of unemployment benefits, pensions paid to the non-elderly and universal benefits (mainly child benefits) in most countries. It would be interesting to further 'dissect' this group of benefits, as their distributional characteristics are likely to be different and to vary among countries.

Appendix

Table 5.A.1 EUROMOD source data

Country	Base dataset for EUROMOD	Date of collection	Reference time period for incomes
Austria	Austrian version of European Community Household Panel	1998 + 1999	annual 1998
Belgium	Panel Survey on Belgian Households	1999	annual 1998
Denmark	European Community Household Panel	1995	annual 1994
Finland	Income distribution survey	1998	annual 1998
France	Budget de Famille	1994/5	annual 1993/4
Germany	German Socio-Economic Panel	1998	annual 1997
Greece	European Community Household Panel	1995	annual 1994
Ireland	Living in Ireland Survey	1994	month in 1994
Italy	Survey of Households Income and Wealth	1996	annual 1995
Luxembourg	PSELL-2	1999	annual 1998
Netherlands	Sociaal-economisch panelonderzoek	1996	annual 1995
Portugal	European Community Household Panel	1996	annual 1995
Spain	European Community Household Panel	1996	annual 1995
Sweden	Income distribution survey	1997	annual 1997
UK	Family Expenditure Survey	1995/6	month in 1995/6

Table 5.A.2 Categorization of public pension and means-tested benefit income components

In this appendix we explain which variables are included in our concepts of *pension incomes* and *means tested benefits* and discuss the issues to be considered in such classifications.

Pension Incomes

Our understanding of pension income can be roughly defined as state enforced savings. However, this includes not only the classical form of social insurance pensions but also general tax financed pension schemes, for example the Danish old-age pension, received by almost all Danes reaching the age of 67 (lowered to 65 in 2004).

We do not consider means-tested old-age schemes as pensions, unless they are an integral part of the pension system. If low pensions are topped up to reach a certain minimum, then we count these supplements as pension income. This distinction can be somewhat arbitrary in practice. Other means-tested schemes for the elderly are included as means-tested benefits (see below).

As in some countries, early retirement pensions are used as a substitute for unemployment benefits, we restrict our pension definition to retirement benefits granted to people aged 65 or older. In the same sense, invalidity pensions are not included in the pensions measure, as they are state insurance for other 'risks' than old age. On the other hand, we include non-means-tested survivor's pensions (for those aged 65+). Where invalidity pensions are paid instead of retirement pensions to people aged 65 or more, then these are treated as pension income.

Finally, some non-pension benefits apply specific rules to the elderly. For example, rules are different for the elderly in Finnish and Danish housing benefits. Such benefits are not included in the pensions category.

The income components included for each country as pensions are listed below:

AUSTRIA
- minimum pension
- minimum pension for civil servants
- child bonus for pensioners
- child bonus for civil service pensioners
- civil servant's pension
- early retirement pension invalidity pension
- old-age pension
- other old age-related schemes or benefits
- survivor pension

BELGIUM
- anticipated pension
- other public pensions
- retirement pension
- survivor pension

DENMARK
- disability pension – basic amount plus supplement
- disability pension – special supplement plus incapacity amount
- disability pension – invalidity amount plus 'augmentation' plus special benefit for disabled with substantial earnings
- old-age pension
- supplementary pension
- survivor pension

FINLAND
- gross state pension income*
- national (basic) pension increases

FRANCE
- minimum old-age pension
- pension benefits
- alimony
- pre-retirement pension

GERMANY
- own old-age pension
- miners' own pension
- civil servants' own pension
- farmers' own pension
- widow/orphan old-age pension
- miners' widow/orphan pension
- civil servants' widow/orphan pension
- farmers' widow/orphan pension
- accident widow/orphan pension

GREECE
- farmers' pension
- social solidarity benefit
- state pension
- invalidity pension (contributory)
- state survivor's pension

IRELAND
- deserted wife contributory benefits
- occupational injury contributory pension
- old age contributory benefits
- retirement contributory benefits
- survivor's contributory benefits

ITALY
- public and private sector old age contributory pensions
- public and private sector contributory disability pensions
- public and private sector contributory survivor's pensions
- supplement paid on old-age pensions – public and private sector
- supplement paid on disability pensions – public and private sector
- supplement paid on survivor's pensions – public and private sector
- foreign pension

LUXEMBOURG
- disability pension
- early retirement pension
- pension received from employment in private sector
- pension received from employment in public sector
- private sector reversion pension
- public sector reversion pension

NETHERLANDS
- state pension
- survivors' benefit

PORTUGAL
- old-age insurance
- old-age agricultural insurance
- survivors related benefits

SPAIN
- old-age pension supplement
- widow pension supplement
- old-age (insurance and early retirement) survivors (widows or orphans, insurance)

SWEDEN
- non-taxable pension
- other taxable pensions

UK
- widow benefit
- basic retirement pension
- state earnings-related pension

---

* includes some occupational pension income.

Means-Tested Benefits

Our definition of means-tested benefits is intended to cover all benefits that depend on an assessment of current income. It includes all benefits with an earnings or income test, even if the limit does not confine entitlement to the poor or near-poor. Thus it includes 'affluence-tested' benefits as well as those targeted on the lowest incomes. Similarly, benefits that are more generous to people with low income than to people with high income are included in the means-tested category, even if the 'rich' are in principle eligible for some amount. So benefits with non-means-tested basic amounts plus means tested supplements are defined here as means-tested. In practice the distinction can be rather arbitrary since there are examples of benefits that are essentially universal, with relatively small means-tested top-ups, or benefits that apply in a similar way to different groups with means-testing only operating in some variants (the Belgian child benefit is an example). The list below shows the benefits that are considered as means tested for each country in this study:

AUSTRIA
- maternity allowance supplement
- new born health check bonus
- provincial family bonus
- social assistance
- small children benefit
- unemployment benefit
- housing benefits

BELGIUM
- income support
- income support for the elderly

DENMARK
- housing benefit
- day care subsidy
- housing allowance
- social assistance

FINLAND
- housing benefit
- home child care benefit
- social assistance benefit
- pensioners housing benefit

FRANCE
- disabled benefit
- young children allowance
- education-related family benefits
- family complement
- housing benefits
- lone parent benefit
- minimum income

GERMANY
- housing benefit
- federal child raising benefit
- direct housing support
- provincial child raising benefit
- social assistance

GREECE
- child allowance
- large family benefit
- third child benefit
- unprotected child benefit
- social pension

IRELAND
- housing benefit
- blind persons non-contributory benefits
- carer's non-contributory benefits
- short-term disabled contributory benefits
- long-term disabled non-contributory benefits

ITALY
- family allowances for single persons with no children
- family allowances for single person with children
- family allowances for couples with no children
- family allowances for couples with children

- deserted wives
  non-contributory benefits
- family income
  supplement
- long-term invalidity
  contributory benefits
- lone parent
  non-contributory benefits
- long-term unemployed
  non-contributory benefits
- old age non-contributory
  benefits
- pre-retirement
  non-contributory benefits
- short-term unemployed
  non-contributory benefits
- social minimum
  non-contributory benefits
- widow's non-contributory
  benefits

LUXEMBOURG
- education allowance
- housing benefit
- maternity allowance
- social assistance

NETHERLANDS
- housing benefit
- social assistance for
  unemployed aged 50–64
  and disabled unemployed
  under 64 with children
- general social assistance
  for families with children
- social assistance for
  unemployed aged 50–64
  and disabled unemployed
  under 64 without
  children
- general social assistance
  for families w/o children
- general social assistance,
  self-employed

PORTUGAL
- child benefits
- income supplement
  to ensure minimum
  income
- social assistance

SPAIN
- child benefit
- old-age social
  assistance
- unemployed social
  assistance for
  those with family
  responsibility
- social assistance
  benefits

SWEDEN
- housing benefits
- housing benefit
  supplement for
  pensioners
- social assistance

UK
- housing benefit
- council tax benefit
- family credit
- income support

Notes

1. Acknowledgements: This paper was written as part of the MICRESA (Micro Level Analysis of the European Social Agenda) project, financed by the *Improving Human Potential Programme* of the European Commission (SERD-2001-00099). We are indebted to all past and current members of the EUROMOD consortium and to Stephen Jenkins for helpful comments on an early draft. The views expressed in this chapter, as well as any errors, are the responsibilities of the authors and do not implicate the institutions to which they are affiliated. In particular, this applies to the interpretation of model results and any errors in its use. EUROMOD is continually being improved and updated and the results presented here represent work in progress. EUROMOD relies on microdata from 12 different sources for 15 countries. These are the ECHP User Data Base made available by Eurostat; the Austrian version of the ECHP made available by the Interdisciplinary Centre for Comparative Research in the Social Sciences; the Panel Survey on Belgian Households (PSBH) made available by the Universities of Liège and Antwerp; the Income Distribution Survey made available by Statistics Finland; the Enquête sur les Budgets Familiaux (EBF) made available by INSEE; the public-use version of the German Socio Economic Panel Study (GSOEP) made available by the German Institute for Economic Research (DIW), Berlin; the Living in Ireland Survey made available by the Economic and Social Research Institute; the Survey of Household Income and Wealth (SHIW95) made available by the Bank of Italy; the Socio-Economic Panel for Luxembourg (PSELL-2) made available by CEPS/INSTEAD; the Socio-Economic Panel Survey (SEP) made available by Statistics Netherlands through the mediation of the Netherlands Organization for Scientific Research—Scientific Statistical Agency; the Income Distribution Survey made available by Statistics Sweden; and the Family Expenditure Survey (FES) made available by the United Kingdom Office for National Statistics (ONS) through the Data Archive. Material from the FES is Crown Copyright and is used by permission. Neither the ONS nor the Data Archive bears any responsibility for the analysis or interpretation of the data reported here. An equivalent disclaimer applies for all other data sources and their respective providers cited in this acknowledgement.

2. Wagstaff and van Doorslaer (2001), Wagstaff, *et al.* (1999). Older studies are Berglas (1971), Kakwani (1977), and Zandvakili (1994). A recent study uses EUROMOD to estimate redistribution and progressivity characteristics of personal income taxes and social contributions for 15 EU countries (Verbist, 2004). O'Donoghue *et al.* (2004) make use of EUROMOD to consider redistribution of taxes and social benefits in the EU-15, with a primary focus on the role of indirect taxes.

3. For the member states of the EU, the ECHP was established in the 1990s. See Eurostat (1996) for details on the methodology. The final wave of the ECHP was collected in 2001 and its successor, the SILC, is planned to provide data from 2004 onwards. For some countries, doubts have been expressed about the accuracy of the ECHP data (Cantillon, *et al.*, 2003; Peracchi, 2002).

4. For example, in an analysis of the redistributive characteristics of income taxes, Wagstaff, *et al.* (1999) use simulated income tax amounts for a sub-set of the countries analyzed.

5. See Immervoll, *et al.* (1999), Sutherland (2000) and visit http://www.iser.essex.ac.uk/msu/emod.php for more information and access to EUROMOD Working Papers.

6. Notable differences across countries in the underlying data sources that should be borne in mind when interpreting results include:

   a) For Sweden, income is aggregated over the narrow family unit (single person or couple plus children aged under 18, such that individuals aged 18 or more are all treated as not living with their parents), whereas for other countries the data allow us to adopt a wider household definition—all people living in one dwelling and sharing some of the costs of living. Also for Sweden, income from capital gains is included, as are the incomes of people living for part of the year. These differences relative to the calculations for other countries are likely to lead to higher measured inequality in Sweden.

   b) The reference time period for incomes for most countries is one year, but for Ireland and the UK it is shorter (a month or a week for most sources of income). Detailed descriptions of the structure of tax-benefit systems as well as validations of EUROMOD results against available external statistics in each country can be found in individual 'country reports' on the website http://www.iser.essex.ac.uk/msu/emod.php.

7. The standard Gini indicator represents one of many possible approaches for aggregating observed income inequalities into one overall measure (using the same weight for each observation regardless of income level (Donaldson and Weymark, 1980; Yitzhaki, 1983). A planned extension of this chapter will use the generalized version of the Gini index to explore the sensitivity of results to alternative weighting schemes giving, for instance, more weight to inequalities at lower income levels.

8. Arguably when adopting the starting point, which includes public pension income in market income, the element of social contributions that covers pensions should also be deducted from market income rather then being considered as part of the redistributive system. This is not done in this chapter, because of the difficulty in some countries in assigning a component of contributions to pensions.

9. This assigns a weight of 1 to the household head, weights of 0.5 to every other adult in the household and 0.3 to each child (person aged below 14) in the household.

10. Incomes in Euro are divided by the OECD purchasing power adjustment factors for GDP as follows: AT: 0.9401, BE: 0.9304, DK: 1.1369, FI: 0.9718, FR: 0.9284, GE: 1.0057, GR: 0.6652, IR: 0.8734, IT: 0.8019, LU: 1.0112, NL: 0.9103, PT: 0.6467, SP: 0.7344, SW: 1.0756, United Kingdom: 0.9341. For Denmark, Sweden and the United Kingdom, respectively, the following Euro exchange rates are used: 7.511, 8.807 and 0.6783.

11. In most countries, total employer social insurance contributions, which are not included in the calculations, are of a similar or greater magnitude to employee-paid contributions (Austria, Belgium, Finland, France, Germany, Greece, Italy, Luxembourg, Portugal, Spain).

12. In fact, 0.3 percent for both taxes and contributions.

13. In most individual countries, 1000 replications were used. For the EU-15 as a whole, 100 replications were carried out.

14. To a degree, this result also captures behavioral incentives associated with tax-benefit systems, where the presence of strong income replacement instruments can result in reduced labor supply by those with low earnings potential, and thus lower market income inequality.

15. Even when measured over the lifetime, public pensions tend to exhibit considerable inter-personal redistribution as a result of widely used design features such as minimum pension guarantees and benefit ceilings in earnings-related pension schemes.
16. Note that, using this approach, the sizes of the effects shown in Figure 5.6 do not sum to the overall *RE* shown in Figure 5.5.
17. An analysis of the individual driving factors of the redistributive effect (size of the tax or benefit instrument, progressivity and re-ranking effect) in European tax-benefit systems is the subject of follow-up work to the present chapter.
18. The division of countries in high, moderate and low redistributive effect through taxes is close but not identical to that found by Verbist (2004), who also uses EUROMOD. The high *RE* countries are Austria, Belgium, Denmark, Finland, Germany and Luxembourg. The group with a moderate *RE* consists of Ireland, Netherlands, Portugal, United Kingdom; and those with a low *RE* are France, Greece, Italy, Spain, Sweden. This study investigates the effect of taxes and contributions in combination, rather than separately.

References

Atkinson A. B. and H. Sutherland (1988) *Tax-Benefit Models*, STICERD (London: London School of Economics).
Atkinson A. B., L. Rainwater and T. Smeeding (1995) *Income Distribution in OECD Countries. Evidence from the Luxembourg Income Study* (Paris: OECD).
Berglas E. (1971) 'Income Tax and the Distribution of Income: An International Comparison,' *Public Finance/Finances Publiques* 26: 532–45.
Boadway R. and M. Keen (2000) 'Redistribution,' in A. B. Atkinson & F. Bourguignon, *Handbook of Income Distribution*, Volume 1, pp. 677–789.
Burniaux J.-M., T.-T. Dang, D. Fore, M. F. Förster, M. Mira d'Ercole and H. Oxley (1998) 'Income Distribution and Poverty in Selected OECD Countries,' Economics Department Working Paper 189 (OECD).
Canberra Group (2001) *Final Report and Recommendations* (Ottawa: The Canberra Group: Expert Group on Household Income Statistics).
Cantillon B., R. Van Dam, K. Van den Bosch and B. Van Hoorebeeck (2003) 'The Impact of the Reference Period on Measures of Household Income from Surveys,' CSB-berichten (Antwerp: Centre for Social Policy).
Deleeck H., K. Van den Bosch and L. De Lathouwer (1992) *Poverty and Adequacy of Social Security in the EC. A Comparative Analysis* (Avebury: Aldershot).
Donaldson D. and J. A. Weymark (1980) 'A Single Parameter Generalization of the Gini Indices of Inequality', *Journal of Economic Theory* 22: 67–86.
Duclos J.-Y. (1993) 'Progressivity, Redistribution, and Equity, with Application to the British Tax and Benefit System,' *Public Finance* 48(3): 350–65.
Eardley T., J. Bradshaw, J. Ditch, I. Gough and P. Whiteford (1996) *Social Assistance in OECD Countries: Synthesis Report* (London: HMSO).
Eurostat (1996) *The European Community Household Panel (ECHP): Survey Methodology and Implementation*, Theme 3, Series E (Luxembourg: Eurostat).
Förster M. and M. Mira d'Ercole (2005) 'Income Distribution and Poverty in OECD Countries in the Second Half of the 1990s,' OECD Social, Employment and Migration Working Papers 22 (Paris: OECD).
Heady C., T. Mitrakos and P. Tsakloglou (2001) 'The Distributional Impact of Social Transfers in the European Union: Evidence from the ECHP,' *Fiscal Studies* 22: 547–65.

Immervoll H., C. O'Donoghue and H. Sutherland (1999) 'An Introduction to EUROMOD,' EUROMOD Working Paper EM0/99, www.iser.essex.ac.uk/msu/emod/publications/emwp0.pdf.

Kakwani N. (1977) 'Measurement of Tax Progressivity: An International Comparison,' *Economic Journal* **87**: 71–80.

Krupp H. J. (1986) 'Potential and Limitations of Microsimulation Models,' in G. Orcutt, J. Merz & H. Quinke (eds), *Microanalytic Simulation Models to Support Social and Financial Policy* (North Holland: Elsevier Science Publishers), pp. 31–43.

Mantovani D. and H. Sutherland (2003) 'Social Indicators and Other Income Statistics Using the EUROMOD Baseline: A Comparison with Eurostat and National Statistics,' EUROMOD Working Paper EM1/03, www.iser.essex.ac.uk/msu/emod/publications/emwp103.pdf.

O'Donoghue C., M. Baldini and D. Mantovani (2004) 'Modelling the Redistributive Impact of Indirect Taxes in Europe: An Application of EUROMOD,' EUROMOD Working Paper EM7/01, www.iser.essex.ac.uk/msu/emod/publications/emwp701.pdf.

OECD (2004) *Benefits and Wages. OECD Indicators* (Paris: OECD).

Peracchi F. (2002) 'The European Community Household Panel: A Review,' *Empirical Economics* **27**: 63–90.

Smeeding T. and A. Grodner (2000) 'Changing Income Inequality in OECD Countries: Updated Results from the Luxembourg Income Study (LIS),' LIS Working Paper 252 (Luxembourg: Luxembourg Income Study).

Sutherland H. (2000) 'EUROMOD,' in Gupta A. & V. Kapur (eds), *Microsimulation in Government Policy and Forecasting* (Elsevier), pp. 575–80.

Verbist G. (2005) 'Replacement incomes and Taxes in the EU: An International Comparison Using EUROMOD,' EUROMOD Working Paper EM2/05, www.iser.essex.ac.uk/msu/emod/publications/emwp205.pdf.

Verbist G. (2004) 'Redistributive Effect and Progressivity of Income Taxes: An International Comparison Across the EU Using EUROMOD,' EUROMOD Working Paper EM5/04, www.iser.essex.ac.uk/msu/emod/publications/emwp504.pdf.

Wagstaff A. and E. van Doorslaer (2001) 'What Makes the Personal Income Tax Progressive? A Comparative Analysis for Fifteen OECD Countries,' *International Tax and Public Finance* **8**(3): 299–316.

Wagstaff A., E. van Doorslaer, H. van der Burg, S. Calonge, T. Christiansen, G. Citoni, U.-G. Gerdtham, M. Gerfin, L. Gross, U. Häkinnen, J. John, P. Johnson, J. Klavus, C. Lachaud, J. Lauridsen, R. E. Leu, B. Nolan, E. Peran, C. Propper, F. Puffer, L. Rochaix, M. Rodriguez, M. Schellhorn, G. Sundberg and O. Winkelhake (1999) 'Redistributive Effect, Progressivity and Differential Tax Treatment: Personal Income Taxes in Twelve OECD Countries,' *Journal of Public Economics* **72**: 73–98.

Whitehouse E. (2000) 'How Poor are the Old? A Survey of Evidence from 44 Countries,' Social Protection Discussion Papers (Washington: World Bank).

Yitzhaki S. (1983) 'On an Extension of the Gini Index,' *International Economic Review* **24**: 617–28.

Zandvakili S. (1994) 'Income Distribution and Redistribution Through Taxation: An International Comparison,' *Empirical Economics* **19**: 473–91.

6
Distributional Effects of Evolving Spending and Tax Policies in Post-Socialist Poland

Leon Podkaminer

6.1 Some prehistory

Poland's socialist economic system, which collapsed in 1989 after a decade of gradual disintegration, was highly egalitarian. Wages and other incomes in the public sector, the main employer, were largely set administratively—with the explicit aim of assuring a 'fair' distribution of income and consumption. Incomes in the private sector were also regulated, either through direct taxation (often quite discretionary) or via administrative controls of prices of that sector's products and of its production inputs supplied by the public sector. Within that system private farming, accounting for about one fourth of total employment, had a privileged position, with the average per capita income consistently higher than in the public sector. The comprehensive incomes policy stipulating low levels of inequality in personal incomes and 'wealth' was complemented by a generous public pension system. All kinds of education were free, as were the services of the public health system. With full employment (endemic and acute shortages of labor), the system did not generate extensive areas of poverty, malnutrition or homelessness.

6.2 'Shock therapy'

At the beginning of 1990, Poland's economic system was radically over-hauled. All administrative controls, including those on prices and incomes, were lifted and the old state apparatus controlling the economy was disbanded. Publicly owned firms, banks, etc. were commercialized, some of them quickly privatized and some went bankrupt and were liquidated within months. Free enterprise of all sorts emerged spontaneously—and the unemployment rate rose from 0 to about 6.5 percent within one year (Figure 6.1). Huge untaxed fortunes were made rapidly while incomes and living standards of large segments of the population (private farmers among others) fell precipitously. In 1990 alone, the average real wage fell by about 25 percent,

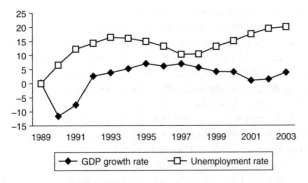

Figure 6.1 GDP growth rate, unemployment rate, 1989–2003

and farmers' real incomes by about 50 percent. Retirement pay lost some 15 percent of its real value.

Initially (in 1990 and 1991), the official policy response to what was happening to incomes and living standards was inaction. First, a new tax legislation had yet to be adopted and a new tax apparatus created, and social spending faced similar challenges. Second, the then prevailing official view was that cuts in incomes were necessary for preventing hyperinflation. Besides, it was claimed (at least in 1990) that income dislocations would quickly correct themselves once the unleashed market forces produced fast growth and full employment. In fact, the high inflation subsided slowly while the GDP fell cumulatively to about 20 percent in 1990–91 and the unemployment rate kept rising until 1993, reaching a (local) maximum of about 16 percent.

The dismal effects of the protracted 'shock therapy' of 1990–91 forced some policy changes on taxation and social spending. In late 1991, the doctrinaire *laissez-faire* ideologists guiding the policy were replaced by more pragmatically minded persons. The former returned to power in late 1997.

6.3 The evolution of the tax system: a general overview

Until 1992, the budgetary revenue came almost exclusively from various taxes and charges levied on the surviving publicly owned firms. In part, that was a consequence of the fact that only those firms maintained proper book-keeping, but there was also an ideological motive. The heavy tax burden placed on publicly owned firms was to encourage privatization. Financially oppressed public firms became easy prey for the emerging private business. Confiscatory taxation facilitated the transfer of public assets into private hands. From 1992, a single corporate tax code has been in force, with a uniform corporate income tax (CIT) rate. The CIT rate was 40 percent from 1992 through to 1996. But foreign direct investment was—and still is—treated preferentially. Larger foreign investors usually enjoy long tax holidays, or even receive subsidies. This extends not only to greenfield investment, as it is not uncommon for foreign investors to buy privatized firms at large discounts—and then receive subsidies and be offered tax privileges. Thereafter, the CIT rate was reduced by 2 percentage points each year, to 24 percent in 2003. The current 2004 rate of 19 percent is likely to remain unchanged for some time, also on account of the reactions of the German and French governments accusing Poland of 'unfair' tax competition.

Personal income taxes (PIT) were also introduced in 1992. The PIT system defines three inflation-indexed income brackets. The initial PIT rates were 20, 30 and 40 percent, and in 1994 these were raised to 21, 33 and 45 percent. Then in 1997 the rates were reduced to 20, 32 and 44 percent. The current rates, 19, 30 and 40 percent, have been in force since 1998. The complex system of tax allowances and deductions has been changing almost continuously.

A new system of indirect taxes, introduced in 1993, replaced the former turnover tax. The basic value added tax (VAT) rate has been 22 percent, which is relatively high. Over time there has been a gradual contraction of the list of items taxed with reduced (7 and 3 percent) VAT rates, or exempt from that tax. Simultaneously there has been a tendency to raise excise tax rates, not only on 'bad goods' such as alcohol and tobacco, but also on fuels and electricity.

Inheritance and property (wealth) other than land are practically untaxed, as is the capital gains income.

6.4   Trends in tax collection

The 'post-shock' recovery, which started in 1992, was associated with a marked change in taxation and spending. Already by 1992 the shares of both revenues and expenditure of the general government in the GDP rose sharply. Both shares increased further in 1993–94 and stayed at relatively high levels through to 1997. Thereafter there was a fast decline in the revenue share—associated with much lower shares of expenditure, including social security transfers (see Table 6.1).

The changes in the taxes collected by the central government, which are a major part of the total revenue of the general government—with the difference between the two made up by non-tax revenues of the central government, such as customs, privatization proceeds, social contributions collected by public pension and health funds, etc.—accurately reflect the changes in the total revenue of the general government. The decline in the share of taxes collected by the central government between the mid-1990s and the early 2000s is about 7 percentage points, while the share of general government's revenue fell some 8–10 percentage points.

The revolutionary (and probably unprecedented) reduction of the shares of taxes/revenues, which took place in 1998–2001, reflects the radical changes in personal income and corporate taxation. In 1999 the share of CIT

Table 6.1 Selected fiscal indicators, 1990–2002 (all items as percent of GDP)

	Revenue gen. govt.	Taxes*	CIT*	PIT*	(CIT+PIT)*	Indirect taxes*	Expenditure	
							gen. govt.	Soc. sec. expend.
1990	46.3	27.6	15.2	0	15.2	7.1	42.6	11.3
1991	39.8	20.2	6.6	0	6.6	7.6	43.4	17.4
1992	45.2	21.4	4.4	6.3	10.7	9.0	50.0	19.9
1993	47.7	23.7	4.0	7.7	11.7	11.4	50.0	20.6
1994	48.3	23.2	3.2	8.4	11.7	12.8	50.4	21.6
1995	47.4	24.8	4.0	8.1	12.2	12.6	49.2	19.8
1996	47.0	22.9	2.7	7.2	10.0	12.9	49.3	18.8
1997	46.5	22.2	3.0	6.7	9.7	12.4	48.1	19.4
1998	44.5	22.3	2.9	6.8	9.7	12.6	43.8	18.5
1999	41.1	18.3	2.4	3.7	6.2	12.1	44.3	18.2
2000	39.7	17.5	2.3	3.2	5.8	11.6	42.8	17.4
2001	38.8	15.9	1.8	3.1	4.9	11.0	43.9	17.2
2002	38.5	16.7	2.0	3.1	5.1	11.6	44.4	17.9

Note: Asterisked items cover taxes collected by the central government.
Source: Yearbooks of the Central Statistical Office. The last column: Mackiewicz *et al.* (2002) for the years 1989–2000, and own calculations (for 2001–02).

collected was halved. The decline in the shares of collected social security contributions, which was also massive, will be discussed later. The share of PIT collected in the 2000s is also about half of what it was over the years 1992–96. The share of indirect taxes collected is roughly constant and the weight of indirect taxes in all taxes has been on the rise.

The falling overall burden of taxation forced cuts in spending, including social security transfers, by about 2–3 percentage points between 1992–95 and 2000–02.

There is little doubt that the policy inaugurated in the late 1990s stipulates a kind of 'reverse-redistribution,' with relatively lower corporate and personal income taxes appearing to be coupled with relatively lower social transfers.

6.5 PIT: a flat tax system for 95 percent of taxpayers

All natural persons receiving income of any sort, including very low retirement and disability payments or unemployment benefits, are taxed with PIT. Individuals whose incomes place them below the official poverty line are liable as well. Only farmers, including the very prosperous, are exempted from PIT. About 95 percent of all taxpayers fall into the first (i.e., the lowest) income bracket, thus for 95 percent of the taxpayers, the PIT is actually a flat tax system. Little is known about the effective PIT tax rates (allowing for deductions and a tax-free income threshold, a very low one) for the first

Table 6.2 Selected data on PIT in 1997 and 2003

		Shares (%)		Effective tax rate (%)
		Number of taxpayers	Taxable income	Tax collected	
1997	1st bracket	94.6	76.7	67.0	15.0
	2nd bracket	4.4	12.4	13.2	18.3
	3rd bracket	1.0	11.0	19.8	30.9
2003	1st bracket	94.7	75.7	65.0	14.1
	2nd bracket	4.1	13.5	15.8	19.3
	3rd bracket	1.2	11.0	19.2	29.2

Source: Author's calculations based on Ministry of Finance reports.

bracket taxpayers. There are good grounds to believe that within that bracket the effective tax rate actually falls with rising taxable income. Major deductions are linked to expenses on upgrading housing facilities and acquisition of flats/homes. The poorest of the first bracket taxpayers are unlikely to have such expenses. Moreover, there are some lower (as well as upper) limits for the expenses in question to be deducible.

The nominal personal income tax rates, reduced in 1998, changed the progression in that taxation across the income brackets. Effective PIT tax rates have also been changing, following the ongoing changes in regulations on various deductions and exemptions. Comparisons of the current and pre-1998 effective tax rates on incomes from different brackets are fraught with difficulties, because in 1999 the definitions of some components of the taxable personal income were changed. An admittedly tentative analysis of the Finance Ministry's statistics on PIT collected in 1997 and 2003, suggests that the effective tax rate fell the most for the highest-income taxpayers (see Table 6.2). The effective tax rate for the second bracket taxpayers appears to have increased. The effective tax rate for the first bracket decreased also.

Interestingly, in absolute terms the number of taxpayers from the first bracket fell by 0.8 percent and by 8 percent in the second bracket. The overall number of taxpayers fell by 0.3 percent. This is one indication of the growing income disparities. Overall, a larger number of persons who had earned taxable income in 1997 had no such income by 2003.

6.6 Taxes, social security contributions, social transfers received in relation to gross disposable income of major sub-sectors of the household sector

Trends in PIT tell only part of the story on the distribution of the actual tax burden. Apart from PIT there are other taxes—first of all, the obligatory social security contributions. The national accounts statistics for the 2000s

Table 6.3 Selected income/tax items for three sub-sectors of the household sector in 2002

	Gross primary income	Taxes on income and wealth	Contributions to social security and public health system	Social transfers	Net tax	Gross disposable income
A. Million zlotys						
Farmers	21,063	1,746	4,852	6,865	−267	21,330
Employees	314,356	14,450	86,995	31,634	69,811	244,545
Employers and the self-employed	176,320	11,975	7,160	5,469	13,666	162,654
B. As % of gross primary income						
Farmers	100	8.3	23.0	32.6	−1.3	101.3
Employees	100	4.6	27.7	10.1	22.2	77.8
Employers and the self-employed	100	6.8	4.1	3.1	7.8	92.2

Source: Author's calculations based on CSO Yearbook 2003.

indicate that the distribution of the burden of all taxes (including social security contributions) is highly uneven. This is exemplified by data for 2002. Unfortunately, owing to the changes in national accounting methodology, comparable data for the 1990s are not available.

As can be seen from Table 6.3, farmers' households receive roughly as much in social transfers as they pay in taxes and in social contributions. Net taxes (taxes plus social security contributions minus transfers received) are a relatively small fraction of the gross primary income of the employers' and self-employed households. However, the share of net taxes in the primary income of employees' households is large.

6.7   The major losers: retirees and the unemployed

The average old-age retirement pay received by a person covered by the general pay-as-you-go (PAYG) pension system ranged between 70 percent and 74 percent of the average wage until 1998. Thereafter, the average pension fell strongly in relative terms (to 52 percent in 2000). Currently it stands at about 56 percent of the average wage. The average old-age pension received by a private farmer was about 42 to 43 percent of the average wage until 1998 and since then has been about 33 percent. It is worth adding that the number of the PAYG retirees has been roughly unchanged and the number of retired farmers has been declining. There was no expansion of the ranks of the retired, which might have perhaps justified what has happened to the average pension.

The unemployed have been experiencing even heavier income losses. The average unemployment benefit was about 33 percent of the average wage until 1998. Since 1999, it has been about 20 percent of the average wage. Although the number of unemployed rose from 1.8 million in 1997 to 3.2 million in 2003, the number of recipients of unemployment benefits was contracting rapidly. In the mid-1990s, about half of the unemployed received benefits. Since then, the share of unemployed receiving benefits has been falling, to about 15 percent in 2003.

Strangely enough, both unemployment benefits and the retirement pay continue to be taxed with PIT.

Shrinking social spending and transfers are reflected in estimates of poverty. In 1998, less than 50 percent of individuals lived below the poverty line—in 2001 about 57 percent. The share of individuals living below the absolute poverty line ('subsistence level') increased from 5.6 to 9.5 percent, respectively.[1]

6.8   The fateful reforms of 1998

The overall successful policy conducted from 1992 through to 1997 was significantly changed when the 'conservatives,' who had administered the 'shock therapy' of 1990–91, returned to power in 1998. They first tried, unsuccessfully, to introduce a general flat tax system (with a 21 percent rate) for all personal incomes. Then in one stroke they overhauled the public education, health and social security systems. Out of three reforms, only the first can be rated as moderately successful. Public spending on education rose slightly, from 5.7 percent of GDP in 1997 to 6.0 percent in 2001.[2]

The health service reform turned out to be a disaster. As such, it has been 'reformed' several times since and further radical changes are currently debated. The health reform promised better quality of the services at a lower cost. Overall, the costs of the public health system turned out to be lower indeed—4.2 percent of GDP in 2001, compared to 4.5 percent in 1997—but the quality and quantity of its services fell precipitously. The reform created an entirely new, huge, overpaid and corrupt network of health service administration (whose task is to monitor costs/quality in the health system proper), which siphoned off vast amounts of money. At the same time, the reform encouraged privatization of hospitals and other public health establishments. In fact, the share of the private sector in the gross output of the whole health service sector rose from 10.6 percent in 1997 to 19.7 percent in 2001. A two-tier health system has emerged, with an under-funded public sub-system for the general public and an expensive commercial sub-system for the rich.

The reform of the public (PAYG) system involved cuts in the contributions of the most affluent employees and of all self-employed (excluding farmers, who are on a separate public system almost exclusively publicly funded). An upper limit on obligatory contributions was introduced, while those contributions remain proportional to income for lower incomes (see Table 6.3). This change alone implied a large loss of revenue of the public pension system. That loss accounted for at least 0.4 percent of the GDP in 2002.

Next the reform introduced the principle of individual accounts for all persons covered, with benefits related to cumulated contributions.

A major novelty was a partial privatization of the pension system. All contributors under 30 years of age had to join one of the 20-odd 'second pillars,' privately managed pension funds, whose mandate was to 'multiply' the value of contributions through shrewd investments. All those under 50 had an option of joining, while all over 50 remained in the old PAYG system. Close to 40 percent of the obligatory contribution charged on a 'member' of a private pension fund is redirected to his/her fund—the rest goes, as before, to the public PAYG system. The resulting loss of the current revenue of the latter is then made up by a subsidy from the central government budget. The budget did not have any difficulty in subsidizing the PAYG system in 1999 and 2000 because of abnormally high privatization revenue (2.2 and 3.8 percent of GDP, respectively). However, as the 'family silver' has been sold, the problem has become acute, with high deficits emerging. To make up for the shortfall of the PAYG revenue, the government has to borrow, additionally, an equivalent of about 2 percent of GDP each year, while trying desperately to economize on other items. Luckily, the private pension funds are eager to purchase government bonds. In this way the government borrows (at a high cost) money, which without the whole reform, it would itself appropriate. Clearly, the pension reform turned out to be a bad deal both for the government and for those who bear the consequences of the resultant cuts in government spending. Also it has turned out to be a bad deal for the 'members' of the private funds. The rates of increase in the market value of the pension funds' investment portfolios trail far behind the interest rate on normal longer-term bank deposits. Moreover, the firms managing the funds (most of them foreign) charge basic fees ranging between 5 and 10 percent on the contributions received, apart from other 'costs,' 'provisions,' etc. At least the owners of the managing firms have no reason to be unhappy.

6.9   Conclusion: dubious merits of 'reverse-redistribution'

Poland's transition to a market economy proceeded in stages, with different policies on taxation and spending. During the first stage (1990–91) the former highly redistributive and egalitarian system was subject to a 'shock' treatment. The 'reverse-redistribution,' which was part and parcel of the 'shock' resulted, rather unsurprisingly, in a fast rise in inequality. This was associated with a deep recession, rising unemployment and—eventually—in a crisis of public finances.

During the second stage (1992–97), the policy was generally much more redistributive. The 'tax-and-spend' policy had the expected impact on inequality and poverty.[3] Neither the high levels of redistribution nor declining inequality impaired the overall growth. On the contrary, the economy performed very well. The average GDP growth rate over that period was 5.8 percent; unemployment was reduced strongly, inflation subsided, the current accounts were under control (with large surpluses until 1996) and the general government deficits moderate. Interestingly, high (40 percent) rates of profit taxation happened to coincide with a fast (on average 13.8 percent p.a.) rise in (real) gross fixed investment.

The third stage started in 1998 and during 2004 showed no signs of nearing an end. The levels of taxation and social transfers were quickly reduced and income inequality increased rapidly. The Gini coefficient of inequality in per capita personal consumption rose from 0.286 in 1996 to 0.316 in 1999. The relative position of the recipients of old-age pensions deteriorated strongly. The unemployed suffered even higher losses and poverty, previously falling, has been on the rise. Falling rates of taxation of corporate profits have been associated first with a slowdown of growth of gross fixed investment, followed by its strong contraction in the years 2001–03 (17 percent cumulatively). GDP growth first slowed down, then stagnated in 2001–02. Unemployment expanded strongly. Misguided reforms of the public health and pension systems created huge unproductive deficits in public finances.

The association between the type of policy conducted and the real economic outcomes appears to be strong in the case of Poland. The policy of 'reverse-redistribution' has happened to coincide with an overall performance that has to be rated as poor (past 1998) or dismal (1990–91). The policy stipulating high levels of distribution appears to coincide with outstanding performance.

Of course, this is not to say that other factors have been irrelevant. The monetary and exchange rate policies conducted in 1992–95 were certainly conducive to high and balanced growth during the initial years of the 'distributive' stage. Conversely, those policies were not helpful, to say the least, throughout much of the 'reverse-redistribution' periods (as well as in the closing years of the 'distributive' period, 1995–98). Thus, a general proposition that high levels of redistribution are good for growth (as well as for equality), which is supported by the Polish experience, requires some caveats. On the other hand, in the light of the Polish experience, the opposite proposition—namely that 'reverse-redistribution' is good for growth—sounds utterly extravagant.

Notes

1. Source: Council on Social and Economic Strategy, Report No. 50, Warsaw, 2004.
2. More recent data on the overall public spending on health, education, etc. are not available.
3. This is documented in L. Podkaminer, 'A Note on the Evolution of Inequality in Poland, 1992–99,' *Cambridge Journal of Economics* (2003) 5: 755–68.

References

Council on Social and Economic Strategy (2004) 'Report No. 50' (Warsaw).

Mackiewicz, M., E. Malinowska, W. Misiag and A. Niedzielski (2002) 'Public Finance in Poland 1989–2001. Case Study of Transformation' (Warsaw: The Gdansk Institute for Market Economics).

Podkaminer, L. (2003) 'A Note on the Evolution of Inequality in Poland, 1992–99,' *The Cambridge Journal of Economics* 27: 755–68.

7

The Distribution of Taxes and Government Benefits in Australia*

Ann Harding, Rachel Lloyd and Neil Warren

7.1 Background

Governments influence income distribution in many ways, including through an extensive web of regulatory and non-budgetary policies. However, the distribution of income is more directly affected through the billions of dollars of taxation revenue that government raises annually and the social programs upon which a large part of that revenue is spent. This study examines the distribution and redistribution of income in Australia in 2001–02.

This is a fiscal incidence study, in that it attempts to estimate the impact of selected outlays and taxes upon the income distribution of households. This means that government outlays are attributed as a benefit to individual households, while taxes are attributed as a burden upon individual households.

Allocating the incidence of taxes and benefits is neither a straightforward nor an uncontroversial task. For example, fiscal incidence studies typically assume that the value of one year of primary education in a government school, to a household containing such a primary school student, is the cost to government of providing that year of education (Harding, 1984; ABS, 2001a). But the cost to government may or may not approximate the value that a particular household places upon education, health or other government provided or subsidized services.

Similarly, the incidence of taxes is not uncontroversial. For example, is a tax levied upon companies shifted to consumers (via higher prices) or to shareholders (via lower dividends)? Equally, a tax collected in a jurisdiction, such as Queensland may actually be incident upon international or interstate visitors, rather than upon Queensland households themselves.

Despite these continuing issues, fiscal incidence studies are now well established in both Australia and overseas (Harding, 1984 and 1995; Johnson *et al.*, 1995; Raskall and Urquhart, 1994; Warren, 1997; Harding *et al.*, 2002). In particular, the Australian Bureau of Statistics (ABS) has published a series of fiscal incidence studies, which build upon the results in its Household Expenditure Surveys (HES), and these now act as a benchmark for many Australian studies (1992, 1996, 2001).

7.2 Overview of methodology

It is important to appreciate that not all taxes and benefits are included within the scope of this study and that the results are heavily dependent upon the quality of the household sample survey data used (Siminski *et al.*, 2003) and our assumptions about the usage and cost of government services. The benefits and taxes included are generally restricted to those that are relatable to particular types of households and/or household expenditure— or for which we had data to determine their incidence.

Household income is increased directly by benefits in the form of regular cash payments, such as the age pension and family payments, and indirectly by government expenditures, such as those on health and education. On the other hand, household income is reduced by personal income taxes (direct taxes) and by indirect taxes passed on in the higher prices households pay for goods and services (ABS, 2001, p. 3). Like the ABS fiscal incidence studies, this study excludes some government taxes and expenditures. On the revenue side, we have not considered Commonwealth taxes such as corporate taxes or any of the taxes levied by the various Australian states and territories. (The exclusion of the taxes levied by the Australian states and territories is likely to mean that we overstate the redistributive impact of the tax system as a whole, given that such taxes are overwhelmingly indirect in nature and thus regressive.) On the outlay side, we have not considered spending on such areas as defence, public safety, transport and communications.

In summary, this paper estimates the distribution in 2001–02 of:

- the major social security cash transfers and family payments;
- income tax and selected income tax rebates and concessions, including the private health insurance rebate;
- the Commonwealth 10 percent Goods and Services Tax (GST) plus excises on tobacco, alcohol, crude oil and LPG; and
- health, housing, welfare and education non-cash benefits.

The methodology used in this study is described in more detail in the Appendix to this chapter. The core data source used in the simulation of the 2001–02 world is the 1998–99 HES unit record file released by the ABS. This file contains a snapshot of the demographic, labor force, income and other characteristics of the Australian population in 1998–99. It is important to note that the scope of the survey is restricted to those living in private dwellings and excludes those living in remote and sparsely settled areas. We made some adjustments to this file to update the private incomes, housing costs and population weights from 1998–99 to 2001–02 levels.

7.2.1   Income concepts used

A number of income concepts are used in this study, and these are summarized in Figure 7.1. Original or private income is the narrowest definition of income used, and comprises income from such sources as wages, superannuation, investments and own business. Adding direct government cash benefits to private income gives gross income, which is the income concept used in many ABS studies (ABS, 2001). Disposable income is derived by subtracting direct (or personal income) taxes from gross income. Disposable income, after adjustment for family or household size through use

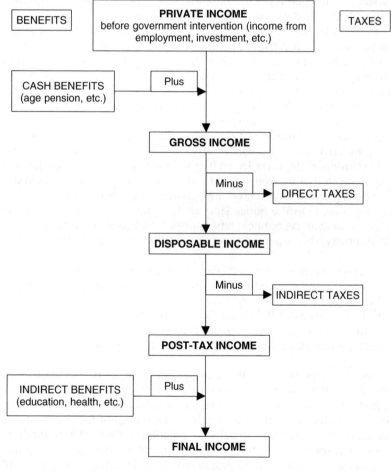

Figure 7.1   Income concepts and stages of redistribution

of an equivalence scale, is the income concept used in the majority of recent Australian studies of income distribution and financial disadvantage (Harding *et al.*, 2001; Saunders, 2001). The ABS also used this income concept for ranking Australians in its latest income distribution survey (2003).

While the payment of income tax is taken into account during the calculation of disposable income, no account is taken of the payment of other taxes or of the services that governments provide that bestow a personal benefit upon households—generally a service that they would otherwise have to buy themselves. Disposable income may thus provide an incomplete picture of the relative living standards of different types of families (Harding, 1995, p. 71). Despite providing only a partial picture, disposable income is widely used in Australian income distribution studies because the requisite data are readily available in the ABS national income surveys.

Broader income measures are used in this study. From disposable income we have subtracted selected Commonwealth indirect taxes—that is, GST and excises. To this *post-tax income*, we have added the value of indirect government benefits—that is, the estimated value of health, education, welfare and housing services provided by government. The resulting income measure is termed *final income* and, in essence, this is our most comprehensive measure of the relative economic well-being of households.

Of the total Commonwealth, State and local government taxation revenue in 2001–02, this study allocates taxes of $124 billion or 57 percent of total government revenue. Of total government expenditure of $262 billion in 2001–02, this study allocates benefits of $139 billion or 53 percent of total government spending. In dollar terms, more benefits than taxes were allocated in the study so that, on average, benefits exceed taxes. This is also the case in the ABS fiscal incidence study and the ABS argues that: 'This outcome is not significant in itself, as there is not a direct correspondence between the level of government benefits provided to any sector and the means used to finance those benefits' (2001, p. 3). However, it should be kept in mind in interpreting the results that we have allocated slightly more benefits than taxes.

7.2.1.1 Equivalent incomes

When attempting to compare the economic well-being of households of differing size and composition, it is important to use equivalence scales. For example, it would be expected that a household of four people would need more income than a single person household, if the two households were to enjoy the same standard of living. However, there is no agreement internationally or nationally about exactly how much more income the four-person household requires than the single-person household. Like the recent ABS income distribution study (2003), our study uses the modified Organisation for Economic Co-operation and Development (OECD) equivalence scale. In our study, this means that we have given the first adult in each household a weight of 1.0, second and subsequent adults a weight of 0.5 points, and dependent children a weight of 0.3 points. The relevant cash income measure is then divided by the sum of the above points, to calculate the household's equivalent income.

It is not clear that equivalence scales designed for use with cash measures of economic well-being can be used when non-cash benefits (such as the value of education consumed) are included within the definition of income (Radner, 1994). The equivalence scales applied to cash income measures are intended to capture the economies of scale that occur when individuals share households. For example, a couple living together require only one bed and fridge rather than two of each required if they lived separately. Following Smeeding *et al.*, we have assumed that there are no economies of scale in non-cash income (1993, p. 240). Most of the output tables in the following section show the total indirect (or non-cash) benefits received by different types of households. For our final measure of economic well-being, 'equivalent final income,' we have added together equivalent post-tax income and per-capita indirect benefits income, following previous practice in studies of this kind (Smeeding *et al.*, 1993, p. 241; Harding, 1995, p. 77).

7.2.1.2 Weighting

Another difficult issue is the appropriate 'weight' to use when analyzing the results of our study. Consider two households, one containing four people and the other containing one person. If we use household weighting, then each household counts once when constructing our estimates. If we use person weighting, then the first household counts four times and the second household counts once. The second approach is considered theoretically the most appropriate, as it does not assume that people living in larger households are less important than people living in smaller households, when assessing the income distribution. The ABS has just moved in its most recent income distribution publication to presenting some results for persons rather than for households (2003, p. 13).

In the output tables in the following section, when dividing the population into income quintiles, we have used quintiles of persons rather than quintiles of households. Thus, the bottom quintile consists of the bottom 20 percent of Australians, rather than the bottom 20 percent of households. Using person weighting to create the quintiles, ensures that our measures are not unduly biased by differences in the average household size within different quintiles. As the ABS notes, this was a problem with their earlier fiscal incidence studies, in which they used quintiles of households rather than quintiles of persons (2001, p. 9).

Apart from the division of the population into income quintiles, another issue is whether the results included within each output table are person or household weighted. While person weighting might be considered the most desirable alternative theoretically, the results are then less accessible to the broad community. Accordingly, we have followed the practice used in the most recent fiscal incidence studies carried out by the ABS and UK Office for National Statistics (ONS), in presenting *averages for households* within each output table (ABS, 2001; ONS, 2003). However, in the case of the three *equivalent* income measures presented in the following tables, the results are person weighted rather than household weighted. This is the same procedure followed by the ABS in its latest study of income distribution (2003, p. 37). In other words, only the three equivalent income measures in the following output tables for income quintiles are for persons rather than households.

7.3 Income quintiles

For this part of our study, all Australians have been ranked by the equivalent disposable income of their household and then divided into quintiles. Thus, the bottom quintile consists of the bottom 20 percent of Australians, not the bottom 20 percent of households.

7.3.1 Overview

Government intervention through the payment of taxes and the distribution of benefits narrows the gap between high and low income households in Australia. Looking at the private income of households, before direct intervention by government, the top quintile receive $2151 a week (Table 7.1 and Figure 7.2). This is about 43 times greater than the private incomes of the bottom quintile. After taking into account the taxes and benefits included within the scope of our study, the ratio between the final incomes of the top and bottom quintiles is reduced to three to one. Overall, the bottom 60 percent of Australians are gainers from the tax and benefit programs considered here, with these gains being financed by the top 40 percent of Australians. For the top 20 percent of Australians, final income is 73 percent of private income. For the bottom 20 percent of Australians, final income is 10 times private income (Table 7.1).

There is clearly substantial redistribution occurring through the tax and benefit programs considered in our study. Which programs have the greatest redistributive impact? Direct cash benefits have an important impact upon the incomes of households at the bottom of the income spectrum, as shown by the sharp increase in income for the bottom quintile as we move from private to gross income in Figure 7.3. In contrast, income tax (or direct tax) reduces the income of middle to higher income families, while having relatively little impact on the incomes of the bottom two quintiles, as shown

Table 7.1 Estimated distribution of household income, taxes and benefits, by quintile of equivalent disposable household income, 2001–02

	Quintile of equivalent household disposable income					
	Lowest 20%	Second quintile	Middle 20%	Fourth quintile	Highest 20%	All
	Average $ per week per household					
Private Income	47.2	377.1	809.9	1236.6	2051.5	893.5
Direct Benefits	247.8	231.9	119.7	52.3	12.1	135.5
Gross Household Income	295.0	609.1	929.6	1288.9	2063.6	1029.0
Direct Tax	4.1	51.7	146.7	255.9	536.8	199.5
Disposable Income	290.9	557.3	783.0	1032.9	1526.9	829.6
Selected Indirect Taxes	60.5	85.9	114.1	133.0	184.3	114.6
Post-tax Income	230.5	471.5	668.9	899.9	1342.6	714.9
Selected Indirect Benefits	258.7	297.5	265.0	206.0	136.0	230.5
Total Education Benefits	66.4	106.0	111.7	92.3	53.3	83.4
Non-Government Schools	7.4	12.2	20.8	19.5	9.0	13.2
Government Schools	40.2	68.2	57.6	40.5	17.2	43.4
All Schooling	50.2	84.9	82.4	63.1	27.4	59.5
Tertiary	16.2	21.1	29.3	29.2	25.9	23.9
Total Health Benefits	118.9	127.6	109.4	92.6	77.9	105.1
Hospital Care	56.6	59.2	46.0	35.7	29.3	45.5
Medical Clinics	31.9	34.7	31.6	28.6	23.4	29.9
Pharmaceuticals	16.1	14.0	9.6	6.1	3.9	10.1
Other Health Benefits	11.2	15.1	15.9	15.2	13.0	13.9
PHI Rebate	3.1	4.7	6.4	7.0	8.2	5.8

Housing Benefits	12.8	3.2	1.2	0.4	0.3	4.1
Total Indirect Welfare Benefits	60.7	60.7	42.7	20.7	4.5	38.0
Child Care Benefits	3.5	7.3	4.6	2.0	0.3	3.4
Soc Sec & Welfare Services	57.1	53.4	38.1	18.7	4.2	34.6
Final Income	489.2	769.0	933.9	1105.9	1478.6	945.4
Total Benefits Allocated	506.5	529.5	384.7	258.3	148.2	366.0
Total Taxes Allocated	64.5	137.6	260.8	389.0	721.1	314.1
Net Benefits Allocated	442.0	391.9	123.9	−130.7	−572.9	51.9
Equiv. Disposable Income	200.5	315.5	422.5	573.1	921.0	486.6
Equiv. After Housing Disposable Inc	154.0	262.2	362.5	504.2	826.1	421.9
Equiv. Final Income	280.8	371.2	449.4	572.9	865.7	508.1
Persons per HH	2.13	2.86	3.01	2.82	2.4	2.6
Adults per HH	1.58	1.87	2.06	2.09	2.06	1.91
Number of Dependants per HH	0.55	0.99	0.95	0.73	0.35	0.69
Number Aged 65+ Per HH	0.49	0.47	0.29	0.16	0.09	0.3
Total No. of Households '000	1807.2	1344.7	1282.3	1369.7	1607.1	7410.9

Note: The quintiles are for persons, ranked by the equivalent disposable income of their household. The bottom quintile thus consists of the bottom 20% of Australians. However, the values within the table are household averages (that is, the results in the table are household weighted rather than person weighted, so as to make interpretation of the results more comprehensible). The only exception to this are the three italicized equivalent income rows, where the results are person weighted to take account of the minor differences in average household size between the deciles.

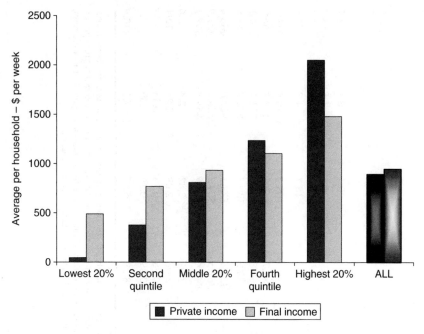

Figure 7.2   Estimated original and final income by quintile groups, 2001–02

by the movement from gross to disposable income in Figure 7.3. The indirect taxes modeled in our study then reduce the income of all households and have only a slightly greater impact upon high income than low income households, as illustrated by the decline in income for every quintile as we move from disposable to post-tax income in Figure 7.3. Moving finally to the indirect benefits provided via the subsidized provision of government services to households, all quintiles use and benefit from these services, although their value to the top quintile is somewhat less than for the bottom four quintiles. The results in Figure 7.3 emphasize again how redistributive the various tax and benefit programs considered in our study are, with the distance between the top and bottom quintiles apparent for private income at the left-hand side of the figure being sharply reduced by the final income stage at the right-hand side of the figure.

7.3.2   Direct cash benefits

The extent of redistribution is again underlined in Figure 7.4, which shows clearly that cash and non-cash benefits are important in boosting the incomes of the bottom three quintiles and taxes are more significant in reducing the incomes of the top quintile. Direct benefits are heavily concentrated

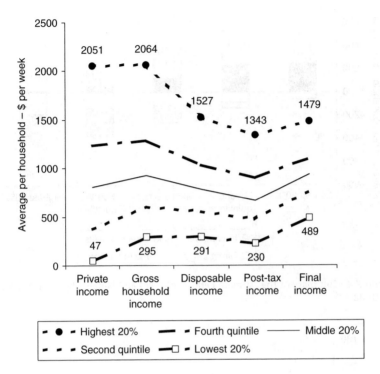

Figure 7.3   Income stages by quintile group, 2001–02

upon the bottom two quintiles, amounting to between about $230 and $250 a week (Table 7.1). In contrast, direct benefits amount to only $12.10 a week for the top quintile. This indicates that direct benefits are highly progressive, amounting to 84 percent of the gross income of the bottom quintile and then falling rapidly to only 0.6 percent of the gross income of the top quintile (Figure 7.5). This high degree of progressivity reflects the tightly targeted nature of direct transfers in Australia, in contrast to the social insurance systems of many European countries. Australian cash transfers are generally both income and asset tested and their level depends on current private income and wealth, rather than on previous workforce experience. Moreover, the private income definition adopted under the welfare system is more comprehensive than that under the personal income tax.

7.3.3 Indirect benefits

Indirect (or non-cash) benefits are particularly significant for the bottom three quintiles, ranging between about $260 and $300 a week for these

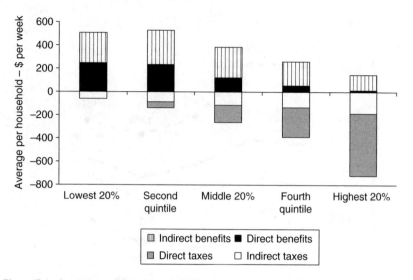

Figure 7.4 Summary of the estimated effects of taxes and benefits by quintile group, 2001–02

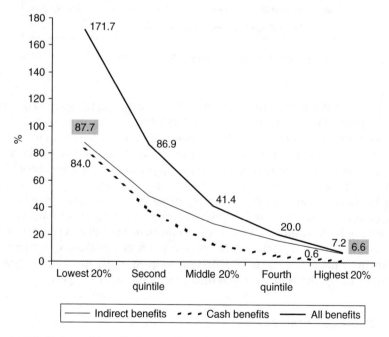

Figure 7.5 Estimated benefits received as a percentage of gross income, by quintile group, 2001–02

quintiles. Indirect benefits are also still important to the fourth quintile, at $206 a week, before declining to $136 a week for the top quintile (Table 7.1). As Figure 7.5 shows, indirect benefits are still highly progressive, although not as progressive as direct cash benefits. As a ratio, indirect benefits are estimated at 87.7 percent of the gross income of the bottom quintile, falling to 6.6 percent of the gross income of the top quintile. The combined impact of all cash and non-cash benefits is also highly progressive, amounting to about 172 percent of the gross income of the bottom quintile and falling sharply to only 7.2 percent of the gross income of the top quintile.

Indirect (or non-cash) benefits are of particular interest, as their value has been increasing more rapidly than cash benefits in recent years. For example, while the average cash benefits received by each household increased by 7 percent between 1993–94 and 1998–99, average indirect benefits increased by 39 percent (ABS, 1996, 2001). While the value of cash benefits is recorded in the regular national income and expenditure surveys covered by the ABS, estimates of non-cash benefits are typically only updated by the ABS every five years in their fiscal incidence studies. Thus, indirect benefits often tend to be an overlooked component of income redistribution in Australia, even though they are becoming an increasingly significant contributor to household economic well-being.

In 2001–02, indirect benefits were worth $231 a week to the average Australian household, making them almost twice as important to the average household as the $136 received in cash benefits (Table 7.1). Which indirect benefits are worth the most to Australian households? The single largest group of indirect benefits is *health* benefits, totalling $105 a week for the average household, and principally representing free or subsidized hospital and medical care and subsidized pharmaceuticals. Hospital benefits are concentrated upon the bottom two quintiles, reflecting the large proportion of older Australians and families with children located in these quintiles (see the 'demographic' panel of rows at the bottom of Table 7.1 and Figure 7.6). Conversely, hospital benefits are lower for the top quintile, partly because of higher usage of private hospitals (which do not attract a hospital subsidy) and the greater representation in this quintile of healthy working age Australians without children. Medical service usage is also somewhat higher among the bottom to middle quintiles than for the top quintile, again reflecting the lower usage of medical services by those in their peak working years and without children.

One program that has attracted much policy debate in Australia is the Private Health Insurance (PHI) rebate, which was introduced in 1999 and refunds 30 percent of the cost of private health insurance. We estimate that the PHI rebate was worth an average of $3.10 a week to bottom quintile households, rising to $8.20 a week for top quintile households. However, the PHI rebate is still progressive, amounting to a higher proportion of the gross income of bottom quintile households than of top quintile households

(1.0 percent versus 0.4 percent). This is because the rebate is more evenly distributed than is gross income. Despite this, more than half of all spending on the rebate is received by the top 40 percent of Australians, with the bottom 40 percent receiving only 28 percent of total outlays on the rebate (Table 7.1).

As found in previous studies (Harding *et al.*, 2004), the Australian Pharmaceutical Benefits Scheme, described briefly in the Appendix, is highly progressive, with its benefits being heavily targeted toward low income concession card holders. Average pharmaceutical benefits for the top quintile are only $3.90 a week—or only one-quarter of those received by the bottom quintile (Table 7.1 and Figure 7.6).

Education is the second big-ticket indirect benefit item, representing $83 a week to the average Australian household. While state government outlays on education tend to be directed toward government schools, the subsidy by the Federal government to non-government schools has been increasing

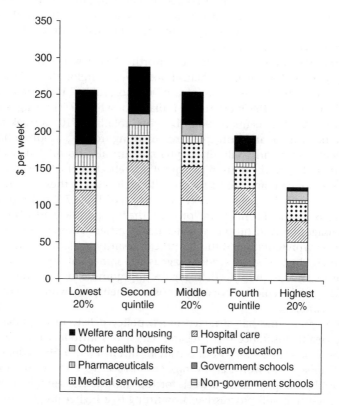

Figure 7.6   Estimated indirect benefits received, by quintile group, 2001–02

more rapidly than that to government schools in recent years, arousing some controversy (Australian Education Union (AEU) 2004).

Looking at all government outlays on education together, government school subsidies are more redistributive toward lower income families than non-government school subsidies, with just over half of all outlays on government schools being directed toward the bottom two quintiles, compared with only 30 percent of all non-government school outlays. School outlays as a whole are concentrated on the bottom three quintiles, which receive 70 percent of total school outlays. Expenditure on tertiary students is somewhat skewed toward the top three quintiles, as shown in Figure 7.6.

The remaining category of non-cash benefits considered is welfare services and housing benefits. Housing benefits are the most progressive of all the non-cash benefits considered in Table 7.1, but total spending on public housing is much lower than for the other services considered here, so they have been grouped with welfare services in Figure 7.6. Welfare services are a rapidly growing category of government expenditure and, as Figure 7.6 illustrates, one that is of major benefit to lower income Australians.

7.3.4   Direct and indirect taxes

Moving now to the tax side, as Figure 7.4 shows graphically, it is the direct tax paid by the top quintile that is particularly striking and an important contributor to the overall redistributive impact of tax and benefit programs. The direct tax paid by the top quintile of about $537 a week is more than double the average direct tax of $256 a week paid by the fourth quintile and about 3.6 times the average direct taxes of $147 a week paid by the middle quintile (Table 7.1). This suggests that income tax in Australia is highly progressive and this is confirmed in Figure 7.7. This figure shows that income tax as a percentage of gross income rises sharply from 1.4 percent for the bottom quintile to 15.8 percent for the middle quintile and 26 percent for the top quintile.

On the other hand, the indirect taxes considered in our study (GST and excise duties) are regressive. As Figure 7.4 shows, all quintiles pay indirect taxes and the magnitude of the indirect taxes paid shows relatively little variation with income, with the $184 of indirect taxes paid each week by the top quintile amounting to only triple the $61 a week paid by the bottom quintile (Table 7.1). The selected indirect taxes amount to an estimated 20.5 percent of the gross income of the bottom quintile, falling to only 8.9 percent of the gross income of the top quintile (Figure 7.7).

While the progressive impact of income tax in Australia is partially offset by the regressive impact of GST and excise duties, the overall impact of the taxes considered in our study remains progressive. As Figure 7.7 illustrates, considering all the taxes studied together, the tax burden increases from 21.9 percent of the gross income of the bottom quintile to 34.9 percent for the top quintile.[1]

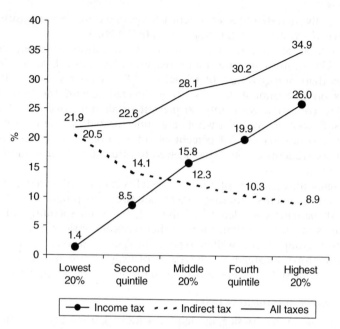

Figure 7.7 Estimated taxes paid as a percentage of gross income, by quintile group, 2001–02
Source: Table 1.1.

7.4 Household type

In this section we have classified households by a combined family type and age categorization, with all households headed by a person aged 65 years and over first selected to be in the 'Head aged 65+ years' category. Of the remaining households, all with heads aged less than 65 years old, those that consist of *only one income unit* were identified and classified into family types.[2] For example, a 'Couple only' household consists of only two people, living as a couple. If such couples live with non-dependent children, other relatives, or unrelated individuals, then they are placed within the 'Other' category. Similarly, 'Couples with dependent children' includes only those households that consist of couples and their dependent children. Again, if such households also include non-dependent children, other relatives or unrelated individuals, then such couples are placed into the 'Other' household category. Thus, the 'Other' household category consists of all multiple income unit and/or multiple family households, including group households, all non-dependent children living with their parents, and two or more families sharing the same household.

Of the household types considered in Table 7.2, the final incomes of aged and sole parent households are affected the most by the redistribution

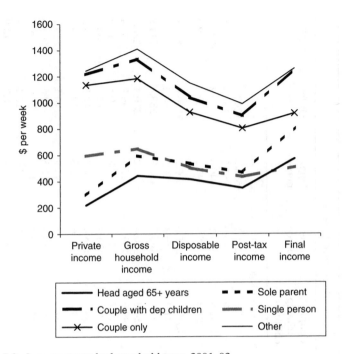

Figure 7.8 Income stages by household type, 2001–02

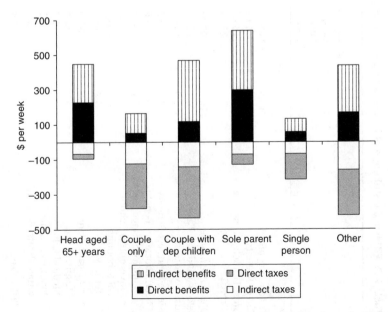

Figure 7.9 Summary of the estimated effects of taxes and benefits, by household type, 2001–02

Table 7.2 Estimated distribution of household income, taxes and benefits, by household type, 2001–02

	Head aged 65+ years	Couple only	Couple with dep children	Sole parent	Single person	Other	All
			Average $ per week per household				
Private Income	218.5	1134.6	1217.0	296.1	594.2	1242.8	893.5
Direct Benefits	225.0	49.1	115.9	298.0	55.2	167.4	135.5
Gross Household Income	443.5	1183.7	1332.9	594.1	649.4	1410.2	1029.0
Direct Tax	27.5	256.4	293.2	58.1	147.2	260.3	199.5
Disposable Income	416.1	927.3	1039.7	536.0	502.2	1150.0	829.6
Selected Indirect Taxes	66.1	122.9	141.3	70.3	68.2	160.4	114.6
Post-tax Income	350.0	804.4	898.4	465.7	433.9	989.6	714.9
Selected Indirect Benefits	222.9	114.0	354.3	340.6	75.2	270.4	230.5
Total Education Benefits	0.4	15.6	199.0	189.6	12.3	96.9	83.4
Non-Government Schools	0.1	0.0	40.7	25.7	0.0	9.5	13.2
Government Schools	0.1	0.3	118.5	134.3	0.0	35.9	43.4
All Schooling	0.2	0.3	168.3	168.0	0.0	47.1	59.5
Tertiary	0.2	15.2	30.7	21.6	12.3	49.7	23.9
Total Health Benefits	158.5	81.0	109.7	80.3	41.9	126.5	105.1
Hospital Care	98.0	31.5	35.9	26.0	17.5	49.5	45.5
Medical Clinics	29.0	24.7	37.4	26.2	12.6	39.3	29.9
Pharmaceuticals	19.1	7.2	7.4	10.1	3.9	12.4	10.1
Other Health Benefits	7.9	10.7	21.5	14.9	5.4	18.2	13.9
PHI Rebate	4.5	6.9	7.4	3.0	2.5	7.2	5.8

Housing Benefits	5.1	1.3	1.5	17.0	6.4	3.2	4.1
Total Indirect Welfare Benefits	58.9	16.1	44.1	53.8	14.6	43.8	38.0
Child Care Benefits	0.0	0.0	10.5	12.4	0.0	1.2	3.4
Soc Sec & Welfare Services	58.9	16.1	33.7	41.4	14.6	42.6	34.6
Final Income	572.9	918.4	1252.7	806.2	509.1	1260.0	945.4
Total Benefits Allocated	448.0	163.0	470.2	638.6	130.4	437.8	366.0
Total Taxes Allocated	93.5	379.3	434.5	128.4	215.4	420.7	314.1
Net Benefits Allocated	354.4	−216.2	35.7	510.2	−85.1	17.2	51.9
Equiv. Disposable Income	337.0	618.2	470.3	333.1	502.2	527.9	486.6
Equiv. After Housing Disposable Inc	366.6	805.2	893.7	419.2	401.5	1028.3	717.9
Equiv. Final Income	432.4	593.3	494.2	412.4	509.1	533.0	508.1
Persons per HH	1.5	2.0	4.0	2.8	1.0	3.4	2.6
Adults per HH	1.5	2.0	2.0	1.0	1.0	3.0	1.9
Number of Dependants per HH	0.0	0.0	2.0	1.8	0.0	0.5	0.7
Total No. of Households '000	1265.5	1204.4	1760.0	397.6	1141.2	1642.2	7410.9

created by the Australian welfare state (Figure 7.8). In 2001–02, the average private incomes of aged households are about $220 a week, and are then roughly doubled by the receipt of cash transfers—predominantly the age pension. Aged households also receive substantial amounts of indirect benefits—and particularly health benefits. Sole parent households receive almost $300 a week in private income, with almost another $300 being added to this in direct benefits, principally via parenting payment. Sole parents receive about another $340 a week in indirect benefits, mainly via the provision of government schooling and health benefits.

Couples with children are on average marginal gainers from the operation of the Australian welfare state, with their relatively high receipt of education and health indirect benefits being largely offset by their direct and indirect tax payments. Couples without children are net payers from the taxes and outlays considered in our study, with their direct and indirect taxes greatly exceeding their direct and indirect benefits. Single person households are also net payers, although not to the same extent as couples without children. However, it must be appreciated that couple without children households consist of two people while single person households by definition consist of only one person. On a per capita basis, the net loss from the welfare state is only slightly higher for couple only households than for single person households. The average benefits received by 'other' households are roughly balanced by their average taxes (Figure 7.9).

7.5   Conclusions

This study assesses the distribution of household income and selected taxes and benefits in 2001–02. Fiscal incidence studies such as this rely on sample survey data and make assumptions about the patterns of receipt and value of various types of benefits and about the payment of selected types of taxes. We faced numerous difficulties with both the sample survey data underlying the study and with the benchmark data used to estimate the taxes received by government and the outlays expended by government. It is also important to appreciate that the benefits and taxes included in our study are generally restricted to those that are either relatable to particular types of households or to household expenditure—or for which we have data to determine their incidence. While we have imputed income tax, the GST and excises in 2001–02, we have not imputed the incidence of such other taxes as capital gains tax, company tax, indirect taxes levied by the States and Territories, and superannuation tax concessions. Similarly, while we have imputed the usage and value of government health, education, housing and welfare outlays that relate directly to particular types of households, we have not included other government outlays such as spending on defence or communications. With these caveats in mind, our study uses a similar methodology to that of other fiscal incidence studies, including those by the ABS (2001) and the UK ONS (2003).

Our study has shown that there is extensive redistribution between households due to the operation of the Australian system of taxes and benefits. This is not unexpected, as this is an intended consequence of the programs of taxes and services included within our study. Our welfare state system has been designed to assist those in our community who are most in need of support. It has also been designed to assist households through the course of their lifecycle, by redistributing income from periods of relative affluence during the lifecycle to periods of relative greater need, such as when there are children or in retirement.

The net impact of the taxes and benefits included within our study is to redistribute income from the most affluent 40 percent of Australians to the less affluent 60 percent. In particular, there is substantial redistribution via the income tax system from the top 20 percent of Australians to the bottom 60 percent. The income tax system is progressive, taking a greater proportion of the gross income of higher income households. The indirect taxes (GST and excise duties) included in our study amount to a smaller proportion of the income of high income households, although in dollar terms the top income quintile pay three times as much in indirect tax as the bottom income quintile. While the indirect taxes included within our study are regressive, this is not sufficient to offset the impact of direct taxes so the combined effect of all the direct and indirect taxes included here remains progressive (although it is important to emphasise again here that state and territory taxes, which are typically regressive, are not within the scope of this study). Direct (or cash) transfers in Australia are also progressive, with three-quarters of total outlays being received by the bottom two income quintiles. While outlays on indirect (or non-cash) benefits are less pro-poor in their impact than this, they are nonetheless also still progressive. Taking both direct and indirect benefits, the bottom two quintiles receive about 60 percent of total outlays, while the top two quintiles receive only 22 percent of total outlays.

The impact of the welfare state also varies greatly by household type, with older Australians and sole parents emerging as the largest gainers from redistribution. Interestingly, while there is substantial redistribution toward lower income couples with children, on average couples with children are not net gainers from the taxes and benefits considered in our study. In recent years the incomes of many such families in Australia have been boosted by falling unemployment and increasing participation in the workforce on a full or part time basis by both parents. This has led to rising income tax payments for couples with children, offsetting the education and health benefits generated by the presence of children. Couples without children, single person households and 'other' households remain net losers from the taxes and benefits considered in our study.

Appendix: Overview of methodology

Data source

The core data source used in the simulation of the 2001–02 world is the 1998–99 Household Expenditure Survey (HES) confidentialized unit record file released by the Australian Bureau of Statistics. This file contains a snapshot of the demographic, labor force, income and other characteristics of the Australian population in 1998–99. It is important to note that the scope of the survey is restricted to those living in private dwellings and excludes those living in remote and sparsely settled areas. We made adjustments to this file to update the private incomes and housing costs of households to estimated 2001–02 levels, using such inflators as average weekly earnings and housing consumer price indexes. We also adjusted the population weights from 1998–99 to 2001–02 levels to allow for the four percent growth in population that occurred over that period. We did not reweight the entire 1998–99 survey to account for possible changes in, for example, labor force and demographic status.

Taxes and cash transfers

In July 2000 Australia introduced a complex tax-mix shift towards indirect taxes, accompanied by extensive social security reforms. As a result, the declared values of these items in the 1998–99 Household Expenditure Survey were redundant. Accordingly, we had to impute the rules of the income tax and social security systems to estimate the income taxes paid by and the transfers received by each of the households in the HES file. This aspect of the modeling employed NATSEM's STINMOD model, which is a long-established static microsimulation model of the Australian tax and transfer system used by government departments for budget policy formulation (Bremner *et al.*, 2002).

The income tax system in Australia in 2001–02 consists of a tax threshold of $6000 and three further marginal tax rate thresholds above that, with the top marginal rate of 47 cents in the dollar cutting in at $60,000 of taxable income. There is also a Medicare levy of 1.5 percent of taxable income, making the effective top marginal tax rate 48.5 percent. There are no social insurance levies on top of this, with the Australian system of means-tested cash payments being financed from general revenue. Australia has a wide range of means-tested payments payable to the aged, unemployed, disabled, sick, sole parents, and families with children. These payments are essentially based on income and assets at the time of payment and, unlike the European social insurance schemes, do not bear any relation to earlier earnings received while in the workforce.

To simulate the impact of the GST and excises we calculated the average tax rates applying to each of the 500 plus detailed expenditure categories contained within the HES for each household. Taxes initially borne by government or business are assumed to be shifted ultimately to consumers, either residents or non-residents. (This differs from the ABS fiscal incidence studies, which only allocate to households those indirect taxes that can be directly assigned to households through their final consumption expenditure.) However, like the ABS, we do not match national accounts estimates of GST and excises collected exactly, because of scope exclusions in the HES and under-statement of tobacco and alcohol consumption by households within the HES.

Indirect benefits

Moving now to indirect benefits, which consist of goods and services provided free or at subsidized prices by the government, our allocation of indirect benefits was restricted, as in the ABS studies (2001), to those arising from the provision of education, health, housing, and welfare services. In most cases, the estimation of the value of an indirect (or non-cash) benefit to households within the HES essentially consists of the following three steps:

1) Identifying those households who are likely to use the service in question and calculating how often they use it within a year;
2) Estimating the cost to government of that usage; and
3) Multiplying the 'amount of usage' by the 'cost to government' to derive the annual estimated value then imputed to the household.

Education benefits

The ABS included on the 1998–99 HES unit record file its estimate of the value of each of the following education services consumed by each household in 1998–99: pre-school, primary and secondary school (divided into government and non-government schools), university, 'technical and further education,' 'tertiary education not elsewhere classified' and 'other education.' We inflated each of these values from their 1998–99 level to 2001–02 estimates, using the best inflator that we could find (generally the percentage change in average benefit per student, derived from such sources as Government Finance Statistics (GFS) and the Ministerial Council on Education, Employment, Training and Youth Affairs).

Health benefits

Health benefits are allocated for hospital care, medical clinics, pharmaceuticals, and other health benefits. *Hospital care* covers expenses relating to acute care institutions, *medical clinics* cover community health services, *pharmaceuticals* covers pharmaceuticals, medical aids and appliances, and *other health benefits* covers public health services, health research and health administration n.e.c.

In our study we calculated new estimates of the value of hospital and medical services and pharmaceuticals consumed. This was either because the program rules had changed so much between 1998–99 and 2001–02 that it was no longer appropriate to use the ABS estimates for 1998–99 or because we wished to use a more sophisticated imputation methodology.

The likelihood of using hospital and medical services was calculated from the 2001 National Health Survey (NHS), and based on such predictive characteristics as age, gender, income quintile and whether the household had private health insurance. Private and public hospital usage was modeled separately, as the latter are far more costly to government.

The likelihood of using prescribed pharmaceuticals was calculated from the 1995 National Health Survey (because the 2001 NHS did not include information on all pharmaceuticals). The Australian Pharmaceutical Benefit Scheme provides highly subsidized pharmaceuticals to 'concession card holders' (generally families and singles on low incomes), with a co-payment per script for this group of $3.50. For other Australians the patient meets the first $21.90 per script and the government meets the full cost of pharmaceuticals listed on the Scheme above this level. We modeled eligibility for concession cards in detail.

To estimate a value for 'other health benefits' we simply inflated the appropriate ABS estimate by the change in 'other health' shown in government finance statistics from 1998–99 to 2001–02, after adjustment for changes in population size.

Private health insurance rebate

One of the innovative features of this study was the simulation of the distributional impact of the Private Health Insurance (PHI) Rebate in the 2001–02 world. The PHI rebate was not simulated by the ABS in its 1998–99 fiscal incidence study, as it was only introduced in 1999 (ABS, 2001). First, the probability of a person having private health insurance was estimated (from the 2001 NHS unit record file) by state, age, sex, income unit type and equivalent gross income unit income quintile. These likelihood estimates were then applied to persons in the HES and used to adjust the numbers in each sub-group who held insurance to match the proportions in the 2001 NHS. We then predicted whether the entire household were likely to be covered by private health insurance or just that individual, using administrative data. We then estimated the average amount paid for such private health insurance (before the rebate), from the amounts indicated on the HES and Private Health Insurance Administrative Council administrative data. Finally, the estimated amount of the PHI rebate was then calculated as 30 percent of the pre-rebate cost of insurance.

Housing benefits

Government expenses relating to housing largely involve building new houses for rent at subsidized cost. These expenses were not allocated amongst HES households in the ABS fiscal incidence study because 'it is difficult to identify likely future recipients of the benefits' (2001, p. 51). Instead, benefits were allocated to households in government rental accommodation according to the value of their rent subsidy. The value of their rent subsidy was taken to be the difference between the rent paid by the households and the estimated value of private market rent according to the State, region, type of dwelling and number of bedrooms. To derive estimates for 2001–02 we multiplied the public housing benefits calculated by the ABS in the HES by the change in the housing Consumer Price Index (CPI) by State over the 1998–99 to 2001–02 period.

Other welfare services

These services exclude cash transfers (dealt with above) and comprise various publicly funded services to assist those who are disabled, aged, have children and so on. In 1998–99 the ABS calculated average indirect benefits for different types of benefit recipients, by dividing indirect welfare GFS expenses by the number of recipients of benefits. Different levels of benefit were calculated for persons receiving age, veterans' affairs, and disability support pensions, and family allowance and parenting payment. Average benefits were allocated to persons receiving similar direct government benefits. Household benefits were the sum of household member benefits. To capture the change in these benefits between 1998–99 and 2001–02, we inflated by the change in total indirect welfare GFS expenses between the two years.

Child care

Expenditure on childcare assistance was treated separately by the ABS, and allocated to households with children under 12 of age, according to household income and the probability that the children were attending eligible childcare. While there was an apparent major change in childcare assistance between 1998–99 and 2001–02 with the GST tax reform package, the rules of the old schemes were effectively largely replicated in the new Child Care Benefit. Accordingly, we simply inflated the childcare benefits shown in the ABS fiscal incidence study by the change in total spending on child-care benefits derived from the relevant departmental Annual Reports (Department of Family and Community Services, 1999, 2002).

Notes

* The authors would like to gratefully acknowledge the input provided to this project by other National Centre for Social and Economic Modelling (NATSEM) staff, particularly Richard Percival, Annie Abello, Elizabeth Taylor, Ben Phillips, Anthea Bill, Rebecca Cassells and Carol Farbotko. We would also like to acknowledge the hard work of those who build and maintain the STINMOD model, particularly Gillian Beer and Matthew Toohey.

NATSEM research findings are generally based on estimated characteristics of the population. Such estimates are usually derived from the application of microsimulation modeling techniques to microdata based on sample surveys. These estimates may be different from the actual characteristics of the population because of sampling and non-sampling errors in the microdata and because of the assumptions underlying the modelling techniques. The microdata do not contain any information that enables identification of the individuals or families to which they refer.

1. It is important to note that taxes levied by State and local governments are not included within our study. Our earlier work has shown that these taxes are regressive (Harding and Warren, 1999) so their inclusion would reduce the degree of progressivity shown in Figure 7.7.
2. An income unit is defined by the ABS as a person or group of related persons living within a household, whose command over income is assumed to be shared. Income sharing is considered to take place within married (registered or *de facto*) couples, and between parents and dependent children. Dependent children are defined as children aged under 15 years, and people aged 15–24 years who are full-time students, live with one or both of their parents, and do not have a partner or child of their own in the household.

References

Australian Bureau of Statistics (2003) 'Household Income and Its Distribution, Australia, 2000–01,' Cat. No. 6523.0 (July).
Australian Bureau of Statistics (2001) 'Government Benefits, Taxes and Household Income 1998–99,' Cat. No. 6537.0 (August).

Australian Bureau of Statistics (1996) '1993–94 Household Expenditure Survey, Australia: The Effects of Government Benefits and Taxes on Household Income,' Cat. No. 6537.0.

Australian Bureau of Statistics (1992) '1998–89 Household Expenditure Survey, Australia: The Effects of Government Benefits and Taxes on Household Income,' Cat. No. 6537.0.

Australian Education Union (2004) Submission to the Senate Inquiry into Commonwealth Funding for Schools, http://www.aph.gov.au/Senate/committee/eet_ctte/schoolfunding/submissions/sub033.pdf.

Bremner, K., G. Beer, R. Lloyd and S. Lambert (2002) 'Creating a Basefile for STINMOD,' National Centre for Social and Economic Modelling, Technical Paper No. 27, University of Canberra (June).

Department of Family and Community Services (2002) Annual Report 2001–02, Canberra.

Department of Family and Community Services (1999) Annual Report 1998–99, Canberra.

Harding, A., A. Abello, L. Brown and B. Phillips (2004) 'The Distributional Impact of Government Outlays on the Australian Pharmaceutical Benefits Scheme in 2001–02,' *Economic Record* **80**(S1): (September).

Harding, A., R. Percival, D. Schofield and A. Walker (2002) 'The Lifetime Distributional Impact of Government Health Outlays,' *Australian Economic Review*, **35**(2): 363–79 (December).

Harding, A., R. Lloyd, H. Greenwell (2001) *Financial Disadvantage in Australia 1900 to 2000: The Persistence of Poverty in a Decade of Growth* (Camperdown, NSW: The Smith Family).

Harding, A. and N. Warren (1999) 'Who Pays the Tax Burden in Australia?,' National Centre for Social and Economic Modelling, Discussion Paper No. 39 (Canberra: University of Canberra).

Harding, A. (1995) 'The Impact of Health, Education and Housing Outlays Upon Income Distribution in Australia in the 1990s,' *Australian Economic Review* (3rd Quarter), 71–86.

Harding, A. (1984) 'Who Benefits?: The Australian Welfare State and Redistribution,' Social Welfare Research Centre Reports and Proceedings No. 45 (Sydney: University of New South Wales).

Johnson, D., I. Manning and O. Hellwig (1995) 'Trends in the Distribution of Cash and Non-Cash Benefits,' Report to the Department of Prime Minister and Cabinet, AGPS (Canberra) (December).

Office of National Statistics (United Kingdom) (2003) 'The Effects of Taxes and Benefits on Household Income, 2001–02' (available at www.ons.gov.uk).

Radner, D. (1994) 'Noncash Income, Equivalence Scales, and the Measurement of Economic Well-Being,' Office of Research and Statistics, Working Paper No. 63 (Washington, DC: US Department of Health and Human Services).

Raskall, P. and R. Urquhart (1994) 'Inequality, Living Standards and the Social Wage During the 1980s,' Study of Social and Economic Inequalities, Monograph No. 3 (Sydney: University of New South Wales).

Saunders, P. (2001) 'Household Income and its Distribution,' in Australian Bureau of Statistics, *Australian Economic Indicators*, Cat. No. 1350.0 (Canberra), pp. 33–55.

Siminski, P., P. Saunders, S. Waseem and B. Bradbury (2003) 'Assessing the Quality and Inter-Temporal Comparability of ABS Household Income Distribution Survey Data,' Social Policy Research Centre, Discussion Paper No. 123 (Sydney: University of New South Wales).

Smeeding, T. M., P. Saunders, J. Coder, S. Jenkins, J. Fritzell, A. J. M. Hagenaars, R. Hauser and M. Wolfson (1993) 'Poverty, Inequality and Family Living Stand-ards Impacts Across Seven Nations: the Effect of Non-Cash Subsidies for Health, Education and Housing,' *Review of Income and Wealth* **39**(3): 229–56.

Warren, N. (1997) 'Recent Trends in Taxation in Australia and their Impact on Australian Tax Incidence,' in J. G. Head and R. Krever (eds.), *Taxation Towards 2000*, Conference Series 19 (Sydney: Australian Tax Research Foundation).

8
Distributional Effects of Personal Income Taxation in Korea

Kwang Soo Cheong[1]

8.1 Introduction

Fairness in income distribution is a basic command of social justice, and redistribution in accordance with tax equity is an important statutory function of the income tax system. Also, an empirical study of the redistributive effects of the system is an important undertaking. It can provide useful policy implications for tax reforms as well as a valuable assessment of the tax system in relation to equity principles. Relating to this, investigations were made of various equity consequences of personal income taxation in Korea, and this chapter summarizes the findings.

The income tax system in Korea is known for the generally low tax burden on taxpayers, which can be attributed to the generous tax allowances and exemptions and the lack of strong and uniform enforcement of tax codes in comparison with other countries. According to Dalsgaard (2000), the average effective tax rate on labor during the period of 1991–97 was only 7.7 percent, which was the lowest among the Organization for Economic Co-operation and Development (OECD) countries and substantially lower than the OECD average of 33.4 percent. Two factors are the importance of the Korean income tax as a revenue source and the extent of the redistributive role of tax and this chapter is an exploration into this proposition.

The redistributive effects of the Korean income tax system, from the perspective of vertical equity, horizontal equity and tax-induced income re-rankings, is considered. Progressivity as a manifestation of vertical equity was examined by means of both a structural measure of average rate progression and a distributional measure of the center of gravity of income distribution (COG). Using this distributional measure, the overall inequality effect was decomposed into the effect on income inequality across income groups and the effect on inequality within income groups. In view of income re-rankings as an equivalent of horizontal inequity, a tax mobility matrix was constructed to give a visual presentation of re-rankings. This matrix measured the extent of re-rankings using a summary statistic of mean squared relative rank-shift. This measure of horizontal inequity was justified by the use of equivalent household income adopted as a money-metric measure of household welfare.

The existing literature on the redistributive effects of the Korean income taxation is not rich but includes a few inspiring studies with important findings that will be referred to in the discussion of empirical findings (Hyun, 1996, 1999; Im, 1996; Lee, 1997; Sung and Lee, 2001). However, this chapter varies from others in several meaningful respects. First, equivalent household income is used as the unit of analysis, which renders the obtained results as welfare interpretations. Second, data is used from all six waves of the Korean Household Panel Study (KHPS) covering the sample period of January 1992 to July 1998. This consistency in the observed households and methods of analysis renders the obtained results meaningfully comparable over the sample years. Most importantly, while existing studies typically focus on either horizontal or vertical equity aspect of the Korean income tax system, vertical equity, horizontal equity and income re-rankings are addressed from a methodical point of view. In particular, tax-induced income re-rankings have been neglected in existing studies and this chapter fills the void.

Section 8.2 discusses the methodology used in this chapter with reference to relevant equity principles. Section 8.3 explains the data source and procedures carried out. Section 8.4 discusses empirical findings in comparison with existing studies in the following order:

- average rate progression in light of (structural) vertical equity;
- tax-induced income re-rankings in light of horizontal inequity; and
- center of gravity and its decomposition in light of (distributional) vertical equity.

Lastly, concluding remarks are in Section 8.5.

8.2 Method of analysis

8.2.1 Equivalent household income

Unlike many previous studies, equivalent household income is used as the income unit of analysis. Equivalent household income is household income adjusted for household structure, using an equivalence scale Γ defined as

$$\Gamma = (A + \rho K)^{\gamma} \tag{1}$$

where A and K are, respectively, the numbers of adults and children in the household, and ρ is a parameter for the weight of a child relative to an adult, and γ is a parameter for the economies of scale within the household.

In an income study, equivalent household income is considered to be a money-metric measure of household well-being, which conveniently allows cross-household comparisons. Abstracted from different abilities-to-pay of households caused by different household sizes and compositions, it is also considered the more appropriate unit of analysis than household income in examining the redistributive effects of income taxation.

As for the parameter values of ρ and γ, there is neither normative theory nor empirical consensus, and different values have been adopted in previous studies. For example, Aronson, Johnson and Lambert (1994), Cheong (2000a, 2001) and Williams, Weiner and Sammartino (1998) set both parameters equal to 0.5. Atkinson, Rainwater and Smeeding (1995) and Kang and Hyun (1998) set ρ to 1 and γ to 0.5, respectively. The OECD generally used the latter set of parameters too.

While recognizing its normative merit, Decoster and Ooghe (2002) concluded that using equivalent income might be ineffective at the empirical level, since welfare results were sensitive to the choice of equivalence scales in their experiment. Their conclusion only signifies the importance of using equivalent income, so calls for empirical efforts to determine reasonable and acceptable equivalent scales for the sample households in Korea. In this study, the choice of Kang and Hyun (1998) is followed, without making further effort to estimate these parameters.

8.2.2 Tax mobility matrix and mean squared relative rank-shift

While there is virtual unanimity that horizontal equity is a worthy goal of any tax system, a workable definition of horizontal equity has been elusive.[2] One approach, such as that of Aronson *et al.* (1994) and Wagstaff *et al.* (1999), is to adhere to the principle of the classical horizontal equity, that is, 'the equal treatment of equals,' and measure the extent of differential tax treatment of equals. In this approach, the ambiguity in the workable definition of horizontal equity is inherited by the definition of pre-tax equals or groupings of unequals, since no two taxpayers are identical. The arbitrariness can be mitigated by using the predicted income distribution estimated non-parametrically from the sample income distribution. This is the usual method of fixing income bands and, if used to group taxpayers as equals, is fundamentally arbitrary and thus likely to make the measure of tax equity sensitive to the choice of income bands.

Another approach is to recognize the existence of tax-induced income re-rankings as a necessary and sufficient condition for the violation of horizontal equity, and measure the extent of changes in income ranking between pre-tax and post-tax income distributions. For example, King (1983) measured the re-ranking of an individual taxpayer using the scaled order statistic defined by the normalized difference between the actual income and the income in post-tax distribution, corresponding to the taxpayer's pre-tax income ranking.

The occurrence of income re-rankings resulting from taxation or the tax mobility in Atkinson's term (1980) is not entirely avoidable in practice.

Tax equity requires differential treatments of households with different needs and abilities to pay, by means of various tax exemptions and deductions and other provisions. Therefore, certain income re-rankings based on income sources and household characteristics are equitable and so intended for a typical progressive income tax system. However, there are income re-rankings that cannot be justified on equity grounds. Some re-rankings may be intentional on efficiency grounds and others may be due to imperfections in the operation of the tax system. Like any other study of the redistributive effects of income taxation, the income re-rankings with no equity justification in assessing the equity consequences of the Korean income tax system is concentrated on here.

In this chapter, tax-induced income re-rankings are considered unjustifiable on the equity basis, unless they reflect the intentional unequal treatment of households with the same income but with different needs. Therefore, it would appear that tax inequity directly measured from household income, whether progressivity, horizontal inequity or the extent of income re-rankings, is necessarily inclusive of equitable differential treatments and hence leads to false judgments.[3] On the contrary, tax inequity measured from equivalent household income is deemed to be free from such intended equitable differences, since their consideration is already factored into the household equivalence scale, which expresses household income in per adult equivalent terms. In light of this normative proposition, any tax-induced re-ranking of equivalent household income is attributed to the violation of tax equity principles.

The extent of the tax-induced re-ranking was measured using the mean squared relative rank-shift, which is the arithmetic average of the squared 'distances' of relative rank-shifts resulting from income re-rankings. First, the relative rank is defined as the (absolute) income rank divided by the total number of households. The relative rank-shift is then obtained as the difference between a household's relative ranking in the pre-tax income distribution and its relative ranking in the post-tax income distribution. If there were no income re-rankings, all distances of relative rank-shifts would be constant at zero and hence the mean squared relative rank-shift would be zero. The mean squared relative rank-shift would increase as the number of re-rankings increases or the distances of rank-shifts increase. The formal definition of the mean squared relative rank-shift is

$$\frac{1}{N} \sum_{i=1}^{N} (p_i - q_i)^2 \qquad (2)$$

where p_i and q_i are household i's relative income rankings in the pre- and post-tax income distributions, respectively. It is noted that the average of relative rank-shifts for all households is necessarily zero and so the mean squared relative rank-shift is the variance of relative rank-shifts itself.

It should be noted that the mean squared relative rank-shift is invariant to replications of the sample population. In other words, this measure satisfies the so-called Dalton's Population Principle often required for a measure of income inequality. For example, merging identical income distributions under the common income tax system would not alter the extent of income re-rankings measured by the mean squared relative rank-shift.

Using a summary statistic, such as the mean squared relative rank-shift to measure certain tax inequity, implies a social welfare function that is inversely related to the variance of relative rank-shifts. One notable implication is that rank exchanges of the same distance would make the same impact on tax equity. Whether it is acceptable or not remains an open question as there is no consensus about welfare weights of rank-shifts in the literature.

As an additional attempt to investigate the tax-induced re-ranking, the so-called tax mobility matrix was constructed following Atkinson (1980). The tax mobility matrix is a transition matrix of which an element m_{ij} represents the percentage share of the ith decile households in the pre-tax distribution that end up in the jth decile in the post-tax distribution. If income taxation were to induce no income re-ranking, all diagonal elements of the matrix would be 100s and all off-diagonal elements would be zeros. Due to the presence of income re-rankings happening across income deciles, the tax mobility matrix is never obtained as a diagonal matrix although its diagonal elements are dominant.

8.2.3   Center of gravity of income distribution

As a measure of income inequality, the COG developed in Cheong (2000b) was used. The COG is the average of households' relative income rankings weighted by their income shares and computed as

$$COG = \sum_{i=1}^{N} \frac{i}{N} \frac{y_i}{Y} \tag{3}$$

where y_i denotes the income of the ith poorest household, N the total population and Y the total income (such that $Y = \sum_{i=1}^{N} y_i$).

By construction, the COG identifies the household on which an ordered income distribution is centered. For example, the computed COG of 0.62 implies that the given income distribution is centered on the 62nd poorest household in percentile income rankings. In other words, the 62 poorest households 'represents' the income distribution provided that there are a total of 100 households in the income distribution.

As intuition would tell, the COG obtains its maximum value of 1 when the income distribution is completely concentrated, so that the income distribution is centered on the richest household. Its minimum value is

$1/2$ when the income distribution is completely equal, so that the income distribution is centered on the midst-income household.

It should be noted that the COG can be expressed as a simple linear transformation of the Gini coefficient, thereby allowing not only an intuitive meaning to the Gini coefficient but also allowing inequality comparison regardless of the Lorenz curve crossings.[4] Another notable benefit of using the COG is that this measure allows an easy yet useful decomposition of an overall inequality change into the change due to within-group inequality and the change due to between-group inequality. Using decile income groups means that an ordered income distribution is partitioned into ten income groups with equal group sizes. Defining the within-group inequality (COG_K) as the center of gravity of income distribution within a group, we have the following relationship:[5]

$$COG = \sum_{K=1}^{10} \frac{1}{K} \frac{Y_K}{Y} COG_K + \sum_{K=1}^{10} \frac{K}{10} \frac{Y_K}{Y} - \frac{1}{10} \qquad (4)$$

where Y is the total income of the whole income distribution and Y_K is the total income of group K. The first term on the right-hand side of Equation (4) is the weighted average of within-group inequalities, with each group's weight being the product of the group's income share and population share. The second term simply computes the center of gravity of group income distribution ($Y_1, Y_2, Y_3, \ldots, Y_{10}$), that is the inequality between groups.

Since Musgrave and Thin (1948) proposed that income tax progressivity, as an implementation of vertical equity, be measured by 'the extent to which a given tax structure results in a shift in the distribution of income toward equality,' the inequality of the pre-tax and post-tax income distributions in terms of the Gini coefficient has been widely used in previous studies. This study takes advantage of the property of the COG as only a linear function of the Gini coefficient. Progressivity measured in this way is distributional progressivity, which was referred to as effective progression by Musgrave and Thin (1948). In this discussion of empirical findings, the notion of progressivity based on average rate progression is also used. Formal discussion of the measurement of progressivity can be found in many existing studies (Dardanoni and Lambert, 2000; Kakwani, 1977; Podder, 1997).

It should be also noted that distributional progressivity would be undermined by horizontal inequity resulting from undesirable income re-rankings induced by the tax system. As will be discussed, the Korean income tax system induced considerable income re-rankings during the sample period. Such income re-rankings may be further investigated by adopting decomposition analysis (Aronson, Johnson and Lambert, 1994; Duclos, Jalbert and Araar, 2000), in which tax progressivity and re-ranking effects are mutually exclusively defined. While it is worthwhile and overdue in the literature of the Korean tax system, an application of such decomposition is put beyond scope of this chapter.

8.3 Data

Both household- and individual-level data from the KHPS conducted by the Daewoo Economic Research Institute was used. The KHPS had been the only source of panel data for Korea until the *Korean Labor and Income Panel Study* (KLIPS) was launched by the Korean Labor Institute in 1998.[6] There had been a total of six waves of the KHPS from 1993 to 1998 and all waves were used in my study.

While each wave of the KHPS covered a sample period of 12 months, the months actually covered in a wave changed in 1994 and 1995. Specifically, the 1993 wave covers a period from January to December 1992. The 1994 wave covers from April 1993 to March 1994. All the subsequent waves respectively cover from the August of the previous year to July of the survey year. Considering these differences, the sample years were renamed as 1992, 1993, 1995, 1996, 1997 and 1998, respectively, in chronological order. For example, the sample year 1998 covers a period of August 1997 to July 1998, which almost coincided with the period of Economic Crisis in Korea.

The sample years of 1992–98 represent a period of moderate economic growth in Korea, with the annual real GDP growth rate being consistently higher than 5 percent until the year of 1998, which was marked with a negative growth rate for the first time in many years. The Economic Crisis erupted in the last quarter of 1997 and brought about dramatic economic downturn unprecedented in the recent economic history of Korea. Also, the unemployment rate, which had been traditionally as low as 2 to 3 percent, abruptly increased to about 7 percent in the wake of socioeconomic consequences.

Tax reforms or piecemeal policy changes implemented in Korea during the sample period may be briefly summarized as follows:[7]

1) In support of the Five Year Plan for the New Economy, Tax Reform in 1993 included policy changes geared toward enhancing tax equity and securing tax revenue by lowering individual income tax rates but also reducing various kinds of non-taxation and tax exemptions;
2) To level the playing field, the 1994 Tax Reform lowered the income tax rates but broadened the tax base by incorporating interest and dividend income into the global income tax system and introducing the self-assessment system for individual income taxes, both of which actually went into effect in 1996;
3) In 1996, individual income tax brackets and their marginal tax rates were adjusted and tax exemption points were substantially raised; and
4) In coping with the Economic Crisis, a series of tax policy measures to prevent excessive revenue shortfalls were implemented in 1998, such as switching the progressive taxation of interest income to a proportional withholding tax and making various exemptions and tax reductions subject to sunset rules.

Due to their complicated nature, it is difficult to determine *ex ante* whether tax equity ought to be improving or worsening as a result of the tax policy changes implemented during the sample period. Horizontal equity would have been improved if all households had become subject to global income taxes based on all sources of income. However, no sample year had policy changes all aligned in the same direction. Implications on vertical equity or progressivity seem to be even more *ex ante* ambiguous due to a series of changes in income tax brackets.[8] It is, however, certain that the rate structure was progressive in every sample year, in that the statutory average tax rate was non-decreasing in income level. This study intends to investigate the effective progressivity (or distributional progressivity) that is a projection of the statutory progressivity on the dimension of household welfare.

8.4 Empirical findings

8.4.1 Equivalence scales and equivalent household income

Using the parameters chosen earlier, an equivalence scale was computed for each sample household as the first step toward computing equivalent household income. Table 8.1 presents the average equivalence scales obtained for each pre-tax income decile and the total sample.[9] First, the average equivalence scale shows little change over sample years, if not a slight decrease. Since the weight of children relative to adults was set at 1, it means the household size varied little during this period. Table 8.1 also shows that equivalence scales, hence household sizes, are generally higher in the middle-income class (of the 3rd to 8th deciles) than in the lower income class (of the lowest two deciles) or the upper income class (of the top two deciles) in every year except for 1998.[10]

Table 8.1 Average household equivalence scale

	1992	1993	1995	1996	1997	1998
Bottom decile	1.69	1.71	1.58	1.60	1.63	1.55
Second	1.93	1.88	1.85	1.76	1.79	1.62
Third	2.00	1.99	1.95	1.90	1.91	1.87
Fourth	1.96	1.99	1.98	1.98	1.92	1.95
Fifth	1.94	1.99	1.99	2.02	2.02	1.99
Sixth	1.99	1.92	1.99	2.02	1.92	2.03
Seventh	1.95	1.97	1.99	2.02	1.98	2.04
Eighth	1.95	2.00	1.98	1.99	1.99	1.99
Ninth	1.90	1.97	1.98	1.99	1.95	2.05
Top decile	1.92	1.95	1.92	1.94	1.95	2.01
All households	1.92	1.94	1.92	1.92	1.90	1.91

As a money-metric measure of household welfare, pre-tax and post-tax equivalent household incomes were computed by applying household equivalence scales to household income and tax amounts. A household's income amount was obtained from the following income sources:

- wage and salary including bonuses;
- income from business activities and professional occupations;
- (imputed) income from farming and fishery;
- income from side jobs and businesses;
- dividends, interest and capital gains; and
- pension, public subsidy, and private gifts.

A household's tax amount was computed as the total of all income taxes paid by household members.

Tables 8.2 and 8.3 present the results of computing pre-tax and post-tax equivalent household income. Since the purpose of these tables was to present a comparison between pre-tax and post-tax equivalent income distributions, two different sets of deciles were used in the tables. The deciles constructed on the basis of pre-tax equivalent income were used for pre-tax figures and the deciles constructed on the basis of post-tax equivalent income were used for post-tax figures. Consequently, households in a pre-tax decile are not necessarily the same as households in the corresponding post-tax decile.[11]

Table 8.2 presents median equivalent household income levels for each decile and the whole sample in 10,000 (nominal) won per month for each sample year. For example, the median pre-tax equivalent household income of the 3rd decile households gradually increased from 400,000 won per month in 1992 to 670,800 won per month in 1997 and then decreased sharply to 416,700 won per month in 1998 due to the Economic Crisis. In fact, this observation of a gradual increase until 1997, followed by a sharp decrease in 1998, is found for every decile.

A simple calculation on the table shows that the median equivalent household income decreased by 21.7 percent on average from 1997 to 1998. It is also found that the percentage decrease for each of the lowest five deciles was higher than this average decrease, whereas the percentage decrease for each of the highest five deciles was below the average. For example, the median equivalent household income of the poorest decile dropped by 46.8 percent, while that of the richest decile dropped by 11.9 percent. The figures in this table are consistent with the popular result in previous studies that show the distributive impacts of the Economic Crisis to be significantly different across different income classes.

Table 8.2 also shows that median post-tax equivalent household income levels were generally close to their post-tax counterparts, indicating that the income taxation in Korea did not significantly affect the size distribution of

Table 8.2 Median equivalent household income (in 10,000 won per month)

	1992		1993		1995		1996		1997		1998	
	Pre-tax	Post-tax	Pre-tax	Post-tax	Pre-tax	Post-tax	Pre-tax	Post-tax	Pre-tax	Post-tax	Pre-tax	Post-tax
Bottom decile	11.79	11.74	13.83	13.84	14.43	14.43	18.07	17.92	25.40	25.26	13.50	13.08
Second	27.21	27.17	31.27	31.08	39.50	38.74	40.41	40.29	48.06	47.73	30.00	30.00
Third	40.00	39.74	47.14	46.58	55.00	54.21	56.67	56.05	67.08	66.40	41.67	41.01
Fourth	50.00	49.20	57.74	56.29	68.57	67.40	71.00	70.29	80.50	80.00	55.00	54.21
Fifth	57.50	55.83	65.32	64.50	76.03	75.31	82.77	81.04	92.00	90.83	71.85	70.67
Sixth	64.47	63.34	74.00	72.50	89.44	87.50	91.92	90.78	102.06	100.00	83.75	81.75
Seventh	75.00	72.92	83.72	82.50	100.00	98.96	103.94	101.98	120.00	116.63	99.00	96.42
Eighth	86.60	84.87	98.39	95.96	115.47	114.40	122.61	120.21	140.00	138.29	115.00	113.13
Ninth	104.72	102.42	115.00	113.06	146.00	143.92	143.88	142.13	165.00	162.00	140.13	136.42
Top decile	150.00	146.39	162.13	158.44	205.00	200.69	200.00	196.04	226.90	223.79	200.00	194.39
All households	60.17	59.58	70.00	68.94	83.00	81.67	88.00	85.88	100.00	97.08	78.26	77.08

Table 8.3 Average equivalent household income (in 10,000 won per month)

	1992		1993		1995		1996		1997		1998	
	Pre-tax	Post-tax	Pre-tax	Post-tax	Pre-tax	Post-tax	Pre-tax	Post-tax	Pre-tax	Post-tax	Pre-tax	Post-tax
Bottom decile	11.43	11.37	13.55	13.55	14.03	13.91	17.20	17.08	22.94	22.78	12.57	12.41
Second	26.98	26.82	31.39	31.21	38.44	38.15	40.20	39.84	47.54	47.22	28.99	28.82
Third	39.99	39.53	46.52	45.96	54.43	53.86	56.45	55.78	66.42	65.80	42.24	41.86
Fourth	49.53	48.75	56.98	56.07	68.25	67.22	70.61	69.67	80.45	79.62	55.13	54.63
Fifth	56.84	55.93	65.71	64.69	77.41	76.30	81.89	80.53	93.30	91.45	71.50	70.17
Sixth	64.39	63.35	73.38	72.25	89.02	87.52	93.13	91.39	102.79	101.05	84.16	82.21
Seventh	73.75	72.62	83.20	81.82	100.58	99.07	104.69	103.00	118.72	116.77	97.88	95.83
Eighth	86.37	84.53	96.88	95.24	116.97	115.38	121.45	119.41	140.06	137.66	115.10	112.90
Ninth	105.50	103.46	115.65	113.46	144.48	142.23	142.82	140.79	166.28	163.56	140.51	137.48
Top decile	178.98	175.85	182.41	178.20	224.30	221.20	229.82	226.66	253.64	250.17	225.41	218.99
All households	69.36	68.17	76.51	75.21	92.68	91.38	95.75	94.33	109.14	107.53	87.08	85.42

income. The same conclusion may be drawn from Table 8.3, which presents the pre-tax and post-tax average equivalent household income levels, using the same template as Table 8.2.

In Table 8.3, both pre-tax and post-tax average equivalent household income levels increased for all deciles from 1992 to 1997. However, the rate of income growth varied over deciles. The average equivalent household income for the bottom decile doubled either in pre-tax or in post-tax terms, whereas that for the top decile grew 1.4 times (either in pre-tax or in post-tax terms). The growth rate for the sample average was only 1.6 times (either in pre-tax or post-tax terms), which was only slightly lower than the growth rate for the middle-income class households.

Table 8.3 also illustrates how different income changed income classes during the Economic Crisis. The percentage decrease in the average equivalent household income for each decile, relative to its 1997 level, was inversely related to its decile ranking, ranging from an 11 percent decrease for the richest decile and a 45 percent for the poorest decile. This table also demonstrates the phenomenon that the upper five deciles suffered less but the bottom five deciles suffered more than the overall average experience, which was a 20 percent decrease in pre-tax terms.

The observation that the growth rates of pre-tax and post-tax average equivalent household incomes from 1992 to 1997 were almost identical per each decile, suggests two possibilities:

1) the tax rate for each decile remained virtually identical between 1992 and 1997; and/or
2) the tax rates were different but they were too low to produce visible differences in the growth rates of pre-tax and post-tax income levels.

However, the first possibility is against the fact that there had been a series of tax reforms in terms of the rate structure as well as tax exemptions and allowances. There remains only the second possibility, as will be shown later. This shows that the effective income tax rates were low relative to the statutory tax rates during the period from 1992 to 1997 and also for 1998.

8.4.2 Distribution of tax burden and effective tax rates

One way to inspect equity aspects of the income tax system is to compare the income shares and tax shares of taxpayers. Table 8.4 presents the pre-tax and post-tax equivalent household income shares and tax shares for deciles. It is noted that pre-tax income shares and tax shares were computed for pre-tax deciles and post-tax income shares were computed for post-tax deciles. As pointed out earlier, households in a pre-tax decile are different from

Table 8.4 Equivalent household income share and tax burden (%)

	1992			1993			1994		
	Pre-tax		Post-tax	Pre-tax		Post-tax	Pre-tax		Post-tax
	Income	Tax	Income	Income	Tax	Income	Income	Tax	Income
Bottom decile	1.65	0.28	1.67	1.77	0.26	1.81	1.52	0.46	1.52
Second	3.89	1.60	3.93	4.11	1.21	4.14	4.14	2.21	4.19
Third	5.77	3.38	5.79	6.07	4.62	6.12	5.87	4.65	5.90
Fourth	7.14	6.76	7.17	7.45	6.66	7.45	7.40	7.36	7.37
Fifth	8.20	7.16	8.18	8.62	7.37	8.61	8.32	8.97	8.33
Sixth	9.29	8.31	9.30	9.59	8.19	9.63	9.61	11.14	9.53
Seventh	10.62	9.81	10.65	10.95	10.53	10.82	10.82	11.78	10.84
Eighth	12.45	14.42	12.39	12.57	12.00	12.69	12.64	12.30	12.63
Ninth	15.19	18.75	15.24	15.10	14.22	15.07	15.64	15.71	15.66
Top decile	25.80	29.51	25.66	23.76	34.94	23.66	24.03	25.42	24.02

Table 8.4 (Continued)

| | 1996 | | | 1997 | | | 1998 | | |
| | Pre-tax | | Post-tax | Pre-tax | | Post-tax | Pre-tax | | Post-tax |
	Income	Tax	Income	Income	Tax	Income	Income	Tax	Income
Bottom decile	1.80	0.40	1.81	2.11	0.82	2.12	1.46	0.30	1.45
Second	4.20	2.74	4.23	4.36	2.00	4.40	3.32	0.73	3.38
Third	5.93	4.41	5.94	6.09	3.45	6.11	4.87	1.15	4.89
Fourth	7.33	6.12	7.34	7.37	5.02	7.46	6.26	3.05	6.41
Fifth	8.56	9.83	8.57	8.55	10.02	8.46	8.75	5.42	8.23
Sixth	9.74	11.53	9.72	9.49	12.33	9.38	9.04	8.55	9.66
Seventh	10.94	13.83	10.93	10.77	11.56	10.89	11.27	14.08	11.27
Eighth	12.70	14.50	12.58	12.84	13.84	12.75	13.31	11.96	13.15
Ninth	14.94	14.48	14.97	15.21	18.33	15.25	16.14	18.75	16.09
Top decile	23.87	22.15	23.92	23.20	22.61	23.18	25.57	36.02	25.48

households in the corresponding post-tax decile to the extent of income re-rankings induced by the tax system.

First, it is shown in Table 8.4 that the income gap between the rich and poor widely sharply during the Economic Crisis, as the income shares of the bottom to sixth deciles all decreased while those of the richest four deciles increased. However, the 1998 income taxation did not effectively mitigate the income gap in the sense that post-tax income shares were not significantly different from pre-tax income shares, although the income shares of the most upper deciles shrank after income taxation. In fact, the year of 1998 was no exception and the Korean income taxation also failed to significantly reduce the pre-tax income gaps in other years.

The principle of vertical equity does not require that the income share of the rich should be lowered and the income share of the poor should be raised as a result of equitable taxation. The equal absolute sacrifice principle may result in proportional income taxation, which leaves income shares intact after tax payments.[12] On the contrary, the equal proportional sacrifice principle may lead to progressive income taxation through which the income share of the poor is raised but that of the rich is lowered.[13] Moreover, equal absolute sacrifice with respect to some utility function may be equivalent to equal proportional sacrifice with respect to another utility function that is a monotonic transformation of the original function.[14] Therefore, the pre-tax and post-tax income shares in Table 8.4 can be compared, in order to investigate the equity consequences of the Korean income taxes. While it is true that they were generally upper income deciles, a majority of the deciles with shrinking income shares after taxation did not relate to each other. For example, the income shares of the 4th, 6th, 8th and top deciles shrank after the 1994 taxation, and the income shares of the 6th, 8th and top deciles shrank after the 1997 taxation. Interestingly, the income shares of as many as six deciles of the bottom, 5th, 7th, 8th, 9th and top deciles decreased due to the 1998 taxation. Therefore, it is difficult to work out what vertical equity principles were implemented by the Korean income tax system and whether the tax system remained truly progressive during the sample period.

Table 8.4 also shows an interesting relationship between pre-tax income shares and tax shares. First, there are three (decile) cases in which the tax share of a decile was lower than that of a lower decile, producing evidence against progressive taxation. They are the 9th decile in 1996, the 7th in 1997 and the 8th decile in 1998. Except in these three cases, tax shares were monotonically increasing in deciles. It is also interesting to observe that the lowest decile with the tax share, being larger than its income share significantly, varied over years. For example, it was only the richest decile that bore the redistributive burden in 1993, while the burden was shared by five different deciles in 1994.

In Table 8.4, one can hardly overlook the phenomenon that the tax share of the poorest decile was significantly lower but that of the richest decile was significantly higher in 1998 than the previous year. This is not surprising given the dramatic income changes during the Economic Crisis shown in Table 8.3. Interestingly, as will be noted in the discussion of Table 8.5, the year of 1998 was also when the average effective tax rate changed most widely from the poorest to the richest decile, potentially indicating highest vertical equity among the sample years. During the Economic Crisis, the Korean government implemented a series of tax policy changes to secure income tax bases in coping with shrinking tax revenues. However, it remains doubtful whether and to what extent the vertical equity aspect of the Korean income tax system was affected. It is presumed that the dramatic changes in income distribution itself were mostly responsible for the changes in the distribution of tax burdens.

Whether a given income tax system is structurally progressive or not may be determined by whether the marginal tax rate is higher than the average tax rate at all income levels, or equivalently by whether the average tax rate monotonically increases in income levels. In practice, an individual taxpayer's effective tax rates is computed as the ratio of the amount of tax paid to the pre-tax income amount. Also, the tax system is considered progressive if a taxpayer with a higher pre-tax income faces a higher effective tax rate. This study computed an individual household's effective tax rate as the equivalized tax amount divided by the pre-tax equivalent household income, which is identical to the tax amount divided by the household income.

Table 8.5 presents the average equivalized tax payment and the average effective tax rates computed for deciles and the whole sample per year. First of all, it is seen that the households in the 9th decile in 1996, the 7th decile in 1997 and the 8th decile in 1998 paid less taxes in absolute amounts than their immediately poorer deciles, respectively. Thus, any conceivable vertical equity principle would not imply such phenomena, not to mention truly progressive taxation. This doubt on the vertical equity and progressivity of the Korean income tax system is further substantiated by the non-monotonic progression of the average effective rates shown in the same table.

If the Korean income tax system is to be progressive on the basis of household welfare measured by pre-tax equivalent household income, the average effective tax rate should be increasing in decile rankings. Table 8.5 shows that the taxation was not truly progressive during the sample period. The average tax rate of the richest decile was not the highest among deciles in as many as four sample years. In any sample year, there were at least three deviating deciles that had lower average effective tax rates than poorer deciles, although one cannot miss the general tendency of average effective tax rates being higher for higher deciles. Moreover, one can hardly find a pattern in the distribution of those deviating deciles. For example, the 5th to 7th deciles had lower tax rates than the 4th decile and the top decile lower than the 9th decile in 1992, while the 3rd decile had lower tax rates than the 2nd decile and the 8th and 9th deciles lower than the 7th decile in 1998. Given these

Table 8.5 Average effective tax rate and equivalized tax payment (in 10,000 won per month)

	1992		1993		1995	
	Tax rate	Tax amount	Tax rate	Tax amount	Tax rate	Tax amount
Bottom decile	0.62%	0.03	0.43%	0.03	0.85%	0.06
Second	0.71%	0.19	0.49%	0.16	0.72%	0.29
Third	1.00%	0.40	1.27%	0.60	1.10%	0.60
Fourth	1.62%	0.80	1.51%	0.86	1.39%	0.95
Fifth	1.49%	0.85	1.45%	0.95	1.51%	1.17
Sixth	1.52%	0.99	1.44%	1.06	1.63%	1.44
Seventh	1.58%	1.17	1.63%	1.35	1.53%	1.53
Eighth	1.96%	1.71	1.63%	1.57	1.36%	1.59
Ninth	2.13%	2.23	1.61%	1.84	1.40%	2.03
Top decile	2.05%	3.51	2.44%	4.55	1.50%	3.32
All households	1.47%	1.19	1.39%	1.30	1.30%	1.30

	1996		1997		1998	
	Tax rate	Tax amount	Tax rate	Tax amount	Tax rate	Tax amount
Bottom decile	0.43%	0.06	0.54%	0.13	0.41%	0.05
Second	0.95%	0.39	0.66%	0.32	0.47%	0.12
Third	1.11%	0.62	0.84%	0.55	0.46%	0.19
Fourth	1.24%	0.87	1.00%	0.81	0.95%	0.51
Fifth	1.71%	1.39	1.72%	1.61	1.18%	0.85
Sixth	1.76%	1.63	1.90%	1.97	1.80%	1.52
Seventh	1.88%	1.96	1.57%	1.88	2.38%	2.33
Eighth	1.69%	2.05	1.60%	2.22	1.70%	1.97
Ninth	1.44%	2.05	1.77%	2.95	2.23%	3.12
Top decile	1.38%	3.16	1.51%	3.64	2.59%	6.06
All households	1.36%	1.42	1.31%	1.61	1.41%	1.66

observations, it seems fair to conclude that the Korean income tax system failed to be progressive in terms of household welfare, despite its statutory progressivity displayed by increasing marginal tax rate for income brackets.

Table 8.5 seems to indicate a decreasing trend in the overall average effective tax rate until 1997, this year being followed by a relatively significant increase by 0.1 percent in 1998. Interestingly, the sample year of 1998 shows the largest increase in the average effective tax rate from the poorest decile to the richest decile. It also happened that the average effective tax rate of the poorest decile at 0.41 percent was the lowest and that of the richest decile at 2.59 percent was the highest among the six sample years. As discussed earlier, this seemingly high progressivity in 1998 should be attributed to the combination of the existing tax structure and distinctive income dynamics during the Economic Crisis rather than the new tax changes implemented during the year.

As explained above, the average effective tax rates presented in Table 8.5 were computed as the average of all individual taxpayers' effective tax rates for each decile. In contrast, previous studies often investigated the progressivity of taxes on the basis of each decile's effective tax rate, computed as the average tax payment divided by the average pre-tax income of all households belonging to the decile. The effective tax rates obtained in this way might not be as revealing or informative because no information about the distribution of tax rates within each decile is reflected in them. This method is equivalent to assuming that each decile is completely represented by a hypothetical household earning the decile-average income and making the decile-average tax payment. Therefore, even if the same equivalent household income were used as the tax base in this method, the obtained rates would be different from the rates computed in this study, because all households within each decile are not homogeneous in terms of income and tax payments.

For the sake of comparison, the effective tax rates were computed using hypothetically representative households, which are juxtaposed with the effective tax rates quoted from comparable previous studies for 1992 and 1996.[15] First, one should note that the effective tax rates for 1992, 1995 and 1996 in this table (that is, the 2nd, 5th and 7th columns of the table, respectively) and the corresponding rates in Table 8.5 show non-negligible differences. The extents were determined by the variation of income and tax payment distributions within deciles. For example, using representative households led to the overall effective tax rates being 1.71 percent in 1992, 1.40 percent in 1995 and 1.48 percent in 1996, each of which is higher than its counterpart of 1.47 percent, 1.30 percent and 1.36 percent in Table 8.5, respectively.

Two previous studies from 1992 (Table 8.6) were based on the KHPS data. As introduced earlier, Im (1996) computed the effective tax rates for two sub-samples of wage earning individuals: one with zero-tax payers included

Table 8.6 Effective income tax rate (%)

	1992 (This study)	1992 (Im, 1996)	1992 (Lee, 1997)	1995 (This study)	1995 (Hyun, 1999)	1996 (This study)
Data coverage			Same as this study		Similar to this study	
Source of tax data for self-employed taxpayers	Survey data	Wage earning individuals	Estimated from income	Survey data	Survey data	Survey data
Bottom decile	0.30	0.59	0.94	0.42	0.16	0.33
Second	0.70	0.69	0.96	0.75	0.23	0.97
Third	1.00	0.87	1.03	1.11	0.37	1.10
Fourth	1.62	0.89	0.96	1.39	0.50	1.24
Fifth	1.50	1.13	1.37	1.51	0.66	1.70
Sixth	1.53	1.17	1.89	1.62	0.81	1.75
Seventh	1.58	1.37	2.26	1.52	0.99	1.87
Eighth	1.98	1.34	2.80	1.36	1.08	1.69
Ninth	2.11	1.64	3.67	1.40	1.23	1.44
Top decile	1.96	3.00	5.07	1.48	1.60	1.38
All households	1.71		3.20	1.40	0.80	1.48

and the other without zero-tax payers, and Table 8.6 presents the tax rates obtained from the latter.

In comparing the tax rates computed in this study and those in Im (1996) (the 2nd and 3rd columns of the table), one should take into account the following differences:

1) The sample unit was a wage-earning individual taxpayer in Im (1996), whereas it was a household with comprehensive income sources in this study;
2) All zero-tax payers were included in Im's (1996) sample, whereas zero-tax payers with income levels higher than their estimated tax exemption points were excluded in this study; and
3) The unit of analysis was the pre-tax earnings defined as the total of wages and bonuses in Im (1996), whereas it was the pre-tax equivalent household income derived from a more comprehensive household income in this study.

Among these three different factors, one would expect that the second factor would lead to Im's (1996) rates being no higher than the rates in this study. However, the first and third factors are presumed to create the opposite bias, given that that the effective tax rates for self-employed taxpayers are generally higher than those for wage earning taxpayers. While the net consequence is thus a priori ambiguous, Table 8.6 shows that Im's (1996) tax rates are mostly lower than the rates in this study, although at varying degrees.

Based on the same KHPS data as Im (1996) and this study, Lee's (1997) study is noted by the following factors:

1) the sample unit was a household like in this study;
2) a) zero-tax payers among wage earning households were included; but
   b) taxes paid by self-employed households were estimated from their reported pre-tax income in order to filter out tax data tainted by tax evasion;
3) the unit of analysis was the pre-tax household income; and
4) compulsory contributions to social security and medical insurance were added to income taxes.

First, the factor of (3) would not create any bias, since tax payments were also equivalized. Apparently, the factor of (2-a) above would lead to Lee's (1997) tax rates being lower than the rate computed in this study, while the factors of (2-b) and (4) would lead to the opposite conclusion. Therefore, it is hard to make an a priori conclusion as to the discrepancies between Lee's (1997) rates and the rates computed in this study. However, Table 8.6 shows that Lee's (1997) rates are not only mostly higher than the rates in this study but also consistently higher than Im's (1996), clearly indicating significant under-taxation of income for self-employed taxpayers.

Hyun's (1999) study quoted in Table 8.6 was based on data from the *National Survey of Household Income and Expenditure* conducted by the Korea National Statistical Office in 1996. The sample period of the survey was the calendar year of 1995, which partially overlapped with our sample years of 1995 and 1996. Hyun's (1999) study is also noted for the following factors:

1) the sample unit was a household like in this study;
2) zero-tax payers were not separately treated;
3) the unit of analysis was the pre-tax equivalent household income as in this study; and
4) the pre-tax income for self-employed taxpayers was estimated from their consumption, under the assumption that consumption behavior was invariant with income sources.

Given that different sample households were selected for a different sample period, one can hardly compare Hyun's (1999) rates with the rates in this study. However, the factors of (2) and (4) would lead to Hyun's (1999) rates being consistently lower than the rates in this study. This is indeed the case, as shown in Table 8.6. Interestingly, it is also seen in the table that the discrepancies between Hyun's (1999) rates and the rates in this study are relatively decreasing in decile rankings, although it is not known whether the phenomenon is due to different sampling or certain systematic bias.

Table 8.6 clearly illustrates how different estimates of effective tax rates can be obtained, depending on the methodology and data used. The above discussion of Table 8.6 is not meant to be a relative evaluation of different studies. However, it would be fair to say that this study stands out in that the same methodology was applied to panel data covering a period of seven years, making it possible and meaningful to compare across different points of time and delineate trends during the sample period, if any.

8.4.3 Tax-induced income re-ranking

The tax mobility matrix is a fractile transition matrix by which income rankings are transformed as a result of taxation. Tax mobility matrices were constructed using the decile rankings of pre-tax equivalent household income for all sample years, which are presented in Tables 8.7–8.12. Two separate tax mobility matrices were constructed for each year, one based on equivalent household income and the other based on household income.

In the household income-based tax mobility matrices, any non-diagonal elements are violations of the classical horizontal equity or the principle of equal treatment of equals. However, as discussed earlier, the equity implication of household income re-rankings is ambiguous in the sense that the acceptable inequity and the unacceptable inequity are inseparably mixed. In this sense, these matrices in Tables 8.7–8.12 only serve illustrative purposes. Here, 'equals' are defined in terms of household size and composition,

Table 8.7 Tax mobility matrix in 1992

Equivalent income	Post-tax deciles									
Pre-tax decile	Bottom	Second	Third	Fourth	Fifth	Sixth	Seventh	Eighth	Ninth	Top
Bottom	98.58	1.42								
Second	1.59	96.72	1.69							
Third		1.83	94.43	3.74						
Fourth			3.64	93.72	2.64					
Fifth				2.77	92.12	5.10				
Sixth					4.50	92.20	3.31			
Seventh					0.45	2.53	94.50	2.52		
Eighth						0.26	2.24	93.05	4.46	
Ninth								4.41	93.59	2.00
Top									2.50	97.50

Household income	Post-tax deciles									
Pre-tax decile	Bottom	Second	Third	Fourth	Fifth	Sixth	Seventh	Eighth	Ninth	Top
Bottom	98.17	1.83								
Second	1.76	96.83	1.41							
Third		1.48	95.07	3.45						
Fourth			3.18	88.71	8.11					
Fifth				8.19	87.41	4.40				
Sixth					4.76	91.57	3.67			
Seventh						3.55	90.16	6.28		
Eighth						0.26	6.02	88.77	4.96	
Ninth								4.97	93.23	1.80
Top									2.10	97.90

Table 8.8 Tax mobility matrix in 1993

Equivalent income	Post-tax deciles									
	Bottom	Second	Third	Fourth	Fifth	Sixth	Seventh	Eighth	Ninth	Top
Bottom	99.27	0.73								
Second	1.02	96.36	2.63							
Third		2.72	95.84	1.44						
Fourth			1.68	93.63	4.69					
Fifth				4.00	89.50	6.49				
Sixth					5.85	90.44	3.71			
Seventh				0.73		3.14	91.44	4.69		
Eighth							4.79	90.39	4.82	
Ninth								4.11	92.63	3.26
Top								0.38	2.67	96.95

(Pre-tax decile)

Household income	Post-tax deciles									
	Bottom	Second	Third	Fourth	Fifth	Sixth	Seventh	Eighth	Ninth	Top
Bottom	98.69	1.31								
Second	1.37	96.45	2.17							
Third		1.91	84.48	13.61						
Fourth			15.27	76.01	8.73					
Fifth				9.23	87.39	3.38				
Sixth					1.53	86.59	11.87			
Seventh					0.88	9.99	84.92	4.21		
Eighth					0.72		3.30	89.79	6.19	
Ninth								5.75	92.52	1.73
Top									1.66	98.34

(Pre-tax decile)

Table 8.9 Tax mobility matrix in 1995

Equivalent income

Pre-tax decile	Post-tax deciles									
	Bottom	Second	Third	Fourth	Fifth	Sixth	Seventh	Eighth	Ninth	Top
Bottom	99.16	0.84								
Second	0.45	99.26	0.30							
Third		0.61	97.39	1.99						
Fourth			2.34	91.83	5.83					
Fifth				5.95	89.84	4.20				
Sixth					4.35	90.81	4.85			
Seventh						4.52	91.73	3.75		
Eighth							3.31	94.95	1.74	
Ninth								1.48	97.46	1.06
Top									1.11	98.89

Household income

Pre-tax decile	Post-tax deciles									
	Bottom	Second	Third	Fourth	Fifth	Sixth	Seventh	Eighth	Ninth	Top
Bottom	99.08	0.92								
Second	0.60	98.94	0.47							
Third		0.74	91.32	7.94						
Fourth			7.89	86.42	5.70					
Fifth				5.59	91.02	3.39				
Sixth					3.99	92.17	3.84			
Seventh						3.25	93.56	3.19		
Eighth							2.58	94.67	2.75	
Ninth								2.53	95.86	1.60
Top									1.49	98.51

Table 8.10 Tax mobility matrix in 1996

Equivalent income

Pre-tax decile	Post-tax deciles									
	Bottom	Second	Third	Fourth	Fifth	Sixth	Seventh	Eighth	Ninth	Top
Bottom	98.61	1.39								
Second	1.79	95.91	2.31							
Third		2.17	93.21	4.62						
Fourth			4.81	83.84	11.35					
Fifth				11.84	79.03	9.13				
Sixth					8.84	82.01	9.15			
Seventh					0.61	9.05	84.92	5.43		
Eighth							5.25	90.98	3.77	
Ninth								3.51	94.65	1.84
Top									1.75	98.25

Household income

Pre-tax decile	Post-tax deciles									
	Bottom	Second	Third	Fourth	Fifth	Sixth	Seventh	Eighth	Ninth	Top
Bottom	99.70	0.30								
Second	0.17	97.96	1.86							
Third		1.79	96.45	1.76						
Fourth			1.96	82.16	15.88					
Fifth				15.70	79.53	4.77				
Sixth					4.89	80.07	15.05			
Seventh					0.61	14.24	80.92	4.23		
Eighth							4.38	92.77	2.85	
Ninth								2.55	95.97	1.48
Top									1.46	98.54

Table 8.11 Tax mobility matrix in 1997

Equivalent income

Pre-tax decile	Post-tax deciles									
	Bottom	Second	Third	Fourth	Fifth	Sixth	Seventh	Eighth	Ninth	Top
Bottom	98.61	1.39								
Second	1.55	96.85	1.60							
Third		1.56	94.11	4.33						
Fourth			4.02	92.29	3.69					
Fifth			0.33	3.90	83.51	12.26				
Sixth					11.92	83.27	4.81			
Seventh						3.78	91.26	4.96		
Eighth							5.09	85.73	9.18	
Ninth								8.99	89.94	1.06
Top									1.34	98.66

Household income

Pre-tax decile	Post-tax deciles									
	Bottom	Second	Third	Fourth	Fifth	Sixth	Seventh	Eighth	Ninth	Top
Bottom	99.22	0.78								
Second	0.77	87.89	11.33							
Third		10.86	86.58	2.56						
Fourth			3.53	91.59	4.89					
Fifth				4.50	83.71	11.80				
Sixth				0.34	11.30	85.31	3.06			
Seventh						3.38	88.54	8.09		
Eighth							7.86	79.91	12.23	
Ninth								12.78	86.10	1.11
Top									1.23	98.77

Table 8.12 Tax mobility matrix in 1998

Equivalent income

	Post-tax deciles									
Pre-tax decile	Bottom	Second	Third	Fourth	Fifth	Sixth	Seventh	Eighth	Ninth	Top
Bottom	98.46	1.54								
Second	1.42	97.01	1.58							
Third		1.43	95.06	3.52						
Fourth			3.42	93.85	2.73					
Fifth				2.75	86.16	11.08				
Sixth					5.29	89.55	5.16			
Seventh					0.64	4.49	92.25	2.61		
Eighth							3.13	89.74	7.14	
Ninth								7.49	90.90	1.62
Top									1.03	98.97

Household income

	Post-tax deciles									
Pre-tax decile	Bottom	Second	Third	Fourth	Fifth	Sixth	Seventh	Eighth	Ninth	Top
Bottom	98.74	1.26								
Second	0.85	96.73	2.42							
Third		2.53	96.45	1.02						
Fourth			0.99	97.90	1.11					
Fifth				0.79	98.58	0.62				
Sixth					1.80	93.00	5.20			
Seventh						4.45	88.32	7.23		
Eighth						0.65	6.72	87.77	4.87	
Ninth								5.96	93.36	0.68
Top									1.02	98.98

thereby encapsulated in the notion of household equivalence scale. It follows then that a re-ranking of equivalent household income indicates an obvious instance of horizontal inequity.

Table 8.7 presents the Tax Mobility Matrix for 1992, showing that 1.42 percent of the pre-tax bottom decile households were promoted to the 2nd decile as a result of redistribution through the income tax system in that year. The 1992 Tax Mobility Matrix is tri-diagonal except for the 7th and 8th (pre-tax) deciles, showing that rank-shifts occurred mostly between immediately neighboring deciles. The 5th decile suffered the most income re-rankings with as much as 8 percent of the households being promoted or demoted to the neighboring deciles. It was the 7th decile that experienced re-rankings most severely in terms of the 'distances' of rank-shifts. It is seen that 0.45 percent of the 8th decile households were demoted to the 5th decile after taxation.

Table 8.8 also shows that income re-rankings mostly happened across the neighboring deciles in 1993. This observation is generally repeated in all sample years. Another common observation is that the 5th decile was subject to most re-rankings in all but 1997 when it was the 6th decile as seen in Table 8.11. In principle, income re-rankings can be caused by various differential treatments of different income sources, such as different statutory tax rates, tax administration or collection procedures and relationships with other taxes. Not only did these differences generally exist among wage income, business income and financial income in Korea during the sample period, they were also more prominent for the middle-income class. According to Tables 8.7–8.12, the 5th and 6th deciles were the two deciles mostly affected by income re-rankings on average throughout the sample period.

Like in 1992, it was the 7th decile that experienced the most distant rank-shifts in 1993. Table 8.8 shows that 0.73 percent of the 7th decile households were demoted to the 4th decile after taxation, while none of the 6th decile households were demoted to lower than 5th decile.

The 1995 Tax Mobility Matrix in Table 8.9 is completely tri-diagonal, unlike the matrices for other years. In addition, its diagonal elements are relatively larger than the corresponding elements in the other matrices, thereby implying that relatively less re-rankings occurred in 1995. As will be discussed later in terms of the mean squared relative rank-shift, it was the year of 1995 that experienced the least extent of income re-rankings among the sample years.

Table 8.10 displays the case of most (cross-decile) re-rankings in all sample years—the 5th decile in 1996. The table shows that as much as 21 percent of the households in the decile ended up in other deciles after taxation. More than half of the affected households were demoted to the 4th decile, while about the same number of the 4th-decile households were promoted to the 5th decile due to taxation. This extent of income re-rankings seems to clearly indicate serious horizontal inequity, although they happened across the adjacent deciles.

In 1997, it was the 5th decile that experienced the highest extent of re-rankings, unlike any other sample year in which it was the 5th decile. Table 8.11 shows that about 17 percent of 6th-decile households were shifted to the adjacent deciles, among which about 12 percent were demoted to the 5th decile. In contrast, about the same number of the 5th-decile households were promoted to the 6th decile.

In comparison with other tables, Table 8.11 also shows another couple of interesting observations peculiar to the year of 1997. Suppose we divide the six deciles of the middle-income class into three sub-classes:

1) the lower-middle class being the 3rd and 4th deciles;
2) the narrowly defined middle-income class being the 5th and 6th deciles; and
3) the upper-middle class being the 7th and 8th deciles.

In all sample years, the order of increasing extent of income re-rankings is the lower-middle class, the upper-middle class and then the rest, when the extent is measured by the percentage of the re-ranked households in all deciles belonging to the sub-class. This is not surprising as the 5th and 6th deciles were the most affected deciles throughout the sample period.

However, the year of 1997 stands out in terms of the difference between the extent of re-rankings happening to the lower-middle class and that of the upper-middle class. The difference was about 10 percent, whereas the second largest difference was about 8 percent shown in 1993 and the smallest difference was less than 1 percent shown in 1992. The year further stands out in terms of the difference between the extent of re-rankings happened to the lower-middle class and that of the narrowly defined middle-income class. The difference in 1997 was as much as 20 percent, whereas the second largest difference was about 16 percent shown in 1996 and the smallest difference was about 4 percent shown in 1992. These observations only signify how different extent of income re-rankings and hence horizontal inequity the Korean income tax system caused in different income groups.

The same exercise also reveals that it was in the year of 1992 that the three sub-groups suffered re-rankings the most evenly, and it was the year of 1996 that each of the three sub-groups suffered the most re-rankings relative to other years. This kind of exercise would become more useful in conjunction with normative considerations as to which income deciles or classes should be weighed relatively more or less in Korean society, such as an endogenous tax model incorporating the Median Voter Theorem. Apparently, there is no consensus about such welfare (or political) weights of income classes, and further considerations are beyond the scope of this study.

Table 8.12 presents the tax mobility matrix for the sample year of 1998, which was the period of the Economic Crisis in Korea. In general, the table shows that re-rankings happened only moderately relative to other years, indicating that income taxation caused less horizontally inequity in 1998 than in other sample years. The table also shows that the 7th decile experienced an extensive re-ranking in that some households were demoted as far as to the 5th decile. As indicated earlier, it would be more appropriate to attribute these phenomena to the distinctive income distribution dynamics during the Economic Crisis rather than tax policy changes implemented in the year.

Although the tax mobility matrix is useful for visually describing income movements induced by taxation, it necessarily neglects income re-rankings taking place within each income decile. In addition, the tax mobility matrix cannot show some important details of re-rankings, such as the distances of rank-shifts. As a complementary instrument to the tax mobility matrix, the mean squared relative rank-shift were computed as a single summary measure of overall income re-rankings, which is presented in Table 8.13. The table also presents other useful statistics of the tax-induced re-rankings.

Table 8.13 shows that most households were rank-shifted after paying income taxes in every sample year. For example, all but 82 of a total of 2873 households experienced tax-induced re-rankings in 1992.[16] In fact, the number of the rank-shifted households amounts to 94–97 percent of the total households over the sample years, of which the magnitude indicates that the Korean income tax system was hardly compatible with the classical horizontal equity. The table shows that the year of 1998 had the fewest re-rankings as the ratio of the rank-preserved households was as high as 6 percent, whereas the ratio was as low as 3 percent in three of the remaining five sample years. Interestingly, however, the percentage of the promoted households in that year was the second highest among the sample years, while the percentage of the demoted households was the lowest.

Whenever an income re-ranking occurs between two adjacently ranked households, the number of promoted households and the number of demoted households will equally increase by one. But if a household is demoted by more than one rank, the number of promoted households will increase exactly by the change in the household's ranking or the distance of the household's rank-shift, while the number of demoted household will increase by one. Therefore, one can understand how large a typical rank-shift was by comparing the numbers of promoted and demoted households.

As for data in Table 8.13, at least the following two observations are notable. First, the number of promoted households was significantly larger than that of demoted households in each sample year, implying that a typical re-ranking did not happen between two rank-adjacent households. Moreover, the ratio of the number of promoted households over the number of demoted households generally decreased from 2.08 in 1992 to 1.81 in 1997.[17] This implies that the distance of a typical rank-shift decreased during the period, and such change should be considered favorable relative to the horizontal equity principle.

Table 8.13 Tax-induced re-ranking of equivalent household income

	1992				1993			
	All households	Promoted households	Remaining households	Demoted households	All households	Promoted households	Remaining households	Demoted households
Number of households	2873	66%	3%	31%	2510	65%	3%	32%
Average equivalent income	69.36	66.46	129.05	70.03	76.51	76.91	42.02	79.35
Average change		0.005		0.011		0.006		0.011
Biggest change		0.032		0.157		0.033		0.269
Measure of overall tax mobility (x10^7)		1893				2173		

Table 8.13 (Continued)

	1995				1996			
	All households	Promoted households	Remaining households	Demoted households	All households	Promoted households	Remaining households	Demoted households
Number of households	2134	61%	5%	34%	1841	63%	4%	33%
Average equivalent income	92.68	90.30	92.75	96.97	95.75	89.55	134.36	102.41
Average change		0.006		0.010		0.006		0.011
Biggest change		0.038		0.110		0.034		0.154
Measure of overall tax mobility (x10^7)		1196				1693		

Table 8.13 (Continued)

	1997				1998			
	All households	Promoted households	Remaining households	Demoted households	All households	Promoted households	Remaining households	Demoted households
Number of households	1663	62%	3%	34%	1486	65%	6%	29%
Average equivalent income	109.14	104.56	105.72	117.76	87.08	85.46	59.42	96.51
Average change		0.007		0.011		0.005		0.011
Biggest change		0.058		0.186		0.027		0.181
Measure of overall tax mobility ($\times 10^7$)	1881				1455			

Given that the average distance of promotions relative to demotions decreased during 1993–97, and also that the percentage of households affected by re-rankings remained stable during the same period, the conclusion may be drawn that horizontal inequity measured by mean squared relative rank-shift must have been decreasing during the period. However, it should be pointed out that the frequency distribution of (relative) rank-shift is tri-modal, with one mode being zero among rank-preserved households, another being negative among demoted households and the last being positive among promoted households. Therefore, a decrease in the average distance of promotions relative to demotions may or may not decrease the overall variation of rank-shifts, even if the fraction of the rank-shifted households were the same. For example, a replacement of a promotion with a 'shorter' one, which reduces the variance of promotions, may increase the variance of (relative) rank-shift.

The distinctiveness of 1998 found in tax mobility matrices is repeated in Table 8.13. First, the percentage of rank-preserved households was the largest among the sample years. In addition, the average distance of promotions relative to demotions was not only the longest but also sharply reversing the decreasing trend until then. These observations lead to the conclusion that the tax-induced rank-shifts affected less households, but more severely so in 1998 than in other years. This conclusion seems to be also supported by the particular observation that, unlike other years, the average equivalent income of the demoted households was exceedingly high in comparison with that of all households, as well as that of the rank-preserved households.

The Economic Crisis in Korea significantly impacted the distribution of income and hence income inequality as found by many previous studies. Yet this study also found that both the frequency and amplitude of the tax-induced income re-rankings in 1998 significantly deviated from their previous trends. While such an aberration does not seem to have stemmed from the 1998 tax changes, the exact causes can be further investigated by future studies.

Table 8.13 also shows that in all years the average equivalent income of demoted households was higher than that of all households, which was then higher than that of promoted households in all years except 1993. This implies that a typical re-ranking happened across the average income household in those five years. It is certainly an interesting phenomenon, yet its equity implications seem to be hardly comprehensible relative to the mean squared relative rank-shift used in this study.

In 1993, the average equivalent income of demoted households was higher than that of promoted households, which was then slightly higher than that of all households. It is also found that the average equivalent income of rank-preserved households was considerably low and comparable to that of the 2nd or 3rd decile in 1993, while the average equivalent income of rank-preserved households was even higher than that of the 9th decile in 1992.

These findings imply that relatively more income re-rankings happened on the higher income side in 1993, and this notable change in equity consequences is deemed to be due to the 1993 tax changes implemented for the purpose of enhancing tax equity and securing tax revenue, such as the reduction of both tax rates and exemptions.

Table 8.13 presents the mean squared relative rank-shift as a measure of the extent of tax-induced income re-rankings. It is seen that its magnitude fluctuated during the sample period, failing to show any obviously increasing or decreasing trend. The mean squared relative rank-shift peaked in 1993, in which both promotions and demotions happened more on the higher income side as discussed earlier. It was least in 1995, in which the percentage of rank-preserved households was second highest and the average distance of promotions relative to demotions was shortest among the six sample years.

As no related previous studies exist, it is hard to make a comparative conclusion on the measure of the mean squared relative rank-shift computed in this study. However, it seems that the measure is sufficiently responsive to the changes in the tax system and/or income distribution, providing additional description of the equity characteristics of the tax system that may not be captured by other single figures, such as the percentage of rank-preserved households and the average distance of rank-shifts.

8.4.4   Tax effect on inequality and decomposition

In this study, the inequality effect—more precisely, distributional progressivity—of the Korean income tax system was first measured by the COG and then decomposed into two components, between-group inequality and within-group inequality. As noted earlier, the tax effect measured in this way is virtually identical to the measure of tax progressivity proposed Kakwani (1977), since the COG is only a linear function of the Gini Coefficient. The computation results are presented in Table 8.14.

First of all, Table 8.14 shows that overall pre-tax (equivalent income) inequality significantly decreased between 1992 and 1997. In 1992, the overall inequality was 0.6752 in terms of the COG (or equivalently, 0.3504 in terms of the Gini coefficient), which implies that the income distribution in 1992 was centered on the household of the 68th poorest percentile. Except in 1995, it gradually decreased every sample year until it became as low as 0.6591 in 1997 (or equivalently, 0.3182 in terms of the Gini coefficient), which implies that the COG of income distribution shifted down by two percentile during the period.

The inequality trend during 1992–97 found in this study seems to make an interesting comparison with previous findings in the literature. Using data from the Urban Household Income and Expenditure Survey (UHIES), Sung and Lee (2001) found that overall inequality measured by the Gini

Table 8.14 Tax effect and inequality decomposition

	1992			1993			1995		
	Pre-tax	Post-tax	Tax effect	Pre-tax	Post-tax	Tax effect	Pre-tax	Post-tax	Tax effect
Overall inequality (COG)	0.6752	0.6744	−0.0008	0.6632	0.6622	−0.0010	0.6680	0.6678	−0.0002
Between-group inequality (COG(K))	0.7207	0.7198	−0.0009	0.7094	0.7086	−0.0008	0.7142	0.7140	−0.0002
Within-group inequality	0.0545	0.0546	0.0001	0.0538	0.0536	−0.0002	0.0538	0.0537	0.0000
% Change in COG(K) relative to change in COG			110.32			81.89			92.19

	1996			1997			1998		
	Pre-tax	Post-tax	Tax effect	Pre-tax	Post-tax	Tax effect	Pre-tax	Post-tax	Tax effect
Overall inequality (COG)	0.6641	0.6640	−0.0001	0.6591	0.6586	−0.0004	0.6875	0.6859	−0.0016
Between-group inequality (COG(K))	0.7098	0.7096	−0.0002	0.7053	0.7050	−0.0004	0.7321	0.7313	−0.0009
Within-group inequality	0.0543	0.0544	0.0001	0.0537	0.0537	−0.0001	0.0554	0.0547	−0.0007
% Change in COG(K) relative to change in COG			189.24			87.92			54.79

coefficient continued to deteriorate from 1995 to 1997, whereas the National Statistical Office announced that the deterioration in 1996 was more than recovered in 1997. According to Cheong (2000a), who measured the COG of equivalent household income distribution using the UHIES data, overall income inequality was improving during the early 1990s or at least until the middle of 1994, and then started to deteriorate until a brief turn to an improvement in the middle of 1997.

It should be taken into account that the KHPS data and UHIES data are different in many respects, such as geographical and occupational coverage of the sample households, coverage of income sources and definition of the sample years. Despite all such differences, this study shares with previous studies the result that income inequality sharply deteriorated during the Economic Crisis, as shown by the significant increase of the COG from 0.6591 to 0.6875 in Table 8.13, which corresponds to a substantial increase of the Gini coefficient from 0.2804 to 0.3801.

Table 8.13 shows that the post-tax inequality closely followed the movement of the pre-tax inequality, implying that the tax effect on income inequality or the distributional progressivity might have not been significant during the sample period. In fact, the tax effect computed as the difference between the pre-tax COG and the post-tax COG ranges between –0.0001 and –0.0016, which corresponds to a range of –0.0002 to –0.0032 in terms of the Gini coefficient. Although all negative numbers imply that the income taxation in Korea was progressive throughout the sample years, the magnitude of the tax effect in such a range is considerably small relative to previous results. For example, the 1995 tax effect, being –0.0004 in terms of the Gini coefficient, is much smaller than –0.0025 in Hyun (1999) and –0.0088 in Sung and Lee (2001).

Although the magnitude of the tax effect is small, its fluctuation relative to the tax mobility seems to illuminate useful information regarding the interpretation of the obtained numbers. It is found that the overall tax mobility presented in Table 8.13 and overall tax effect in Table 8.14 did not fluctuate in the same way, nor did they fluctuate in the opposite ways. Compared to the corresponding immediately previous sample years, they moved together in the same direction in 1993, 1995 and 1997, but they deviated in the opposite directions in 1996 and 1998. If they always move differently, it would mean that vertical equity is always complementary to horizontal equity by way of reduced income re-rankings. On the contrary, if they always move together, it would mean that vertical equity is enhanced always at the expense of income re-rankings and vice versa. In other words, there is an unavoidable trade-off between vertical equity and horizontal equity. However, the existence of such trade-off is denied by the results in Tables 8.13 and 8.14, which otherwise would restrict the flexibility in the government policy toward tax equity.

On the other hand, one should note that, in principle, the non-existence of income re-rankings is a premise of vertical equity. In this sense, the usefulness of a progressivity measure based on the COG or the Gini coefficient, which does not filter out the effects of re-rankings, seems to be seriously undermined when the tax in consideration caused as many re-rankings as seen in Korea.

Table 8.14 also presents the overall pre-tax and post-tax inequality respectively decomposed into between-group inequality and within-group inequality. It is not surprising that within-group inequality was dwarfed by between-group inequality and hence the change of overall inequality was mostly driven by the latter in all sample years. However, it is an intriguing finding that the percentage change in between-group inequality relative to the change in the overall inequality exceeded 100 in 1992 and 1996, implying that within-group inequality increased rather than decreased due to the income taxation in those years. A truly progressive tax should be progressive on any subset of income distribution, as a higher income household should face a higher tax rate. In this sense, the observation of increased within-group inequality is inconsistent with the alleged progressive nature of the Korean income tax system. Put another way, income taxation in Korea does not seem to be as progressive as is suggested by the usual distributional measure of progressivity, not to mention the statutory rate structure.

Again, the sample year of 1998 warrants additional attention. First, the tax effect on overall inequality was most prominent in this year. Further, within-group inequality was most improved by taxation in the same year. Therefore, one may say that income taxation was most progressive in 1998, aside from the issues on true progressivity raised above. This conclusion seems to be in line with an earlier observation that the 1998 taxation showed higher progressivity than any other sample year in terms of the faster average rate progression presented in Table 8.5.

However, one should also recall from Table 8.13 that income re-rankings affected least households but the average distance of re-rankings was longest in the same year. From the perspective of vertical equity, it is desirable for income tax to improve inequality without causing re-rankings. Given the diverse income sources and their differential treatments in tax codes, income re-rankings cannot be completely avoided in reality. This line of thinking, along with the previous observations, leads one to conclude that income taxation in Korea was most consistent, with vertical equity during the year of the Economic Crisis, among the six sample years.

Lastly, Figure 8.1 is a visual presentation of pre-tax and post-tax inequality trends in Table 8.14. The figure illustrates how closely pre-tax inequality and post-tax inequality moved together, whether in terms of inequality among all households or inequality across income deciles. It is also clearly illustrated how sharply income inequality was worsened during the Economic Crisis.

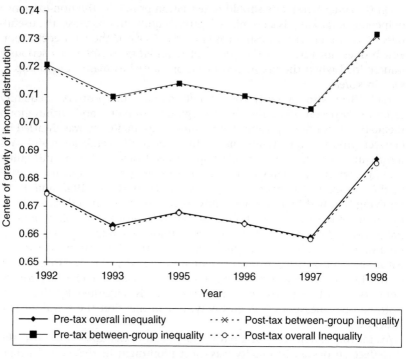

Figure 8.1   Pre- and post-tax inequality trends

8.5   Concluding remarks

Distributive justice is an important normative foundation of the income tax system, and the redistributive effects of the Korean income tax system are emerging as a popular topic in socio-economic policy debates in Korea. Applying newer methods of analysis to panel data from the KHPS, various equity consequences of the Korean income tax system during the period of 1992 to 1998 were empirically explored.

On the surface, the overall tax effects were not strong in terms of the welfare changes for individual households or the reduction of welfare gaps between the rich and the poor. Whether it is measured using the structural measure of average rate progression or the distributional measure of the COG, the extent of vertical equity implemented by the tax system was not significant throughout the sample years, despite the apparent statutory progressivity.

While these results are basically in the line with previous studies, substantial evidence against the principle of progressive taxation was found. First, the average effective tax rates computed for equivalent income deciles failed to consistently increase in decile rankings in each sample year. In addition, there are three cases in which income taxation incurred more welfare sacrifice to a lower decile than a higher decile. Decomposition analysis further found that the within-group inequality was negatively affected by income taxation despite the unambiguous improvement in overall inequality during the sample years of 1992 and 1996.

The undesirable redistributive effects of income taxation in Korea were even further signified by the extent of the tax-induced re-rankings analyzed by means of the tax mobility matrix and the mean squared relative rank-shift. From the re-ranking analysis being yet another addition to the literature, it was found that the Korean income tax system induced re-rankings of equivalent household income so extensively as to affect most households in all sample years. General, the middle-income class of the 5th and 6th deciles were most rank-shifted to adjacent deciles.

The high frequency of the tax-induced re-rankings not only indicates a serious violation of horizontal equity but also significantly undermines effective progressivity measured in any fashion. As a summary of overall re-rankings, the mean squared relative rank-shift was computed to help delineate a better understanding of tax inequity during the sample period. While fluctuating significantly over years, the mean squared relative rank-shift displayed no obvious trends such as effective progressivity. However, the average distance of rank-shifts gradually decreased from 1992 until 1997 and then sharply increased in 1998. Given these observations, it cannot be concluded that a series of tax policy changes implemented during the sample period were visibly effective in alleviating horizontal inequity in taxation.

The sample year of 1998, which largely overlapped with the Economic Crisis in Korea, was worthy of note compared to the prior years. In that year, the progression of effective tax rates was most prominent. The distributional tax effect on income inequality was also prominent, yet the percentage of rank-preserved households was highest and the extent of the tax-induced re-rankings was the second lowest. Thus, the year is marked with significantly less tax inequity than the other sample years, which seems to be attributed to the combination of the existing tax peculiarities and the distributive impacts of the Economic Crisis.

In this chapter, while agreeing with the general understanding that the redistributive effect of the Korean income tax system has been only moderate in terms of effective progressivity, existing studies were extended by highlighting equity implications based on the tax-induced re-rankings, which have been long overdue in the literature. In summary, the unfavorable redistributive effect in terms of re-ranking and hence horizontal inequity has been substantially large, although the significance has fluctuated over years. It should be noted, however, that all findings and conclusions made in this chapter may have inherited the limitations of the particular data set and methodology used, and thus they must be considered with caution.

Notes

1. I thankfully acknowledge the financial support from the Korea Institute of Public Finance. The opinions expressed in this study are my own, not to mention any remaining errors.
2. This sentence draws on Auerbach and Hassett (1999).
3. In the same vein, Wagstaff *et al.* (1999) noted that the classical horizontal inequity might be more appropriately called horizontal inequality, since some horizontal inequality may be considered equitable.
4. See Cheong (2000b) for further discussion of the COG relative to the Gini coefficient.
5. See Cheong (2000b) for proof of Equation (4).
6. The KLIPS is mainly focused on labor market activities and does not address tax questions.
7. This summary heavily draws on Ministry of Finance and Economy of Korea (1999). More details may be found in the source or similar government publications.
8. As illustrated by Dardanoni and Lambert (2000), income brackets with low marginal tax rates can be more progressive because it matters for progressivity where the taxpayers are located.
9. Unless specified otherwise, income deciles are defined on the basis of pre-tax equivalent household income levels in this study.
10. There is no consensus about the definition of the middle-income class in the literature, and the conventional usage by the Korea National Statistical Office is followed in this chapter.
11. A pre-tax decile and the corresponding post-tax decile would include the same households, if household income rankings were preserved through income taxation. However, it is far from true in Korea, as will be discussed later.
12. A logarithmic utility function is an example of this case.
13. This would be also true for the equal marginal sacrifice principle as income distribution is completely equalized after taxation under this principle.
14. See Tresch (2002) for related discussion.
15. These previous studies have different scopes than this chapter and, therefore, discussion of their effective tax rates quoted here are not meant to be overall comments on them.
16. Due to the sampling weights of households, the numbers of households obtained for Table 8.14 were not necessarily natural numbers, and were rounded up for the sake of presentation.
17. It is useful to compare the average distance of promotions and the average distance of demotions in the table, since the sum of promotion distances must be identical to the sum of demotion distances.

References

Aronson, R., P. Johnson and P. Lambert (1994) 'Redistributive Effect and Unequal Income Tax Treatment,' *The Economic Journal* **104**(423): 262–70.

Atkinson, A., L. Rainwater and T. Smeeding (1995) 'Income Distribution in OECD Countries: Evidence from the Luxembourg Income Study' (Paris: OECD).

Atkinson, A. (1980) 'Horizontal Equity and the Distribution of the Tax Burden,' in Henry Aaron and Michael Boskin (eds), *The Economics of Taxation* (Washington, DC: The Brookings Institution).

Auerbach, A. and K. Hassett (1999) 'A New Measure of Horizontal Equity,' NBER Working Paper 7035.

Cheong, K. S. (2001) 'Economic Crisis and Income Inequality in Korea,' *Asian Economic Journal* **15**(1): 39–60.

Cheong, K. S. (2000a) *Distributive Inequality and Demographic Characteristics of the Worker Households in Korea: Long-term Trends and Changes after the Economic Crisis* (in Korean), Korea Development Institute.

Cheong, K. S. (2000b) 'A New Interpretation and Derivation of the Gini Coefficient,' *Seoul Journal of Economics* **13**(4): 391–405.

Dalsgaard, T. (2000) 'The Tax System in Korea: More Fairness and Less Complexity Required,' OECD Economic Department, Working Paper 271.

Dardanoni, V. and P. Lambert (2000) 'Progressivity Comparisons,' The Institute for Fiscal Studies, Working Paper 00–18.

Decoster, A. and E. Ooghe (2002) 'Weighting with Individuals, Equivalent Individuals or not Weighting at all. Does it matter empirically?,' CES (Belgium: KULeuven), mimeo.

Duclos, J.-Y., V. Jalbert and A. Araar (2000) 'Classical Horizontal Inequity and Reranking: An Integrated Approach' (Canada: Université Laval), mimeo.

Hyun, J. K. (1999) 'Income Distribution and Tax Policy' (in Korean), Korea Institute of Public Finance Policy Analysis 99–02.

Hyun, J. K. (1996) 'The Distributional Effects of Taxes in Korea: Empirical Evidence by Using 1991 Household Data,' Korea Institute of Public Finance, Working Paper 96–05.

Im, J. Y. (1996) 'A Study of Vertical Equity of the Personal Income Tax System Using the Equal Sacrifice Hypothesis,' in Jin Kwon Hyun (ed.), *Tax Policy and Income Redistribution*, Seoul: Korea Institute of Public Finance.

Kang, S. H. and J. K. Hyun (1998) 'An International Comparison of the Korean Income Distribution' (in Korean), *Research in Economics* **46**(3): 145–67.

Kakwani, N. C. (1977) 'Measurement of Tax Progressivity: An International Comparison,' *The Economic Journal* **87**: 71–80.

King, M. (1983) 'An Index of Inequality: With Applications to Horizontal Equity and Social Mobility,' *Econometrica* **51**: 99–116.

Lee, S.-Y. (1997) 'Tax Evasion and the Redistributive Effects of the Korean Tax system,' Ph.D. Dissertation, Seoul National University.

Ministry of Finance and Economy of Korea (1999) *Korean Taxation*.

Musgrave, R. and T. Thin (1948) 'Income Tax Progression, 1929–1948,' *Journal of Political Economy* **56**: 498–514.

Podder, N. (1997) 'Tax Elasticity, Income Distribution and the Measurement of Tax Progressivity,' *Research on Economic Inequality* **7**: 33–60.

Sung, M.-J. and M.-H. Lee (2001) 'A Study on the Estimation of Redistributive Effects of Taxation: A Cross-Country Comparison in Terms of the Gini Coefficient,' Korean Institute of Public Finance.

Tresch, R. (2002) *Public Finance A Normative Theory* (Second edition), Academic Press.

Wagstaff, A., E. van Doorslaer, H. van der Burg, S. Calonge, T. Christiansen, G. Citoni, U.-G. Gerdtham, M. Gerfin, L. Gross, U. Häkinnen, J. John, P. Johnson, J. Klavus, C. Lachaud, J. Lauridsen, R. Leu, B. Nolan, E. Peran, C. Propper, F. Puffer, L. Rochaix, M. Rodríguesz, M. Schellhorn, G. Sundberg and O. Winkelhake (1999) 'Redistributive Effect, Progressivity and Differential Tax Treatment: Personal Income Taxes in Twelve OECD Countries,' *Journal of Public Economics* **72**: 73–98.

Williams, R., D. Weiner and F. Sammartino (1998) 'Equivalence Scales, the Income Distribution, and Federal Taxes,' Congressional Budget Office, Technical Paper Series, 1999–2.

Part III

International Comparisons

9
Income Distribution and Social Expenditures*

Jonathan A. Schwabish, Timothy M. Smeeding and Lars Osberg

9.1 Introduction

> America's high earners—the fortunate top fifth—thus feel increasingly justified in paying only what is necessary to insure that everyone in their community is sufficiently well educated and has access to the public services they need to succeed
>
> Reich (1991)

Economic inequality, actual or perceived, plays an important role in influencing the set of goods and services that are subsidized by the public sector. Public expenditures on defense, police and fire services, roads, foreign aid, or research and development may (or may not) have benefits for all citizens. However, except for those directly employed in these activities, such expenditures do not directly affect the well-being of households. In this chapter, we focus on public expenditures that provide income or goods and services directly to households. This implies that we are primarily concerned with public expenditure on the provision of 'private goods,' including cash and near-cash transfers.[1]

We first document the trends in social spending as we have defined it and quickly review the existing literature that links social expenditures and inequality. We then construct and estimate a new model of the empirical relationship between inequality and social expenditures. Our main questions deal with the effects that inequality and trust have in the provision of public expenditures. We use trust as a proxy for citizen belief in altruism, help for those around them who are afflicted or in need—regardless of their beliefs as to whether government should facilitate these altruistic desires. Our estimates imply that more trustful societies are associated with higher levels of public spending, while measures of inequality, especially the ratio of the top market income to the middle market income, are indicative of lower spending as defined above.

First, we review and summarize the literature in the area that links social expenditures and inequality. Then we present some summary data linking inequality and trust variables from the International Social Survey Programme (ISSP) data set. In Sections 9.3 and 9.4, we present the data used in our empirical analysis followed by a review of our results. Finally, we bring the issues together in the conclusion of Section 9.5.

9.2   Social spending, inequality and the literature on public redistributive goods and inequality

We briefly review the growing literature on redistribution by governments and inequality. However, before doing so, we examine the trends in social spending and the measures of inequality used to explain its relationship to economic inequality. We offer some clues as to the way in which we review the literature and why we model the relationship between the two, as we do in the next section of this chapter.

9.2.1   Patterns of social spending

Redistributive social expenditures vary greatly across nations. In the developed countries, total social expenditures as a percent of gross domestic product (GDP) (in 1998) ranged from 15 percent in the United States to 26 percent in the United Kingdom to over 30 percent in Sweden (Organization for Economic Co-operation and Development, OECD, 2002a).[2] The available evidence (Smeeding, 2002b) indicates that social expenditures as a fraction of total government spending in OECD nations range from 0.67 in Australia to 0.90 in Denmark and Sweden. That is, 67 to 90 percent of all government spending is made up of redistributive cash or in-kind benefits.[3] Thus, the topic of social expenditure is mainly about what most governments actually do.

We begin by tracing the trend in non-elderly cash and near cash (food, housing) benefits for OECD countries over the past 20 years, using data from the OECD (2002a). We present these estimates in comparable format in Figure 9.1. Here, 17 OECD nations—all of the major nations except for the Central and Eastern Europeans—have been grouped into clusters: Scandinavia and Finland (Finland, Norway, Sweden); Northern Europe (Belgium, Denmark, Netherlands); Central and Southern Europe (Austria, France, Germany, Italy, Luxembourg, Spain); Anglo Saxony (Australia, United Kingdom, Canada); the United States and Mexico.[4]

The Scandinavian and Northern Europeans follow similar patterns—high levels of spending showing responsiveness to the recession of the early 1990s in Sweden and Finland, and a tapering after these events. The Central and Southern Europeans and the Anglo-Saxon nations show remarkably similar spending patterns, again rising in the early 1990s but overall at a level

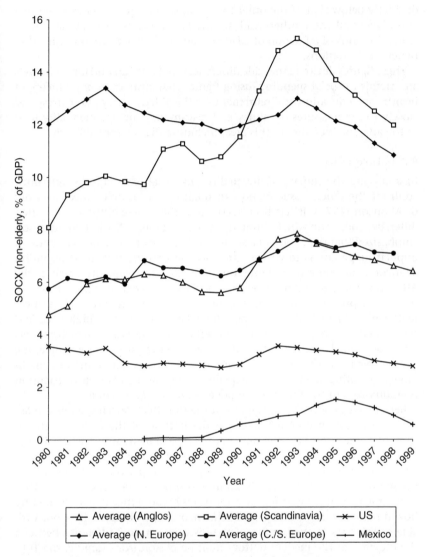

Figure 9.1 Non-elderly social expenditures in 6 sets of 17 nations*

Note: *Total Non-elderly Social Expenditures (as percentage of GDP), including all cash plus near cash spending (for example food stamps) and public housing but excluding health care and education spending. OECD (2002b). Anglos include Australia, UK, Canada; Scandinavia includes Finland, Norway, Sweden; Northern Europe includes Belgium, Denmark, Netherlands; Central/Southern Europe includes Austria, France, Germany, Italy, Luxembourg, Spain.

distinctly below that of the other two groups. The United States is significantly below all these others and, by the late 1990s is spending at a level closer, in terms of a fraction of GDP per capita, to Mexico than to the other richer OECD nations.

These figures illustrate the wide differences that one can find for both levels and trends in social spending, using figures that abstract from financing of health care, education and retirement for the elderly. They also correspond closely to the measures of money and near-money income inequality used in the analytic literature in this area, including that presented below.

9.2.2 Inequality

In analyzing the impact of 'inequality' on social expenditures, one must confront the crucial issue of how inequality is measured. Since the work of Atkinson (1970), it has been recognized that inequality rankings often differ, depending on which summary measure of inequality is used. Atkinson emphasized that the choice of a summary measure of inequality contains an implicit judgment as to which differences in each part of the distribution of income are more important. Some measures of inequality (such as the Atkinson index) weight more heavily the differences between the incomes of the most deprived and the 'mainstream' of society. Whether these differences matter most,[5] or whether it is the difference between the middle class and the affluent (captured better by the coefficient of variation) which matters more, depends largely on which question is being asked. For example, the gap between the affluent and the middle class is an important variable in models of voting behavior but inequality at the lower end of the distribution is emphasized in the literature on poverty and social outcomes.

Because we believe that inequality at the top affects social spending *differently* than does income inequality at the bottom of the distribution, our work makes use of robust measures of each type of inequality, specifically the ratio of the top income groups to the middle income group (90th percentile person divided by the median or 50th percentile person) and the ratio of the middle group to the bottom group (50th percentile person to the 10th percentile person). We prefer these measures because they explicitly identify how differences in specific parts of the income distribution affect our variable of interest. At the bottom of the distribution, the difference between the incomes of the median bottom quintile person (for example, the 10th percentile) and the middle income person (the median or 50th percentile) may show a need for redistribution in the society and hence the larger this difference, the larger is the 'demand' for redistribution.

The arguments for the significance of the top versus middle income comparisons are different. Here we want to test the assertion that there may be a 'tipping point' in overall national levels of inequality (for example, at high levels of the 90/50 ratio), beyond which affluent citizens become less civically engaged and so less likely to support public policies that benefit all of society. This might occur, for example, when a critical mass of high-income parents decide to pull their children out of the local public school system or when well paid employees decide that paying taxes for income security programs or social insurance are a waste of money because it is easier to self-insure at lower cost. As a consequence, it is essential to know *which part* of the distribution of income is becoming more unequal and how each part affects the variable of interest.[6]

9.2.3 The literature on inequality and spending

There are at least three main threads of economic research specifically relevant to the current analysis. The three strands of the economics literature that we review include:

1) the literature on social capital and inequality;
2) the median voter models of inequality and social spending; and
3) the literature on social spending and economic growth.

Then there is additional institutional literature on politics and social spending in the political science literature. We summarize our reading of the literature at the end of the section.

9.2.3.1 Social capital and inequality

The first grouping of literature in this area examines the relationship between specific measures of social capital and inequality (Knack and Keefer, 1997; Alesina and La Ferrara, 1999, 2001; Costa and Kahn, 2001; Putnam, 2001).[7] The intent of this literature is to capture national or jurisdictional (for example, US states; Canadian provinces) tastes for redistributive and collective goods. These specific measures include such 'taste parameters' as community heterogeneity and community participation (for example, membership in social groups such as churches, sport clubs, etc.) and are used either as dependent (Costa and Kahn, 2001) or independent (Knack and Keefer, 1997; Alesina and La Ferrara, 1999, 2001; Costa and Kahn, 2001) variables in the various empirical models. Alesina and La Ferrara (2001) extend these ideas by addressing perceptions of economic and social mobility as they affect people's taste for redistribution within the United States. They report that: 'people who believe that American society offers equal opportunities to all are more averse to redistribution in the face of increased mobility.' Those that do not perceive there to be an equal chance or a great deal of mobility do not find social mobility as a good substitute for redistributive policies. Thus, the political economy approach from the economists' point of view suggests that preferences for redistribution are tied to beliefs about equality of opportunity and social and economic mobility. However, it should be emphasized that Alesina and La Ferrara are examining differences in attitudes within the United States, for example, within a common context of understanding of the acceptable domains of inequality and a common perception of basic human rights. Such intra-country attitudinal differences may be a poor guide to international differences, as we argue (and estimate empirically) in this chapter.

Closely associated to the social capital studies is literature that relates various measures of trust to economic outcomes. Recent work by Slemrod (2002) and Slemrod and Katuscak (2002) use the same data used in this study to look at the impacts of trust on income. Slemrod and Katuscak show that 'on average, a trusting attitude has a positive impact on income, while trustworthiness has a negative impact on income.' Other work in this area, including studies by Knack and Keefer (1997) and Zak and Knack (2001), make similar conclusions. Knack and Keefer find that trust exhibits a strong and positive relationship to growth while Zak and Knack introduce other influences on growth, including formal institutions, social distance and discrimination. In the latter paper, a percentage point increase in trust is found to have slightly over a 1 percent effect on growth, while our empirical results imply a slightly smaller effect of trust on social expenditures. Finally, Blinder and Krueger (2004) assert that public attitudes toward taxes, social security and other social spending are strongly affected by ideology and beliefs, as well as by media portrayal of social issues. We try to frame our empirical work with these papers in an effort to expand what we believe is an important yet relatively unexplored factor in both the economic growth and the inequality literature.

9.2.3.2   *Median voter models*

The second research thread tests the median voter hypothesis (and the closely related issue of social mobility) or other closely related hypotheses (for example, social affinity hypothesis), relating them to inequality and its effects on growth or on social spending within and across countries. These papers (Milanovic, 2000; Bassett *et al.*, 1999; Alesina and La Ferrara, 2001; Kristov *et al.*, 1992) are typically motivated by the relationships between measures of income and income inequality (for example, median income levels or Gini coefficients) and growth, but they focus on the impact of the inequality decision-making process of the median voter. If the median voter model is to be believed, greater levels of inequality at the top of the distri-bution produce more redistribution because there is more for the poor and middle classes to gain from taxing the rich.

Our work is a departure from the median voter hypothesis, since we believe political influence differs within the population. As previously noted, more affluent individuals may become less civically engaged at some 'tipping point.' The same individuals may be better able to further their own interests (which may or may not benefit those at the other end of the distribution) through political contributions, greater political knowledge, higher probab-ility of voting or greater access to elected officials. So while money may not 'buy' votes, it may buy access, hence tying voting to lobbying (see Ansolabehere *et al.*, 2003 and American Political Science Association (APSA) Task Force on Inequality and American Democracy, 2004). In fact, in a recent study by Bartels (2002), constituents at the 75th percentile of the income distribution are shown to have almost *three times* as much influence on US senators' voting patterns as those at the 25th percentile. McCarty *et al.* (2003), also using the United States, show that political partisanship increased substantially over the last half of the twentieth century and in addition has become more stratified by income. Comparing partisanship and income over the period, the authors speculate that 'richer voters represented by both parties are . . . less likely to favor redistribution and social insurance than were the counterparts of these voters a half-century earlier.' Of course, political institutions differ by nation and political system but we believe that for most developed countries, especially the nations in our analysis, this basic framework makes conceptual sense.[8]

Milanovic (2000) uses the Luxembourg Income Study (LIS) data set to build a model that regresses three measures of inequality on the extent of redistribution.[9,10] The paper does not, however, present any data on median voters or their incomes compared to the average incomes in society. Since it is not generally true that the outcomes of the median voter are measured by these different indices of inequality,[11] there is only a loose link between the model of voting behavior and the inequality measures he seeks to motivate. Further, the largest effects of greater inequality resulting in greater social spending by governments in Milanovic's work seem to come from social retirement expenditures.

Kristov *et al.* (1992) use a political economy approach to examine a 'pressure group' model of spending.[12] In their 'pressure group' model, citizens join groups that promote or fight specific income-transfer programs that have a likely chance of legislative approval. Such categories may translate into a conclusion about the relationship between growth and inequality. They note:

> Growth might be a negative influence on commitment to social transfers for a reason linked to the social-affinity hypothesis: the greater the recent rate of growth the stronger the perception of upward mobility, reducing sympathy with those presently poor.

It will be seen that this formulation conflates societal and individual income growth. As already noted, the relationship between growth in average income and redistribution has often been put in terms of social spending being a normal good—hence higher rates of growth of average income should lead to higher rates of public spending. However, we must also be aware of the assumption that changes in average incomes measure typical individual experiences of income change. It is possible for individuals to experience a faster rate of change in their personal incomes over their life-times, even as aggregate growth slows, if the age/earnings profile becomes sufficiently steep. A third and more recent paper by Mahler (2002) fits into this literature and measures the impact of globalization and domestic political factors on income distribution. Not only does he use the standard measures of income, but he constructs a measure of the difference between pre- and post-tax and transfer income. This 'fiscal redistribution' variable is sensitive to his linear model but continues to perform well. Overall, the author finds 'only scattered evidence of relationships between integration into the global economy and internal income inequality.' However, strong and positive relationships are exhibited between domestic political variables and egalitarian distribution of income. Hence, in a global world, individual national tastes for redistribution appear to remain important determinants of the level and pattern of social spending.

The remaining recent literature on social spending and inequality, such as papers by Moene and Wallerstein (2001, 2002) and by like minded political scientists and sociologists of an empirical bent, such as Kenworthy and Pontusson (2002) and Bradley *et al.* (2001), have several common features. They all purport to test the 'median voter' model, such as differences being expressed as the difference between the mean and median incomes or voters, but they then use earnings inequality for all earners (not voters alone and not among households) to express this difference. Voting turnout is then used as a measure of intensity of preferences and institutions are represented by right or left government parties.[13]

One new and appealing feature in Moene and Wallerstein (2002) is their argument that investigations of the determination of social expenditures and its relationship to inequality should be carried out on a disaggregated basis. That is, there is no a priori reason why national levels of welfare spending, unemployment insurance, health care, pensions and education should all have the same determinants. Indeed social insurance, targeted social assist-ance and universal benefits (like child allowances) may reflect different tastes, values and mechanisms for redistribution—and different conceptu-alizations of the acceptable domains of inequality and redistribution. This thinking is consistent with the different tastes for cash versus goods and services that we have already identified and leads to a belief that one should model demand for social goods on a policy by policy basis. However, we also feel that one may also go too far down this path, ignoring the built-in relationships between different programs that are part of each nation's social history and institutions. However, some disaggregation is to be preferred. In fact, Moene and Wallerstein (2002) find that higher levels of inequality in pre-tax earnings are associated with lower levels of spending for policies that insure against income loss for working persons. While they find different determinants for different types of social spending, they find no category of social spending that is positively related to income inequality. This is a radical departure from the older literature discussed above but the results are similar to our empirical work found below.

9.2.3.3 Inequality and growth

The final strand of the literature deals with issues of inequality and growth, particularly as they are both affected by redistributive public spending. This literature in general is a huge area of inquiry,[14] akin to the growth and savings literature popularized by Romer and Mankiw. Here we are much more specific in our interests. The effects of health and education benefits on growth, as well as public cash benefit provision, are particularly relevant for our purposes. This literature regarding inequality and redistribution and their interactions with economic growth includes papers by Perotti (1992, 1996), Bassett *et al.* (1999), Persson and Tabellini (1994), Alesina and Rodrik (1994), Osberg (1995) and Bénabou (1996, 2000). It also concludes the seminal work of Lindert (2004) and a survey article by Gordon and Wang (2004).

This area has been the subject of recent surveys and includes work by Arjona, Ladaique and Pearson (2001), Lindert (2004), Gordon and Wang (2004), and Scarth (2000). Although the high level of inequality and low level of redistribution in the United States is an important counter-example, Arjona, Ladaique and Pearson find support for the hypothesis that higher levels of pre-government ('market') income inequality lead to *greater* levels of redistribution. In turn, they suggest that the form of additional redistribution is also important and that policies that reduce market income inequality directly, by raising the market incomes of the poor, may be good for growth. The example they give is greater education for the poor, which produces lower market income inequality. They admit that other interpretations are also relevant, for example, that more redistribution causes lower market incomes (due to poverty traps and lower labor supply) and that in turn these phenomena may reduce economic growth. They conclude that they cannot say which interpretation best fits the data. The historical record surveyed by Lindert (2004) suggests that public spending for social services and income security (which reduces disposable income inequality) enhances economic growth and efficiency rather than detracting from it. The literature on growth, inequality and social spending therefore suggests that wise social welfare expenditures may in fact enhance economic growth and efficiency more than they harm it.

9.2.3.4 Institutional and political economy literature

In the political science field, the new literature on cross-national 'social policy preferences' is typified by the work of Iversen and Soskice (2001, 2002), Hall and Soskice (2001) and Iversen (1999). The approach, while akin to the earlier 'worlds of welfare capitalism' work of Esping-Andersen (1990), is also somewhat different. This literature offers a more institutionally driven and sophisticated argument about national preferences for redistribution. The argument is that coordinated nations—those with a high degree of cooperation between business, industry and labor—invest in human capital in different ways than nations that are of the liberal market economies, where competition replaces consensus seeking. Skill training is more specific (for example, vocational training), job tenure is longer and job changing is less in these coordinated economies than it is in societies with more general training (for example, college educated). In these latter types of economies, market competition rewards high skills with high 'winner take all' wages and low skills are punished with low wages. They term this latter group the risk-taking 'liberal economies.'

In the liberal economies, the costs of social protection are perceived to outweigh the benefits, and so we find less employment protection and less wage protection. However, in the coordinated economies is found strong employment protection and wage protection from within and outside companies, coupled with high unemployment benefits, adequate and early take-up social retirement and various other trappings of the European welfare state. This also suggests that, as market based earnings inequalities grow, more redistribution will take place because of the built-in stabilizers in western coordinated economies (Kenworthy and Pontusson, 2002).

It turns out that the most market-oriented societies are those with the least equality, while the coordinated nations have the least degree of inequality. These findings fit our original hypotheses but seem to be independent of income inequality as a driving force. Rather it is argued that lessened inequality and greater social spending are the joint product of the broader systems of social and economic cooperation that they find in these societies (which they call 'business social capital'). This hypothesis is difficult to examine conclusively since clearly there must be some set of processes to generate any particular pattern of inequality but a number of different processes might generate the same level of inequality.

A recent study group of the APSA Task Force on Inequality and American Democracy (APSA, 2004) reaches a different conclusion. They provide convincing evidence that influence and 'voice' in American democracy are becoming increasingly skewed toward the rich as economic inequalities continually widen in America. Using a variety of sources of evidence on voting, policy preferences and government actions, they find that political action and participation more closely track high wealth and income than any other variable.

9.2.4   Summary

In this summary of the literature, we have been careful to select only articles that seem relevant to our particular interests and hypotheses. However, in a longer review article (Osberg *et al.*, 2004), we offer an expanded review of these same issues. We have not delved into the literature on education and health spending and inequality, leaving these to other projects (for example, Mullahy *et al.*, 2002 and Berkman *et al.*, 2002 on health spending).

We conclude that the older literature in this area has primarily focused on the United States (Kristov *et al.*, 1992) and includes several different models, all attempting to predict which characteristics will lead to higher social spending. They tend to suggest that higher inequality leads to more social spending. The newer political science literature follows many of the same threads that we have followed here but without differentiating between the effects of the top and bottom of the distribution. They also do not clearly untangle the ways in which preferences for a fair society are translated into actual programs and policies via social and political institutions. The literature also tends to ignore how lobbying or other uses of political and economic power in highly unequal societies may prevent progressive social policies from being formulated and passed.

9.2.5 General conclusions

More specifically, the review that we have carried out so far leads us to the following conclusions:

- Inequality and poverty are different and a single summary measure of inequality—for example, the Gini or the 90/10 ratio—will not allow us to differentiate amongst explanations that hinge on forces which differentially come from different parts of the income distribution.
- The relationship between economic inequality and social spending is one of mutual interdependency and therefore it is crucial to distinguish the measure of income inequality that best captures its effect on social spending.
- Most models are of a reduced form, with little attention paid to desired levels of redistribution (or national differences in the taste for redistribution) in combination with the institutions and voting mechanisms (parties, lobbies, etc.) legitimizing these tastes.
- Leaps of analytic belief are often made in the current literature (such as the assumption that political preferences can be measured on a left/right domestic spectrum that is comparable internationally), which are crucial to the models developed but which seem to us to be questionable in a cross-national context.

9.3 Theories, models and data

All the nations that we have been examining are 'democracies,' yet their governments play different roles in the level and type of social expenditures. If we are to model the interaction of inequality of income and public expenditures, it seems important to understand more clearly why the citizens of different countries may make different demands of their political

systems. This first leads to a discussion of a theory of how differing attitudes toward inequality (or tastes and values for redistribution) may affect
public policy, using ISSP preference data. We then present our reduced-form
model and follow that with a detailed description of the data we use in our
empirical work.

9.3.1 Modeling inequality and the perception and provision of public expenditure

International differences in how inequality is perceived can be expected to
affect the link between public expenditures and inequality. The standard
'political economy' model of the median voter skips a number of crucial
steps. In a standard 'median voter' model, there is nothing complicated about
the line of connection between relative income and voting behavior. Votes
are assumed to be directly transformed into policy outcomes. Individuals are
presumed to directly perceive their self interest and to get results when the
median voter opts for a specific policy.

However, we believe it is more realistic to recognize that citizens
do not necessarily get what the majority wants. Political systems differ
considerably—for example, in the constraints they place on campaign financing or in the ease with which new parties that represent a particular point
of view can be formed. Greater inequality does increase the number of relatively poor but it also gives some citizens incentives and resources to lobby
and make donations to the candidates who will protect and augment their
wealth. These citizens may also hold considerable influence on policy makers
through greater access and connections, associations with interest groups
and greater coordination between lobbyists, individuals and political action
groups (Bartels, 2002; Ansolabehere *et al.*, 2003; APSA, 2004).

While less affluent citizens may want to make demands of the political
system, whether or not they vote depends on their sense of individual political efficacy. In some jurisdictions it will be individually rational (given
that each person can observe the impact of campaign donations on the
process) for the less affluent to conclude that the effort of voting is pointless
(and it is observable that voter turnout has declined precipitously in many
affluent nations). Discontent with the available political options can only be
expressed by voting for new entrants, if party entry is feasible. However, if
entry is not feasible, the absence of a party to represent a point of view (for
example, the absence of a Labor party or a Socialist party) is likely to produce
abstention by its potential voters. The bottom line is that political and social
institutions, such as collective bargaining arrangements and unionization,
are likely to play an intervening role in determining the relationship between
inequality and public spending.

Although statistical data can reveal whether, in an objective sense, income
inequality is increasing, the political attitudes and behavior of individuals
actually depend on the subjective awareness that individuals have of income

inequality. These attitudes also depend on the subjective evaluation of this perceived degree of inequality relative to an individual's own norms of 'fair' income differentials. A fascinating series of questions in the ISSP of 1987, 1997 and 1999 asked respondents about their perceptions and beliefs of inequality (see our unpublished paper for a more thorough exploration of this data (Osberg *et al.*, 2004)).

For purposes here, we focus on the questions that the ISSP asks about attitudes to redistribution. It should be carefully noted that international differences in responses seem to be sensitive to how exactly the role and responsibility of government is framed. Two nearly identical items were asked at different points in the questionnaire:

1) 'On the whole do you think it should be or should not be the government's responsibility to reduce income differences between the rich and the poor? Possible responses coded from 1 (Definitely should be) to 4 (Definitely should not be).'
2) 'What is your opinion of the following statement: It is the responsibility of the government to reduce the differences in income between people with high incomes and those with low incomes? Possible responses coded from 1 (Strongly agree) to 5 (Strongly disagree).'

These items have slightly different coding but the results are consistent— on average, United States respondents are least likely to agree that it is the responsibility of government to reduce income differences. The degree to which Americans hold this belief is by an especially impressive margin, given that respondents in the United States are starting from a considerably higher base rate of inequality in income (see Table 9.1). Asking whether it is the 'responsibility of government' to reduce income differences mingles the twin issues of whether income differences should be reduced and how it should be done. As already noted, the United States and other countries have similar attitudes to the fact of income inequality. Thus, Table 9.1 can be interpreted largely as indicating a disinclination by Americans to assign to government the responsibility for reducing inequality.

Further, although it is logical to expect attitudes to redistribution by government to be similar to those in favor of progressive taxation, the attitudes evoked by wording about the 'responsibility of government' may differ from those probed in the item:

Some people think those with high incomes should pay a larger proportion of their income in taxes than those who earn low incomes. Other people think that those with high incomes and those with low incomes should pay the same proportion of their earnings in taxes. Do you think those with high incomes should: 1 (Pay much larger amount) to 5 (Pay much smaller amount)?

Although the average United States respondent is still clearly less likely than the average respondent elsewhere to be in favor of progressive taxation, the differences with other nations are not nearly as pronounced as in the other items in Table 9.1.

In the neighboring columns of Table 9.1, each of the ISSP variables is scaled to the unit interval so that it can be compared to the World Value Survey (WVS) data, which appears in the final column. The WVS trust variable—which we use in our regression framework (see below)—is a broader measure of trust and asks respondents whether most people 'can be trusted' (= 1) or if people 'can't be too careful' (= 0). This is a broader measure of trust and has different effects on the rankings of the countries in the table. For example, with the ISSP data, the United States consistently ranks at the bottom of the distribution. However, with the WVS data the United States is closer to the middle of the pack, ranking ninth. Norway ranks somewhere in the middle in the first three columns but is the second least trusting country in the table under the WVS header. Thus, because trust from the WVS is measuring something much broader than the ISSP variables, countries appear different in their relationship to one another. This difference will have important consequences for our empirical work, which we discuss in the following sections.

In short, there is strong evidence for international differences in attitudes to the role government might play in reducing inequality[15] but much less strong evidence for systematic differences in attitudes to income inequality in itself. This raises the issue of how attitudes to government are formed and what influence the evolution of inequality may have on those attitudes.

To make one final note before detailing our empirical work, we acknowledge several conceptual problems with the trust data. A particular problem with the WVS trust data that we use in our regression framework is that the binary measure is an ordinal measure and does not differentiate between those who 'really' trust and those who 'somewhat' trust. In addition, persons in different countries may have different concepts of what is and what is not trustworthy. For example, what people in Sweden consider trustworthy may be distinctly different than in the United States. We also recognize that this trust measure mixes issues of general trust, altruism and egalitarianism. Nevertheless, we use the trust measure since it at least provides a baseline measure of these concepts.

9.3.2   Model and data

Thus far we have focused on previous work in the area of inequality and social expenditures as well as the levels and trends of trust across the world. We begin the final sections of the chapter by specifying a reduced form equation to explore the relationship between inequality and social expenditures:

$$\text{Social Expenditures} = f \{\text{Inequality, Values, Growth,}$$
$$\text{Institutions, Immigrants}\}.$$

Table 9.1 Inequality and the role of government

	A1		A2		A3		A4
Data set	ISSP		ISSP		ISSP		WVS
	Should government reduce income differences between the rich and poor? 1 (definitely) to 4 (definitely not)		It is the responsibility of government to reduce income differences? 1 (strongly agree) to 5 (strongly disagree)		Those with high incomes should pay: 1 (much more) to 5 (much less) tax than those with low incomes		Would you say people can be trusted or you can't be too careful? 1 (most people can be trusted) to 0 (can't be too careful)
Country	Average	Average/4	Average	Average/5	Average	Average/5	Average
Australia[1]	2.54	0.63	1.82	0.36	2.15	0.43	0.48
Austria[2]	1.96	0.49	1.36	0.27	1.86	0.37	0.32
Canada[3]	2.47	0.62	1.84	0.37	2.14	0.43	0.51
Denmark[4]	2.64	0.66	–	–	–	–	0.57
France[5]	1.77	0.44	1.33	0.27	2.09	0.42	0.24
Germany[6]	2.08	0.52	1.51	0.30	1.80	0.36	0.34
Italy[7]	1.87	0.47	1.39	0.28	1.84	0.37	0.29
Netherlands[8]	2.15	0.54	1.68	0.34	–	–	0.51
Norway[9]	1.97	0.49	1.58	0.32	2.09	0.42	0.60
Spain[10]	1.62	0.41	1.32	0.26	1.92	0.38	0.35
Sweden[11]	2.19	0.55	1.50	0.30	2.09	0.42	0.62
Switzerland[12]	2.44	0.61	–	–	–	–	0.43

Table 9.1 (Continued)

Data set	A1 Should government reduce income differences between the rich and poor? 1 (definitely) to 4 (definitely not)		A2 It is the responsibility of government to reduce income differences? 1 (strongly agree) to 5 (strongly disagree)		A3 Those with high incomes should pay: 1 (much more) to 5 (much less) tax than those with low incomes		A4 Would you say people can be trusted or you can't be too careful? 1 (most people can be trusted) to 0 (can't be too careful)
	ISSP		ISSP		ISSP		WVS
Country	Average	Average/4	Average	Average/5	Average	Average/5	Average
UK[13]	2.07	0.52	1.55	0.31	1.98	0.40	0.39
US[14]	2.80	0.70	1.98	0.40	2.21	0.44	0.48
Overall average	2.18	0.55	1.57	0.31	2.01	0.40	0.44

Notes:

[1] Years averaged for Australia: A1: 1998, 1996, 1992, 1991, 1990, 1987, 1985; A2: 1999, 1996, 1993, 1990, 1985; A3: 1999, 1990, 1985.

[2] Years averaged for Austria: A1: 1998, 1992, 1991, 1987, 1985; A2: 1999, 1985; A3: 1999.

[3] Years averaged for Canada: A1: 1998, 1996, 1992; A2: 1999, 1996, 1993; A3: 1999.

[4] Years averaged for Denmark: A1: 1998.

[5] Years averaged for France: A1: 1998, 1996; A2: 1999, 1996; A3: 1999.

[6] Years averaged for Germany: A1: 1998, 1996, 1992, 1991, 1990, 1987, 1985; A2: 1999, 1996, 1993, 1990, 1985; A3: 1999.

[7] Years averaged for Italy: A1: 1998, 1996, 1992, 1991, 1990, 1987, 1985; A2: 1996, 1993, 1990, 1985; A3: 1990, 1985.

[8] Years averaged for the Netherlands: A1: 1998, 1991, 1987; A2: 1993.

[9] Years averaged for Norway: A1: 1998, 1996, 1992, 1991, 1990; A2: 1999, 1996, 1993, 1990; A3: 1999, 1990.

[10] Years averaged for Spain: A1: 1998, 1996; A2: 1999, 1996, 1993; A3: 1999.

[11] Years averaged for Sweden: A1: 1998, 1996, 1992; A2: 1999, 1996; A3: 1999.

[12] Years averaged for Switzerland: A1: 1998, 1987.

[13] Years averaged for the UK: A1: 1998, 1996, 1992, 1991, 1990, 1987, 1985; A2: 1999, 1996, 1993, 1990, 1985; A3: 1999, 1990, 1985.

[14] Years averaged for the US: A1: 1998, 1996, 1992, 1991, 1990, 1987, 1985; A2: 1999, 1996, 1993, 1990, 1985; A3: 1999, 1990, 1985.

Source: ISSP; WVS 2002.

We are most interested on the effects that Inequality and Values (as measured by trust) have on Social Expenditures. The remaining covariates are included as controls for various social, economic and political institutions.

Our estimation strategy is rather straightforward and we use a simple Ordinary Least Squares (OLS) approach. To test the significance of the estimated coefficients, we estimate the standard errors by not only correcting for heteroskedasticity by using a Huber-White 'sandwich' robust estimator, but we also cluster the observations by country. Since our data are pooled in unevenly spaced year observations, this clustering technique may be preferred to the simple robust standard errors (Mahler, 2002). In some cases, the clustered standard errors are larger than in the robust case (not reported) and some are smaller. The latter case can occur when the intra-cluster correlations are negative, that is, some variation in the variable is being cancelled out in the clustering technique (Stata Corporation, 2002). Statistical significance tests however, are generally consistent between the two approaches.

Before detailing the data used in the empirical model, there is one particular issue in the recent literature on inequality and redistribution that demands our attention. As we have seen, our assertion that inequality affects social expenditures through the level and distribution of publicly provided goods is not unique. Recently, Kenworthy and Pontusson (2002) have argued the opposite case, that household earnings inequality can be determined by employment controls and measures of household income combinations and those changes in redistribution are a function of *changes* in employment, unionization, GDP, trade and other political controls. Beramendi (2001) and Bradley *et al.* (2001) also argue that reductions in inequality can be at least partially determined by measures of social expenditures (overall social expenditures in the former and taxes and transfers in the latter). This is not a surprising view, because the goal of social expenditures and public goods is, at least in some part, to redistribute wealth and reduce inequality.

These conflicting theories force us to consider the endogeneity of inequality in regression models. The key then, is to find a variable that determines inequality but is exogenous to the social expenditure decision— and such instruments are hard to come by. Moene and Wallerstein (2002) use wage-setting institutions and political variables as instruments for inequality (their inequality measure is the logarithm of the 90/10 wage ratio). However, the exogeneity of these factors to social expenditures can be difficult to argue convincingly, for instance, if institutions directly affect wage levels (for example, minimum wages) and employment and training policies.

Thus, while our framework addresses the effects of inequality on government spending, the reverse causality begs our attention. In short, we believe that our focus on pre-tax and transfer income, or market income, removes most if not all of the endogeneity of the inequality measures. Such income is measured before taxes and transfers are accounted for and so have yet to reflect the degree to which taxes and transfers serve to redistribute income. However, it is well established that taxes and transfers affect behavior (specifically in terms of labor market behavior), which in turn affects our inequality measure and the subsequent social expenditure decision. Thus the reverse causality does not work directly through our measures of inequality but indirectly through (labor market) responses to such policies (Beramendi, 2001). Consequently, as tax rates or transfer payment generosity changes, citizens revise their labor market response, which ultimately changes inequality as the market adjusts. We note that instrumental variable attempts were unsuccessful and we briefly explore our efforts in Section 9.4.

9.3.3 Data: sources and details

We have constructed a data set with 57 different sets of observations for 17 countries, using data from the LIS (on various measures of inequality), the OECD on growth and social expenditures (Soc Ex) and the WVS data sets on values, as expressed by trust for others. Most countries enter with multiple observations, though five is the maximum number of observations we have for any one nation.[16] The main variables of concern (trust, 90/50 (MI), 50/10 (MI) and Gini (MI)) are graphed along with Social Expenditures in Appendix Figures 9.A.1–9.A.4. What is particularly interesting in these figures is how the Nordic countries (Belgium, Denmark, Finland, Sweden and Switzerland) tend to lie above the regression lines, while the Anglo countries (Australia, Canada, United Kingdom and the United States) tend to lie below.

For the empirical model, the OECD Social Expenditure, Education at a Glance and Health Expenditure databases (OECD 2002a, b and c) offer us few practical options for dependent variables:

a. Total social expenditures (elderly and non-elderly; cash only); and
b. Non-elderly spending (total, cash and non-cash, categorical).

These data sets are fairly comprehensive, both in terms of number of countries and years covered but are lacking in a number of other dimensions. Here we concentrate on non-elderly social spending for the reasons given above. Once this decision is made, there is no straightforward way to split health care expenditures between the elderly and non-elderly and to include the role of employer benefits in the United States. In addition, there exists no consistent education series that covers most or all of the years for which we have the other variables of interest. Hence, we concentrate our analysis on models using non-elderly cash and near cash social expenditures (excluding education and health care expenses) since these are less sensitive to public retirement funding and more sensitive to a nation's age structure. To avoid some of the problems associated with purchasing parity and inflation variation, we measure our dependent variable as a percentage of GDP.[17]

A wide variety of comparable measures of inequality can be directly generated from the LIS database, including:

a. Both market income and disposable income inequality; and
b. Pre- or post-tax and transfer poverty rates.

The measures of inequality include the 90/50; 50/10; 90/10 percentile ratios, and many single parameter measures of inequality (Gini, Theil, Atkinson). These are easily estimated from the LIS data set and are comparable to previously published numbers and publicly available series available directly from LIS. The 90/50 and 50/10 ratios or poverty rates are less sensitive to changes in the top or the bottom of the distribution than are the single parameter estimates (Atkinson *et al.*, 1995). These measures also separate two effects:

1) the effect of the economic distance of the rich from the middle class (90/50 ratio); and
2) the effects of poverty or relative low income (50/10 ratio) on support for income transfers.

We present results using both 'market income' defined as pre-government tax and transfer income, largely consisting of pre-tax market earnings for households plus property income; and 'disposable income' defined as post-tax and transfer income, which includes the effects of direct taxes and cash social redistribution on market income.[18] Thus, our empirical work uses market income-based measures of inequality, as well as distinct measures of inequality (Gini ratios and percentile ratios), measures which other studies do not generally use.

Our data on values come from the WVS results from the 1981–84, 1990–93 and 1995–97 surveys (WVS, 2002). The WVS question that is universally asked is about trusting others—very few nations also ask about trusting government. In addition, variables that measure trust in government may primarily reflect attitudes to the government of the day rather than to the institution of government. Also, current political popularity fluctuates for many reasons unrelated to the issues of this paper. In some cases, the surveys are limited to some nations-periods, but not others (for example, Gallup, ISSP, Euro barometer). Due to the small number of surveys performed with respect to our data set, we were forced to impute some (less than 15 percent) WVS trust figures to other years for the same country. The absence of these variables in the research summarized in Section 9.2 (with the exception of the papers by researchers such as Slemrod, Keefer, Knack, and Zak) leave something to be desired in the literature. Such trust variables are critical for determining the 'tastes' for redistribution and are especially powerful when combined with political and institutional variables that measure the forces that move governments to act via redistributive measures.

We therefore employ a set of variables that can express the efficacy with which preferences are transmitted and enacted. One variable measures the way that labor market institutions affect inequality via their effect on the stability of market incomes and in political circles (Koeniger *et al.*, 2004). These are typified by union representatives or by the fraction of centrally bargained wages. Iversen (1998) has developed a consistent centrally bargaining series for a number of countries between 1973 and 1993 but we are then left with only 31 observations. Since variation over time for the same country is relatively small, we increase the degrees of freedom in the regressions with the centralization measure. We do this by filling in the missing observations by using own-country averages—the coefficient on the centralization measure was virtually unchanged by this procedure.[19]

Another approach is to use political or voting variables, such as voter turnout. Voter turnout is a rough indicator of the extent to which a nation's citizenry is involved in its political process. The political science literature has done much with voter turnout but we are unconvinced that the measures used in the literature are accurate and so we do not include them here. Following the literature, we have experimented with measures of governance, such as left governing party seats as a percent of all legislative seats and left party legislative seats as a percent of all legislative seats (both from Marshall and Jaggers, 2000). Neither variable entered the regressions statistically significantly or had much effect on the other covariates. Hence, specifications with these variables are not included in the tables below.

There may be an income elasticity of demand for public social spending, especially health care and education. Several authors cited above have found that economic growth generally leads to greater generosity for redistributive spending. We test for this by using the average growth rate over the five years prior to the year of observation (see OECD, 2002d).[20]

Some additional demographic differences from LIS are reasonable proxies for factors that would almost automatically produce demand for social goods, both cash and in-kind. However, we believe demographic variables—such as the percent of single parent families and the percent elderly—contaminate other covariates and are thus not included in the empirical specifications below. Specifically, because single parent families often receive a significant amount of social transfers and generally find themselves at the bottom end of the income distribution, we infer that this variable contaminates the 90/50 ratio. Also, since the elderly receive a disproportionate share of the largest social expenditure categories—social retirement and health care—we believe there are spillover effects to the other covariates and to cash spending on the non-elderly as well. Thus, we do not include these variables in the regressions that follow.

The percent of foreign born, or the number of immigrants in a society, is a different kind of demographic variable, one that may positively affect the demand for social services and expenditures[21] but may also directly and negatively affect voters' taste for redistribution, depending on attitudes toward minorities and on program eligibility rules. Using data from OECD (2000), LIS and the US Census Bureau, we enter this variable in our model as an additional control of demand for services.

9.4 Empirical results

This chapter has presented a review of the literature and our heuristic model of how preferences toward equality affect redistributive spending via voting, lobbying and related institutions. In this final section, we present the single equation approach to modeling inequality and public social spending.

Following the single equation format outlined in the previous section, we regress total cash and near cash social expenditures on the non-elderly as a percentage of GDP on a set of demographic, political and macroeconomic covariates (see previous section and table notes for sources and definitions of covariates). We choose to use expenditures on the non-elderly since we know that social expenditures on the elderly are heavily driven by the population's age structure and are relatively poorly modeled by direct state expenditures (which do not include tax expenditure incentives for private pensions). The covariates include trust, inequality measures (Gini coefficient and 90/50–50/10 percentile ratios), macroeconomic controls (percent foreign born and an index of centralization of union wage bargaining) and per capita GDP growth rate. Summary statistics, sources and details for the variables are found in Table 9.2.

We focus on Tables 9.3 and 9.4, which contain the results using market-income based measures of inequality.[22] The GDP growth rate variable is negative and significant in the two tables, confirming our prior expectations. Converting the point estimates to elasticities implies that a 1 percent increase in previous GDP growth decreases non-elderly social expenditures by approximately 0.2 percent. Recall that in these tables, trust is measured as the percentage of survey respondents who agree with the statement that they believe that people can generally be trusted. The interpretation is that a positive coefficient would indicate that more cohesive and trusting societies are more willing to share economic resources through the state. Table 9.3 shows that trust is strongly significant (and the inequality measure is not) if the Gini index is used as our measure of inequality. When one uses measures of social distance at the bottom (the 50/10 ratio) and at the top (the 90/50 ratio) in Table 9.4, the measures are significant (with opposite signs) and the trust variable maintains both its significance and magnitude. The elasticity estimates are about the same as those found in Zak and Knack (2001)—a 1 percent increase in trust increases social expenditures by approximately between 0.40 and 0.90 percent.[23]

Table 9.2 Summary statistics

Variable	Obs	Mean	Std. dev.	Min	Max	Source
Total Social Expenditures, Non-elderly	55	8.44	3.78	2.85	15.82	SOC-X
Gini	55	0.38	0.05	0.27	0.46	LIS
Gini (DPI)	55	0.27	0.04	0.20	0.37	LIS
90/50 (MI)	55	2.06	0.18	1.71	2.49	LIS
50/10 (MI)	55	11.70	17.41	1.84	97.99	LIS
90/50 (DPI)	55	1.79	0.18	1.51	2.15	LIS
50/10 (DPI)	55	1.95	0.29	1.58	2.80	LIS
Trust	55	0.44	0.12	0.23	0.66	WVS
GDP	55	1.79	1.20	−1.84	5.65	OECD
% Foreign Born	49	8.21	8.52	0.05	26.49	OECD, LIS, U.S. Census
Centralization	50	0.28	0.15	0.07	0.58	Iversen

Sources and definitions:
Total Social Expenditures, Non-elderly: percentage of GDP from OECD (2002a).
Trust: 'most people can be trusted (= 1) or can't be too careful (= 0).' *World Values Survey* (2002).
Gini, 50/10, 90/50: authors' calculations, Luxembourg Income Study.
GDP: Average annual percent growth over five years preceding year of observation. OECD (2002d).
% Foreign Born: OECD (2000), various years; LIS, various years; U.S. Census.
Centralization: See text for definition. Iversen (1998). Country average used to impute for missing data. (Luxembourg and Spain omitted with zero observations.)

The other two structural controls—percent foreign born and the centralization index—are both typically statistically significant and consistent in magnitude in both Tables 9.3 and 9.4. The foreign born variable is consistently negative (between –0.16 and –0.20), indicating that more open (less homogeneous) societies are less willing to spend on social goods. The centralization index is positive and large in magnitude, suggesting that centralized wage bargaining does help transfer social policy preferences into programs and policies that support greater spending.[24]

Comparing the results in Tables 9.3 and 9.4 demonstrates the importance of using different inequality measures. When a single summary statistic of inequality (the Gini) is used and income inequality is measured before taxes or transfers, it is statistically insignificant. However, Table 9.4 indicates that the inequality in market income between the middle classes and the poor (as indicated by the 50/10 ratio) has a *positive* impact on social spending.[25] Inequality in market income between the middle class and the affluent (as captured by the 90/50 ratio) has a statistically significant and *negative* (and larger) impact. Hence, the aggregate insignificance of aggregate inequality in market income is arguably due to the *offsetting* influences of inequality at the top and at the bottom of the distribution of income before taxes and transfers. Therefore, it may well be that once inequality at the top of the

Table 9.3 Measure of Inequality: Gini (MI)

	(1)	(2)	(3)
Gini (MI)[1]	−17.1093	−14.2006	−8.7146
robust, clustered standard error	(15.5484)	(16.0815)	(10.1840)
Trust	15.9276	12.5683	5.4299
robust, clustered standard error	(4.4345)**	(4.2071)*	(3.7907)
GDP	−0.9260	−1.0700	−0.9116
robust, clustered standard error	(0.3288)*	(0.2576)**	(0.1554)**
% Foreign Born		−0.1794	−0.2007
robust, clustered standard error		(0.0667)*	(0.0771)*
Centralization			10.2339
robust, clustered standard error			(3.8968)*
Constant	9.4924	11.7138	10.1065
robust, clustered standard error	(6.6316)	(6.4416)	(4.1993)*
Observations	55	49	47
R-squared	0.34	0.49	0.65

Notes:
Dependent variable: Total Social Expenditures, Non-elderly (as percentage of GDP). OECD (2002a).
[1] These variables are measured using market income.
* significant at 5 percent.
** significant at 1 percent.
Sources and definitions:
Trust: See Table 9.2 for definition. *World Values Survey* (2002).
GDP: Average annual percent growth over five years preceding year of observation. OECD (2002d).
% Foreign Born: OECD (2000); LIS; U.S. Census, various years.
Centralization: See text for definition. Iversen (1998). Country average used to impute for missing data. (Luxembourg and Spain omitted with zero observations.)
Authors' Calculations.

income distribution reaches a particular 'tipping' level, further support for public expenditures that benefit all of society is lost.

The results in Table 9.4 indicate that a widening of income gaps between the poorest 10 percent and median incomes has a small positive impact on expenditures, while the impact of widening differentials between the top end and the middle class is far larger in magnitude and strongly negative. This finding seems to counter much of the other literature, which finds the reverse sign (Milanovic, 2000 and Kristov *et al.*, 1992) and may reflect the changing times of the post-1980s where inequality continues to grow and incomes are growing more slowly. These measures of inequality reflect differences in the impact of inequality at the top and bottom of the distribution and are thus preferable to single parameter estimates, which cannot differentiate between these effects. In fact, different exogenous and endogenous forces are driving changes in the 90/50 as opposed to the 10/50 in most rich nations (Smeeding, 2002a). The F-test statistics, found in the last row of Table 9.4, test the joint hypothesis that both the 90/50 and 50/10 measures equal zero. The F-test statistics unanimously and overwhelmingly reject the hypothesis

Table 9.4   Measure of Inequality: 90/50 and 50/10 (MI)

	(1)	(2)	(3)
90/50 (MI)[1]	−9.0161	−8.3684	−5.6742
robust, clustered standard error	(2.5216)**	(2.6982)**	(2.3244)*
50/10 (MI)[1]	0.0449	0.0419	0.0348
robust, clustered standard error	(0.0209)*	(0.0168)*	(0.0143)*
Trust	10.6192	7.8869	4.2085
robust, clustered standard error	(4.1896)*	(3.6657)	(3.4367)
GDP	−1.0431	−1.2425	−1.1253
robust, clustered standard error	(0.3127)**	(0.2309)**	(0.1540)**
% Foreign Born		−0.1602	−0.1836
robust, clustered standard error		(0.0468)**	(0.0607)*
Centralization			6.8840
robust, clustered standard error			(2.9406)*
Constant	23.6032	25.2885	19.7082
robust, clustered standard error	(6.0687)**	(6.1186)**	(5.3301)**
Observations	55	49	47
R-squared	0.51	0.64	0.71
F-statistic	9.97**	9.44**	5.27*

Notes:
Dependent variable: Total Social Expenditures, Non-elderly (as percentage of GDP). OECD (2002a).
[1] These variables are measured using market income.
* significant at 5 percent.
** significant at 1 percent.
Sources and definitions:
Trust: See Table 9.2 for definition. *World Values Survey* (2002).
GDP: Average annual percent growth over five years preceding year of observation. OECD (2002d).
% Foreign Born: OECD (2000); LIS; U.S. Census, various years.
Centralization: See text for definition. Iversen (1998). Country average used to impute for missing data. (Luxembourg and Spain omitted with zero observations.)
Authors' Calculations.

that *both* the 90/50 and 50/10 variables equal zero. Overall, the model fits well with an R-squared around 0.60 but is obviously sensitive to the covariates used.[26]

Clearly, in a single equation cross-sectional model, establishing causation is problematic. We would argue that causation plausibly runs from the right-hand side and thus a larger income gap between the median and the poorest may well produce greater needs for social expenditures.[27] However, a widening income gap at the top end may plausibly be reflected in an increased influence in the political process of those with a preference for lower taxes (see Section 9.3 and APSA, 2004). Although one can argue that wider income gaps in market income imply a greater 'need' for social spending, the same differentials also increase the resources available to those who oppose higher social spending.

Table 9.5 Country effects: U.S. and Mexico

	US only results from Table 4			Include US and Mexico[+]			Without US or Mexico		
	(1)	(2)	(3)	(4)	(5)	(6)	(7)	(8)	(9)
90/50 (MI)[1]	−9.0161	−8.3684	−5.6742	−5.2012	−4.9271	−4.3550	−6.2783	−4.6542	−2.4539
robust, clustered s.e.	(2.5216)**	(2.6982)**	(2.3244)*	(1.2913)**	(1.2375)**	(0.6500)**	(3.5741)	(2.9628)	(3.0079)
50/10 (MI)[1]	0.0449	0.0419	0.0348	0.0455	0.0426	0.0345	0.0408	0.0366	0.0300
robust, clustered s.e.	(0.0209)*	(0.0168)*	(0.0143)*	(0.0212)*	(0.0165)*	(0.0139)*	(0.0218)	(0.0156)*	(0.0131)*
Trust	10.6192	7.8869	4.2085	12.0531	9.0209	4.1122	11.9811	9.4009	5.7293
robust, clustered s.e.	(4.1896)*	(3.6657)	(3.4367)	(4.1171)**	(3.8669)*	(3.6605)	(4.6057)*	(3.9715)*	(3.5803)
GDP	−1.0431	−1.2425	−1.1253	−0.7353	−0.8865	−0.9280	−0.9325	−1.0510	−0.9353
robust, clustered s.e.	(0.3127)**	(0.2309)**	(0.1540)**	(0.2786)*	(0.2471)**	(0.1561)**	(0.2994)**	(0.1698)**	(0.1481)**
% Foreign Born		−0.1602	−0.1836		−0.1727	−0.1889		−0.1741	−0.1997
robust, clustered s.e.		(0.0468)**	(0.0607)*		(0.0491)*	(0.0642)*		(0.0566)**	(0.0668)*
Centralization			6.8840			7.8315			5.9593
robust, clustered s.e.			(2.9406)*			(3.3158)*			(2.9205)
Constant	23.6032	25.2885	19.7082	14.6375	17.2365	16.5068	17.4280	17.0900	12.8003
robust, clustered s.e.	(6.0687)**	(6.1186)**	(5.3301)**	(3.6486)**	(3.6110)**	(2.6068)**	(8.6177)	(6.5800)*	(6.6128)
Observations	55	49	47	58	52	50	51	45	43
R-squared	0.51	0.64	0.71	0.55	0.68	0.76	0.45	0.62	0.69
F-statistic	9.97**	9.44**	5.27*	12.20**	13.64**	45.83**	3.00	5.03*	2.97

Notes:
See Tables 9.2–9.4 for variable definitions and sources.
[1] These variables are measured using market income.
* significant at 5 percent level.
** significant at 1 percent level.
[+] Sample includes three observations for Mexico (1994, 1996, 1998).
Source: Authors' Calculations.

One might question if the results that we capture are merely reflections of the United States alone or of other nations as well. In order to test this hypothesis, we included observations for Mexico, for which we have both OECD measures of social spending and LIS measures of income inequality, identical to those found for the other nations.[28] In Appendix Figure 9.A.2b, we illustrate the way that Mexico continues the pattern of inequality compared to social spending that we find in the other rich OECD nations. Were we able to easily add to this continuum with other similar nations, we would do so, but we believe that Mexico helps make our point. Table 9.5 includes a series of regressions akin to Table 9.4, both with and without the United States and Mexico observations. It is clear that adding Mexico to the sample has little impact on the overall conceptual story. The 90/50 coefficients are somewhat smaller but coefficients on both the 50/10 and trust variables are stable and statistically significant. Our hypothesis continues to hold in the last three columns, where both the United States and Mexico are eliminated from the sample. Although the coefficient on the 90/50 ratio is statistically insignificant, both sign, magnitude and significance are maintained on the remaining covariates. So from this exercise we conclude that the United States is not an outlier but among the richest nations. Rather it is at one end of the continuum of the OECD and middle income nations. Were we to add more nations with greater inequality, the same patterns would hold and still greater support for the tipping point hypothesis would be found.

The results in these tables provide evidence for two stylized facts. First, variable inclusion/exclusion and especially variable measure may have a profound effect on the outcome of the model. The changes we see are expected a priori, given our understanding of the differences between disposable and market incomes. Second, trust and distributional measures of inequality (especially the 50/10 and 90/50 variables) play large and significant roles on social spending. In the future, more sophisticated estimation techniques with better, more consistent international data will enable researchers to pin down these causal effects more precisely.

9.5   Conclusion

The hypothesis we have presented in this chapter is that high levels of income inequality reduce public support for redistributive social spending. Were we able to also include consistent measures of publicly provided goods (such as health care and education), which benefit poor and rich alike, we believe our results would be even stronger. Indeed this is our next priority area for additional research. Our empirical work strongly suggests that inequality and trust have important impacts on public spending but also suggests that future work can better tackle endogeneity and the measurement issues discussed above.

Our results are consistent with the hypothesis that higher levels of market income inequality (or market income poverty, or low income) mean higher outlays for these goods but that higher levels of market driven pre-government inequality lead to lower levels of non-elderly social spending once we control for economic conditions, trust and social institutions (unions, wage setting behavior).

The results suggest that as the 'rich' become more distant from the middle and lower classes, they find it easier to opt out of public programs and to either self insure or to buy substitutes in the private market. The implication is that 'two-income' households with two highly educated parents have little need for redistributive cash and new cash social benefits because they are unlikely to directly benefit from such transfer programs. The conclusion is that higher economic inequality produces lower levels of those publicly shared goods that foster greater equality of opportunity, income insurance and greater upward mobility.

The results also suggest that the median voter model is simplistic in its ignorance of the maldistribution of political influence. Having greater numbers of rich in a nation does not lead to additional redistribution because the lower and middle classes do not have the political power, voice and access to legitimize these claims (APSA, 2004).

We believe the analysis has important policy implications. Our comparison of attitudes to inequality in the United States and other countries has emphasized the essential similarities between countries in attitudes toward income inequality itself. But it is the dissimilarities in the institutions that represent social and economic rights in the political arena that determine redistributive government spending. Our discussion suggests that ideology and efficacy may both matter. Ideology—in the sense of national understanding of the meaning of fairness, altruism and basic human rights—may play a crucial independent role in defining the acceptable domains of inequality. But efficacy in the ways in which social institutions and political parties can influence government is likely to be crucial in understanding whether demands are made of the political system to reach these objectives.

The many factors that affect public social expenditures are complex and intertwined. Certainly, social values and institutions in the United States differ from those found in other nations and our belief in the market system is much more central and critical to social outcomes than in other advanced nations. Yet even within these beliefs, it seems clear that we do not possess the social institutions or political movements that might bring about greater levels of redistribution, even for those who are more clearly deserving because of their work effort or other factors. And it is clear that the high level of market driven economic inequality that we tolerate is in large part a determinant of the social outcomes and social policy outcomes which we observe.

Appendix

Table 9.A.1 Measure of Inequality: Gini (DPI)

	(1)	(2)	(3)
Gini (DPI)[1]	−56.2449	−51.3368	−42.1754
robust, clustered standard error	(9.1094)**	(9.4218)**	(10.0100)**
Trust	7.7198	5.7767	4.9367
robust, clustered standard error	(3.4471)*	(2.5548)*	(2.6353)
GDP	−0.8959	−0.8581	−0.8901
robust, clustered standard error	(0.1494)**	(0.1644)**	(0.1358)**
% Foreign Born		−0.1358	−0.1486
robust, clustered standard error		(0.0308)**	(0.0414)**
Centralization			3.1652
robust, clustered standard error			(2.6300)
Constant	21.9413	22.6205	19.8297
robust, clustered standard error	(3.3768)**	(2.8543)**	(3.0673)**
Observations	57	51	49
R-squared	0.63	0.71	0.73

Notes:
Dependent variable: Total Social Expenditures, Non-elderly (as percentage of GDP). OECD (2002a).
[1] These variables are measured using disposable personal income.
* significant at 5 percent.
** significant at 1 percent.
Sources and definitions:
Trust: See Table 9.2 for definition. *World Values Survey* (2002).
GDP: Average annual percent growth over five years preceding year of observation. OECD (2002d).
% Foreign Born: OECD (2000); LIS; U.S. Census, various years.
Centralization: See text for definition. Iversen (1998). Country average used to impute for missing data. (Luxembourg and Spain omitted with zero observations.)
Authors' Calculations.

Table 9.A.2 Measure of Inequality: 90/50 and 50/10 (DPI)

	(1)	(2)	(3)
90/50 (DPI)[1]	−4.5793	−0.8065	0.5358
robust, clustered standard error	(6.1279)	(4.5701)	(4.6875)
50/10 (DPI)[1]	−6.0395	−7.4914	−7.5841
robust, clustered standard error	(3.4494)	(2.5793)*	(2.3670)**
Trust	10.7593	10.5068	10.1476
robust, clustered standard error	(4.7959)*	(3.4910)**	(3.3826)*
GDP	−0.8028	−0.7217	−0.7276
robust, clustered standard error	(0.1367)**	(0.1870)**	(0.2118)**
% Foreign Born		−0.1246	−0.1407
robust, clustered standard error		(0.0294)**	(0.0332)**
Centralization			0.9936
robust, clustered standard error			(1.7617)

Constant	25.0971	22.4004	20.2906
robust, clustered standard error	(6.7873)**	(4.6198)**	(5.2032)**
Observations	57	51	49
R-squared	0.69	0.80	0.80
F-statistic	25.77**	47.72**	53.49**

Notes:
Dependent variable: Total Social Expenditures, Non-elderly (as percentage of GDP). OECD (2002a).
[1] These variables are measured using disposable personal income.
* significant at 5 percent.
** significant at 1 percent.
Sources and definitions:
Trust: See Table 9.2 for definition. *World Values Survey* (2002).
GDP: Average annual percent growth over five years preceding year of observation. OECD (2002d).
% Foreign Born: OECD (2000); LIS; U.S. Census, various years.
Centralization: See text for definition. Iversen (1998). Country average used to impute for missing data. (Luxembourg and Spain omitted with zero observations.)
Authors' Calculations.

Table 9.A.3 Measure of Inequality: Gini (MI) – SOCX <15%

	(1)	(2)	(3)
Gini (MI)[1]	−14.6013	−13.3417	−10.5088
robust, clustered standard error	(16.1810)	(16.8665)	(10.7682)
Trust	14.3405	11.5259	4.3828
robust, clustered standard error	(4.6520)**	(4.2533)*	(3.8777)
GDP	−0.5189	−0.7073	−0.7684
robust, clustered standard error	(0.3042)	(0.3045)*	(0.2378)**
% Foreign Born		−0.1638	−0.1915
robust, clustered standard error		(0.0676)*	(0.0792)*
Centralization			10.0642
robust, clustered standard error			(3.8702)*
Constant	8.2293	10.8886	10.8487
robust, clustered standard error	(7.1639)	(7.0452)	(4.5352)*
Observations	52	46	44
R-squared	0.27	0.42	0.60

Notes:
Dependent variable: Total Social Expenditures, Non-elderly (as percentage of GDP). OECD (2002a).
[1] These variables are measured using market income.
* significant at 5 percent.
** significant at 1 percent.
Sources and definitions:
Trust: See Table 9.2 for definition. *World Values Survey* (2002).
GDP: Average annual percent growth over five years preceding year of observation. OECD (2002d).
% Foreign Born: OECD (2000); LIS; U.S. Census, various years.
Centralization: See text for definition. Iversen (1998). Country average used to impute for missing data. (Luxembourg and Spain omitted with zero observations.)

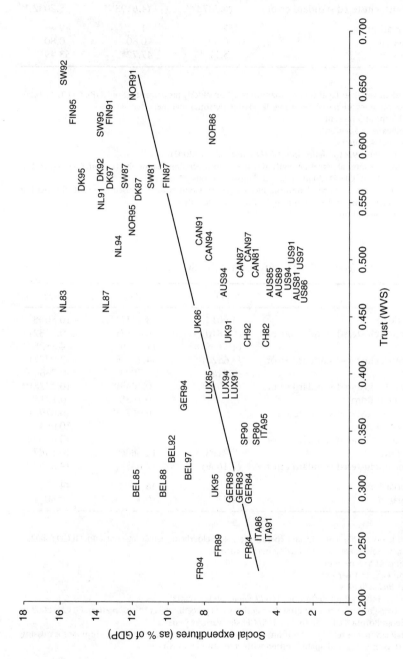

Figure 9.A.1 Social expenditures – trust

Source: Authors' Calculations using LIS data and OECD (2002b).

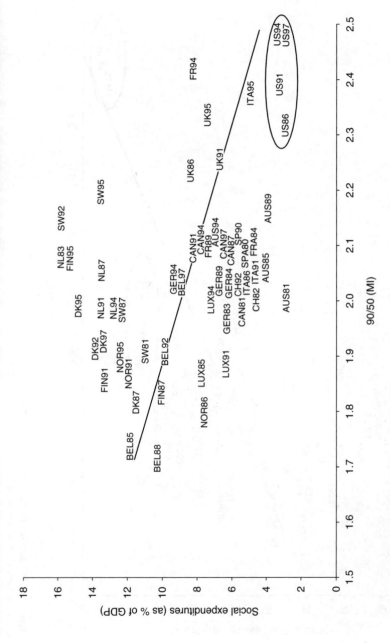

Figure 9.A.2a Social expenditures – 90/50 (MI)
Source: Authors' Calculations using LIS data and OECD (2002b).

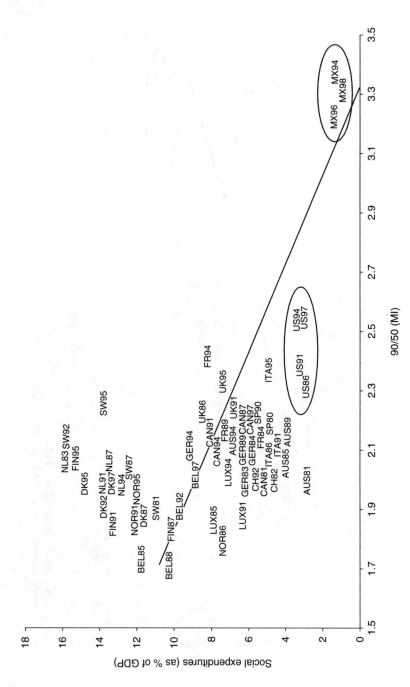

Figure 9.A.2b Social expenditures – 90/50 (MI)

Source: Authors' Calculations using LIS data and OECD (2002b).

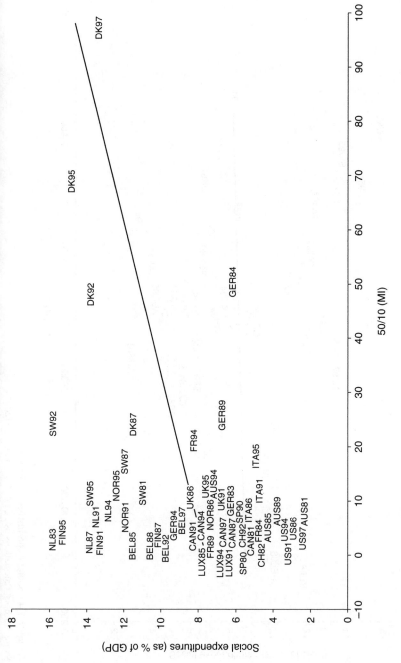

Figure 9.A.3 Social expenditures – 50/10 (MI)
Source: Authors' Calculations using LIS data and OECD (2002b).

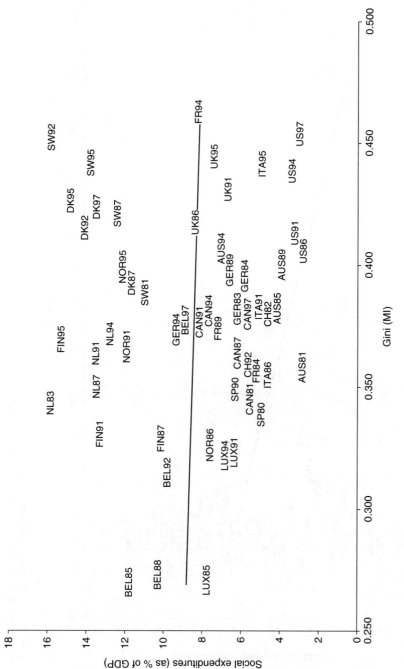

Figure 9.A.4 Social expenditures – Gini (MI)
Source: Authors' Calculations using LIS data and OECD (2002b).

Table 9.A.4 Measure of Inequality: 90/50 and 50/10 (MI) – SOCX <15%

	(1)	(2)	(3)
90/50 (MI)[1]	−8.9705	−8.5723	−6.4032
robust, clustered standard error	(2.3209)**	(2.4061)**	(2.1246)*
50/10 (MI)[1]	0.0524	0.0468	0.0379
robust, clustered standard error	(0.0184)*	(0.0134)**	(0.0122)**
Trust	8.8975	6.6228	3.3331
robust, clustered standard error	(4.0449)*	(3.5200)	(3.3042)
GDP	−0.5936	−0.8086	−0.8612
robust, clustered standard error	(0.2352)*	(0.2577)**	(0.1869)**
% Foreign Born		−0.1398	−0.1673
robust, clustered standard error		(0.0448)**	(0.0583)*
Centralization			5.8405
robust, clustered standard error			(2.3067)*
Constant	23.0511	25.0492	21.0644
robust, clustered standard error	(5.5977)**	(5.4847)**	(5.0075)**
Observations	52	46	44
R-squared	0.52	0.64	0.70
F-statistic	13.01**	15.10**	9.13**

Notes:
Dependent variable: Total Social Expenditures, Non-elderly (as percentage of GDP). OECD (2002a).
[1] These variables are measured using market income.
* significant at 5 percent.
** significant at 1 percent.
Sources and definitions:
Trust: See Table 9.2 for definition. *World Values Survey* (2002).
GDP: Average annual percent growth over five years preceding year of observation. OECD (2002d).
% Foreign Born: OECD (2000); LIS; U.S. Census, various years.
Centralization: See text for definition. Iversen (1998). Country average used to impute for missing data. (Luxembourg and Spain omitted with zero observations.)
Authors' Calculations.

Notes

* The authors would like to acknowledge the assistance of Michael Eriksen and Joseph Marchand from the Center for Policy Research. The authors thank The Russell Sage Foundation, the ISER at the University of Essex, and the SPRC at The UNSW, Sydney, Australia, for support while working on this paper. Helpful discussions were had with Christopher Jencks, Irv Garfinkel, Sara McLanahan, David Brady, Robert Haveman, David Soskice and Robert Goodin. Helpful comments were made by Dan Rosenbaum, Janet Gornick, Pablo Beramendi and Nancy Folbre, and at seminars at the Center for Advanced Study, Standford, CA; ANU, Canberra Australia; Syracuse University; and the Special Program on the Social Dimensions of Inequality Conference in Washington, DC. The authors wish to thank Andrea Johnson, Lynn Lethbridge, JoAnna Moskal, Mary Santy, Martha Bonney and Kati Foley for their excellent help with manuscript preparation. All errors are our own.

1. We concentrate on social expenditures in cash or near cash terms, for example, food stamps, housing allowances, active labor market programs, for the non-elderly. We cannot include health care or education at this time because of lack of data on these areas of social spending for the nations and years that we are analyzing. Tax expenditures are not included nor are employer provided benefits, but refundable tax credits such as the earned income tax credit are. This definition of social expenditures is consistent with the definitions of market and disposable income employed in the income inequality literature.
2. The variation in non-elderly total social expenditures is even more pronounced. The Northern European (Belgium, Denmark, Netherlands) and Scandinavian (Finland, Norway, Sweden) countries spend markedly more (as a percentage of GDP) on social expenditures than do the Anglo (Australia, Canada, United Kingdom, United States) countries (OECD, 2002a).
3. We estimate this ratio by adding OECD Social Expenditures and OECD Final Government Outlays and dividing this total into OECD Social Expenditures. For more on this method, see Smeeding (2002b) and OECD (2002a). Both we and the OECD do not include tax expenditures as public benefits in these calculations.
4. No consistent comparable time series exists that includes both health care and education spending over the past 20 years.
5. In the European literature, the current emphasis on 'social exclusion' as a major social problem reflects both a concern with the multidimensionality of economic and social deprivation and an analysis that social outcomes are heavily influenced by the economic distance between the bottom and the middle parts of the distribution.
6. In unpacking this issue, we also recognize the fact that social expenditures *do* influence the 'real' level of inequality within and across societies (Beramendi, 2001). We discuss this endogeneity issue more completely below.
7. The World Bank also has useful annotated bibliographies on social capital and research on the connection between inequality and violence—visit http://www.worldbank.org/poverty/inequal/abstracts/violence.htm and http://www.worldbank.org/poverty/scapital/index.htm.
8. The study by Mulligan *et al.* (2002) is cross-national in nature and investigates the empirical connection between Social Security programs and democracies. Although they show that Social Security programs vary by demographic and economic factors, democracies and non-democracies are surprisingly similar in their provision of Social Security benefits.
9. Milanovic defines the dependent variable as 'how the share of (i) the bottom half of (ii) the bottom quintile (ranked by factor income) increases when we move from factor to disposable income'.
10. Milanovic's paper outlines one economic theory of social expenditures and inequality as follows:

> When individuals are ordered according to their factor (or market) incomes, the median voter (the individual with the median level of income) will be, in more unequal societies, relatively poorer. His or her income will be lower in relation to mean income. If net transfers (government cash transfers minus direct taxes) are progressive, the more unequal is income distribution, the more the median voter has to gain through joint of taxes and transfers, and the more likely he or she is to vote for higher taxes and transfers. Based on the median-voter as decisive, more unequal societies will therefore choose greater redistribution.

11. The median voter will be, for example, completely unaffected by changes in the share of income received by the bottom quintile.
12. A paper closely related in terms of methodology is by Plotnick (1986), who constructs a similar model by individual states of the United States using AFDC data.
13. We in turn experiment with these political variables in our empirical work (see Section 9.4).
14. For a useful summary and guide to the literature, visit http://www.worldbank. org/poverty/inequal/econ/index.htm.
15. There is some evidence that Americans and Europeans may have different attitudes to the responsiveness of government.
16. The country-years used in the analysis include: Australia (AUS) (1981, 1985, 1989, 1994); Austria (AUT) (1987, 1995); Belgium (BEL) (1985, 1988, 1992, 1997); Canada (CAN) (1981, 1987, 1991, 1994, 1997); Denmark (DK) (1987, 1992, 1995, 1997); Finland (FIN) (1987, 1991, 1995); France (FR) (1984, 1989, 1994); Germany (GER) (1983, 1984, 1989, 1994); Italy (IT) (1986, 1991, 1995); Luxembourg (LUX) (1985, 1991, 1994); Netherlands (NL) (1983, 1987, 1991, 1994); Norway (NOR) (1986, 1991, 1995); Spain (SP) (1980, 1990); Sweden (SW) (1981, 1987, 1992, 1995); Switzerland (CH) (1982, 1992); UK (1986, 1991, 1995); and US (1986, 1991, 1994, 1997). We also use Mexico (1994, 1996, 1998) in later illustrative regressions.
17. When the dependent variable is measured in per capita terms, the magnitudes of the estimated coefficients are different but the (mean) elasticities are virtually unchanged.
18. We relegate the results with disposable income to Appendix tables.
19. Index of centralization from Iversen (1998): 'The operational definition of centralization—C—is the sum of $(w_j{}^*p_{ij}^2)^*(1/2)$, where wj is the weight accorded to each bargaining level j (sum of $w_j = 1$) and p_{ij} is the share of workers covered by the union (or federation) i at level j.'
20. The per capita GDP growth rate reported here is the growth rate of per capita GDP at current prices and current PPPs (US dollars) over the five years preceding the year of observation. Three other measures of per capita GDP were also included in the specification with minor differences in the results. Since this growth measure is the average annual growth rate over the five years prior to the year of observation, we believe this is sufficient to be considered exogenous to the *current* social expenditure decision by a nation.
21. We would like to thank David Richardson for suggesting the use of ethnic fractionalization measures as a proxy for immigration and centralization. However, ethnic fractionalization measures are not available for multiple years. We did impute ethnic fractionalization data from Alesina *et al.* (2002) for each country and while it did enter the model statistically significantly, we do not report the results with the variable below.
22. The analogous regressions using the disposable personal income definition are repeated in Appendix Tables 9.A.1–9.A.2. The results are sensitive to the new inequality variable measures. In Appendix Table 9.A.1, the coefficient on trust is still positive and significant, though of slightly smaller magnitude. Estimates on other covariates also differ somewhat from their MI counterparts. The estimate on the percent foreign born variable maintains its sign, magnitude and significance. The coefficient on Iversen's Centralization variable is again positive and of smaller magnitude but no longer significant. The reader is left to further investigate the differences on her own.

23. It might also be interesting to examine the determinants of our trust measure. While the WVS provides microlevel survey data, not all demographic or income variables are available for all country-years. However, we are able to estimate trust as a function of demographics (ratio of elders to total population, ratio of children to total population and percent of households that are single parent families), economics (unemployment rate and per capita GDP) and government activity (voter turnout) from our main data set. We estimate several different linear (OLS) specifications and mostly the equations fit poorly (R-squared under 0.05), although the unemployment rate (and percent single parent family) enter negatively (positively) and statistically significantly. Overall, we expect trust to depend on the economic and demographic characteristics of a nation and feel that continued research in this area could prove worthwhile.

24. It is also important to note that we included a control for total union membership (from Visser, 1996 contained in Huber *et al.*, 1997) but the estimated coefficient was approximately zero, statistically insignificant in all runs and took overall precision out of the model. A third set of regressions were estimated using just the 90/50 as the inequality control (not reported) with results similar to those found in the tables. As noted above, two political variables were also included in the specification but both proved to be statistically insignificant and close to zero. An alternative trust measure was used from the ISSP data set (various years) but due to the small number of observations, the model fits too poorly to report any results. Finally, we note that our GDP measure confounds issues of level and growth. Hence, we included current levels of per capita GDP but noted the probable endogeneity of this measure. We then included lagged values ($(t-1)$ and $(t-2)$) of per capita GDP (separately) but all were statistically insignificant and virtually equal to zero.

25. The statistical significance of the coefficient on the 50/10 variable may be driven by two Denmark observations (1995 and 1997); see Appendix Figure 9.A.3. When those two observations are not included in the analysis, however, the estimates on all of the variables maintain their magnitudes. The only change is a statistically insignificant coefficient on the 50/10 ratio. However, the magnitudes are very similar.

26. In Appendix Tables 9.A.3–9.A.4, we estimate the same regressions for the sample without countries that spend more than 15 percent of their GDP on social expenditures. Eliminating these countries (Finland 1995, Netherlands 1983, Sweden 1992) has significant effects on the coefficients. For the regressions with the market income 90/50 and 50/10 measures (Appendix Table 9.A.3), trust is no longer statistically significant in a majority of regressions, although it maintains its sign and magnitude. The inequality measures maintain their sign and are statistically significant in every column.

27. We tried several separate experiments to deal with the endogeneity issue. First, we used the other covariates in the basic model as instruments for the inequality variable. However, because of the small number of observations and subsequent lack of adequate variation in the sample, we were unable to deal with the collinearity of the predicted variable of interest. In a second approach, we used inflation as an instrument for inequality since inflation has been shown to positively affect inequality (Albanesi, 2001) but as expected the instrument was weak. Third, we reduced the model in Tables 9.3 and 9.4 to the basic demographic, trust and growth variables. Then, using combinations of the remaining covariates as instruments, we predicted the appropriate measure of inequality. Finally, we used

several state variables as possible instruments, none of which generated significant results. Such instruments included trade and financial openness, measures of imports and exports (Mahler, 2002) and lags in the dependent variable. Again, the fit was poor and the resulting estimates statistically insignificant.

28. Due to other data constraints, however, we were forced to impute the average values of trust, centralization and the percent foreign born for the three Mexico observations (1994, 1996, 1998).

References

Albanesi, S. (2001) 'Inflation and Inequality,' *CEPR Working Paper* (Italy: Bocconi University).

Alesina, A., A. Devleeschauer, W. Easterly, S. Kurlat and R. Wacziarg (2002) 'Fractionalization,' *NBER Working Paper* 9411 (Cambridge, MA: National Bureau of Economic Research) (December).

Alesina, A. and E. La Ferrara (2001) 'Preferences for Redistribution in the Land of Opportunities,' *NBER Working Paper* 8267 (Cambridge, MA: National Bureau of Economic Research) (May).

Alesina, A. and E. La Ferrara (1999) 'Participation in Heterogeneous Communities,' *NBER Working Paper* 7155 (Cambridge, MA: National Bureau of Economic Research) (June).

Alesina, A. and D. Rodrik (1994) 'Distributive Politics and Economic Growth,' *Quarterly Journal of Economics* 109(2) (May): 465–90.

American Political Science Association Task Force on Inequality and American Democracy (2004) 'American Democracy in an Age of Rising Inequality' (June), http://www.apsanet.org/Inequality/index.cfm.

Ansolabehere, S., J. M. de Figueiredo, and J. M. Snyder Jr. (2003) 'Why is There so Little Money in U.S. Politics?,' *Journal of Economic Perspectives* 17(1) (Winter): 105–30.

Arjona, R., M. Ladaique and M. Pearson (2001) 'Growth, Inequality, and Social Protection,' *Labour Market and Social Policy Occasional Paper* 51 (Paris: OECD) (June).

Atkinson, A. B. (1970) 'On the Measurement of Inequality,' *Journal of Economic Theory* 2(3) (September): 244–63.

Atkinson, A. B., L. Rainwater and T. M. Smeeding (1995) *Income Distribution in OECD Countries: The Evidence from the Luxembourg Income Study (LIS)*, Social Policy Studies 18 (Paris: OECD) (October).

Bartels, L. (2002) 'Economic Inequality and Political Representation,' unpublished manuscript (Princeton University) (November).

Bassett, W. F., J. P. Burkett and L. Putterman (1999) 'Income Distribution, Government Transfers, and the Problem of Unequal Influence,' *European Journal of Political Economy* 15(2) (June): 207–28.

Bénabou, R. (2000) 'Unequal Societies: Income Distribution and the Social Contract,' *American Economic Review* 90(1) (March): 96–129.

Bénabou, R. (1996) 'Inequality and Growth,' in Ben S. Bernanke and Julio Rotemberg (eds), *NBER Macroeconomics Annual 1996* (Cambridge, MA: MIT Press), 11: 11–74.

Beramendi, P. (2001) 'The Politics of Income Inequality in the OECD: The Role of Second Order Effects,' *Luxembourg Income Study Working Paper* 284, Center for Policy Research (New York: Syracuse University) (September).

Berkman, L. F., D. Cutler, E. Meara, D. Acevedo-Garcia and A. M. Epstein (2002) 'Social Inequality and Health: The Impact of Socialisms Economic and Health Policies on Population Health,' unpublished manuscript, Harvard University Working Group on Social Inequality (June).

Blinder, A. S. and A. B. Krueger (2004) 'What Does the Public Know about Economic Policy, and How Does It Know It?,' *NBER Working Paper* 10787 (Cambridge, MA: National Bureau of Economic Research) (September).

Bradley, D., E. Huber, S. Moller, F. Nielsen and J. Stephens (2001) 'Distribution and Redistribution in Post-Industrial Democracies,' *Luxembourg Income Study Working Paper* 265, Center for Policy Research (New York: Syracuse University) (May).

Costa, D. L. and M. E. Kahn (2001) 'Understanding the Decline in Social Capital, 1952–1998,' *NBER Working Paper* 8295 (Cambridge, MA: National Bureau of Economic Research) (May).

Esping-Andersen, G. (1990) *The Three Worlds of Welfare Capitalism* (Cambridge, UK: Polity Press).

Gordon, P. and L. Wang (2004) 'Does Economic Performance Correlate with Big Government?,' *Econ Journal Watch* 1(2) (August): 192–221, www.econjournalwatch.org.

Hall, P. A. and D. Soskice (2001) *Varieties of Capitalism* (New York: Oxford University Press Incorporated).

Huber, E., C. Ragin and J. D. Stephens (1997) 'Comparative Welfare States Data Set,' created by Northwestern University and University of North Carolina.

International Social Survey Programme, various years, http://www.gesis.org/en/data_service/issp/index.htm.

Iversen, T. (1999) *Contested Economic Institutions* (Cambridge, MA: Cambridge University Press).

Iversen, T. (1998) 'Wage Bargaining, Central Bank Independence, and the Real Effects of Money,' *International Organization* 52(3) (Summer): 469–504.

Iversen, T. and D. Soskice (2002) 'Political Parties and the Time Inconsistency Problem in Social Welfare Provision,' unpublished manuscript, Center for European Studies (Cambridge, MA: Harvard University) (March).

Iversen, T. and D. Soskice (2001) 'An Asset Theory of Social Policy Preferences,' *The American Political Science Review* 95(4) (December): 875–93.

Kenworthy, L. and J. Pontusson (2002) 'Inequality and Redistribution in OECD Countries' (Cornell University) (March).

Knack, S. and P. Keefer (1997) 'Does Social Capital Have an Economic Payoff? A Cross-Country Investigation,' *Quarterly Journal of Economics* 112(4) (November): 1251–88.

Koeniger, W., L. Nunziata and M. Leonardi (2004) 'Labour Market Institutions and Wage Inequality,' *IZA Discussion Paper* 1291 (September), www.iza.org.

Kristov, L., P. Lindert and R. McClelland (1992) 'Pressure Groups and Redistribution,' *Journal of Public Economics* 48(2) (July): 135–63.

Lindert, P. (2004) *Growing Public: Volume 1, The Story: Social Spending and Economic Growth since the Eighteenth Century* (Cambridge, UK: Cambridge University Press).

Mahler, V. (2002) 'Economic Globalization, Domestic Politics, and Income Inequality in the Developed Countries,' paper presented at the 2002 Southern Political Science Association meeting (7–9 November 2002).

Marshall, M. and K. Jaggers (2000) 'Polity IV Project. Political Regime Characteristics and Transitions, 1800–1999: Dataset Users Manual,' Integrated Network for Societal Conflict Research (INSCR) Program and the Center for International Development and Conflict Management (CIDCM) (December), pp. 1–84.

McCarty, N., K. T. Poole and H. Rosenthal (2003) 'Political Polarization and Income Inequality,' *Russell Sage Foundation Working Paper* 201 (February).

Milanovic, B. (2000) 'The Median-Voter Hypothesis, Income Inequality, and Income Distribution: An Empirical Test with the Required Data,' *European Journal of Political Economy* 16(3) (September): 367–410.

Moene, K. O. and M. Wallerstein (2002) 'Income Inequality and Welfare Spending: A Disaggregated Analysis,' unpublished manuscript (Princeton University) (February).

Moene, K. O. and M. Wallerstein (2001) 'Inequality, Social Insurance and Redistribution,' *American Political Science Review* **95**(4): 859–74.

Mullahy, J., S. Robert and B. Wolfe (2002) 'Health, Income, and Inequality: Review and Redirection for the Wisconsin Russell Sage Working Group,' *Russell Sage Foundation Working Paper*.

Mulligan, C. B., R. Gil and X. Sala-i-Martin (2002) 'Social Security and Democracy,' *Universitat Pompeu Fabra, Economics and Business Working Paper* 621 (May): 1–56.

Organization for Economic Cooperation and Development (OECD) (2002a) *Social Expenditures* (Organization for Economic Cooperation and Development: Paris).

Organization for Economic Cooperation and Development (OECD) (2002b) *Education at a Glance* (Paris: Organization for Economic Cooperation and Development).

Organization for Economic Cooperation and Development (OECD) (2002c) *Health Care Expenditures Database* (Paris: Organization for Economic Cooperation and Development).

Organization for Economic Cooperation and Development (OECD) (2002d) *National Accounts of OECD Countries Volume I* (Paris: Organization for Economic Cooperation and Development).

Organization for Economic Cooperation and Development (OECD) (2000) *Stocks of Foreign Born Population by Country of Origin: 2000 Release 1* (Source OECD International Migration Statistics: Paris) (November).

Osberg, L. S. (1995) 'The Equity/Efficiency Tradeoff in Retrospect,' *Canadian Business Economics* **3**(3) (April–June): 5–20.

Osberg, L. S., T. M. Smeeding and J. A. Schwabish (2004) 'Income Distribution and Public Social Expenditure: Theories, Effects and Evidence,' in K. Neckerman (ed.), *Social Inequality* (New York: Russell Sage Foundation), pp. 821–59.

Perotti, R. (1996) 'Growth, Income Distribution, and Democracy: What the Data Say,' *Journal of Economic Growth* **1**(2) (June): 149–87.

Perotti, R. (1992) 'Income Distribution, Politics, and Growth,' *American Economic Review* **82**(2) (May): 311–16.

Persson, T. and G. Tabellini (1994) 'Is Inequality Harmful for Growth?,' *American Economic Review* **84**(3) (June): 600–21.

Plotnick, R. D. (1986) 'An Interest Group Model of Direct Income Redistribution,' *Review of Economics and Statistics* **68**(4) (November): 594–602.

Putnam, R. D. (2001) *Bowling Alone: The Collapse and Revival of American Community* (New York: Touchstone Books).

Reich, R. B. (1991) 'Secession of the Successful,' *New York Times Magazine* (January 20): 16–23. Reprinted at www.-personal.umich.edu/~gmarkus/secession.html.

Scarth, W. (2000) 'Growth and Inequality: A Review Article,' *Review of Income and Wealth* **46**(3) (September): 389–97.

Slemrod, J. (2002) 'Trust in Public Finance,' *NBER Working Paper* 9187 (Cambridge, MA: National Bureau of Economic Research) (September).

Slemrod, J. and P. Katuscak (2002) 'Do Trust and Trustworthiness Pay off?,' *NBER Working Paper* 9200 (Cambridge, MA: National Bureau of Economic Research) (September).

Smeeding, T. M. (2002a) 'Globalization, Inequality, and the Rich Countries of the G-20: Updated Results from the Luxembourg Income Study (LIS) and other Places,' unpublished manuscript, Center for Policy Research (New York: Syracuse University) (May).

Smeeding, T. M. (2002b) 'Real Standards of Living and Public Support for Children: A Cross-national Comparison,' unpublished manuscript, Center for Policy Research (New York: Syracuse University) (December).

Stata Corporation (2002) 'How can the Standard Errors with the Cluster( ) Option be Smaller than those Without the Cluster( ) Option?,' FAQ Statistics, www.stata.com/support/faqs/stat/cluster.html.

Visser, J. (1996) *Unionisation Trends. The OECD Countries Union Membership File, Amsterdam* (Amsterdam: Centre for Research of European Societies and Labour Relations CESAR: University of Amsterdam).

World Values Survey (2002) http://wvs.isr.umich.edu.

Zak, P. J. and S. Knack (2001) 'Trust and Growth,' *The Economic Journal* **111** (April): 295–321.

10
The Generosity of the Welfare State Towards the Elderly

Mathieu Lefèbvre and Pierre Pestieau

10.1 Introduction

Imagine a casual discussion involving three Eurocrats in a café on the Brussels Grand Place. They are attending a meeting on the 'Future of Pensions in the EU' and are talking about the generosity of pensions. Each one contends that his country is the most generous. The Belgian contends that his country is by far the most generous as it allows workers to retire as early as age 50 and that Belgium has the earliest effective age of retirement, that is, 57 years for men. The Italian disagrees with this view, as in his country the rate of replacement at age 65 is the highest, and that is the relevant measure of generosity. The third one, a Dutchman, completely disagrees with his two colleagues. 'Generosity to whom?' he says: 'In my country, pensions reduce the poverty rate among the elderly more than in any other country and that is what matters.'

This imaginary discussion illustrates what this chapter is all about. The concept of generosity is important, but at the same time very ambiguous. We distinguish three types of generosity:

1) one relying on average benefits;
2) one focusing on early retirement; and
3) one concerned with alleviating intragenerational inequality or poverty.

A fourth definition would be one dealing with intergenerational redistribution, but is outside of the scope of this chapter.

Two questions are dealt with in the rest of this chapter:

1) What is the statistical correlation among our three concepts of generosity?
2) Has this relation evolved over time, and to what extent is this evolution linked to economic openness?

But before answering these questions,[1] we provide some theoretical predictions as to the relationships among the three types of generosity.

10.2 Theoretical predictions

10.2.1 Political support of contributory systems

In order to discuss the relationship between average and redistributive generosity, we have to introduce a traditional distinction between two extreme types of pension systems. The first one provides earnings-related benefits, which is also labelled Bismarckian or contributive. At the other extreme, there are pension systems whose benefit structure is such that the replacement rate (benefit to earning ratio) declines as earnings increase. These are also called redistributive or Beveridgean, with flat rate benefits. In reality, pension systems usually fall between these extremes, with Germany and France closer to the Bismarckian pole and the United Kingdom and the Netherlands closer to the Beveridgean pole.

10.2.1.1 *Programs for the poor are poor programs*

A number of recently developed political economy models argue that the size of a program depends on its degree of contributiveness. People vote for two parameters that reflect the two features of contributiveness and size. These votes are either sequential[2] or simultaneous.[3] In either case and under plausible assumptions, there is a negative relation between size and contributiveness. This formalizes a well-known political economy proposition that targeting the benefits to the lower part of income distribution is unsustainable because of a lack of political support. This idea is popularized by the sentence: 'Programs for the poor are poor programs.' In other words, a broad program that caters to everyone, rich and poor, is most likely to get more political support than a program focusing just on the poor.

10.2.1.2 *Rich programs are good for the poor*

We have just seen that contributory programs tend to be larger than redistributive ones. Do they improve the standards of living of the poor? Almost certainly, they do. Within the Bismarckian tradition, is found the idea of a so-called minimum pension guarantee. This is a guarantee provided by the government that brings pensions to a minimum level, possibly by topping the existing entitlements if there are any. If this guarantee is sufficient to lift a sizeable fraction of poor retirees out of poverty, then a contributory system can end up being very costly, having not much incidence on income redistribution while being efficient at alleviating poverty.

10.2.2 Unavoidable distortions

As shown by Gruber and Wise (1999), one of the main factors of early retirement is the implicit tax on prolonged activity, which is high in some countries. Implicit taxation can be explained by the concern of governments with regard to the unemployment of young people. But even without such a concern, no government that tries to achieve some redistribution can avoid tax distortions. In an ideal world, it might be possible to redistribute income in a non-distortionary way, in other words, in maintaining equality between the marginal disutility of one more year of work and its marginal productivity. In a less perfect world, non-distortionary taxes are not available. Hence any redistribution entails taxes and pension benefits that induce workers to retire earlier than they would in a market economy, or in the ideal world.[4] Such an observation would imply some positive correlation between early retirement generosity and redistributive generosity.

However, it can be shown that when the implicit taxes are too distortionary, reducing them could have a double dividend—an improvement of income inequality among retirees and an increase in revenue.[5] To conclude, the question of whether or not early retirement and either redistribution or poverty alleviation are positively correlated, can only be answered empirically.

10.2.3 Race to the bottom

One of the main alleged pitfalls of the ongoing economic integration is that it would impede redistributive policies at the national level, plus threaten the future of the welfare state. The basic idea is that mobile factors of production, labor or capital, can adjust their location to any international differentials in taxation or benefits. Therefore, national governments cannot abstract from such potential reactions when designing redistributive policies. To illustrate this point, assume a small open economy that provides retirees with a minimum pension benefit regardless of the value of their contributions. Assume also that workers can move freely across countries. It is likely that low-income workers will move in and that high-income workers will move out to other countries that have a contributory system. This would lead our small open economy to an unsustainable outcome, as it would be forced to adopt a less redistributive system. This is what is called 'the race to the bottom,' a notion that does not seem as radical as one could have feared a few decades ago.[6]

10.3 Statistical relationship

10.3.1 The data

We use two types of data for the average generosity of the pension system. Average generosity (AVGEN)1 is simply the share of public pension spending in gross domestic product (GDP), and AVGEN2 is the rate of replacement at 65. This rate of replacement that comes from the Organization for Economic Co-operation and Development (OECD) is compiled for six typical households distinguished by earnings and marital status. Both are presented on Table 10.1 for the year 1995. Table 10.2 presents two coefficients of correlation, the Pearson and Spearman[7] ones, between these two indicators. The most and least generous countries according to AVGEN1, are Italy and Australia, respectively. According to AVGEN2, the more generous is again Italy and the least is now Norway. These two concepts are not perfectly correlated, as AVGEN2 comes from the rate of replacement of only those retirees who are covered, whereas AVGEN1 includes the rate of replacement, but also the rate of coverage that varies across countries.

For the generosity toward early retirement, we also use two indicators:

1) Early retirement generosity (ERGEN)1 is the effective age of retirement of male workers; and
2) ERGEN2 is the ratio of replacement at 55.

As be seen, this generosity is equal to 0 in some countries that do not have any such schemes. ERGEN1 ranges from 66.5 in Japan to 58.8 in the Netherlands and ERGEN2 ranges from 0.7 in Italy to 0 in the United States, Norway, New Zealand, Japan, Canada and Australia. There can be seen some intersection between ERGEN1 and ERGEN2—countries characterized by generous rates of replacement for early retirees also count more early retirees than the others (implicit tax rates on prolonged activity are linked to these replacement rates).

Finally we have two indicators of redistributive generosity:

1) The first one concerns poverty alleviation (the difference between poverty without and with net public transfers). It is denoted poverty alleviation generosity (POVGEN) and ranges from 78 percent in France to 25 percent in Japan.
2) The second redistributive indicator consists of the ratio of the income share of public pensions in the first quintile to the same share in the top quintile. It is called income share generosity (INEGEN) and ranges from 8.9 in Australia to 1 in France.

These two indicators should be positively related but this is not the case, as shown in Table 10.2. Poverty is just one aspect of inequality. A pension system can be distributively neutral on most of the income scale and at the same time provide the poor retirees with a good minimum pension. Also it can reduce inequality without alleviating poverty.

10.3.2   Correlations

Table 10.2 presents the correlation coefficients (Spearman and Pearson) for all these indicators. We have already discussed the correlations between indicators measuring the same type of generosity. We now turn to the relationships for which we have some theoretical predictions.

Table 10.1 Indicators of generosity, 1995

	AVGEN1	AVGEN2	POVGEN	INEGEN	ERGEN1	ERGEN2
AUS	3.798	0.376	57.000	8.9	61.8	0.000
CAN	5.400	0.571	46.854	3.4	62.3	0.000
DNK	9.718	–	65.270	3.6	62.7	–
FIN	9.739	0.594	30.831	3.9	59.0	0.528
FRA	12.106	0.783	77.979	1.0	59.2	0.499
DEU	11.174	0.525	70.100	1.4	60.5	0.370
ITA	13.324	0.800	55.675	1.4	60.6	0.700
JAP	5.915	0.637	25.400	3.6	66.5	0.000
NLD	8.002	0.589	59.700	3.1	58.8	0.687
NZ	5.580	0.439	70.200	3.2	62.0	0.000
NOR	7.507	0.321	58.200	2.2	63.8	0.000
SWE	10.627	0.735	73.205	1.2	63.3	0.250
GBR	8.740	0.457	53.387	3.5	62.7	0.232
USA	6.348	0.545	36.461	3.7	63.6	0.000

Source: OECD (2004, 2003), Förster (2003), Blöndal and Scarpetta (1999).

10.3.2.1   *Redistribution and average generosity*

It appears that using both AVGEN1 and AVGEN2 and either correlation coefficient, there is a negative relation between redistribution and average generosity. This seems to vindicate the political economy theory that says that the more contributory a pension scheme, the more generous it will be in average terms. Does that mean that average generosity is good for the poor? In fact, it appears that rich programs are in this instance good for the poor.

10.3.2.2   *Poverty alleviation and average generosity*

Indeed, there is a positive though hardly significant relationship between poverty alleviation and average generosity. This implies that schemes that are generous on average include programs that alleviate poverty.

10.3.2.3   *Early retirement and redistribution*

It is interesting to note a high correlation between ERGEN2 based on the replacement ratio offered to early retirees and either measure of average generosity. That indicates that there is no trade-off between early retirement and normal retirement. Instead, if we use the other indicator, ERGEN1, the coefficient is negative, but not significantly so. This implies that countries with generous but restricted early retirement are also those that have, on average, a generous pension system.

Concerning the link between redistributive generosity and early retirement, we have a negative but not significant correlation between INEGEN and ERGEN2, which does not vindicate the idea of a double dividend.

Table 10.2 Correlation coefficients of generosity indicators, 1995

		AVGEN1	AVGEN2	POVGEN	INEGEN	ERGEN1	ERGEN2
AVGEN1	P	1.000					
	S	1.000					
AVGEN2	P	0.678**	1.000				
	S	0.610**	1.000				
POVGEN	P	0.392	0.081	1.000			
	S	0.371	0.000	1.000			
INEGEN	P	−0.733***	−0.552*	−0.351	1.000		
	S	−0.617**	−0.407	−0.694***	1.000		
ERGEN1	P	−0.458*	−0.253	−0.358	0.130	1.000	
	S	−0.370	−0.258	−0.268	0.173	1.000	
ERGEN2	P	0.786***	0.611**	0.223	−0.425	−0.777***	1.000
	S	0.829***	0.633**	0.236	−0.451	−0.748***	1.000

*** significant at 1%.
** significant at 5%.
* significant at 10%.

10.4　Changes over time

The previous section was based on data concerning 14 countries and the year 1995. We also have data for 1985 and 2000 (see the Appendix). This allows us to first check if the coefficients of correlation just discussed are changing over time. Then we look at the question of social dumping, given that the period 1985–2000 is one of increased economic integration.

10.4.1　Stability of correlations

On the basis of the previous section, we are going to focus on three relationships:

1) the one between AVGEN1 and INEGEN;
2) the one between AVGEN1 and POVGEN; and
3) the one between AVGEN2 and ERGEN2

to see how they evolve over time, namely over the period 1985–2000 (see Table 10.3). It appears that there has been little change in these correlations among these types of generosity.

10.4.2　A race to the bottom?

Table 10.4 gives the variations in generosity for the years 1985–95, along with an indicator of economic openness,[8] the trade openness indicator (TOI), which will be used to test the existence of a 'race to the bottom.'

Table 10.3 Evolution of coefficients of correlation

		1985	1995	2000
AVGEN1 and INGEN	P	−0.662	−0.733	−0.601
	S	−0.626	−0.617	−0.649
AVGEN1 and POVGEN	P	0.558	0.392	0.364
	S	0.582	0.371	0.349
AVGEN2 and ERGEN2	P	0.711	0.611	0.542
	S	0.769	0.633	0.584

Three evolutions are worth noting:

1) DPOVGEN, the variation in the extent of poverty alleviation due to social security is positive in eight countries and negative in six. In other words, there does not appear to be any trend toward less poverty alleviation;
2) DINEGEN, the income share generosity, which is negative in 10 out of 14 countries, shows a trend toward less reduction in inequality or alternatively toward more contributiveness; and
3) DERGEN1 is the change in the effective age of retirement. Interestingly, DERGEN1 is negative everywhere.

Thus it seems that for reasons of globalization or ageing, all concerned countries are under pressure to reduce the generosity of their social security systems toward early retirement. Appendix Table 10.A.5 gives the changes in generosity for the period 1995–2000. We observe more or less the same pattern.

Table 10.4 Change in indicators of generosity and trade openness, 1985–95

	DAVGEN1	DAVGEN2	DPOVGEN	DINEGEN	DERGEN1	DERGEN2	TOI
AUS	−0.003	0.017	8.600	−2.010	−0.9	0.000	7,20
CAN	1.339	−0.003	−0.170	−0.804	−1.5	0.000	7,60
DNK	1.464	–	9.010	−0.090	−1.8	–	7,10
FIN	1.578	0.039	−10.723	−0.665	−1.1	0.093	6,70
FRA	1.444	−0.009	9.869	−0.132	−2.1	−0.046	6,50
DEU	0.272	−0.082	−1.400	−0.041	−1.7	−0.034	8,50
ITA	2.323	0.000	7.157	−1.152	−1.0	0.000	7,40
JAP	1.052	–	12.200	−0.010	−0.7	–	6,50
NLD	−0.125	−0.048	−0.100	0.092	−2.6	−0.035	8,40
NZ	−1.358	−0.015	6.000	0.510	−0.9	0.000	7,50
NOR	1.522	−0.036	4.400	−0.067	−2.2	0.000	7,40
SWE	1.435	−0.029	−10.867	0.323	−1.3	−0.026	7,80
GBR	1.149	0.072	−7.270	0.278	−1.9	−0.024	8,50
USA	−0.133	0.028	2.467	−0.247	−0.6	0.000	7,80

Source: TOI (CATO, 2001).

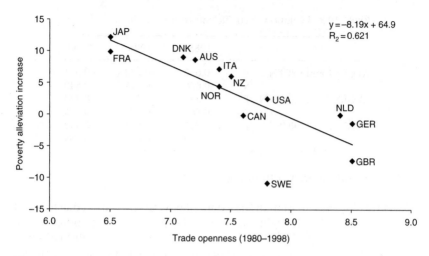

Figure 10.1   Poverty and openness, 1985–1995

If there is any race to the bottom, it is likely to be more intense in open economies, the indicator of openness being quite stable. Thus, using the change in TOI instead of the level of TOI did not generate any significant result. Accordingly we try to see to what extent changes in POVGEN can be explained by the openness of the countries concerned. Appendix Tables 10.A.6–10.A.9 give the coefficients of correlation for the two periods and for the whole sample of countries with and without Finland. Finland's figure for poverty alleviation is doubtful since part of the social security benefits are not taken into account. Indeed, Figure 10.1 presents results that show that variation in poverty alleviation is negatively related to the degree of openness for the period 1985–95. The R^2 is 0.62.

10.5   Conclusion

The main idea of this paper is that a social security system—including not only old-age pension systems but also disability and unemployment insurance, early retirement scheme and welfare programs—can be labelled generous in three different ways:

1) It can be generous toward early retirement by offering workers aged 55–65 relatively high benefits;
2) It can be generous toward people who retire at the normal age (generally 65); and
3) It can be generous toward the poor retirees by giving them benefits well above their contributions.

To conclude, we have provided evidence for these three definitions of generosity, and shown that they are not closely correlated. The main result is that Bismarckian contributory programs tend to offer generous pensions that in turn benefit the poor. This is a vindication of the idea that programs for the poor are poor programs, and that rich programs are good for the poor. We also note the link between economic integration and redistribution. All in all, variation in poverty alleviation is related to the openness of the economies concerned.

Appendix

Table 10.A.1 Indicators of generosity, 1985

	AVGEN1	AVGEN2	POVGEN	INEGEN	ERGEN1	ERGEN2
AUS	3.801	0.359	48.400	10.9	62.7	0.000
CAN	4.062	0.575	47.024	4.2	63.8	0.000
DNK	8.254	–	56.260	3.7	64.5	–
FIN	8.161	0.555	41.555	4.6	60.1	0.435
FRA	10.663	0.792	68.110	1.1	61.3	0.545
DEU	10.902	0.607	71.500	1.5	62.2	0.404
ITA	11.000	0.800	48.518	2.5	61.6	0.700
JAP	4.863	–	13.200	3.6	67.2	–
NLD	8.127	0.637	59.800	3.0	61.4	0.722
NZ	6.937	0.454	64.200	2.7	62.9	0.000
NOR	5.985	0.357	53.800	2.3	66	0.000
SWE	9.192	0.765	84.072	0.9	64.6	0.276
GBR	7.591	0.385	60.657	3.2	64.6	0.255
USA	6.481	0.517	33.994	3.9	64.2	0.000

Source: OECD (2004, 2003), Förster (2003), Blondal and Scarpetta (1999).

Table 10.A.2 Indicators of generosity, 2000

	AVGEN1	AVGEN2	POVGEN	INEGEN	ERGEN1	ERGEN2
AUS	5.576	0.351	50.000	9.7	60.5	0.000
CAN	5.167	0.566	48.878	3.7	60.8	0.000
DNK	8.285	–	61.240	4.3	60.4	–
FIN	8.575	0.588	23.270	6.1	58.6	0.517
FRA	12.123	0.750	78.699	1.1	58.3	0.456
DEU	11.904	0.499	72.000	1.4	60.4	0.348
ITA	13.831	0.800	58.700	1.4	59.0	0.420
JAP	7.961	0.598	32.400	3.2	65.5	0.000
NLD	7.151	0.614	60.600	2.9	58.8	0.693
NZ	4.900	0.528	67.100	4.2	63.4	0.000
NOR	6.833	0.320	63.400	2.3	62.6	0.000
SWE	9.852	0.696	69.893	1.3	63.0	0.233
GBR	8.871	0.481	50.518	3.4	61.0	0.194
USA	6.015	0.556	35.474	3.8	62.0	0.000

Source: OECD (2004, 2003), Förster (2003), Burniaux, Duval and Jaumotte (2004).

Table 10.A.3 Correlation coefficents, 1985

		AVGEN1	AVGEN2	POVGEN	INEGEN	ERGEN1	ERGEN2
AVGEN1	P	1.000					
	S	1.000					
AVGEN2	P	0.734***	1.000				
	S	0.790***	1.000				
POVGEN	P	0.558**	0.357	1.000			
	S	0.582**	0.322	1.000			
INEGEN	P	−0.662***	−0.550*	−0.413	1.000		
	S	−0.626**	−0.496	−0.771***	1.000		
ERGEN1	P	−0.501*	−0.458	−0.314	−0.058	1.000	
	S	−0.438	−0.522*	−0.117	−0.053	1.000	
ERGEN2	P	0.786***	0.711***	0.238	−0.386	−0.678**	1.000
	S	0.819***	0.769***	0.283	−0.341	−0.694**	1.000

*** significant at 1%.
** significant at 5%.
* significant at 10%.

Table 10.A.4 Correlation coefficients, 2000

		AVGEN1	AVGEN2	POVGEN	INEGEN	ERGEN1	ERGEN2
AVGEN1	P	1.000					
	S	1.000					
AVGEN2	P	0.620**	1.000				
	S	0.538*	1.000				
POVGEN	P	0.364	0.145	1.000			
	S	0.349	0.099	1.000			
INEGEN	P	−0.601**	−0.540*	−0.517*	1.000		
	S	−0.649**	−0.503*	−0.623**	1.000		
ERGEN1	P	−0.414	−0.297	−0.153	−0.037	1.000	
	S	−0.473*	−0.330	−0.099	0.083	1.000	
ERGEN2	P	0.589**	0.542*	0.190	−0.302	−0.754***	1.000
	S	0.681**	0.584**	0.263	−0.422	−0.777***	1.000

*** significant at 1%.
** significant at 5%.
* significant at 10%.

Table 10.A.5 Change in indicators of generosity and trade openness, 1995–2000

	DAVGEN1	DAVGEN2	DPOVGEN	DINEGEN	DERGEN1	DERGEN2	TOI
AUS	1,778	−0,025	−7,000	0,805	−1,3	0,000	7,20
CAN	−0,234	−0,006	2,024	0,346	−1,5	0,000	7,60
DNK	−1,433	–	−4,030	0,753	−2,3	–	7,10
FIN	−1,164	−0,006	−7,561	2,243	−0,4	−0,012	6,70

Table 10.A.5 (Continued)

	DAVGEN1	DAVGEN2	DPOVGEN	DINEGEN	DERGEN1	DERGEN2	TOI
FRA	0,017	−0,033	0,720	0,134	−0,9	−0,042	6,50
DEU	0,730	−0,026	1,900	−0,033	−0,1	−0,021	8,50
ITA	0,508	0,000	3,025	0,043	−1,6	−0,280	7,40
JAP	2,045	−0,038	7,000	−0,410	−1,0	0,000	6,50
NLD	−0,851	0,025	0,900	−0,201	0,0	0,006	8,40
NZ	−0,680	0,089	−3,100	1,070	1,4	0,000	7,50
NOR	−0,674	−0,002	5,200	0,048	−1,2	0,000	7,40
SWE	−0,775	−0,040	−3,312	0,166	−0,3	−0,018	7,80
GBR	0,131	0,024	−2,870	−0,133	−1,7	−0,038	8,50
USA	−0,333	0,011	−0,987	0,092	−1,6	0,000	7,80

Source: TOI (CATO, 2001).

Table 10.A.6 Correlation coefficients of changes, 1985–95

		DAVGEN1	DAVGEN2	DPOVGEN	DINEGEN	DERGEN1	DERGEN2
TOI	P	−0.327	−0.238	−0.482*	0.283	−0.336	−0.464
	S	−0.433	−0.246	−0.678***	0.397	−0.212	−0.384

*** significant at 1%.
** significant at 5%.
* significant at 10%.

Table 10.A.7 Correlation coefficients of changes, 1995–2000

		DAVGEN1	DAVGEN2	DPOVGEN	DINEGEN	DERGEN1	DERGEN2
TOI	P	−0.148	0.328	−0.002	−0.379	0.145	0.047
	S	−0.031	0.390	0.050	−0.335	0.108	0.027

*** significant at 1%.
** significant at 5%.
* significant at 10%.

Table 10.A.8 Correlation coefficients of changes, 1985–95 (without Finland)

		DAVGEN1	DAVGEN2	DPOVGEN	DINEGEN	DERGEN1	DERGEN2
TOI	P	−0.279	−0.105	−0.788***	0.246	−0.302	−0.180
	S	−0.376	−0.160	−0.920***	0.387	−0.177	−0.292

*** significant at 1%.
** significant at 5%.
* significant at 10%.

Table 10.A.9 Correlation coefficients of changes, 1995–2000 (without Finland)

		DAVGEN1	DAVGEN2	DPOVGEN	DINEGEN	DERGEN1	DERGEN2
TOI	P	−0.280	0.338	−0.192	−0.192	0.211	0.080
	S	−0.168	0.373	−0.077	−0.273	0.149	0.020

*** significant at 1%.
** significant at 5%.
* significant at 10%.

Notes

* We acknowledge financial support from the Belgian FNRS and from the European RTN research project. We are grateful to Michael Förster for his comments and remarks. Pierre Pestieau initiated this research while visiting DECVP at the World Bank.

1. This paper is an examination of Pestieau (2004b).
2. Casamatta *et al.* (2000, 2002).
3. Conde-Ruiz and Profeta (2003).
4. Cremer *et al.* (2004).
5. Cremer and Pestieau (2003).
6. Pestieau (2004a).
7. Pearson and Spearman are two different ways of measuring correlation. The first one assumes that the variables are distributed in a specific way, whereas the second one does not make such an assumption.
8. This indicator was published by the CATO Institute in its 2001 report. It is richer than the usual ratio of exports plus imports GDP. We use it for the 1980–98 period.

References

Blöndal, S. and S. Scarpetta (1999) 'The Retirement Decision in OECD Countries,' Working Paper 202 (Paris: OECD).
Burniaux, J. M., R. Duval and F. Jaumotte (2004) 'Coping with Ageing: A Dynamic Approach to Quantify the Impact of Alternative Policy Options on Future Labour Supply in OECD Countries,' Working Paper 371 (Paris: OECD).
Casamatta, G., H. Cremer and P. Pestieau (2002) 'The Political Economy of Social Security,' *Scandinavian Journal of Economics* 102: 503–22.
Casamatta, G., H. Cremer and P. Pestieau (2000) 'Political Sustainability and the Design of Social Insurance,' *Journal of Public Economics* 75: 315–40.
CATO (2001) *Economic Freedom of the World 2001*, Fraser Institute.
Conde-Ruiz, J. and P. Profeta (2003) 'What Social Security: Beveridgean or Bismarckian,' unpublished.
Cremer, H., J.-M. Lozachmeur and P. Pestieau (2004) 'Social Security, Retirement Age and Optimal Taxation,' *Journal of Public Economics* 88: 2227–58.
Cremer, H. and P. Pestieau (2003) 'The Double Dividend of Postponing of the Age of Retirement, *International Tax and Public Finance,*' 10: 419–34.
Duval, R. (2003) 'Early Retirement Incentives and the Participation of Older Workers to the Labour Force,' OECD, unpublished.

Förster, M. (2003) 'Income Inequalities, Poverty and Effects of Social Transfer Policies in Traditional OECD Countries and Central Eastern Europe. Patterns, Trends and Driving Forces in the 1990s,' PhD Thesis, University of Liège.

Gruber, J. and D. Wise (1999) *Social Security Programs and Retirement Around the World* (Chicago: University of Chicago Press).

OECD (2003) 'Replacement Rates,' OECD, unpublished.

OECD (2004) *Social expenditures database, 1980–2001* (Paris: OECD).

Pestieau, P. (2004a) 'Globalization and Redistribution,' unpublished.

Pestieau, P. (2004b) 'Social Security and the Well-Being of the Elderly. Three Concepts of Generosity,' unpublished.

Author Index

Subject Index